'ON GOD'S SIDE'

GEORGE TYRRELL

'ON GOD'S SIDE'
A Life of George Tyrrell

NICHOLAS SAGOVSKY

CLARENDON PRESS · OXFORD

*This book has been printed digitally and produced in a standard specification
in order to ensure its continuing availability*

OXFORD
UNIVERSITY PRESS

Great Clarendon Street, Oxford OX2 6DP

Oxford University Press is a department of the University of Oxford.
It furthers the University's objective of excellence in research, scholarship,
and education by publishing worldwide in

Oxford New York

Auckland Bangkok Buenos Aires Cape Town Chennai
Dar es Salaam Delhi Hong Kong Istanbul Karachi Kolkata
Kuala Lumpur Madrid Melbourne Mexico City Mumbai Nairobi
São Paulo Shanghai Singapore Taipei Tokyo Toronto
with an associated company in Berlin

Oxford is a registered trade mark of Oxford University Press
in the UK and in certain other countries

Published in the United States
by Oxford University Press Inc., New York

ISBN 0-19-826728-2

For my parents

It is . . . easy to throw oneself heartily into the 'liberal' school or into the 'conservative', but to combine what is right in both is certainly not a 'cheap' position to take up; yet surely it is best to be on God's side and detached from every faction and party.

George Tyrrell to Maude Petre, 25 April 1899.

Often Divine Providence allows even good men to be driven out of the Church by the factious intrigues of the worldly. And if they endure this reproach and injustice with all patience for the peace of the Church and do not start any new heresy or schism they will hereby teach men how to serve God with pure affection and disinterested love. The aim of such men will always be to make for the port again as soon as ever the wind falls; or if that is impossible, either because the same storm still rages or a worse would be excited by their return, they will steadily determine to labour for the interests of those very men of whose turbulence and agitation they are the victims, and abstaining from all schismatical separation, to defend with their blood and to assist with their testimony that same faith which they acknowledge to be taught in the Catholic Church. Such men the Father who seeth in secret doth secretly crown. Their case may seem a rare one, but it is not unexampled, nay it is far commoner than might be supposed.

St Augustine, De Vera Religione,
translated and quoted by George
Tyrrell in 'Beati Excommunicati'
(manuscript in Petre Papers,
dated 18 May 1904).

Introduction

WHAT was it about Tyrrell that so captivated his friends and contemporaries? Intelligence, integrity (up to a point), compassion, humanity, wit: all these were there. He was a complex, wounded, attractive person, as eloquent in condemnation as in the giving of tender, sympathetic support. It was said of him that he could 'see through a stone wall'. Certainly he could see through any wall of hypocrisy, pretence, or dishonesty. He was as much feared as he was admired. He was dangerous not only to his enemies, but to his friends, for he assumed that they would be as ready as he was to expose pomposity and fraud, to give themselves in support of the weak and the exploited. He expected no less of the Society of Jesus. His writings represented a sustained protest against the intellectualism, the rationalism, into which the Catholic Church and the Society of Jesus had fallen. With supreme intelligence and knowledge of the human heart, he articulated the feelings, the doubts, and the certainties of those who could not find their home in an alienated Catholicism. He wrote as he felt, enjoying and admiring intellectual systems, but distrusting them as untrue to the shifting nature of human experience. The proof of his Christianity was not the readiness with which he sacrificed his spiritual peace; rather it was his utter unselfconsciousness in doing so.

It has taken nine years to complete this biography. I began by writing a thesis on the thought of Tyrrell and Matthew Arnold, and that became a book. All the while what I really wanted to write was a biography of Tyrrell, because it seemed that only in the context of his life could the vigour and fertility of his thought truly be demonstrated. Only in a biography could one show the integrity of the spiritual counsellor, the devotional writer, and the thinker whose thought ranged over every major theological issue that has reverberated throughout the twentieth century. Biographical work was also needed to trace out the threads of Tyrrell's clashes with authority, and to reassess the tragedy of his Jesuit vocation.

Maude Petre's work remains irreplaceable for its comprehensiveness. It is a remarkable tribute from a remarkable woman to a remarkable man. However, as one would expect, after seventy years there are other sides to the story that have now become clearer.

Tyrrell's attitude to Maude Petre was deeply ambivalent. There were aspects of his life about which she probably knew very little, such as his friendship with the Shelleys at Clapham. The accessibility of material in Jesuit archives has transformed our understanding of Tyrrell's relations with his superiors, who were well out of their depth in their attempts to deal with someone of Tyrrell's complex personality and mercurial intelligence—especially when he recognized few of the norms by which the Jesuits of his time were governed. Where I believe Maude Petre was substantially accurate was in her judgement that von Hügel should bear some (but by no means all) of the blame for what happened.

A word needs to be said about the policy I have followed over notes. In order to avoid a text and notes overweighted with numbers and references, I have tried to keep these to a minimum. I have therefore not given individual page references in the text for the many quotations from Tyrrell's books and articles. The source for any quotation should always be clear from the context, and, in the case of books, the page reference should be speedily located with the help of the initial note. In the case of articles, I have not given specific page references. With manuscript material, especially letters, I have always given the reference in the notes, but I have not repeatedly given the whereabouts of such material. This can be ascertained by consulting the list of 'major unpublished sources' in the Bibliography.

I have accumulated many debts during the writing of this book, some I am sure unnoticed or unremembered. Amongst those who should be thanked for generous and courteous help are Miss Elizabeth Poyser, archivist of the Archdiocese of Westminster; Mme Callu and the staff of the Manuscripts Room at the Bibliothèque Nationale, Paris; Father Osmund Lewry of Blackfriars, Oxford; the staff of the Bodleian Library, Oxford; the staff of the British Library Manuscripts Room; the staff of the Cambridge University Library; Mme A. L.-David; Dom Mark Pontifex of Downside Abbey; Father Francis Edwards, SJ, formerly archivist of the English Province of the Society of Jesus; Father Edward Lamalle, SJ, formerly archivist of the Roman Archive of the Society of Jesus; Professor N. L. A. Lash; the staff of the National Library of Scotland; Mrs K. Pirenne; Dr J. Root; Mr R. N. Smart and Mrs C. Gascoigne of the Manuscripts Department, St Andrews University Library; Father D. J. Schultenover, SJ; Father Michael Clifton, archivist of the Archdiocese of Southwark;

Father André Venard and Professor Marc Venard. Special thanks are due to Father R. Butterworth, SJ and Dr E. Duffy, who read the whole typescript and provided invaluable criticism, most of which I readily accepted and some of which I obstinately ignored. My work would have been impossible without the herculean bibliographical labours of Dr T. M. Loome; the pioneering work of Father Schultenover in the Roman Archive of the Society of Jesus, and the hospitality of many friends, especially Dr and Mrs P. J. Drudy in Dublin. It would also have been impossible without generous financial assistance from the Cleaver and Leverhulme Trusts, and a sabbatical term from my work at the Edinburgh Theological College. For the typing I am indebted to Mrs J. Wallace-Hadrill, Mrs E. Glass, and Mrs S. Jenkins. The staff of the Oxford University Press have been exemplary in their patience and attention to detail. Throughout the nine years my wife Ruth has supported me; for the latter part of it my children, Alexander and Kate, have distracted me—but I am grateful to them too.

Clare College, Cambridge   Nicholas Sagovsky
15 July 1988

Contents

Abbreviations

AAW	Archive of the Archdiocese of Westminster
AL1	*The Autobiography of George Tyrrell* (London, 1912)
AL2	M. D. Petre, *The Life of George Tyrrell from 1884 to 1909* (London, 1912)
AEPSJ	Archive of the English Province of the Society of Jesus
ARSJ	Roman Archive of the Society of Jesus
BL	British Library (British Museum)
BN	Bibliothèque Nationale
CCR	G. Tyrrell, *Christianity at the Cross-Roads* (London, 1909)
CM	A. R. Waller (attributed; in fact by Tyrrell), *The Civilizing of the Matafanus: An Essay in Religious Development* (London, 1902)
CP	Clutton Papers, Oxford
DS	H. Denzinger and A. Schönmetzer (eds), *Enchiridion Symbolorum Definitionum et Declarationum de Rebus Fidei et Morum*, 34th edn. (Freiburg, 1967)
EFI	M. D. Petre (ed.), *Essays on Faith and Immortality* (London, 1914)
FM1, 2	G. Tyrrell, *The Faith of the Millions: A Selection of Past Essays*, 1st and 2nd series (London, 1901)
GTL	M. D. Petre (ed.), *George Tyrrell's Letters* (London, 1920)
LN	*Letters and Notices* (house journal of the English Jesuits)
OD	*Our Dead: Memoirs of the English Jesuits who Died between June 1939 and December 1945* (Roehampton, 1947–8)
REEPE	*Registrum Epistolarum ad Exteros Praelatos et Ecclesiasticos*, iv (1898–1908)
RPA	*Registrum Epistolarum ad Provinciam Angliae*
SAUL	St Andrews University Library
SDA	Southwark Diocesan Archive
TSC	G. Tyrrell, *Through Scylla and Charybdis: or, the Old Theology and the New* (London, 1907)

I

A Dublin Lad

DUBLIN today sprawls for twenty miles around the bay, from Howth to Killiney, north and south of the River Liffey, as far as the eye can see. The city has spread all along the coastal plain, eating up villages and hamlets, its onward progress checked only by the hills to south and west which rise in the distance to become the Wicklow Mountains. A hundred and thirty years ago most of this land was open country. Old Dublin did not stretch for two miles on either side of the river, but all through the latter part of the nineteenth century the inexorable growth of the city provided work for navvies, who, rather than emigrate, remained behind to lay railways and tramlines, to build new quays, to erect terraces of red-brick houses across the fields, and, often enough, to starve. Already the elegant Georgian buildings in the centre of town were coated with grime, and once well-kept town houses had declined to become tenement slums. As the city expanded, the middle classes began to settle in fashionable suburbs to the south: Rathmines, Pembroke, and Irishtown. The centre was left to the very rich and the very poor. Walking along Dorset Street or round Mountjoy Square in St George's parish, just a mile to the north of the river, one is overwhelmed today by the atmosphere of pure dereliction. In the late nineteenth century this was the home of some of Dublin's most prominent citizens.

In this city George Tyrrell grew up: a city of wealthy, absentee landowners and day-labourers on the breadline; of lawyers, civil servants, soldiers, and academics who belonged, by and large, to the Protestant ascendancy; of dressmakers, domestic servants, and traders who were almost always Catholic. It was a city riven in two by social and religious differences. 'In the Dublin of 1861,' wrote a schoolfriend of Tyrrell's, 'everybody was necessarily a member of one of two contending hosts.'[1] Tyrrell himself was brought up to feel that Roman Catholicism was 'the religion of the Helots, and of vulgar and uneducated classes in Ireland'.[2] His own family was staunch for Protestantism and for the Reformation, members of the

Dublin 'professionocracy', doctors, lawyers, and clergymen, mocked by the *Whitehall Review* because they closed ranks rather than admit wealthy tradespeople to their society.[3] Tyrrell's grandfather came from Oxfordshire shortly before 1800, and is described in the register of St George's as a 'merchant'. Two of his sons were clergymen, and George's father became an overworked journalist, sub-editor of the *Dublin Evening Mail*, then a well-known organ of Protestant Toryism, and Irish correspondent for *The Times*. In the next generation, cousins rose to prominence in the law, the army, the diplomatic service, and the academic world. The name Tyrrell became one of the most outstanding at Trinity College, the Protestant university which dominated the intellectual life of Dublin. Here, Professor Robert Yelverton Tyrrell, George's first cousin, gained a chair in Latin at the age of 25. He is remembered for his edition of Cicero's letters and his wit: 'There is no such thing', he once remarked, 'as a large whiskey.'[4]

George never knew his father. William Tyrrell died at the end of December 1860, five weeks before the birth of his son on 6 February 1861. He left a pregnant wife and two small children: William, aged 9, already stunted by an accident a year earlier; and Louisa, aged 1. There was little money. In his *Autobiography*, a deliberately self-denigrating account of his early life, Tyrrell recalls that his father, when only about 19, married a Roman Catholic widow so much older than him that he was actually younger than some of her children. It is hard to know why they married. She was not wealthy, but she was 'the painted remains of a once beautiful woman'.[5] The marriage lasted for twelve years, during which her health declined and her husband nursed her to the end. A year after her death William Tyrrell married Mary Anne Chamney at St George's, close to which church they both lived. Their first child, Melinda, was born about 1849. From the time of her birth William affected indifference. He flatly refused to be in the same room as the child, who lived only a year, but when she died he was so distraught that after the funeral he had to be helped into a cab and driven home with the blinds down. In later years George discovered how much he took after the father he never knew. Both were quick in all they did, easily irritated, compulsive writers, great dog-lovers. They even had similar handwriting. Like his son, the father was warm-hearted, wounded, and headstrong. Unfortunately, the marriage was not happy, and as a child George heard little but ill of his father. Only in later years did he become convinced that the man he never knew was a finer character than he had ever been led to believe.

His mother he adored. He broke off his *Autobiography* at the point of her death, unable, even after twenty years, to cope with the pain. She was the light of his lonely and insecure childhood. It was to George that she turned for comfort and friendship as she struggled to bring up her children. Friends noticed that mother and son shared the same sense of the ridiculous. Mary Anne Chamney was the daughter of a solicitor prominent enough to have Daniel O'Connell, 'the liberator' and nationalist leader, for a client. Tyrrell concluded that rather than loving his father, she 'admired and feared' him, and that his father's nature, like his own, craved an affection that his mother could never provide for a husband. Her affection was directed towards the children, especially after the death of her husband and her eldest son.

Willie was already in the hands of the surgeons by the time George was born. A fall in the nursery had fractured his spine, and he never grew above 4 feet 10 inches. All his energies were poured into achieving such academic excellence that his younger brother found it impossible to compete. While George was growing up, Willie was usually away at school or college. When he did come home he was bitter or sarcastic. Not until the last summer of Willie's life, when George was 15, did the two brothers draw closer together. It was Louy who was George's childhood friend and playmate. Later they drew apart as she went away to school, and it became evident that she did not share her brothers' intellectual gifts.

Tyrrell remembered his early years with astonishing clarity. They were dominated by financial insecurity and the struggle to keep the family together. When George was only 1, a sudden set-back deprived his mother of most of her small income, and she had to take a job as a lady's companion. Willie was away at school, and the younger children went to board with a certain Mrs Meyers. Suddenly his mother became a shadowy figure who only visited when she could. George clearly remembered the trauma of this separation, which lasted for about two years. The financial situation then improved enough for his mother to rejoin her children. Before long they were also joined by his mother's widowed sister.

Aunt Melinda brought a little much-needed money, but she also inflicted on the family a severe and unwelcome Calvinistic faith. She immediately began to force the pace of the children's religious upbringing. There were burdensome family prayers, and Sunday had to be observed with full Presbyterian rigour. Tyrrell's mother bent with the wind, and the children had to put up with the new regime. In later years Tyrrell spoke scathingly of Calvinism, but acknowledged the debt that he owed to his mother's quiet, low-church, Anglican faith.

Not long after Melinda's arrival, Willie became too ill to be kept at school. For the sake of the invalid the family moved to the coast, where there were more relatives; when Willie improved, they returned to Dublin. By 1867 both brothers were at the same school. Willie subsequently went on to Rathmines School, where he became the most brilliant student the school had ever produced; in 1870 he won an outstanding classical sizarship to Trinity College. On the strength of this, his headmaster, Dr Benson, offered to educate the younger brother free. Such an offer could not be refused. In the shadow of his elder brother's success, George arrived at Rathmines School.

Dr Benson often said that his hobbies consisted of 'three Bs': boys, boats, and birds. He was a remarkable man for any boy to have as his headmaster: a passionate sailor, astronomer, and gardener, Ireland's leading ornithologist, irrepressibly enthusiastic and compassionate. He offered affection and inspiration more than discipline, and this brought out the best and the worst in his complex new pupil. Looking back, Tyrrell could only see that he had responded badly to the Doctor's gentleness. He felt guilty that he had taken advantage of an easygoing nature, and did not reward Benson's generosity with the kind of academic distinction that Willie had attained. He saw himself as idle and undisciplined, but it is clear that as a schoolboy he needed to hide behind a studied indifference. Outside the classroom he responded to all that Benson had to offer. He also appreciated the way in which each morning the Doctor, the captain of the school, and the prefects (of which George was never one) donned their gowns and processed into the long schoolroom. Morning prayer included psalms, hymns, and an exposition by the Doctor: 'Really, dear boys, I do think that, *without any exception*, this is the most remarkable text *in the whole Bible*.'[6]

A tougher regime might have given him more peace. When he was 12 he was sent to board at Middleton College, where he was drilled in grammar and hit if he did not know his paradigms. Typically, Tyrrell interpreted the move as a punishment for his ungovernable temper, and actually welcomed the cruelty of a violent teacher who 'took my measure exactly, and dealt with me for the deceitful little devil I was'.[7] All the time he was failing by his brother's standards, and so by his own. Where Benson was lenient, Tyrrell had to punish himself, or find punishment. He had not been a term at Middleton before his mother became seriously ill, and there was no money to keep him on. With characteristic generosity, Benson took him back, and his mother, against all expectation, recovered. Separation from her and anxiety about her health were the worst aspects of life at this time. It is significant that his rages were directed solely towards his mother. So much within the family had already been lost. He needed to find out if she too could be destroyed by his supposed wickedness.

Anger was a symptom of the insecurity that formed the background to Tyrrell's early life. He had been moved from a school where he was happy to one where he struggled, and unexpectedly brought back again. He had been separated from his mother, brother, and sister, and reunited with his mother only when she was expected to die. His aunt had come and was now gone. Money was always short. They had no settled home. 'Not to have had a home, in the strict sense of the word,' he wrote, 'was as grave a loss as not to have had a father.'[8] In all this, he drew closer to his mother. When Louy was away at school and Willie at Trinity College, he became in effect an only son, on whom his mother, her face haggard from unremitting stress, leaned for support.

Tyrrell returned to Rathmines School at the age of 13. Once again there were violent outbursts of temper. It was about this time that Aunt Melinda died and left enough money for him to board with a master who taught at the school. This lasted just over a year—a year in which Willie took an outstanding degree at Trinity College, and George went to All Saints' Church, Grangegorman, for the first time.

In his *Autobiography* Tyrrell makes much of his adolescent questioning and misbehaviour. Certainly, he used his wit and quickness of intelligence as it suited him, not as Willie had done. In later years he wrote to a friend: 'From my earliest days I had the gospel of brains preached at me till I got to loathe it. I had my brother and my cousins flung at my head so often, that I conceived a detestation of learned and brainy people that I have never got over . . . Cleverness is in my mind an attribute of monkeys.'[9] At school he struck his friends as idle and shallow, though he did make a name for himself for his comic recitations with a friend. These became a regular feature of the monthly concerts at Rathmines. His mother wrote most of his material and, presumably, rehearsed it with him. Although he later lamented the weakness of his memory, he was in fact laying the foundations for a considerable ability to memorize Scripture and poetry.

Early specialization was discouraged at Rathmines School. Until the age of 15 the boys received a broad general education in the classics of English, Latin, and Greek literature. However much he wasted the opportunities given him, Tyrrell gained a good knowledge of the Bible, of Shakespeare, Swift, and Goldsmith, of Virgil and Homer—or, at least, he was made aware of what he was missing. Despite his under-achievement, there can be no question of the distortion in his self-evaluation: 'I was now pretty well all undone; I had reached bottom. I was untruthful, violent, irreligious, idle, and good for nothing except ineffectual tinkering.'[10] The clue to such extreme self-denigration is given in the same passage of his *Autobiography*, where he compares himself to the unconverted Augustine, whose *Confessions* he obviously had in mind. Like Augustine, he is at pains to demonstrate his need of salvation, and then to demonstrate the grace of God, who provided for his need.

Such provision came not only through good Dr Benson, but also through Grangegorman Church. Only in Ireland could Grangegorman, which Tyrrell now began to attend regularly, be reckoned a 'high' church. It had no elaborate ritual, but Dr Maturin, the vicar, said the prayer of consecration at the Eucharist with his back to the people. He was a notorious figure in the Church of Ireland. In 1866 he had outfaced a mob, which probably included one of Tyrrell's uncles, intent on wrecking morning prayer because he intoned rather than read the service. 'If I were to live for one hundred years,' Dr Maturin declared, 'I shall never yield what I believe to be right.'[11] He never did. In 1872 he was tried and condemned under the new canons of the Church of Ireland, a proceeding which Maturin characteristically ignored. At St George's Tyrrell had worshipped in a church dominated by a central pulpit; at All Saints' the focus was an altar with flowers and a coloured frontal. This appealed to his sense of the quixotic and the mysterious: 'Popery in a Protestant Church ... the birettas and cassocks made the fibres of one's Protestantism quiver. I had almost discovered a new sin, and found the sensation novel and agreeable.'[12]

Of course, Grangegorman was in no way a ritualist or crypto-papist church. Dr Maturin once wrote, with ill-advised self-congratulation:

I have been a parish clergyman in Dublin since I was admitted to Holy Orders, and for more than a third of a century I have served in that capacity without intermission, first at the south, and next at the north side of the city . . . and I can state that during the entire . . . time I have mentioned, I never knew or heard of a single individual who was under my instruction having become a Roman Catholic.[13]

That boast was made ten years before George Tyrrell came under his instruction. Maturin was a Prayer-Book man of the early Tractarian type, with a 'high' doctrine of the Church and the Eucharist. He was also an excellent preacher. It was this, more than his admitted delight in running against the grain, that drew Tyrrell so deeply. Twenty years later, he wrote:

Frankly, I have never seen, inside or outside the Church, any form or style of worship so reverent, dignified and devout as that of Grangegorman. It was absolutely free of any sign of that sham-Romanism and unreality which made any sort of ritualism perfectly intolerable to me . . . We had no lights, no incense, no insane paradings and prancings . . . In short, there was no irrational element in that worship, and yet the sense and the imagination were not starved. As far as feeling goes, the quiet early Communions and the Church evensongs at Grangegorman appealed to me as nothing has done since.[14]

Like the worship at Rathmines School, the worship at Grangegorman was free from any hint of religious narcissism. Tyrrell, at 15, was longing for the security of a religion that he could make his own, but any step that he took towards belief would have to pass the test of his own self-criticism and Willie's acid scepticism. Bit by bit, he was drawn in. Within a year he was confirmed and began to take Communion regularly. Grangegorman, however, was only a stepping-stone, for it was to Catholicism that he was increasingly attracted. As yet, though, the attraction was romantic and theoretical. A Tyrrell, like a Wilde or a Shaw, could expect to have little experience of Roman Catholicism, the religion of the common people around him.

In March 1876, however, Mrs Tyrrell had finally settled in lodgings owned by a Miss Lynch, a sincere and self-effacing Roman Catholic whose goodness and faith Tyrrell quickly came to respect. Exactly a month after moving into these lodgings, Tyrrell was reading Montalembert's *Monks of the West*. The description of St Benedict caught his imagination, and in a moment of desperation, when saying compline, he threw his Protestant conscience to the winds and prayed to the saint. The words he read immediately afterwards passed, burning, into his soul:

Quoniam in me speravit, liberabo eum; protegam eum quoniam cognovit nomen meum; clamabit ad me et ego exaudiam eum; cum ipso sum in tribulatione, eripiam eum et glorificabo eum. (Because he hoped in me, I will deliver him; I will protect him because he knew my name; he will call on me and I will hear him; I am with him in trouble, I will rescue him and honour him.)[15]

Significantly, he does not quote the next verse: 'With long life I will satisfy him.' He was always convinced that, like Willie, he would die young. It was the preceding words that spoke unmistakably to him in his unhappiness.

In the summer of 1876 Willie came home from Cambridge, where he had been studying for a year. Expecting to be rebuffed, George told him of his tentative belief. To his surprise, Willie heard him quietly and admitted that he too needed a faith. If ever he became a Christian, which at that stage seemed intellectually impossible, he would be a Roman Catholic. Academic success did not compensate for his deformed body and the constant pain it brought him. Inwardly he was lost. In one of their last conversations George asked Willie where he thought the soul went after death, and Willie replied: 'Where the flame goes when the candle is burnt out.' George contemplated his riposte while Willie was away visiting a friend in Tipperary, but on 29 August he was called to see Dr Benson, who handed him a telegram: 'Willie Tyrrell died here last night; tell his mother and friends.' George brought home the news of Willie's death, but it was actually Miss Lynch who told his mother, whose first thought was that her son had committed suicide, an idea George specifically repudiates in the *Autobiography*. Two months later, on All Saints' Day 1876, George committed himself yet more deeply to the life of Grangegorman Church by joining the Guild. Willie's early death had cemented his brother's Anglican faith.

In the last two years at Rathmines Tyrrell specialized in Hebrew under the tuition of Charles Osborne, who had been just ahead of him at school and was now at Trinity College, but his heart was not in the work. The Rathmines School magazine recorded his position in the sixth-form examination for 1877: bottom, with 13 marks out of 110. In 1877 and 1878 the brother of William Tyrrell failed the Trinity College Hebrew sizarship dismally. Though he scraped entry in the autumn of 1878, without a scholarship there was not the money for him to take up his place. Where Willie and his cousins had achieved such triumphant success, George failed ignominiously. As always, lack of application let him down. He had not yet found the things he really wanted in life. He was far keener to discuss questions of religion with Osborne on their long walks in the hills around Dublin than to work at his Hebrew. Osborne responded to this readily, as he was a convinced, moderate high-churchman, who later became a well-known Anglican vicar. Their sunny, open friendship lasted until Tyrrell's death.

About this time Tyrrell was drawn into the orbit of a far more mercurial character—Robert Dolling. More than any other single person, Dolling made Tyrrell what he was. He came from the landed Protestant gentry, and managed estates from Dublin. At Harrow and Cambridge he had been one of a group of Christian Socialists, who brought together Catholic devotion and service to the poor. Dolling had rooms built at the back of his house so that he could entertain the young men he cheerfully drilled in the rudiments of the faith, and with whom he spent hour after hour in animated conversation. With his indifference to theological niceties, and his outsize personality, he swept Tyrrell, who always responded to a strong lead, quite off his feet. His young friend was proud to help with the setting-up of a library at Mountjoy Square, where Dolling lived. By getting Tyrrell to arrange the books, Dolling guided his reading at an important stage in his development. At the age of 17, Tyrrell was already reading the works of theologians like Wilberforce and Liddon. This was where he first read Aquinas. In later years he paid Dolling an affectionate tribute: 'All my love of the *benignitas et humanitas Dei Salvatoris nostri*; all that people care for in *Nova et Vetera*; all my evangelical sympathies; all my revolt against the Pharisee and the canon-lawyer, is the outgrowth of the seeds of his influence.'[16] At a time of failure and distress, Dolling cared for the boy: he gave him the courage to set light by the ecclesiastical and social rules.

Tyrrell had once made his confession to Dr Maturin of Grangegorman, but he had found him a grim disciplinarian who withheld absolution when he was not satisfied that all, or enough, had been told, and forbade Tyrrell to come to Communion every week. Dolling thought this simply scandalous, and encouraged Tyrrell to confess elsewhere. Tyrrell began to go to confession at the Roman Catholic church in Marlborough Street, but he continued to communicate at Grangegorman. He was also attending mass at the Jesuit church in Gardiner Street, but he did not receive Communion there. Being of a less breezy temperament than Dolling, he could not sustain this irregularity for long. He was being forced to a decision.

By now he had left school. The future looked distinctly uncertain. As a beginning, he took a teaching job in Wexford, where he found that there was no religious *via media*, like Grangegorman, on offer. The school was out-and-out Protestant, and *that* he knew he could not abide. The appointment in Wexford only lasted until Christmas, but in that time he clearly saw where he now stood. He found himself a Catholic in all but name, though still he recoiled from 'the dirt and tinsel and flashy gew-gaws' in the Catholic chapels, from 'the essential "commonness" of Romanism'. When the blow of his conversion finally fell, what pained his mother was 'that a son of mine should go to Mass with the cook'.[17]

On his return to Dublin it was not easy to pick up the threads at Grangegorman. Dr Maturin, who for all his 'high-church' views remained solidly anti-papist, had heard of Tyrrell's attendance at Gardiner Street and confronted him with it. Tyrrell was forced to resign from the Guild of All Saints in January 1879, and Dolling was blamed for leading him astray. His young friend wanted only to find a way of leading a whole-hearted Christian life, without intellectual or moral compromise, and was appalled by the snobbery of Dublin Protestantism. When Maturin forced the issue, the result was inevitable. Already Tyrrell had a secret altar in his bedroom and had begun to think about the Jesuits. When Dolling (who did not share his sense of boundaries) invited him to London to see the life of a real ritualist church and to join him in his work amongst postmen, Tyrrell saw a way out of Dublin and accepted at once. Dolling was not deceived: he predicted the conversion of his young friend. On the day Tyrrell left, Miss Lynch gave him a rosary—where he was going, no one would be shocked when he used it.

NOTES

1. C. E. Osborne in the *Church Times*, 23 July 1909, p. 121.
2. *AL1*, p. 34.

3. *Whitehall Review*, 20 Jan. 1877, p. 179.
4. R. M. Kain, *Dublin in the Age of William Butler Yeats and James Joyce* (Norman, Okla, 1962), p. 162.
5. *AL*1, p. 4.
6. Ibid., p. 61.
7. Ibid., p. 88.
8. Ibid., p. 72.
9. Tyrrell to Thurston, 15 Nov. 1891 (AEPSJ).
10. *AL*1, p. 93. Mr Hogan, curate at Grangegorman Church, who knew Tyrrell from the time he began to attend, said after reading the *Autobiography*: 'I do not believe that the young man there depicted ever existed . . . I used to see George Tyrrell . . . very often; he was utterly unlike what later on he said of himself. (Letter from W. Stockley, undated (SAUL, Ward Papers, VII 294.)) When he began to write his *Autobiography*, Tyrrell told Maude Petre: 'I mean to flay myself ruthlessly.' (*AL*1, p. vi.)
11. *Dublin Evening Mail*, 23 Apr. 1866.
12. *AL*1, p. 98.
13. Letter to Lord Bishop of Cashel, 1867, quoted in the *Irish Ecclesiastical Gazette*, 23 July 1887, p. 623.
14. *AL*1, pp. 126–7.
15. Ps. 91: 14–15.
16. *AL*1, p. 129.
17. Ibid., p. 34.

2

Conversion to Catholicism

As an older man, Tyrrell was to take a sardonic delight in the date of his coming to England. He arrived on All Fools' Day 1879, a sandy-haired, insecure boy of 18, with a low opinion of his own worth, conscious of physical ugliness and the longing for a spiritual home. For three years the church at Grangegorman had offered him old-fashioned high-church teaching without ritual extravagance, but he still remained unsatisfied. In the last months he had been to mass more often than to Holy Communion, though he did not communicate at mass. As yet he was unconvinced by the claims of Rome, though he was unhappy in his Anglicanism. Dolling, who had no idea how much his own criticism of Grangegorman had unsettled his young friend, tried to help him find his way, as he himself had done, in extreme Anglo-Catholicism. It was not a position that Tyrrell could hold for long.

The two friends had agreed that Tyrrell should come to London and earn his living by helping at a mission for postmen that Dolling now ran in Southwark. The mission was an outpost of St Alban's, High Holborn, where the vicar, Father Mackonochie, and his team of assistant clergy exercised a controversial ministry of flagrant ritualism and outstanding pastoral care. Such a blend appealed enormously to the cheerful extroversion and ready compassion of Robert Dolling. At the Borough Road house where Dolling lived and worked when in London, an endless stream of the deprived, the lonely, and the downtrodden were welcomed without patronage and with genuine love. Tyrrell was immediately enlisted as a valued helper. He joined enthusiastically in the life of the house: the meals in common; animated discussions under a pall of pipe-smoke; earnest prayers led by 'Brother Bob'; uninhibited singsongs; unforced counselling and friendship. This was the sort of practical Christian living that he respected all his life.

Yet he remained unhappy. However much Dolling's way of life appealed to him, he could not share his breezy indifference to externals. Dolling was happy at St Alban's because he did not take the liturgical extremism all that seriously. If the vestments, the candles, and the processions added colour to lives that were otherwise drab, and if they made the truths of the Gospel live for the poor, well and good. Tyrrell could not take it that way at all. For him, unless these were the lineaments of authentic Christianity, they were an offensive show. On his first Sunday at St Alban's, Palm Sunday, he loathed what he saw as an insincere charade, and fled in confusion.

Outside he paced up and down waiting for Dolling. At just this time the largely Irish congregation of St Etheldreda's, Ely Place, was assembling for mass. Tyrrell found himself irresistibly drawn to the crypt church. Here he found none of the splendour and urbanity of St Alban's, but, 'Oh! the sense of reality! here was the old business, being carried on by the old firm, in the old ways; here was continuity, that took one back to the catacombs; here was no need of, and therefore no suspicion of, pose or theatrical parade; its aesthetic blemishes were its very beauties for me in that mood.'[1] From this morning, six days after Tyrrell's arrival in London, Dolling's expedient had failed. While Dolling himself would continue to go happily to St Alban's, Tyrrell went only to please his friend, and with a sinking heart. Once more he began slipping off to Catholic churches to hear mass.

About this time he found the money to buy a fervent little book called *Jésuites!*.[2] Looking back, he was astonished that he could have fallen under the spell of such naïve adulation of the Society, but at the time it was precisely the emotionalism of the book that appealed to him. The birth of the Jesuits appeared as a burst of light upon a darkened Europe; Ignatius called his followers to new deeds of heroism, sacrifice, devotion, and obedience; like the first six companions of Ignatius, the Society of Jesus was ready to obey the call. This was the challenge that Tyrrell had been waiting for, presented not in the uncertain light of ritual extravagance, but in the clear daylight of militant truth. Tyrrell wrote to Miss Lynch, and through her obtained an introduction to the English Jesuits. This he took to Father Albany Christie of Farm Street, who had been a fellow of Oriel with Newman, and, like Newman, had been received into the Roman Church in 1845. At the first interview, Christie gave Tyrrell a Penny Catechism, which solved nothing and only raised new question about the intellectual cogency of Catholicism. There were more visits to Farm Street—Tyrrell being both attracted by the apparent stability of Catholicism and tormented by his sceptical nature and terror of being deceived. Before too long Father Christie, taking the offensive, put to him his standard question for wavering young Puseyites: 'How can you, who have so clear a conviction that Christ founded on earth a Church that was His Spouse, be content with such a miserable mass of inconsistencies as the Anglican Communion?' By this stage Tyrrell's inward resistance had collapsed. Despite his doubts and hesitations, 'convinced by a syllogism', on 18 May he made his confession and became a Roman Catholic.

Already he hoped to join the Jesuits, but he had such a low opinion of his own worth that he hardly dared raise the question with Father Christie. To his surprise, Christie could see no reason why a man who had neglected his Greek should not think of the priesthood, and even of the Jesuits. A new world beckoned. Before long Tyrrell had visited the Jesuit novitiate at Roehampton, and Christie, who must have been something of an enthusiast, gave him to think he might start in September. Tyrrell was giddy from it all. It seemed that he had found a spiritual home and a future of unlimited promise all in a matter of weeks. Perhaps it had been too easy? Although his predominant emotion was one of wonder and joy, the doubt remained.

Before any move could be made, there was a summer to pass. Dolling had wished Tyrrell well in his new-found faith, and certainly would not have thrown him out for his change of heart. However, he had to return temporarily to Ireland, and there was no place for Tyrrell at Borough Road. He found himself lodgings and settled to the lonely wait, broken only by occasional tutoring which barely brought him enough money to survive. He went daily to mass and to vespers, read voraciously, and battled with his loneliness and self-doubt. Still, it was only for a time. In the event, Father James Jones, Provincial of the English Jesuits, proved more cautious than Father Christie. Not unreasonably, he thought Tyrrell too new a convert to go straight to Roehampton, and suggested a year abroad. It so happened that Father Henry Schomberg Kerr, chaplain to the British forces in the newly ceded territory of Cyprus, had recently written asking for an Englishman 'fresh from his Greek' who would learn the modern language quickly and help him set up a school in Limassol, where learning English was all the rage. Tyrrell arrived in Cyprus at the beginning of November.

He had travelled on the *Fortuna*, and was surprised to receive the following note on his arrival: 'Sir,—I am expecting a friend by the *Fortuna*; will you kindly look after him and convey him to Limassol.'

To his knowledge there had been no Jesuit on board, and he did not know who else might be a friend of Father Kerr. He left the matter, and made his way to the nearest English hotel. When he signed his name in the register, the proprietor showed him a letter he had received from Father Kerr: 'Dear Mr Tyrrell,—I have asked Mr Lewsly to look after you. He is a respectable young man; but as the company at his table is rather mixed, you had best keep your counsel and say nothing as to the purpose of your coming, etc.'[3] Father Kerr had clearly sent Tyrrell the note intended for Lewsly. Such a beginning appealed to Tyrrell's highly developed sense of the ridiculous.

Tyrrell always held Henry Schomberg Kerr in the greatest affection; he spoke of him as 'my veritable novice-master'.[4] Kerr was ex-navy: bluff, hearty, and full of common sense, in many ways not unlike Dolling. Most of all, he was utterly uncomplicated. Tyrrell took to him at once, and they would go on long evening walks together, like father and son, Kerr striding out with his stick clasped across his shoulders, Tyrrell, himself a fast walker, keeping pace. When they said their office together in the open air, Tyrrell marvelled at Kerr's ability to make a nonsense of Latin. Sometimes Kerr would • march into the bazaar or even into a garden, appropriate the vegetables he wanted, and hand over what he thought just payment —no more, no less—oblivious of all protestation. He was as amazed at Tyrrell's grasp of theology and Greek as Tyrrell was at his naïve admiration for all that the Society said and did. The third member of this unlikely household was Father Riotta, a portly Sicilian Jesuit, who spoke Greek, and whose principal academic interest was the Photian Schism between the Churches of Rome and Constantinople.

For a time the school did well. Numbers rose from eight to thirty, and there was a party to celebrate, but then disaster struck. Father Riotta had been a little too free with his opinions on the Photian Schism. The local orthodox priest became alarmed at the teaching of the school, and went round the boys' parents denouncing the English teaching as a Jesuit plot. Next morning the place was deserted; there was not a single student. At first the three foreigners were puzzled, but then, when Father Kerr took in the whole situation, to Tyrrell's delight he responded with enormous gusts of laughter, and his young assistant could do nothing but follow suit. Only Father Riotta was not amused when notices were posted in the neighbourhood which read:

Inasmuch as certain persons have given cause for scandal by professing to interest themselves in the teaching of English, while in fact they were designing evil and impious things against our orthodox faith—and scandal, moreover, of such kind that all right-minded men are anxious to uproot such tares, and rid the community of baneful teaching, the undersigned offers his own class hours, gratis, for the teaching of English, in our own Greek school, until the want of a suitable professor of English shall have been satisfied . . .

O. I. Jasonides[5]

After the collapse of the school, Kerr returned to Malta to consult with the Provincial. For a month Tyrrell and Riotta were left alone, to all intents abandoned on the island. Now Tyrrell's fears and fantasies revived in the enforced idleness. By the time he was recalled to Malta he was asking himself what will-o'-the-wisp had led him to flee Ireland and England, family and friends—in fact, whether he wanted to be a Jesuit at all.

In Malta Tyrrell was far less free than he had been in Cyprus. He was to teach at a Jesuit school that had been established some two years previously. An international staff of twelve was teaching a hundred boys, all of whom were the sons of well-to-do Maltese. The shock for Tyrrell was immense. Far from the dedicated and harmonious atmosphere he had expected, he found pettiness, suspicion, and strife. The members of the teaching community did not get on with each other. The boys spoke virtually no English, and the community no Maltese. Tyrrell was still in the first flush of conversion, but he found no one there to share his enthusiasm. What was to him new and exciting was to the others merely commonplace. Moreover, since he was not a Jesuit he did not share fully in the life of prayer, though he was instructed to pass himself off as a member of the Society lest the parents should discover that a non-Jesuit was in charge of their children. All he had to do was to drive the school bus to and from Valletta, and teach five or six of the most difficult boys at the bottom of the school. Things improved towards the end of his stay, but the impression Tyrrell leaves in his *Autobiography* is one of loneliness and disappointment. 'Unutterably shocked and disgusted by the general tone of the community',[6] he withdrew into himself and found himself all but ostracized.

Real friendship came from the lay brothers, and solace from the countryside. This was an oft-repeated pattern. In Malta it was Brother Masseurs the gardener, a stormy petrel, who attracted Tyrrell by his rugged ordinariness. The friendship was cemented five years later, when Tyrrell returned as a Jesuit scholastic. If he recoiled from the community, he loved the college, which was set above St Julian's Bay, where the better-off inhabitants of Valletta came for their holidays. On clear days, Mount Etna and the Sicilian coast could be seen across the straits. The garden, where Tyrrell often sat and read, stretched down on three levels to the sea. He had time to watch the waves and wonder if he really belonged. By the end of the year nothing had been resolved. He still did not know whether the Jesuits of his imagination or the Jesuits of Malta were the reality. In this frame of mind he returned to England.

For a few days Tyrrell stayed with Dolling, but there was no going back to Dolling's religion. He was determined to become a Jesuit novice. Dolling's last words to him were: 'You will be out in six months.'[7]

NOTES

1. *AL*1, p. 153.
2. P. Féval, *Jésuites!*, 5th edn. (Paris, 1877).
3. The Hon. Mrs Maxwell-Scott, *Henry Schomberg Kerr* (London, 1901), p. 155.
4. *AL*1, p. 172.
5. *LN*, 13 (1880), p. 152.
6. *AL*1, p. 183.
7. C. E. Osborne, *The Life of Father Dolling* (London, 1903), p. 22.

3

Jesuit Novitiate

TYRRELL was 19 when he arrived at Manresa House, Roehampton in September 1880. There were twenty-one novices that year, fifteen of whom came straight from Jesuit schools, 'boys in years, boys in mind, boys in character'.[1] In his *Autobiography* Tyrrell describes the shock of being ushered into the 'dismal little guest parlour' that evening, and being asked by Alfred Hulley which college he came from—The Mount? or Stonyhurst? or Beaumont? 'When I explained that I came from none of them he seemed to conclude that I had come from nowhere, and lapsed into silence.' From the first Tyrrell was made to feel different because he was one of the small number of novices who came 'from the world'.[2]

Manresa House was a Georgian mansion that had been built for the Bessborough family on the edge of Richmond Park. Once a centre of gracious living, it had now become the very opposite, a house of considerable austerity. A later entrant wrote: 'My first impression of the house of novices was bleakness; that impression was never quite obliterated in the two years I spent there.'[3] Inside, the house had been stripped of creature comforts. There were fine, high ceilings where chandeliers had once hung. Rumour had it that the walls of the Novices' Hall had been covered with frescos of classical subjects, but these had been boarded up to protect the eyes of the innocent from so much naked flesh: hence the dull pine panelling. Each novice was given a cubicle in a dormitory, 'like stalls in a well-kept stable, except for the red curtains that could be drawn across the front'.[4] In the cubicle there was an iron bedstead, a wash-stand with pitcher and basin, and a discreetly placed chamber-pot. One oblong strip of carpet lay on the bare boards. Each novice had a small desk that might at times be withdrawn into the cubicle for more private reading or meditation. The day's routine was governed by the ringing of a bell that had to be obeyed instantly.

The bare outlines of day-to-day events in the novitiate can be followed closely, as one of the novices, called the Porter, was deputed to keep a journal. A journal was also kept by the Father Minister, who noted events in the life of the house as a whole, including the menu for special occasions, and any medical problems that occurred. Both journals record the arrival of twenty-one new novices, among them Tyrrell, on 7 September. Brothers Smith, Atteridge, Worden, and Jinks were appointed 'angel guardians' to make the new arrivals feel welcome, to introduce them to the daily routine, and to shepherd them round the house. Tyrrell arrived in the late afternoon and 'took recreation' with the others until supper. In the evening he and all the new novices went to benediction and confession. Lights went out in the house at ten.

The next day was the Feast of the Nativity of the Blessed Virgin Mary, and, as it happened, an outstandingly important day in the life of the Jesuits at Manresa. At the 6.30 a.m. mass, twenty-one men who had completed their novitiate took the vows of poverty, chastity, and obedience, the largest number hitherto to have taken their vows at Manresa. From that time they were true religious, though it might be another ten or twelve years before they finished all their training and made their 'final profession', which, for those considered suitable, included the fourth vow peculiar to Jesuits, that of obedience to the Pope. Later that morning minor orders, a stage on the way to the priesthood, were conferred on twenty-six men by the Bishop of Amycla. When the Bishop had finished saying mass, everyone made their way to the Novices' Hall, where the Provincial, Father Purbrick, read a letter from the General appointing Father John Morris as Rector and Master of Novices. For Tyrrell, though he did not yet know it, this was a fateful appointment. Dinner that day ('Fowls, chops, beef, mutton, jellies, blanc mang and Grapes, Pears, Peaches, Plums'[5]) was eaten at 'long tables', a festal arrangement that broke down something of the usual segregation between the groups in the house. Wine was served four times, and the health of the new Rector was proposed by the Provincial. Not for two more days did the novices settle to the normal routine.

The tenth of September was almost a normal day. Almost, because the novices were as yet spared the rigours of a 5.30 a.m. start and an hour's meditation. This would come in a fortnight. They were called late, at 6.30 a.m., for the 7.00 a.m. mass. After breakfast there was a reading from *Rodriguez on Christian Perfection*. Tyrrell deplored 'the daily half hour wasted over the banalities and fallacies of Rodriguez's mischievous and much overrated book'.[6] Both morning and afternoon there were 'indoor works' and 'outdoor works'. The new novices had to study the rules of the Society and the 'Summary of the Constitutions', including the papal bulls of particular relevance to the Jesuits. Their 'angel guardians' instructed them in the routine of the house. Before lunch and before retiring for the night they had to examine their consciences for any sin into which they might have fallen. The whole day was parcelled out in units of prayer, work, and recreation. 'During that time', wrote Tyrrell, 'we were drilled, and trotted about, and taken out for walks, and exhorted and instructed by our "angel guardians"; and never did I in my life feel so isolated, so absolutely out of sympathy with my company, as with these raw schoolboys,'[7] some of whom in fact became his close friends. One of the few bright spots was the daily reading of à Kempis, whose 'Christian Buddhism' became a lasting influence. No other work, apart from the Bible, is quoted anything like so often in Tyrrell's devotional writings.

In some ways the whole experience of the novitiate was one long retreat, intended to cultivate a devout and obedient spirit.[8] It had been the intention of St Ignatius that new novices should immediately embark on a thirty-day retreat, but this was found to be too taxing (in itself a comment on their immaturity), and in the 1870s the Long Retreat was postponed until the month before Christmas. So Tyrrell had a short retreat from 19 to 25 September, and a thirty-day retreat from 25 November. After the short retreat the new novices exchanged their lay clothes for shabby Jesuit gowns, and were formally reckoned to be novices of the Society. On this day, perhaps to their surprise, they were given a set of 'examen beads' threaded on a wire, which they had to pin on to the inside of their clothing and use as a tally to count the number of times they fell into some fault that they might be trying to overcome. At the midday and evening 'examens' of conscience the total was noted in a book, which would hopefully show a diminishing score of iniquity. They were also given a small spiked chain for the upper leg, and a scourge or 'discipline', the use of both being governed by strict rules—not for fear that they should be used too little, but too much. For most of the novices, who easily became spiritually overheated, this restraint was necessary, but the story is told of one novice who walked and genuflected with conspicuous ease on those mornings when the others were visibly stiff from the pain of their spikes. Only when another novice found the courage to ask how he managed it was it borne in on him that the spikes were worn *under* the trousers and that they should be pointing

inwards. Tyrrell, predictably, had no time for these crude mortifica-
tions, being of the opinion that 'cold baths and interesting work are
of more help than disciplines and chains'.[9] He would readily have
agreed with the novice who sensibly commented: 'If we were made to
cut off the two back buttons of our trousers or take a bath in treacle
and then put on our clothes we should be quite uncomfortable
enough and free from any temptation to spiritual pride.'[10]

For the next two years the dominant influence on Tyrrell and on all
the novices was Father Morris, whom Tyrrell called 'a man of very
pronounced personality, *i.e.*, a narrow intense man, with an un-
wavering belief in the opinions and the cause he had embraced, and
an absolute incapacity of seeing the other side'.[11] He was an uncom-
promising enthusiast for Christ, for the Roman Church, and for the
Society of Jesus, all adored and obeyed with the same perfervid
devotion. As a convert and a late entrant to the Society who had not
himself been through a full Jesuit training, he was a surprising choice
for a Master of Novices, but he was a man of ardour who lived to
kindle the same devotion in others. He was, in his own way, a master
builder who came to Manresa from Malta, where he had established
the Jesuit College and ruined his health. Under Morris, building
restarted on St Joseph's Church in the grounds of Manresa, and it
was quickly finished. He had another wing added to the house. For
six years he laboured with prodigious and unstable energy, and then
broke down once more.

It was Father Morris who conducted the Long Retreat. For thirty
days, broken only by three rest-days, the novices were kept in silence;
they meditated for five hours a day on 'conferences' given to them by
Father Morris; they rose early and prayed late. The first week of the
programme laid down in the *Spiritual Exercises* is perhaps the most
disturbing: a prolonged meditation on sin, judgement, and hell that
brings the exercitant to the foot of the Cross. For ten to twelve days
the meditations then concentrate on the Kingdom of Christ, challenging the retreatant to fight under Christ's banner rather than that
of Satan. Four or five days are then spent on the Passion, and the final
two or three days on the Resurrection and Ascension. There are three
days of total recreation to recover from the inevitable mental fatigue.
The Spiritual Exercises end on a high note of self-surrender: 'Take,
Lord, into Your possession, my complete freedom of action, my
memory, my understanding and my entire will, all that I have, all that
I own: it is Your gift to me, I now return it to You. It is all Yours, to be

used simply as You wish. Give me Your Love and Your Grace; it is all I need.'[12] This is from the 'Contemplation for Achieving Love'. When Father Morris came to this point in his own novitiate, he wrote: 'It is worth going through the Exercises to make this meditation.'[13]

Tyrrell was both inspired and wounded by Morris. It was said by Tyrrell and by others that 'personal love of our Lord amounted in him almost to a passion'.[14] Tyrrell, who had never known a father, attributed to this devotion the undoubted power that Morris had over him. Swept along by it, he accepted as he would never have done from a less enthusiastic guide what he would later come to repudiate: 'the dull, "commonsense", uncritical system of the Society, and all its traditions.'[15] Morris was cultivated, eloquent, and devoted, but he could also be cruel. Tyrrell wrote that 'he knew exactly how and where to wound, and was rather fond of displaying his skill'.[16] Morris knew this, and struggled with it. He once wrote in a letter: 'I saw the colour in a man's face yesterday at something I said . . . , but he bore it beautifully. It won't do though. Will you help me to conquer it?'[17] Externally he was sallow, cold, and strict; internally he was passionate and sensitive. He was continually overstretched, and something of this communicated itself to the novices. In 1881 Gerard Manley Hopkins, then a tertian at Manresa, wrote to his mother: 'Fr Morris's novices bear his impress and are staid: we used to roar with laughter if anything happened, his never do.'[18]

However gentle the Master of Novices (and Morris was not), the psychological pressure on these young men in their late teens and early twenties was unremitting. Every novice had from time to time to endure the public admonition or 'ring'. For this he knelt on the floor in front of the Rector. The other novices would be invited to make their criticisms of the unfortunate penitent, criticisms which might be elaborated upon by the Rector. Sometimes the tension and shame were too great, and the man in the centre gave way to tears, which was considered by the others a great loss of face. Tyrrell, who said of himself that he was 'always vulnerable from the side of [his] affections',[19] would have had to steel himself consciously for the ordeal. Gerard Manley Hopkins records two occasions in his novitiate when he suddenly found himself crying uncontrollably.[20] Such was the tension of life that novices were prone to fits of giggling at the slightest pretext, and many suffered from headaches.

The real problem for Tyrrell, however, was the clash of personality between himself and the man he was supposed to obey in all things short of sin, between an open, questioning mind, and one that was closed and domineering. When Tyrrell brought to Morris his questions about the Society, the low standards he had seen at Malta, and the lack of mature commitment among some of the novices who had come straight from school, Morris was at first angry, and then the tears stood in his eyes. When Tyrrell contrasted the wealth of the Church with the poverty of Christ, he was accused of having a critical spirit and told he would understand better later. Early in his second year he found it had been all but decided that he should leave the Society. Tyrrell was bitterly hurt and infuriated, for he had worked hard at cultivating an obedient and tractable disposition, and, however conspicuous his lack of success, he felt that Father Morris was trying to trap him into providing cause for his dismissal. He was determined either to stay or to leave in his own time. This time he won, though he did not get away with his riposte. He had already prepared a sermon on St Ignatius's 'Letter on Obedience' which was to be preached on a day of his own choosing. He decided to preach it that same night, but at the last minute the plan came to the ears of Father Morris and it was stopped. After the clash Tyrrell wrote to Father Purbrick, the Provincial, and it was agreed that he should stay, but that his vows should be deferred. In the event the sermon was preached later, Father Morris was delighted with it, and Tyrrell took his vows at the same time as the other novices.

Tyrrell had been attracted to Catholicism by the sense of reality he found within the liturgy. Not that it was necessarily well done, but it put him in touch with the unbroken tradition of the Church. The liturgical life of Manresa was an important factor for all the novices: the daily mass, benediction, the feasts, fasts, vigils, processions, and solemn masses. In 1881 St Joseph's, the new parish church in the grounds, was ready for use. At dawn on a cloudless March morning the Blessed Sacrament was taken there in solemn procession. A month later the church was used for Holy Week services. There was as yet no organ, but the choir sang Gounod's *Messe des Orphéonistes* on Easter Sunday. 'We firmly believe', wrote an enthusiastic reporter, 'that a more spirited and splendid piece of music was never produced by a body of twenty voices, a harmonium, and a violin.'[21]

A high point in the year was the Corpus Christi procession. In June 1882 this involved half the house, with a robed choir, eight juniors in copes and dalmatics, six priests in chasubles, four juniors to carry the canopy over the Sacrament, and Subdeacon, Deacon, and President, all in white vestments. Singing all the way, they processed from the chapel to an outside walk, and back into the house by another route, stopping in the hall for elevation of the Sacrament and benediction before returning to the chapel. One of the visitors on this occasion was Robert Bridges, to whom Gerard Manley Hopkins wrote: 'I wish our procession, since you were to see it, had been better: I find it is agreed it was heavy and dead.'[22] As a novice, Tyrrell may have felt the same, but it would not have been his place to voice it. Besides, he wanted to survive until he could take his vows and had proved that he would be a good Jesuit. At this stage he still took Jesuit life as Father Morris wanted him to, with extreme seriousness.

The Porter's Journal[23] helps greatly in building a picture of day-to-day life in those two years. Games of cricket and football are recorded, as are the regular trips to local parishes to give catechetical instruction. On Holy Innocents' Day the juniors and novices were given a shilling and allowed to go to London. Favourite destinations were Westminster Abbey and St Paul's. Occasionally a 'seance' or evening entertainment took place. In the first year Baron Friedrich von Hügel came for four days' retreat in October; on 14 January there was skating for the juniors but not for the novices; twenty novices were vaccinated during dinner on 31 May; on 4 June there should have been a 'ring', but it was omitted through the Porter's mistake; work in the hayfield, always a popular diversion, began on 24 June; and on 29 June, the Feast of Saints Peter and Paul, leave was granted to visit the Carmelites and the Oratory. The Journal records: 'Card. Newman was at the Oratory. Most of the novices went to the Oratory, none to the Carmelites.' On 2 August leave was granted to go to Clapham and hear Cardinal Manning preach. On 28 August, the Minister records, Brother Tyrrell and a stranger were confirmed. When the new novices arrived on 7 September Tyrrell had proved Dolling wrong—he had survived not six months, but a full year.

The Porter's Journal mentions changes in the rules, but it does not dwell on those rules that were taken for granted. From his earliest days the novice learnt that he must avoid all physical contact with other novices; he must show a proper respect by not looking directly in the eye of anyone in authority, but slightly lower; he must not expect to go on walks alone, but with one or two companions selected by the Master of Novices, and for the first half-hour of such walks all conversation had to be in Latin. Years after, Robert Steuart, who had been a novice in 1893, remembered the walks with horror:

To have to go out for long walks two and two, and find yourself landed with a person with whom you had absolutely nothing in common, no mutual interests; whose whole background and trend of thought were on utterly different lines; that—he used to burst out with deep feeling fifty years later—that—yes, I think it was almost the worst of all.[24]

There were to be no special friendships. For all conversations there were approved subjects, and subjects on which novices did not dwell. If it was wet, recreation was taken by sitting in a circle and making edifying conversation, which would be concluded by a *pia fabula*, or listening to an edifying story told by one of the novices. One of the problems they all had was finding anything to talk about. For two years they read no fiction, no poetry except religious verse, and no newspapers; only spiritual reading of the officially approved kind was permitted.

A life as intense as this tended to cut the novice off from family and friends. Tyrrell worked hard to stay in touch with his mother and sister. His mother had been ill with breast cancer, which was operated on in Dublin. She was to live for four more years. Together with Louy, she came to London and was received into the Roman Church in 1881. Thereafter, they visited Manresa a number of times before moving to Bonn for the sake of Louy's German. The parting was one that Tyrrell always remembered with pain. He felt that he had cut himself off from his family, and all his life he was haunted by guilt for what he had done.

At this stage he was not unhappy. He believed he had found what he was looking for, the pearl of great price, and threw himself heart and soul into his novitiate. He was incapable of being a model novice, but at 21 he was still too young to see that the model novice would not make the best priest. His potential was evident to others, though he was often silent and withdrawn. It took him years to formulate his criticisms of the novitiate, and these might well have been less savage if it had not been for his unfortunate relationship with John Morris. As it was, he wrote: 'I find it most difficult to explain the effect of the noviceship upon my thoughts and judgments; but I am satisfied that, upon the whole, it was mischievous, and that it has taken me years to recover the violent warp that I received during those two years.'[25]

NOTES

1. *ALi*, p. 196.
2. Ibid., p. 195.
3. D. Meadows, *Obedient Men* (London, 1955), pp. 6–7.
4. Ibid., p. 14.
5. Minister's Journal (AEPSJ, *Manresa Journal*, ii, 1875–84); *LN*, 13 (1880), pp. 322–4.
6. *ALi*, pp. 223–4.
7. Ibid., p. 200.
8. See especially R. F. Clarke, 'The Training of a Jesuit', *The Nineteenth Century*, 40 (1896), pp. 211–25; A. Thomas, *Hopkins the Jesuit* (London, 1969); Meadows, *Obedient Men*.
9. J. P. Thorp, *Friends and Adventures* (London, 1931), p. 39.
10. Ibid., p. 40.
11. *ALi*, p. 204.
12. *The Spiritual Exercises of St Ignatius*, trans. T. Corbishley (Wheathampstead, 1973), p. 80.
13. J. Morris, *Journals Kept during Times of Retreat* (London, 1894), p. 59.
14. J. H. Pollen, *The Life and Letters of Father John Morris* (London, 1896), p. 236.
15. *ALi*, p. 206.
16. Ibid., p. 208.
17. Pollen, *Life of Morris*, p. 238.
18. C. C. Abbott (ed.), *Further Letters of Gerard Manley Hopkins*, 2nd edn. (London, 1956), p. 161.
19. *ALi*, p. 208.
20. H. House and G. Storey (eds.), *The Journals and Papers of Gerard Manley Hopkins* (London, 1959), p. 195.
21. *LN*, 14 (1881), p. 242.
22. C. C. Abbott (ed.), *The Letters of Gerard Manley Hopkins to Robert Bridges* (London, 1935), p. 148.
23. The Porter's Journal is preserved in the AEPSJ.
24. K. Kendall, *Father Steuart* (London, 1950), p. 36.
25. *ALi*, p. 201.

4

A Hidden Decade

TYRRELL missed a stage in the normal Jesuit training. He expected
to remain at Manresa for one or two more years for a course in
classics, but he was moved straight to Stonyhurst in Lancashire to
study philosophy. Although he found the idea laughable, he was
considered proficient in Latin and Greek. Having travelled north
alone, he arrived at the seminary knowing virtually nobody, and
from the day of his arrival found himself thrown almost totally on to
his own devices. Term had not yet begun, so after the tight timetable
of Manresa, there was nothing particular that he had to do in the
long September days. He was free to read what he wanted, to talk to
whom he wanted, to go where he wanted. How different from the
novitiate, and how perplexing! After the observant novices, the
second-year scholastics seemed positively lax. Had the burning
commitment instilled by Father Morris been extinguished by just a
year of philosophy? Here, to his amazement, he heard Father Morris
spoken of as a rigorist who lacked the spirit of the Society. For two
years, to Tyrrell, he had *been* the Society. His approval had meant
everything, and now all that had been learnt to win that approval had
to be unlearnt. He felt duped and disorientated and, like Gerard
Manley Hopkins before him, homesick for Manresa.

St Mary's Hall, the seminary at Stonyhurst, 'a big rectangular
barrack of three floors and the attic',[1] stands about a quarter of a
mile from the magnificent Elizabethan buildings of the school. In
Tyrrell's time the house had just been extended, and, however
unimaginative the design, with rooms all alike, the scholastics still
welcomed the privacy after the cubicles of Manresa. Those at the
front looked across gardens and open fields to Pendle Hill. In 1870
Hopkins rejoiced in his view of 'a beautiful range of moors dappled
with light and shade'.[2] He also commented: 'It has rained many
times already and I know it will go on so to the end of the chapter.'[3]
At the back the building was surrounded by woods and farmland.

'Schools' began on 2 October. At 5.30 a.m. *Deo gratias* echoed
along the corridors to waken the students. As at Manresa, the day

was briefly offered to God—a sort of chapel parade—before the hour of meditation. Tyrrell was becoming a convinced opponent of this silent hour, which had been introduced by Acquaviva, the fifth General of the Jesuits, in place of the 'Little Office' of Our Lady that Ignatius had intended. Community mass followed at 7.00 a.m. There were two lectures in the morning and a long period of private study in the early evening. Three times a week there was a formal Latin debate, or 'circle', for an hour in the afternoon. One student began by giving a quarter-hour synopsis of the professor's last two lectures; for half an hour the 'objicients' challenged him at every possible point; and for the last quarter of an hour the professor himself was cross-questioned by the students. Once a month there was a 'Blandyke', a complete day off, when the seminarians thought nothing of walking twenty or thirty miles across the moors.

Tyrrell arrived at a time of particular intellectual ferment. Only three years earlier, Pope Leo XIII had called the Catholic Church to a renewed study of St Thomas Aquinas by the encyclical *Aeterni Patris*. Traditionally, the Jesuits had taught Aquinas as interpreted by Suarez and other approved commentators, but Tyrrell now passed under the influence of a man who rejected all that, and taught 'Aquinas, his own interpreter'.[4] This was Thomas Rigby, Professor of Logic, Acting Superior of the house, and first-year lecturer. Rigby was something of a philosophical genius, but he lacked the capacity to make things simple. One of his pupils wrote: 'I learned more from him than from all the professors I ever sat under: but the diet which he supplied was not "milk for babes".'[5] Students were attracted to him by his natural openness and friendliness, even if they did not understand what he taught. They appreciated his freedom of approach, far-sightednes, and insistence on a philosophy related to life. Tyrrell later remembered him as 'a very amiable, puzzleheaded good old thing whom everyone likes and laughs at'.[6] He was devoted to Rigby.

The habit of teaching Aquinas filtered through the mind of Suarez died hard for some. One of these, stolidly loyal to the main body of Jesuit teaching and opinion, was Bernard Boedder, Professor of Special Metaphysics and teacher of the second-year students. By the time they came to him the students had been thoroughly awakened by Rigby. Tyrrell wrote of Boedder: 'I never met a man more self-restrained and Aloysius-like on all other occasions, and more like a wild beast unchained when his views were attacked in the lesser or greater disputations.'[7] At the Greater Disputations Rigby would be present too, and there was nothing the students liked better than to set the one against the other. From top to bottom the house took sides, a situation that could not be allowed to last. In 1884 Rigby was removed to British Guiana, where he remained for fifteen years. When, in 1903, the Provincial proposed that he should become Prefect of Studies at St Beuno's, the General wrote back in amazement at the suggestion, and insisted that Rigby should never again be given charge of students.[8]

Tyrrell recognized that he was attracted to Rigby before he was attracted to Aquinas, but through the one he came to love the other. Once he began to appreciate Aquinas, he was thrilled by the sweep, the perspicacity, the insight he offered, so that long after he had rejected Thomism for its static and ahistorical nature, he could still write: 'Whatever order or method there is in my thought, whatever real faculty of reasoning and distinguishing I have acquired, I owe it to St Thomas.'[9] At St Mary's Hall his mind for the first time became thoroughly engaged. He was committed to the Catholic faith; Aquinas was the supreme teacher of Catholicism; from Aquinas he would learn. In the examination at the end of the first year he came out top.

In the debates Tyrrell began to develop a reputation as a shrewd and original thinker. He could never be a docile adherent of the Catholic system. He had to fight for his faith all the way, something that caused Father Morris to shed tears, but which won the admiration of Joseph Rickaby, spiritual and academic director of the house. In him Tyrrell found a guide of an entirely different order, tolerant, understanding, and gentle. Rickaby had the intelligence to value a questioning mind, and to support Tyrrell as he groped his way to a surer faith, based, for the time being, on the teaching of Aquinas. It was probably Rickaby who first encouraged him to read Newman.

Tyrrell made two important friendships at St Mary's. William Roche, whom he had known in Malta, shared his enthusiastic response to Rigby. Though utterly different in temperament and approach, he and Tyrrell were both avid students of Aquinas, lovers of Dante and Tennyson. When Roche said, 'The first thing a philosopher or theologian should realize, is the limitation of the powers of the human intellect,'[10] it might have been Tyrrell speaking. In his first year of theology Roche disturbed one of his seniors by maintaining a view without reference to any accepted theologian simply because it seemed true. Again, how like his friend! Edward Lawless, another close friend, was a Dubliner of similar background to Tyrrell who shared his taste in poetry. In later years he left the Society, and Tyrrell helped him through a breakdown. Lawless recalled that Tyrrell knew the whole of *In Memoriam* by heart.[11] Tyrrell called his 'walks and wanderings by the Hodder and in the woods and over the fells' with Lawless 'some of the brightest pictures' in his memory.[12] In particular he remembered one frosty Christmas morning when the two Irish converts listened spellbound to the bells of the old church at Mitton: two young hopefuls destined to leave the Society in despair.

Tyrrell was at St Mary's Hall for three years. He studied logic, ontology, mathematics, physics, psychology, and natural theology, delighting in the speculative philosophy of Aquinas, loathing the way his thought had been coarsened and materialized by later generations. Already he despised the triumphalism of the Catholic Church. Twenty-five years later a book was published by Richard F. Clarke, a fellow Jesuit, which expressed exactly the attitude that Tyrrell was learning to abhor:

In the philosophy of the Church there can be no new discoveries, but only developments of Truth already possessed. For fresh discovery means a setting aside of what exists already, and if what exists already is the perfect Truth, to set it aside is but to introduce the destructive poison of error. We cannot, therefore, be surprised if the Method of Discovery did not flourish among the Scholastic philosophers. Nor can it ever be the adopted method of the Catholic Church. She will ever look on, from her throne upon the Rock, and will watch unmoved the discoveries of modern science, knowing that they will contribute sooner or later, one and all, to illustrate the truth of her philosophy. She will watch the rise and fall of one system of philosophy after another, knowing that amid their dismantled ruins she will remain in her unshaken supremacy the true Queen of all Science and the Mistress of all Philosophy. For to her all arts and all sciences minister, but none more than the Art and Science of Logic, since the Catholic Church alone can challenge the world to point out a single inconsistency in her teaching, or a single weak point in the perfect system of Divine philosophy which God through her has given to the world.[13]

It was to take Tyrrell twenty-five years to formulate a searing critique of such nonsense. As a student, he only knew it was not to his taste. As a professor, he let Aquinas himself speak in refutation of such crudity. When he began to write for *The Month*, the Jesuit periodical, he never ceased to urge an attitude of responsible humility towards the discoveries of science.

Tyrrell was in his second year at St Mary's Hall when his mother's cancer took a turn for the worse. Clearly dying, she set out to return from Germany to Dublin, but she collapsed at the home of her brother in London, and by the time George reached her she was unconscious. She died shortly thereafter, leaving her son beside himself with guilt-ridden grief. 'I saw poor mother laid quietly in her grave on Friday—God rest her dear soul!', he wrote to his cousin.[14] Now, in a new way, the Society was his father and mother. In this year he barely passed his examinations. Just as after the death of Willie, bereavement, compounded by antipathy to the teaching of Bernard Boedder, destroyed his power to work. When he left Stonyhurst a year later it was with a bare 'pass' in the final examination. At the age of 24, he returned to Malta to be form-master for the first-year class.

Almost nothing is known of this period of his life. Under the Jesuit system, scholastics teach for a number of years. Tyrrell's three in Malta were a relatively short assignment. He went up the school with his class, who might well have expected him to see them through more of their school career. By his own account he was a good teacher. Like Dr Benson, a natural enthusiast, he must have drawn out the best in the boys and they the best in him. It would have been a source of wry amusement to him that one of his tasks was to teach writing, for he always maintained that he had held his pen wrongly from childhood, though he had a clear, flowing script. In his last year, in addition to the school work, he taught philosophy at the University of Valletta.

Malta could be a most uncomfortable place to live and work. One teacher complained that the masters' ignorance of Maltese made it impossible to get close to the boys. He called the island 'a rock with a few handfuls of earth dropped upon it, here and there'.[15] Tyrrell could cope with a temperature of 85°F in the shade for half the year, but everyone was troubled by the mosquitoes and sand-flies. Sea-bathing was the only escape. In 1887 cholera raged in Valletta, and three or four people died daily. The college was sufficiently far away not to be unduly alarmed. It had a hundred or so pupils, but Tyrrell's teaching load would not have been unreasonable. In his first year he read Newman's *Grammar of Assent* for the first time. It effected a 'profound revolution'[16] in his thought just when he was beginning to see the limitations of scholasticism. Newman's stress on the moral and intuitive dimension of certainty in religious belief provided a necessary complement to the intellectualism of nineteenth-century scholastic teaching. In 1886 Tyrrell found time to produce an extended review for *The Month*. He was beginning to write seriously. A lover of children, he called the three years in Malta 'the three purest and best years in some ways since I entered the hardening school of religious life'.[17]

Tyrrell now moved to St Beuno's in North Wales to study theology. It was ten years since Gerard Manley Hopkins had left the place where he wrote some of his most famous poetry: 'The Wreck of the Deutschland', 'The Windhover', and 'Pied Beauty'. Hopkins had been thrilled by the Vale of Clwyd, and by St Beuno's itself: 'The house stands on a steep hillside, it commands the long-drawn valley of the Clwyd to the sea, a vast prospect, and opposite is Snowdon and its range, just now it being bright visible but coming and going with the weather.' As for the college, 'It is built of limestone, decent outside, skimpin within, Gothic, like Lancing College done worse. The staircases, galleries, and bopeeps are inexpressible: it takes a fortnight to learn them. Pipes of affliction convey lukewarm water of affliction to some of the rooms, others more fortunate have fires.'[18] Jesuits always liked patent heating systems, but they caused no end of trouble. Term had barely started in 1888 before some of the hot water-pipes burst.

Students at St Beuno's were expected to work hard. Hopkins wrote of 'hours of study very close—lectures in dogmatic theology, moral ditto, canon law, church history, scripture, Hebrew and what not'.[19] He once complained to Robert Bridges: 'The close pressure of my theological studies leaves me time for hardly anything: the course is very hard, it must be said.'[20] On three days a week there were two lectures in the morning and three in the afternoon, plus a 'circle'. Ordination came at the end of the third year, and the pressure of lectures ceased in the fourth as the students prepared themselves for a final examination. Tyrrell was taught by Bernard Tepe, 'a German refugee of a solid Suarezian exhaustiveness in speculative matters, but no historian of dogmas',[21] John Pope, and John Rickaby, another dedicated Suarezian, but a forward-looking Scripture scholar who was carefully watched by Rome. The teaching at St Bueno's was particularly dry in this period, and discipline was at a low ebb. By the end of his course Tyrrell was rebellious and frustrated. Throughout the whole of his time at St Beuno's he clashed with Tepe. In 1889 he wrote an article setting out his view that Aquinas should be studied in seminaries not as an oracle of philosophical and theological certitude, but as a master of thought who might well be wrong yet was always instructive.[22] On such an occasion he gave an article to Roche for criticism. Roche advised against expressing his views as he had, because it would only cause trouble: 'Don't put it that way, Father, it will only cause trouble.' 'But I want to cause trouble,' replied Tyrrell, 'I am going to cause trouble.'[23]

The Beadle's Journal[24] gives a full picture of life at St Beuno's: the arrival of new students in August and September; the start of 'schools' on 1 October; the masses, concerts, and feasts at Christmas, including the annual Oyster Supper on 29 December; skating throughout the winter; epidemics of flu in February and March; the ending of fires in April; extra masses for Holy Week and Easter; examinations in July; the holiday at the villa in Barmouth each August; the annual retreat and the ordinations in September. A note was kept of defendants and objicients at the monthly formal disputations, and of any cases of illness in the house. On one occasion the Beadle recorded a particularly serious operation on Caesar, the dog, who suffered from constipation. The visit of Father Loftus, a secular priest from Ireland ('height 6ft. 6in. and broad and stout in proportion'), created something of a stir, as did the ability of Tyrrell's friend, Father Thurston, to walk more than fifty miles in a day. In Tyrrell's time a whole generation of famous converts, including Cardinals Newman and Manning, and Father Christie, died, and news of these losses is duly recorded. There were constant visits to and from the French Jesuits at Mold. Henri Bremond, later to be Tyrrell's closest friend, was so unhappy at the college there (a recently disused prison) that he felt that 'Abandon hope all ye who enter here' should be written on the high walls.[25] Names are not usually entered in the Journal, but Bremond was at St Beuno's just after Easter 1891, for Ash Wednesday, and for eight days over Easter 1892, the year in which he was due to be ordained. Although Tyrrell was away preaching at Holywell on Easter Day, they must have met. Bremond probably took every opportunity to escape to the peace of St Beuno's.

Tyrrell was active in both the Debating Club and the Essay Society.[26] When the students debated the motion, 'It is advisable that there be introduced into this country a political and moral censorship of all printed matter to be conducted by competent authority,' he predictably led the opposition. (The motion was carried.) He defended the proposition that 'In the English pulpit gesticulation should be the exception not the rule.' There was nothing he loathed more than preachers who practised gesticulation in front of a mirror. He also moved that, 'Apart from the divine prohibition, no valid reason has been adduced so far against the practice of lying.' This he won, despite an amendment that 'the above proposition is to be condemned as offensive to pious ears, pernicious, impious, scandalous, captious, rash and savouring of heresy'. It is not surprising that on this issue Tyrrell was a minimalist. When it suited him, he was capable of some extremely evasive interpretation of the divine prohibition.

Tyrrell also wrote a number of essays 'to amuse the monks'.[27] Perhaps the most topical—certainly the most cheeky—was 'Cramming and Other Causes of Mental Dyspepsia',[28] a thinly veiled attack on the intellectual diet at St Beuno's. Four others, published in *The Month*, share a common debt to Swift. By imagining trips to far-away places Tyrrell demonstrates the folly which surrounds us at home. Naturally, the supreme folly is pride of intellect and blindness to God. The real theme of these early essays is the problem of religious knowledge. Twice Tyrrell uses a favourite analogy: it is as difficult for man, in all his limitation, to understand God as it is for a blind man to know the meaning of colour. If he is to understand anything, it will be by the use of analogy, and if that is the case it is imperative that he realize the limits of his understanding. In 'The Contents of a Pre-Adamite Skull'[29] Gulliver meets a race who lack the senses of hearing, touch, and smell, but are endowed with a highly developed sensual apparatus through which they have a fuller knowledge of God than any post-Adamite. 'Among the Korahites'[30] describes the opposite situation: a blind people who mock at the notion of vision, and indignantly repudiate the truths of religion in the name of science. So Tyrrell, like Swift, cuts men down to size. It is not so much that we are wicked, more that we are stupid—and at our most stupid when we fail to recognize the limitations of human understanding. We should learn that what we know is very limited, but it is enough, because it brings the humble and the wise to the knowledge of God. For Tyrrell, the problem of knowledge is not ultimately intellectual, but moral.

Tyrrell was two years behind his friend William Roche at St Beuno's, and since ordination came at the end of the third year, he had been at the college just a year when he wrote some verses for the day his friend became a priest. They give an insight into his own feelings when, two years later on three successive days, 18, 19, and 20 September 1891, he became subdeacon, deacon, and priest:

> Send forth, O Lord, Thy Truth and Light
>   To be my comfort still,
> For they have led my steps aright
> Through all the dark and dreary night
>   Unto Thy Holy Hill.
>
> And onward to Thy dwelling place
>   Have brought me on my way
> Until at last before Thy Face
> Here at the Altar-throne of grace
>   I stand with joy today.
>
> O Christ, my joy from early youth
> Thou art that Light and Thou that Truth,
>   Be with me still I pray;
> In youth Thou wert my earliest friend,
> Be with me, Jesu, to the end
>   Nor suffer me to stray.
> Be with me 'till the morning break
>   And shadows flee away'.[31]

One close friend who missed Tyrrell's ordination was Herbert Thurston. He had just completed his fourth year and had left for London to become a staff writer on *The Month*. A cautious and careful historian, he applied the tools of historical criticism to uncritical hagiography in a way that Tyrrell admired, but found too painstaking for his taste. A number of letters from Tyrrell to Thurston survive.[32] They are skittish, with an underlying note of bitterness. Just before his ordination he told Thurston: 'I write all day from morning till night regardless of the price of stationery. It is the only narcotic that is strong enough to make me forget myself and my imaginary woes.'[33] The real trouble was that he had so few outlets. He had joined the Jesuits in the expectation of heroic service. At the end of seven years of study, eleven of preparation in all, he had ceased to believe that he could ever be useful or fulfilled. In April 1892 he wrote:

I have not the remotest idea what is going to be done with me next year; and I am sure I don't care, unless it be that I hope I may close my books for ever and begin to be worth from ten to fifteen shillings a week, which after all is a very moderate ambition for a man who has spent thirty years preparing to begin life.[34]

There was in Tyrrell some deep inner pain and self-disgust which could only be assuaged by active involvement with others, by writing or study. When he had time on his hands he immediately felt worthless, a chronic wastrel forever condemned to rue his profligacy. 'I am sorry you and Roche have formed ideas of my capabilities which will certainly never be realised,' he wrote to Thurston. 'Even if I had the native facility with which you credit me, there is an Irish improvidence in my blood that would prevent my ever making much use of it.'[35] The improvidence was indeed there, but so was the ability. Tyrrell could have been a doughty fighter for the Jesuits, not against them. This was, of course, what he always wanted, but came to believe was impossible. As yet, though, the 'preparation for the beginning' was still not over. Many Jesuits go to a parish or other employment between their theology and their tertianship. Tyrrell went on 'supply' to Preston, but due to his intellectual gifts and potential as a teacher, he was not allowed to remain in parish work. In October he was sent back to Manresa as a tertian.

NOTES

1. D. Meadows, *Obedient Men* (London, 1955), p. 138.
2. C. C. Abbott (ed.), *Further Letters of Gerard Manley Hopkins*, 2nd edn. (London, 1956), p. 112.
3. Ibid.
4. *AL1*, p. 242.
5. *LN*, 32 (1913–14), p. 132.
6. Tyrrell to Bremond, 3 Jan. 1904 (BN, Fonds Bremond).
7. *AL1*, p. 245.
8. Martin to Colley, 18 Oct. 1903 (ARSJ, *RPA*, v).
9. *AL1*, p. 248.
10. *OD*, p. 378.
11. E. Lawless to Norah Shelley, 25 July 1909 (SAUL, MS 30756B).
12. *AL1*, p. 261.
13. R. F. Clarke, *Logic* (Manuals of Catholic Philosophy, Stonyhurst Series; London, 1889), p. 483.

14. Tyrrell to William Tyrrell, 18 May 1884 (*AL1*, p. 279).
15. *LN*, 19 (1887–8), p. 247.
16. Tyrrell to R. Gout, 26 May 1906 (*AL2*, p. 209).
17. Tyrrell to Maude Petre, 2 Jan. 1901 (BL, Petre Papers).
18. Abbott, *Further Letters*, p. 124.
19. Ibid.
20. C. C. Abbott (ed.), *The Letters of Gerard Manley Hopkins to Robert Bridges* (London, 1935), p. 31.
21. J. Crehan, *Father Thurston* (London, 1952), p. 22.
22. 'Aquinas Resuscitatus', *American Catholic Quarterly Review*, 16 (1891), pp. 673–90.
23. *OD*, p. 381.
24. The St Beuno's Beadle's Journal is preserved in AEPSJ.
25. A. Blanchet, *Henri Bremond* (Paris, 1975), p. 38.
26. A. Thomas, 'George Tyrrell: From Student Days', *Heythrop Journal*, 11 (1970), pp. 170–2.
27. Tyrrell to Thurston, 15 Nov. 1891 (AEPSJ).
28. *The Month*, 67 (1889), pp. 410–19.
29. Ibid., pp. 56–73.
30. Ibid., 72 (1891), pp. 81–93.
31. *LN*, 57 (1949), p. 3.
32. These have been collected as R. Butterworth (ed.), *A Jesuit Friendship: Letters of George Tyrrell to Herbert Thurston* (London, 1988).
33. Tyrrell to Thurston, Sept. or Oct. 1891 (0075).
34. Tyrrell to Thurston, 16 Apr. 1892.
35. Tyrrell to Thurston, 15 Nov. 1891.

5

Early Thought of a Young Priest

THE tertianship is the third year of the Jesuit novitiate and the last of training. Having completed his philosophy and theology, become a priest, and accumulated some experience as a pastor and teacher, the tertian father has to return to the life of work and prayer he lived when he first joined the Society. Once more he makes a thirty-day retreat, and he now studies the constitutions of the Society in depth. Tyrrell could not leave the grounds without permission, and could read nothing but spiritual books. Hopkins explained the point of all this in a letter to his friend, R. W. Dixon

This Tertianship or Third Year of Probation or second Noviceship . . . is not really a noviceship at all in the sense of a time during which a candidate or probationer makes trial of our life and is free to withdraw. At the end of the noviceship proper we take vows which are perpetually binding and renew them every six months (not *for* every six months but for life) till we are professed or take the final degree we are to hold, of which in the Society there are several. It is in preparation for these last vows that we make the tertianship; which is called a *schola affectus* and is meant to enable us to recover that fervour which may have cooled through application to study and contact with the world.[1]

In Tyrrell's time the tertian was once more enclosed in the little world of Manresa. He had few opportunities to write letters, and heard virtually no news of the world outside. Although as fellow tertians he had friends like Charles Blount, Henry Farmer, and Herbert Thurston, Tyrrell must have found the renewed confinement and inactivity almost beyond endurance.

This time he had a far more intelligent guide than Father Morris. Edward Purbrick, Master of Tertians, had been at school with Edward Benson, Archbishop of Canterbury, and J. B. Lightfoot, Bishop of Durham, and had remained on intimate terms with them, though he was a noted ultramontane who welcomed the growing Rome-centredness of the Catholic Church that he had seen in his lifetime. As a former Provincial, he was a man of great experience, strong, orderly, and firm. Nothing is known of the Long Retreat which took place in October and early November, though scraps of Tyrrell's commentary on the *Spiritual Exercises* survive in *The Soul's Orbit*.[2] The basic ideas were undoubtedly worked out by 1893, so they give some hint of the way in which he would have approached the retreat. The five hours' meditation each day he undoubtedly found difficult. With typical exaggeration, he wrote to Thurston in 1896: 'I have meditated a good deal, in bed, at meals, and elsewhere, but never have I made a meditation, nor do I profess to understand that mysterious art of thinking to order.'[3]

Despite this disclaimer, Tyrrell made the *Exercises* thoroughly his own, and, in view of his later development, it is important to remember that they were a major influence upon him. Two important principles to which he always adhered come ultimately from the *Exercises*. The first is a profound belief in the ability of the individual soul to recognize its own good. Ignatius wrote: 'In the course of these spiritual exercises, it is more appropriate that, in the search for the divine will, the Creator and Lord should be left to deal Himself with the soul that belongs to Him.'[4] Tyrrell's approach as a spiritual counsellor was based on the assumption that individuals would be drawn in the right direction if they responded to interior spiritual indications, what Ignatius calls 'consolations' and 'desolations'. Tyrrell commented:

It is thus that the greatest experts in the spiritual life have taught us to teach ourselves; amongst them St Ignatius of Loyola, who bids us feel our way along by observing the inward movements of 'consolation' or 'desolation' which attend certain actions or purposes of action, according as they foster or retard our true spiritual growth and union with God.[5]

The job of the spiritual director is to stay in the background as much as possible and let the Holy Spirit do his work. This links up with the second important point, that the fundamental human level is not that of thought but that of feeling. Tyrrell writes: 'From the first "annotation", as it is called, to the very end, the book of the *Spiritual Exercises* is pervaded by the principle that, on the whole, what we think depends on what we feel far more than our feeling depends on our thought.'[6] It was this conviction that led to Tyrrell's enthusiasm for thinkers like Newman, Blondel, and Bergson, who recognized the importance of the will, as opposed to the exaggerated stress on reason in the scholastic teaching he had received. More than this, the *Spiritual Exercises* fed his concern for religion as a practical activity, his concern with experience, with conscience, and with Christ. The generous, whole-hearted, and imaginative spirit of Ignatius appealed to him immensely. He found it committed but never inflexible.

Tyrrell arrived for the tertianship on 1 October 1892, and three days later went into the thirty-day retreat. A major highlight that year was the sudden visit of the General just before Christmas. There was barely time to fling up a few garlands both outside and inside the house; to practise a welcome chorus written by Father Farmer, together with the national anthem; and to rehearse the cheering so that it would not be ragged. Father Martin could only stay to lunch before moving on, but the welcome he was given, and the request that the day be commemorated annually, made a particularly warm impression. This was the man whose health was to suffer as a result of worrying over Tyrrell, and of whom Tyrrell recognized that 'he was *comparatively* temperate, and as sincere as possible for an official'.[7] Tyrrell preached at high mass on Christmas Day, and in February left for Lenten Missions at Chesterfield, Westminster, and Wolverhampton. In April he returned, and in July heard that after an eight-day retreat at the end of the month, he was to go to Oxford so that he would have time for writing. Edward Purbrick's confidential report described him as 'a good religious, regular, best suited to intellectual work, who also possesses an outstanding gift of communication, which leads one to hope particularly that he applies himself in work of this kind, using the fruit of his wide reading in philosophy and theology, disciplines to which he brings a mind devoted to St Thomas'.[8]

Once he had moved, Tyrrell speedily produced a review of Wilfrid Ward's life of his father, W. G. Ward, who played a prominent part in the Oxford Movement and became an ultramontane Catholic. Part I of the book had been read to the community at St Beuno's. The review brought Tyrrell into correspondence with Ward, and led him to pay increased attention to Newman's *Grammar of Assent*, which he was reading for the fourth time. At this stage he hoped that the study of Newman would enable the Church 'to pour Catholic truth from the scholastic into the modern mould without losing a drop in the transfer'.[9] In this way he could hold on to the best of Newman and Aquinas. It was a hope that was later to be dashed. Tyrrell was unhappy in Oxford, and soon requested a transfer. After only a few months he was moved to the 'Lowe House' Mission in St Helens.

Here, for one year, he did the work he most enjoyed and for which he was in many ways best suited: preaching, hearing confessions, and visiting among the poor. The only record of this time is in two small volumes of manuscript sermons.[10] These show the longing for whole-heartedness in the service of God, the central thrust of Ignatian spirituality. Tyrrell talks of 'the unhappiness which many experience in the service of God because they are themselves half and half and not thorough'.[11] He enthusiastically embraces the Catholic Church as the vehicle for his own whole-heartedness:

Look for a moment, Dear Brethren, at the great Kingdom of God the Catholic Church whose root is at Rome the old centre and capital of the Gentile Empire, and whose branches are in all lands, stretching from sea to sea and to the uttermost bounds of the earth; look at her highly developed organisation, her hierarchy, her discipline, her doctrine. What a gigantic power she is! How rationalists and misbelievers are at loss to account for her origin, her spread, her persistence.[12]

This is Tyrrell's version of *securus iudicat orbis terrarum* ('firm is the judgement of the whole world'), the words which were instrumental in Newman's conversion. One cannot deny the smugness of the language. How could Tyrrell of all people talk in such terms? Here is the contradiction of his faith. As an incorrigible idealist, he believed in the Roman Church with a kind of visionary fervour, and at this stage of somewhat uncritical orthodoxy he still accepted that the Roman system, intellectual and institutional, worked to promote these visionary aims. Bit by bit, he lost his confidence in the system, but the more this happened, the more he clung to his hope for a renewal of the Church by a return to the sources; in its essence, a return to the concerns of the saints rather than those of the Curia. In this early sermon Tyrrell glories in the 'gigantic power' of the Church. In later years he would not identify that power, which he saw as spiritual in both origin and nature, with the hierarchy, discipline, or doctrine of the present Church, but only with the Church of the future, renewed and transformed by the 'gigantic power' of the spirit. Looking back on his early sermons, Tyrrell lamented that he could not express 'how much of his sanity and balance he lost by the practice of preaching or how difficult it is to regain the first elements of common sense'.[13] It was a typical overstatement.

Nevertheless, as a young priest, Tyrrell could be very defensive. In view of later developments it is ironical to hear him warning,

Unconsciously and by force of example with our natural imitativeness or sheeplike tendency to follow the crowd, we come to adopt non-Catholic phrases, modes of speech which gradually work their way into our mind, non-Catholic axioms and maxims, views and theories, until, while we still retain the substance and profession of the faith, the whole temper and tone of our mind is protestant.[14]

This is so totally uncharacteristic of the later Tyrrell that it shows quite another facet of his youthful character: as in his struggles with Father Morris, he still needed to prove to the world that he could be a good Catholic. By using such language, Tyrrell allowed himself to play on the fears and prejudices of his hearers. The irony is that little by little, often learning from Protestant critics—and at times sounding like one—Tyrrell would come to accuse the whole Catholic Church of departing from its Catholicism, while the Church accused him of falling victim to the very tendency he is warning against here.

In many ways these early sermons show the clear outline of Tyrrell's later thought. He says of the Church: 'She is merely the extension of Christ; she carries on or rather carries out the work of the Incarnation,'[15] a theme he was to develop in *External Religion*. What he says of revelation and mystery in an undelivered sermon is typical:

For us, Dear Brethren, revelation and mystery are two names for one thing. Eternal Truth is *revealed* to us so far as God gives us a twilight glimpse of its rough outline, or of some little corner of the picture here and there. It is a mystery because so much of the detail is unrevealed, because the connection and relation of part with part is for the most, past all conjecture.[16]

Tyrrell roundly attacks the contempt for the body that was rife in Catholic thinking. Characteristically, he relates his vision of the whole man to the whole doctrine of the Trinitarian God:

There is no such thing as a divided charity which loves the soul and is careless for the body. We must love all that God the Father created, all that God the Son redeemed; all that God the Holy Ghost sanctifies and consecrated; that is the whole man; with all his capacities for joy and for sorrow earthly and heavenly, temporal and eternal. If a man say I love my neighbour's soul, and is indifferent to his temporal sorrows he is a liar and the truth is not in him.[17]

Tyrrell's writing and preaching were always refreshing, arresting, dangerous. Despite the deference to contemporary apologetic, bringing that unexpected note of triumphalism into his preaching, there is at every point such a firm hold on Christianity as a sacramental religion that Tyrrell is never in danger of confusing what *is* with what *ought to be*. What is, in terms of the Church, is only the pointer to what ought to be, and one day will be. The danger was that it needed only a shift in the balance between what is seen and what is unseen, a shaking of confidence in the visible Church, for the carefully balanced ecclesiology to turn into a searing indictment of an over-confident religion, which, like the Grand Inquisitor of Dostoevsky's *The Brothers Karamazov*, has traded the hope of a spiritual kingdom for the embattled certitude of an earthly one. Over the next decade this is the shift that took place.

Tyrrell spent a year in the parish. To his great regret, he was then moved back to St Mary's Hall to teach philosophy. Despite his reluctance, he was told he had to go. The records show that he arrived just after the start of term, and even then he did not begin lecturing immediately. For anyone with eyes to see, it was obvious that there would be trouble. Bernard Boedder was still teaching the Suarezianism that Tyrrell and Roche had repudiated a decade before. Joseph Thorp, a student in 1894 and a devoted supporter of Tyrrell, described how the students used to cheer Boedder's 'passionate disquisitions', and how hurt the guileless professor was when he discovered that all this enthusiasm was simulated.[18] Roche was already teaching logic at the seminary when Tyrrell arrived in an aggressive mood, believing that his own devotion to Thomas, independent of all commentators, had been endorsed by the Pope himself.

During Tyrrell's first year at St Mary's he seems to have been less prominent than Roche as an opponent of Boedder, but more popular. Things came to a head at a formal debate, or *Menstruum*, before the Provincial. An essay was read attacking Boedder's position, Boedder responded, and a row developed between Boedder and Roche. 'At the end each party seemed satisfied that the other was quite off the point.'[19] In the summer Tyrrell wrote to Thurston: 'You hear we are losing Roche. Don't believe it for a month at least. I shall not survive him long if it proves true.'[20] It was true. Tyrrell's response was to write to the Provincial asking to be released from his teaching post at St Mary's Hall, as he could see that the Provincial had decided for the 'anti-papal' faction ('anti-papal' because Tyrrell believed the Pope had encouraged the study of Aquinas rather than his commentators) when he removed Roche.[21] Roche left at the end of the vacation. The Beadle's Journal for 30 September 1895 reads:

'Fr Roche left us this morning for St Beuno's, where he is to teach the short course. He is much regretted by all—especially by those who are of the "Roman" . . . school, of which he was a staunch upholder. All came down to the door to bid him farewell.'[22] Five months later the General wrote to the English Provincial, asking for Tyrrell to be watched and the Provincial kept closely in touch with the situation at St Mary's.[23]

This was the result of Tyrrell's first serious clash with authority. During his first year's teaching at St Mary's he had produced a defence of his theological method, which involved direct reading of Aquinas and the use of Cajetan and Ferrariensis, both Dominican commentators. In this he believed he was following the explicit instructions of Rome. Mindful of past clashes, he sent a copy of his essay to Bernard Tepe, his old Professor of Scholastic Theology at St Beuno's, still an unyielding follower of the Jesuit Suarez among the commentators on Aquinas, and a fierce critic of all that younger men like Tyrrell and Roche now stood for. Tyrrell also sent his piece to Cardinal Mazzella, a Jesuit, the Pope's Prefect of Studies, and one of the most influential voices in Rome. Tepe, for whom Tyrrell's position represented a kind of treason, predictably wrote a heated response, calling Tyrrell 'our Reformer' and 'the adversary'. Mazzella, as Tyrrell had intended, wrote sympathetically, supporting Tyrrell's defence of what he and Roche had been doing as following the wishes of Rome. Somewhat disingenuously, Tyrrell had appealed to the General for guidance in this matter, turning over to him his initial correspondence with Tepe. The General diplomatically sounded out the English Provincial before he replied, asking Scoles what sort of man Tyrrell was. Scoles replied that he was 'eminently well-intentioned, but that an agitated mood impaired his judgement'. Whatever the theological merits of Tyrrell's case, there was nothing wrong with his political judgement. Once he could quote Mazzella in his favour, he knew that he could defend himself against all but the most determined assaults. The General wrote back cautiously, and let events unfold.[24]

The new academic year had begun badly. Two days before the beginning of term there was a dispute over the number of lectures to be held each week. Tyrrell, as Professor of Ethics, refused to lecture, and Roche, so soon to depart, publicly joined in the complaints. Further eruptions followed. The General complained that Tyrrell 'thought he knew more of St Thomas than all the rest of the

Society'.[25] When the Provincial visited St Mary's Hall he was disconcerted to find that there was no essay from the logicians at the *Menstruum*, 'owing to a disagreement between the essayist and the professor'.[26] There can be little surprise that he was driven to remove the most provocative member of staff at the end of the academic year.

Amongst some members of the community Tyrrell was idolized, amongst others he was disliked and distrusted. Writing to Mazzella offered only short-term advantages. Tyrrell was always ready to take up his pen, as was his right, and address himself to those at the very top, but playing off the Cardinal against the General and the Provincial was a dangerous game that won him few friends in high places. Considerations of prudence, however, he dismissed as beneath contempt, for caution had no part in his nature. He once told Thorp: 'Ask questions, inconvenient questions. Satire may be your best weapon.'[27] This was not a prescription for popularity. If he detected any hint of insincerity he was utterly caustic. Some of the scholastics worked for weeks to produce a comic opera, *The Philosopher's Stone*, which went down well in the community. Thorp unwisely fished for praise from Tyrrell. All he got was the crushing enquiry: 'And are you going to be a priest or a dramatic author?'[28] It was with the lay brothers that Tyrrell was most at ease. Here he could take out his pipe and relax as he had done in the company of 'Brother Bob' Dolling. Even at the end of his life, when he had left the Society, he wrote to Brother Everard: 'You plod on in your old ways, but some of us must follow our own.'[29]

Tyrrell made no secret of the line he took in his teaching. He sincerely believed that he was acting in accordance with the Pope's wishes as expressed in *Aeterni Patris*, which had commended a return to the 'golden wisdom' of St Thomas, though not a slavish adherence to all the conclusions of the scholastics. The encyclical had warned that this wisdom should be drawn from the 'fountains' of Thomas himself, or at least—and this was the source of the confusion—'from those streams that are derived from the fountain itself and still flow entire and untainted'.[30] Did this, or did this not, include Suarez? An editorial in *The Tablet* provided further support for Tyrrell's reading of the encyclical when it argued that 'It is not St Thomas's "body of doctrines"—preeminently valuable as they are —but the *method* of St Thomas, which the Pope holds forth as an ever victorious weapon in the fight against error', and when it added: 'It is the study of the great authorities at first hand which he so earnestly inculcates.'[31] This was precisely what Tyrrell wanted, and he pushed the licence given him by *Aeterni Patris* to the limit. In the house magazine he wrote an account of the *Tabula Aurea* of Peter de Bergamo, which was a comprehensive index to the works of Aquinas.[32] Tyrrell called it 'the clearest, safest, surest guide to the doctrine of Aquinas', for it could be used to gain an understanding of Thomism as a system; with a characteristic twist, he added: 'This, rather than truth, should be our direct aim so far as Aquinas is to be an instrument of education.'[33] He wrote to Thurston: 'If D[ivus] T[homas] were studied as Dante is studied, it would be at least an education in a classic, even though no one were to assent inwardly to his teaching.'[34]

Teaching Thomas rather than Suarez was one thing—Thomas Rigby had done that—deliberately prescinding from the *truth* of Thomism was quite another. This was a position that horrified Boedder, who publicly told Tyrrell that if his views were taken to their logical conclusion they would end in agnosticism. In later years Tyrrell came very close to this. To his critics, the view he was advocating looked like a prescription for anarchy.

In the next fifteen years Tyrrell's mind, and his pen, worked at white heat. He was a man in a frenzy to question, to provoke, to tear down and rebuild, and eventually to proclaim. For all this he found licence in the Church of the past and the future, but little freedom in the Church of the present, which to him was hidebound and petty. Where was the sovereign moral freedom and fearlessness of Christ, the sanctified restlessness of saints like Ignatius, the imaginative and intellectual boldness of Aquinas? Where was the urgent commitment to changing so much that needed to be changed? The inner pain from the past and the outer pain of misunderstanding drove him to unremitting activity. He told Thurston:

> I only write because I must,
> And sing but as the linnets sing.

It is a relief to address myself to an inane sheet of paper which at least if not sympathetic, is silent . . . It is a sense of approaching extinction that harries me to write down all I have to say before the funeral.[35]

In this case he is talking about extinction as a Jesuit, though the thought of imminent death never left him.

Writing helped to clear Tyrrell's mind. In these years the medi-

tations that were to become *Nova et Vetera* poured out. Paradoxically disgusted with himself, Tyrrell suggested that they be called
Gemitus Columbae ('The Groaning of a Dove') or *Excrementa
Hirundinis* ('The Droppings of a Swallow').[36] He wrote controversial articles of unimpeachable orthodoxy on the sacraments and
'zoophily' (in this controversy with the Quaker Frances Cobbe he is
both arrogant and condescending); besides books by Wilfrid Ward,
he reviewed works on *The Foundations of Belief, Social Evolution,*
and *Modern Science and Modern Thought.* Much the most important essay was one calling for 'A Change of Tactics' in Catholic
apologetic.[37] The Protestant controversy, argued Tyrrell, had
absorbed Catholic energy and distorted Catholic self-understanding
for long enough. Now it was time to show the Catholic faith in all its
beauty and cohesion to the unbelieving world. This needed men who
could interpret the age to the Church, and the Church to the age.
Among those specifically called to this role were the Jesuits. It was
usual to argue 'that the Order . . . was manifestly raised up by God to
combat the new-born heresy of Luther, to vindicate the principles of
obedience and authority, and to carry the doctrine of the Papacy to
its final development in the Vatican Council,'[38] but all this, Tyrrell
argues, had been achieved, and it was time for the Society to address
itself to the wider questions raised by contemporary science and
culture. By implication, Tyrrell was criticizing the Jesuits for a kind
of sclerosis and a backward-looking mentality. It was simply naïve of
him to think that this would win approval or go unremarked
—particularly as there was so much truth in what he had to say.
Characteristically disappointed and crudely self-deprecatory, he
wrote to Thurston: 'The reception accorded to my last menstruation
(of Febr.) by "the faculty" at S. Beuno's made me throw up my hands
in despair.'[39] But what did he expect? It was not, according to most
Jesuits, 'interpretation' and 'understanding' that the age needed, but
conversion. Tyrrell was calling the Society and the Church to that
with which, in the eyes of those in authority, it was more than
satisfactorily engaged.

Disaffected himself, Tyrrell continued to spread disaffection. The
debates he had witnessed as a student were renewed, with him
pushing his ideas about Thomism to the limit, as he held forth against
the conservative Boedder. Tyrrell was clearer, more witty, and more
determined than his old teacher Rigby. The clashes had to be
stopped. As soon as 'schools' began in October 1896 he was moved

to Farm Street, but the incident was not yet quite closed. In December Tyrrell wrote to tell the General that he had no wish to teach again, as he now knew that he was not trusted by the Society. What had really offended him was that 'Superiors have not had the courage or the charity to remonstrate with me or point out what was wrong or excessive. To this moment I have not been told definitively the causes of complaint against me.' He went on: 'At the age of 36 I find myself out of place and not wanted in the Society.' However, he had no intention of leaving the Jesuits, nor would he do so as long as he remained in sympathy with the fundamental principles of St Ignatius, but he would rather leave than 'be paralysed by a mysterious reputation as a dangerous man'.[40] When the General explained that complaints had come from certain Fathers and from scholastics that Tyrrell's mind was reported not to be docile and modest enough, that he lacked the inner quiet needed for the formation of scholastics, and that, anyway, the Provincial was quite within his rights to move him, Tyrrell did not take up the argument over Thomas again, but sadly admitted that he might indeed have harmed his students: 'Perhaps I did not take enough account of their weak constitution, and gave adult food to babes, who really needed milk.'[41]

NOTES

1. C. C. Abbott (ed.), *The Correspondence of Gerard Manley Hopkins and Richard Watson Dixon* (London, 1935), p. 75.
2. Published under the name of Maude Petre (London, 1904). Tyrrell wrote chaps. 1–5, 9, 11, 14 (*AL2*, p. 83).
3. Tyrrell to Thurston, 9 Aug. 1896 (AEPSJ).
4. *The Spiritual Exercises of St Ignatius*, trans. T. Corbishley (Wheathampstead, 1973), p. 16.
5. *The Soul's Orbit*, p. 10.
6. Ibid., pp. 11–12.
7. Tyrrell to Thurston, 4 May 1906.
8. ARSJ, ANGL. 1007, XI.30.
9. Tyrrell to Ward, 12 Dec. 1893 (SAUL, Ward Papers).
10. These are kept in the AEPSJ.
11. Sermon of 12 Nov. 1893.
12. Sermon of 19 Nov. 1893.
13. W. J. Williams to Ward, undated (SAUL, VII 318a (2)).
14. Sermon of 24 Dec. 1893.
15. Sermon of 10 Sept. 1893.

16. Sermon of 7 Jan. 1894.
17. Sermon of 'Pentecost 6' 1894.
18. J. Thorp, *Friends and Adventures* (London, 1931), pp. 29–30.
19. Philosophers' Beadle's Journal, 31 May 1895 (AEPSJ).
20. Tyrrell to Thurston, undated (0006).
21. Tyrrell to Scoles, autumn 1895 (ARSJ, ANGL, 1021, IA.8).
22. Philosophers' Beadle's Journal, 30 Sept. 1895.
23. Martin to Scoles. 14 Feb. 1896 (ARSJ, *RPA*, iv, p. 179).
24. The sources for this paragraph are collected in ARSJ, ANGL. 1021, IA; for Mazzella's involvement, see *AL2*, p. 42.
25. *AL2*, p. 42.
26. Philosophers' Beadle's Journal, 22 May 1896.
27. Thorp, *Friends and Adventures*, p. 39.
28. Ibid., p. 38.
29. P. Caraman, C. C. *Martindale* (London, 1967), p. 82.
30. *The Tablet*, NS22 (23 Aug. 1879), p. 238.
31. Ibid., p. 229.
32. 'The "Tabula Aurea" of Peter de Bergamo', *Heythrop Journal*, 10 (1969), pp. 275–9.
33. Ibid., pp. 275, 278.
34. Tyrrell to Thurston, undated (0006).
35. Tyrrell to Thurston, undated (0007).
36. Tyrrell to Thurston, 9 Aug. 1896.
37. *The Month*, 86 (1896), pp. 215–27.
38. Ibid., p. 226.
39. Tyrrell to Thurston, undated (0007).
40. Tyrrell to Martin, 26 Dec. 1896 (ARSJ, ANGL. 1021, IA.11).
41. Tyrrell to Martin, 14 Jan. 1897 (IA.12).

6

Farm Street Writer

TYRRELL was brought to London to work as a writer. A small scriptorium had been established at the back of the Jesuit complex in Mount Street, Mayfair. Here, in the Farm Street building, *The Month*, journal of the English Jesuits, was produced. Sydney Smith, the editor, was convinced that an intellectual journal would show the people of England that not all Catholics were credulous and uneducated. He encouraged a controversial tone, writing on Anglican questions himself, and looking to Tyrrell for contributions on ethics, science, and modern society. Thurston wrote learned pieces on liturgical and medieval matters. John Pollen wrote on the Elizabethan age and its martyrs. In the first three months Tyrrell did not produce a great deal, but from the end of 1896 he wrote a steady stream of articles—some of very poor quality.

He arrived at a time of considerable ferment. The papal bull *Apostolicae Curae*, in which Anglican orders were condemned as 'absolutely null and utterly void', had just been published. Not until early 1897 did Tyrrell join the fray with a controversial piece criticizing the New Year pastoral of the Archbishop of York. He mocked him for demonstrating how, in effect, 'by a sudden and adroit movement, the Church of England has placed her left eye against the fist of the Church of Rome'.[1] Two months later he took up the dispute as to whether sacrificial terminology was appropriate for the Anglican Eucharist. He found that 'the whole present Anglican position rests on the fiction of continuity, itself dependent on an equivocation and the fruitful mother of innumerable equivocations'.[2] In July, however, he returned to a more eirenic tone with an essay that saw in the Anglo-Catholic movement 'the direct action of God'.[3] This article was moderate enough to attract a grateful letter from Lord Halifax, whose work for unity between Canterbury and Rome lay in ruins after *Apostolicae Curae*. Tyrrell wrote back, telling Halifax frankly that he thought he had been too sanguine in his hopes for corporate reunion between the two Churches, but deploring the bitterness engendered by the controversy.[4] He was obviously beginning to recover from the 'taint of the virus of the controversial and theological fever'[5] which he later looked back upon with shame.

Apart from general reviews and occasional pieces, Tyrrell's main concern was mysticism and devotion. In May 1897 his first book, *Nova et Vetera*,[6] subtitled *Informal Meditations for Times of Spiritual Dryness*, appeared. He called it 'a record of private musings'. It was in fact the product of years of meditation, pen in hand, so there was no shortage of material. He was not trying to say anything new, but he wanted to jolt his readers; he wanted them to 'stop and listen' and relearn truths they had known but forgotten. It was a dangerous tactic, open to serious misinterpretation, as it carried an implicit criticism of the way devotion was taught, and it meant that Tyrrell's most orthodox statements might be misread as heresy simply because they sounded different. Not that Tyrrell cared if he raised suspicion: he had no use for self-preservation, especially when he so regularly met people who, like himself, were stifled by the banality of conventional devotion. Maude Petre, a grateful reader, remembered how 'to many silent sufferers in convents, but not convents only, the informal meditations of *Nova et Vetera* came as a breath of fresh air into a close room'.[7]

Tyrrell achieved his effects by directness and honesty. The book was a success because it was written out of immediate personal experience, avoiding spiritual clichés. Few readers would have guessed how much of his childhood he was revealing when he wrote: 'All love what they labour for—even as God loves the troublesome souls, or mothers their crippled children, or scapegrace, thankless sons.' Already Tyrrell knew that 'There is no harder cross than loneliness and isolation, the sense of being out in the cold, not wanted, perhaps to some extent "boycotted"; and there is no greater charity than that which lightens it.' By looking into his own heart he found the key to understanding and loving others.

Theologically, he expressed himself in the language of immanence, basing himself securely on the teaching of Ignatius. The book returns several times to the conviction that God 'uses the human heart as an instrument whereby to love Himself, and long for Himself, and praise Himself; and to love and praise all else in Him and for Him; to love those whom He loves and as He loves them'. That is, as it were, to look at human experience from God's side. What man knows, in the words of the 'First Principle and Foundation' of the *Spiritual*

Exercises, is that he 'has been created to praise, reverence and serve our Lord God, thereby saving his soul', and that 'everything else on earth has been created for man's sake, to help him to achieve the purpose for which he has been created'.[8] God is clearly transcendent, but we have to recognize his immanent activity

> in matter, giving it existence,
> in plants, giving them life,
> in animals, giving them consciousness,
> in men, giving them intelligence,
> . . . in me, giving me existence, life, consciousness, intelligence.[9]

Nature, then, is 'the garment of God'. Man is the temple of God: 'As God is always serving us and labouring for us in Nature, and we do not recognize it, so He is continually speaking to our inmost heart.' Too often we fail to hear him because we think of him amiss. 'Many "safe" people', warned Tyrrell, 'will be damned for their mean conceptions of Almighty God.'[10]

Nova et Vetera is shot through with the potential goodness of man and of the world. 'Whence comes this devil's doctrine which gives us a God of nature, and a God of grace at enmity with one another?' 'Christ has not come to destroy human nature, but to fulfil, to perfect, to elevate.' It is typical of Tyrrell to insist that 'We mostly love God far more than we think.' In the same way he believed that 'there is a perverted truth in every error; and a distorted sense of justice at the bottom of every conflict'. This was vastly more attractive than the carping and controversial attitudes that were widespread in religious debate, and it was securely based on Ignatius's premiss in the *Spiritual Exercises* that 'Every good Christian will be more inclined to put a good construction on another's statement than to fault it.'[11] This was Tyrrell's charter for sympathetic dialogue with Protestants and with those for whom contemporary scientific progress had raised a host of new questions about the truth of Christianity.

Above all, *Nova et Vetera* is a sensible book, rooted in extensive knowledge of the Bible and of favourite authors like Augustine and Thomas à Kempis. Where ascetic teaching had become overblown, Tyrrell punctured it in the name of Ignatius:

Some well-meaning persons think it a profanation to bring to ascetic teaching the touchstone of reason and consistency; or to suppose for an instant that the maxims of holy people can ever embody pernicious and soul-destroying fallacies. Ignatius of Loyola thought far otherwise. A man may be an admirable artist, though an execrable art-critic; and conversely.

He held the highest view of the priesthood, but hated priests who took themselves too seriously. 'If one realized what a priest should be, no one would ever get ordained. God has to be content with such rubbish as He gets.' No wonder that many of his more cautious, or conservative, or jealous colleagues regarded him with suspicion: Tyrrell was rapidly becoming one of the most sought-after Jesuits in London.

This was a turning-point in his career. From the time that *Nova et Vetera* appeared, Tyrrell began to attract increasing attention as a writer, confessor, preacher, and giver of retreats. More and more, however, he came to loathe the atmosphere of genteel devotion and tea-time gossip amongst the congregation at Farm Street, and he moved his base to Wimbledon College at the first opportunity. His intellectual horizons began to widen out of all recognition, largely under the tutelage of the man who first wrote to him on 20 September 1897:

Dear Reverend Father,
    For some time already I have been wanting to give myself the pleasure of writing and thanking you most sincerely for all the furtherance and encouragement that I have so abundantly found, in your *Nova et Vetera*, of ideas and tendencies that have now for so long been part and parcel of my life, its aims and combats. I wanted also to find out whether you perhaps could and would come up here to luncheon some day, at one, and get a walk and talk with me afterwards?[12]

On the afternoon of 9 October Tyrrell visited Baron Friedrich von Hügel in Hampstead for the first time, and so began a friendship in which he was to be by turns attracted, awed, perplexed, and infuriated, and through which, in his own words, he would grow 'from a boy to a man'.[13]

Von Hügel brought Tyrrell into touch with a new world of contemporary thought, but they first became friends on the ground of a common opposition to the defensiveness of the Roman Church. Little by little, von Hügel demonstrated to Tyrrell the breadth of his own horizons as an international scholar with contacts all across Europe. He was unashamedly Catholic, but enjoyed respect and friendship from a number of traditions. Being fluent in German, French, and Italian, and an indefatigable correspondent, he acted as a self-appointed go-between for a whole range of European scholars, of whom Tyrrell was now to be one. At 45, von Hügel was a respected biblical critic with a particular concern for the academic freedom of scholars within his own communion. Nobody in England was more aware of the need for the Roman Church to catch up in an area that had been sadly neglected because of the fears such study aroused. The great danger was that the door now half-opened by critics like Alfred Loisy, with whom von Hügel was in touch from 1893, would be slammed shut. The encyclical *Providentissimus Deus* of that year left very little room for manœuvre. In von Hügel, son of a diplomat and a baron of the Holy Roman Empire, there was none of the belligerent and controversial Catholicism that had begun to revolt Tyrrell, but a wider sympathy with truth as a common endeavour of scholars and saints whose natural, but not exclusive, home was the Roman Catholic Church.

Von Hügel's first approach to Tyrrell was made at a time of particular need. He was about to leave with his family for six months in Rome, but his eldest daughter Gertrud, then aged 20, was in the throes of a spiritual crisis. Von Hügel described to Tyrrell her 'sadly overwrought state of nerves and imagination'.[14] She was reacting against the pressures of her upbringing and her father's determination to involve her in his work. Von Hügel thought Tyrrell might be able to help, and Gertrud was eager to see him. When she stayed in England for the winter, he managed to bring her through a crisis of faith that might have led to complete mental breakdown.

Von Hügel was anxious because she had lost 'not simply faith in the Church and even the fundamental Christian dogma, but (which is surely a further and a still graver matter) true *creatureliness* of mind'.[15] Tyrrell discovered that she was not really in intellectual difficulties, but simply experiencing 'a total alienation of affection, amounting, in certain paroxysms, to violent aversion'.[16] Gently, he tried to explain to von Hügel what had gone wrong:

In a word, you neglect St Paul's caution against giving to babes the solid food of adults. The result is indigestion. Things that your formed mind can easily swallow without any prejudice to simple faith, may really cause much uneasiness in a mind less prepared . . . If you want your daughter's company you must shorten your steps and walk slowly, else she will lose her breath in her desire to keep up with you.[17]

Immediately, von Hügel saw that he was right, and wrote back in pained humility:

I see so increasingly plainly the triple fault and undermining character of my influence—, the dwelling so constantly and freely on the detailed humanities in the Church; the drawing out and giving full edge to religious difficulties; the making too much of little intellectual and temperamental differences between myself and most Catholics . . . I have dropped my own child, my First-born, whom God gave me to carry and to guard.[18]

No one, least of all the fatherless Tyrrell, could be unmoved by such a letter, but he should also have been warned by what he had seen. Though so much more experienced than Gertrud, he was also impressionable, and he did not share the Baron's unfailing sense of the presence of God, whatever the intellectual difficulties. He might also have taken note of von Hügel's concern to preserve 'a reputation for substantial orthodoxy, and even for prudence', which would be harmed if Gertrud's present state were widely known. As it was, there was little to worry about because she was already recovering in her father's absence. Tyrrell wrote praising the Baron's intellectual courage, but rubbing in the obvious lesson that von Hügel found so difficult to learn:

It was your anxiety to secure a clear-sighted faith that would fear no facts, and need no blinding, that would not be scandalised to find heavenly treasure in earthen vessels, and men rather than angels the ministers of the Gospel . . . that led you, as you say, to emphasise the human side of the Church too exclusively and to forget that the other side which was so apparent to your own mind had not yet seized hold . . . It is just because your faith is so much stronger than [that of others] that you can afford to make so many concessions, to allow the existence of so many adverse facts and difficulties.[19]

By the time von Hügel returned to England in late May 1898 the crisis was over, and shortly afterwards Gertrud returned to the sacraments. Her father had feared, with good reason, that others would see her as 'but speaking out, acting out, the unadmitted or undeveloped premises or conclusions of my mind'.[20] To some extent, it was not Gertrud but Tyrrell who later did this.

Besides discussing these personal matters, von Hügel began to send Tyrrell selected articles and papers. In the early months of their friendship he particularly encouraged him to read philosophers like Maurice Blondel and Lucien Laberthonnière; he lamented that Tyrrell could not cope with the German of Rudolf Eucken, and sent him his own paper on the Hexateuch. Tyrrell avidly set about this new reading, finding in Blondel a criticism of contemporary apologetic with which he whole-heartedly agreed, and the encouragement to think thoughts that he had previously rejected as too rash. He welcomed the clarity of Laberthonnière, restating Blondel's position without Blondel's obscurity. Von Hügel's paper reawakened an interest in biblical studies that he had deliberately suppressed at St Beuno's because he knew that if he were to make any significant contribution in that field, he would have to devote himself to it exhaustively, and he was not prepared for that.

Temperamentally, Tyrrell was quite unsuited to the painstaking work of the Scripture scholar, but he recognized that it was crucial. Within the scholastic framework, the historical, critical study of the Bible was not important, but now that scholasticism was breaking down, it was essential for the Church to face the historicity of the biblical record, whatever the cost. For the moment Tyrrell had no idea how extreme the cost might be. Von Hügel guessed, but managed to hold together a considerable historical scepticism with deep and orthodox piety. It was a perplexing mixture which Tyrrell, the convert, never really understood, least of all when he first fell under the Baron's considerable spell.

Throughout 1898 Tyrrell's circle of friends continued to expand. In July he received a letter from Henri Bremond, soon to be his closest Jesuit friend, almost his *alter ego*. Bremond, who was four years younger than Tyrrell, shared both his literary interests and his dissatisfaction with the Society. Having noticed Tyrrell's articles in *The Month*, he was seeking out a kindred spirit. A warm response encouraged him: until Tyrrell's death the two men corresponded regularly.[21] From the beginning Tyrrell was outspoken about the way in which he had to 'retard [his] pace so as to keep more or less in line with the very conservative body' to which they both belonged.[22] In his second letter he spoke of the need for 'the elasticity of the spirit of S. P. N. [Ignatius] . . . to mediate between the old and new, and to interpret them one to another'.[23] This was exactly what Bremond was longing to hear, and he began to open his heart. Within a year he was consulting Tyrrell about his vocation, and discussing reasons for being a Christian at all.

During this year also Tyrrell was making an ever-deeper impression on Maude Petre, at that time Superior of an order for lay women called the *Filles de Marie*, and a regular user of the Farm Street library. Even more than Bremond, she was to share his eventual fate. Maude Petre belonged to one of the most ancient and

distinguished Catholic families in England. Her father was the
younger son of the thirteenth Lord Petre. As a girl, she had studied
theology in Rome, astonishing her professors by her obvious compe-
tence. She had a kind of intellectual and moral fearlessness, but at
times she could be painfully intense, something Tyrrell loathed. She
was very plain. Initially she looked to him for spiritual guidance
when she was carrying a good deal of responsibility, and he probably
became her confessor. As with von Hügel, who also became her
friend, they shared a common interest in mysticism. Tyrrell referred
to her in the early days of their friendship as 'rather narrow but
intelligent and I hope redeemable'.[24] The tone of condescension is
unmistakable.

Wilfrid Ward was yet another whom Tyrrell began to recognize
—this time prematurely—as a kindred spirit. In February he reviewed Ward's *Life of Wiseman*,[25] taking particular note of the
epilogue in which Ward expounded his own ideas on the ways in
which the Church should respond in the spirit of Newman and
Wiseman to the challenge of the times. Ward argued that they had
shared a commitment to two positions in particular: that the Church
in communion with the Pope has been the one, true Church from the
beginning; and that this Church should follow a policy of accommodation, allying itself with 'the better tendencies of modern
thought'.[26] Tyrrell accepted, but did not stress, the first point. It was
the second that he developed enthusiastically in his review. He
agreed with Ward that the Church should involve itself in every
department of science and art, as Wiseman had done, thereby
creating the 'wish to believe' in those who would not otherwise see
what Catholic Christianity had to offer. Of course, he did not deny
the right of the Church to set limits to this dialogue, but the whole
drift of his argument was towards openness and optimism. He still
believed that

The Church is always more willing to loose than to bind; and that she binds
only so far as she is absolutely urged by necessity; that definitions are simply
forced from her by the cavillings of the rationalistic or heretical mind; that
though final, so far as they exclude some definite error, her dogmas are never
final in the sense of stating exhaustively truths that, being supernatural, are
inexhaustible; that if she arrests the inopportune discussion or proclamation
of some new discovery in history or science, it is really in the essential interest
of truth, lest the wheat should be uprooted with the tares, and the minds of
millions perplexed in matters of supreme practical consequence for the sake

of a detail of little or no practical consequence; or it is because the truth is urged in an heretical spirit, not as creating an interesting difficulty, but as founding a right to doubt.[27]

While he held to this line he could still be called a 'liberal Catholic', but he soon came to reject it as hopelessly unrealistic. Where Tyrrell moved on to a revolutionary 'modernism'—an ecclesiastical position born of frustration and despair—Ward remained the obedient optimist.

Throughout the year Tyrrell remained in close contact with von Hügel, who spent the autumn struggling over an article on St Catherine of Genoa. An important letter sets out some of his fundamental ideas for Tyrrell, criticizing the mystics who teach that the soul is purified by turning away from the particular to the general, from 'the particularity of the creature to the simplicity of the Creator'.[28] This leaves no place for scientific endeavour, which is pre-eminently concerned with the concrete and the particular. God, for von Hügel, was 'the supremely concrete, supremely individual and particular, and the mental and practical occupation with the particular must ever remain an integral part of my way to Him'.[29] Tyrrell readily agreed, adding that God 'is apprehended (*as every personality is apprehended*) rather by a certain *sense* or *gustus*, than by any reasoning process'.[30] Giving his thought a characteristic twist towards ethics, he added:

The sensitiveness of this sense (which I take it is simply our whole moral and spiritual being regarded as attracting and attracted by its like, as repelling and repelled by its unlike), depends on the purification of the heart and affections whereby they are brought into sympathy with God; and this again is the chief end of life and experience and education of every kind.

This appealed greatly to von Hügel, who did not yet recognize the danger of a total loss of confidence in the 'reasoning process' when Tyrrell failed to stress the place of *doctrine* in educating the 'whole moral and spiritual being'. His immediate concern was in finding the most tactful way of handling the difficult question of St Catherine's obvious hysteria. For once it was Tyrrell who urged the Baron to be cautious. The article, which von Hügel called 'the biggest grind' he had been through as a writer,[31] was too long, and he asked Tyrrell to help him prune it. Just as with the two volumes of *The Mystical Element of Religion* that grew from it over the next ten years, Tyrrell was responsible for the original article's extensive revision—in this case with such success that the publisher asked von Hügel for a short book, and von Hügel asked Tyrrell, in preference to Ward or anyone else, to write a preface.

Writing prefaces was one of Tyrrell's most regular chores at this time. In 1898 he introduced four volumes in Duckworth's series, *The Lives of the Saints*, three more in 1899, and two in 1900. It was hack work, since Tyrrell was disappointed in the quality of the biographies,[32] but it gave him an opportunity to debunk the kind of nonsense that was often regarded as 'edifying'. He firmly believed that 'We need less than formerly to be dazzled with the wonderful, and more to be drawn to the lovable.'[33] He saw that we are attracted if the saints are regarded not as a species apart, but as human beings like ourselves, only more advanced in the love of God. 'If love be mysticism,' said Tyrrell, 'then we have the key to all mysticism within ourselves.'[34]

Two of Tyrrell's articles for *The Month* in 1898 were of particular importance. In an article on ' "Liberal" Catholicism'[35] he covered himself by a half-hearted attack on the sort of liberal Christianity that identified the Gospel with human progress, and then proceeded to suggest that it was equally wrong for the Church to go to the opposite extreme. He argued that we should 'treat the relation of the Church to modern progress and civilization as in nearly every way parallel to that which obtains between grace and nature in the individual'. This means that 'The Church may neither identify herself with "progress" nor isolate herself from it. Her attitude must always be the difficult and uncomfortable one of partial agreement and partial dissent.'[36] This was perilous ground, as only thirty-three years before, in the *Syllabus of Errors*, Pius IX had rejected the belief that 'The Roman Pontiff can and should reconcile and adapt himself to progress, liberalism, and modern civilization.'[37] In his article Tyrrell even contrived to suggest that those who are impatient with 'the suicidal over-caution, the apathy, the lethargy of the Catholic body' have a point. Edmund Bishop, the distinguished liturgist and a secret sympathizer with the liberal cause, spotted the aggression in Tyrrell's tone, and called this 'the "beating of the tom-tom" article'.[38]

A month later, in June 1898, Tyrrell reviewed *The Vitality of Christian Dogmas* by Auguste Sabatier.[39] Sabatier argued that the heart of religion lies in 'emotion or sentiment or vital instinct', not in the dogmas in which we try, by use of the intellect, to express what we have experienced. Since religion is a living process, dogma itself grows, develops, and dies. 'The vitality of a dogmatic creed is therefore the vitality of a language, some words dying, others being born, others slowly changing their sense till change ends in death.' Tyrrell claimed that this is Protestantism worked out to its logical conclusion:

As soon as faith is asserted to be an internal sentiment, and not to be a blind assent to an infallible external teacher; as soon as revelation is declared to be merely a stirring up of feeling, and not an instruction of the mind, this is the conclusion we must come to—Christianity is a certain sensation or emotion, which tends to awake conceptions, theories, and images in the mind which have no absolute objective value whatever.

We should note the polarization. It was already clear from almost everything Tyrrell wrote that he did not see faith as 'blind assent', nor did he believe revelation to be more than secondarily instruction of the mind. In this article he was forced to reaffirm his commitment to the approved definition of Christian dogma as 'the divinely-chosen expression of those truths and external realities on which the eye of Christ rested'; at the same time he was coming to appreciate more and more the very human process by which dogma had evolved. Within three years he stood with Sabatier on almost every major issue raised by this article.[40] His orthodoxy was built on sand.

The year finished with the publication of a hefty successor to *Nova et Vetera*, 'much more destructive of widely received views about the spiritual life than the ordinary reader will ever divine'.[41] Rather than offering a large number of 'informal meditations' of perhaps a page or half a page in length, Tyrrell now offered eighteen major essays on mystical theology and ethics, entitled *Hard Sayings*.[42] Von Hügel was quick to admire a recurring stress on 'the immanence of God, Heaven and Hell in each individual soul',[43] or, as Tyrrell puts it, the teaching that 'Eternal life is God *in* the soul. God is the soul's soul . . . We speak too exclusively of entering into Heaven, into life, into God; forgetting that the relation is truly—perhaps more truly—expressed by saying that God, and Heaven, and life, enter into us.' Encouraged by his reading of Blondel, Tyrrell attacked the kind of theology that made the supernatural *extrinsic* to man: 'Grace is not another soul over and above our natural soul; but it is a new radiance given to the soul by a new indwelling of God.' Under the influence of grace, the finest natural qualities are perfected; they are 'supernaturalized'. In this process, man is called upon to co-operate by a union of will with his Maker.

For Tyrrell, conscience is the human faculty that brings this about. 'It is as bringing us into will-relations with God that conscience differs so generically from any other act of our mind.' For the stress on conscience Tyrrell was indebted to Newman; for the description of union with God as a union of will he went back to Augustine. Both emphases were perfectly orthodox, provided that there was a complementary stress on God as the transcendent 'Other' who instructs our minds as well as our hearts by revealing information that we would not otherwise know. Tyrrell's emphasis on the immanence of God and the place of the will (or heart) in knowing him was a necessary corrective to a widespread and exaggerated stress upon the transcendence of God and the place of reason in knowing him. Had von Hügel seen that when Tyrrell developed his ideas further he would hardly be able to hold the place of head and heart together, he might have been more muted in his praise of what his friend had to say. Blondel, the careful but obscure teacher of the 'method of immanence', which found in the world and in man an unfulfilled need of the transcendent, was to prove far more cautious here. Tyrrell welcomed what Blondel had to say—when he understood it—because it supported his sacramental view of the world. 'Matter, no less than spirit', he wrote in *Hard Sayings*, 'is God's dear creature; and as spirit is not destroyed, but perfected and elevated by its subjection to divinity; so matter is transfigured, glorified, and exalted by its impregnation with spirit.'

As to faith, Tyrrell followed Newman when he acknowledged that men are not Catholics solely because they have been persuaded intellectually. He talks of faith in the Church as 'the effect of an impression produced on our mind and heart by her whole concrete reality', for which, of course, intellectual cogency is indispensable. He sees the whole of the Catholic faith—which in this instance means 'body of dogmas', but since he reminds us that a dogma is 'simply the skeleton of a living concrete reality', may be taken to mean the whole *life* of the Church, including its teaching—as 'an exquisite harmony so delicate, so exact in composition, that no element can be removed, or disturbed without destruction to the whole'. There is, as it were, a 'mystical body' of truth held in trust by the mystical body of Christ, which is the Church. Just as every part of that truth is integral to the perfection of the whole, so is the

participation of every member in the life of the whole. Tyrrell did not
yet draw out the consequences of this in terms of a theology of the
laity, but that soon followed.

When von Hügel offered a careful critique, Tyrrell was quick to
admit the unevenness of the book. There were relics of more assertive
days, such as his complaints about 'this de-Christianized country,
where Catholics find it so hard, so impossible, to keep mind or heart
free from the infectious pestilence of unbelief, misbelief, and moral
corruption'. There were frightening echoes of authoritarian teaching
when he wrote:

All human society, secular or ecclesiastical, entails sacrifice and self-
repression upon its members; nor has any individual just cause of complaint
if in many ways his liberties are restricted, his talent injured and left idle, his
capacities squandered, sometimes through force of inevitable circumstances,
sometimes through the blunderings or the faults of those in command,
sometimes through the selfishness and blindness of his fellow-members.

Tyrrell would put this to the test before long.

As yet, though, there was no crisis. Even though Tyrrell had little
affection left for the Society, he still hoped for better things. In 1896,
the year of his arrival in London, he wrote on the title-page of his
breviary: 'Thou shalt see from afar the land which the Lord God will
give to the Children of Israel, but thou shalt not enter therein.' He
was the 'coming man' amongst the London Jesuits, committed to
them for life, like a man in a bad marriage. When all love was lost,
there would still be duty and the example of the father he never knew
to sustain him. In this spirit he took his final vows on 2 February
1898, 'recognising them as contained in the contract I had already
made when, as a boy in my credulity, I thought the S. J. was as Paul
Féval painted it'.[44] He himself was still hoping to find a 'middle way',
as he explained to Maude Petre when they discussed *Hard Sayings*: 'I
do think', he wrote,

that the conception of the Church as the creator and saviour of true liberty
has become obscured even in the eyes of Catholics in modern times, and that
our endeavour ought to be to set this truth free again; to destroy the notion
that narrowness and orthodoxy go hand in hand; to show that the deeper we
dig into Catholic truth and the closer we hold to her words, the broader we
can afford to be; that the narrow is always the less truthful way, depending
on a partial view. It is, as you say, easy to throw oneself heartily into the
'liberal' school or into the 'conservative', but to combine what is right in

both is certainly not a 'cheap' position to take up; yet surely it is best to be on God's side and detached from every faction and party.[45]

Where there is no 'middle way', being 'on God's side' will mean something quite new: an attempt to transcend the terms of the debate which will probably be misunderstood by all concerned. Being 'on God's side', for Tyrrell, meant opening himself to justified charges of arrogance; it meant being committed to all, and to none; it meant paying the inevitable price.

NOTES

1. *The Month*, 89 (1897), p. 137.
2. Ibid., p. 364.
3. Ibid., 90 (1897), p. 15.
4. Tyrrell to Halifax, 24 July 1897 (Borthwick Institute, Halifax Papers).
5. AL2, p. 61.
6. *Nova et Vetera: Informal Meditations for Times of Spiritual Dryness* (London, 1897). Quotations are from pp. iii ('a record . . .'); ibid. ('stop and listen'); 18 ('All love . . .'); 304 ('There is no harder . . .'); 385 ('uses the human heart . . .'); 127 ('the garment of God'); 356 ('As God is always . . .'); 320 ('Many "safe" . . .'); 163 ('Whence comes . . .'); 287 ('Christ has not come . . .'); 105 ('We mostly . . .'); 346 ('there is a perverted . . .'); 119 ('Some well-meaning persons . . .'); 329 ('If one realized . . .').
7. AL2, p. 64.
8. *The Spiritual Exercises of Saint Ignatius*, trans. T. Corbishley, (Wheathampstead, 1973), p. 22.
9. Ibid., p. 80.
10. In later editions of *Nova et Vetera* he toned this down to 'may be damned'.
11. *Spiritual Exercises*, p. 21.
12. Von Hügel to Tyrrell, 20 Sept. 1897 (BL, Petre Papers).
13. Tyrrell to von Hügel, 5 Dec. 1902.
14. Von Hügel to Tyrrell, 19 Oct. 1897.
15. Von Hügel to Tyrrell, 26 Jan. 1898.
16. Tyrrell to von Hügel, 16 Feb. 1898.
17. Tyrrell to von Hügel, 6 Dec. 1897.
18. Von Hügel to Tyrrell, 26 Jan. 1898.
19. Tyrrell to von Hügel, 16 Feb. 1898.
20. Von Hügel to Tyrrell, 26 Jan. 1898.
21. Only Tyrrell's letters survive. These have been translated into French

and published in A. L.-David (ed.), *Lettres de George Tyrrell à Henri Bremond* (Paris, 1971).

22. Tyrrell to Bremond, 6 July 1898 (BN, Fonds Bremond).
23. Tyrrell to Bremond, 2 Oct. 1898.
24. Tyrrell to von Hügel, 31 Dec. 1897.
25. *The Month*, 91 (1898), pp. 142–50.
26. W. Ward, *The Life and Times of Cardinal Wiseman*, 2 vols. (London, 1897), ii, pp. 533–4.
27. *The Month*, 91 (1898), pp. 149–50.
28. Von Hügel to Tyrrell, 26 Sept. 1898.
29. Ibid.
30. Tyrrell to von Hügel, 28 Sept. 1898.
31. Von Hügel to Tyrrell, 27 Oct. 1898.
32. Tyrrell to Waller, 5 Sept. 1900 (BL, Waller Papers).
33. *The Month*, 90 (1897), p. 603.
34. Ibid., p. 610.
35. Ibid., 91 (1898), pp. 449–57.
36. Ibid., pp. 454–5.
37. DS, 2980.
38. N. Abercrombie, *The Life and Work of Edmund Bishop* (London, 1959), p. 238; for Bishop's liberal and modernist sympathies, see A. R. Vidler, *A Variety of Catholic Modernists* (Cambridge, 1970), pp. 134–52.
39. *The Month*, 91 (1898), pp. 592–602.
40. See J. A. Laubacher, *Dogma and the Development of Dogma in the Writings of George Tyrrell* (Baltimore and Louvain, 1939).
41. Tyrrell to Maude Petre, 19 Apr. 1899 (BL, Petre Papers).
42. *Hard Sayings: A Selection of Meditations and Studies* (London 1898). Quotations are from pp. 2 ('Eternal life . . .'); 305 ('Grace is not . . .'); 52 ('It is as . . .'); 301 ('Matter, no less . . .'); 439 ('the effect of . . .'); ibid. ('simply the skeleton . . .'); 130 ('an exquisite harmony . . .'); 240 ('this de-Christianized . . .'); 288 ('All human society . . .').
43. Von Hügel to Tyrrell, 31 Dec. 1898.
44. Tyrrell to Bremond, 22 Dec. 1899.
45. Tyrrell to Maude Petre, 25 Apr. 1899.

7

'External Religion' and its Dangers

THE year 1899 marks the high point of Tyrrell's Jesuit career. By now he was well known in London and far beyond. He was constantly in demand as a confessor, spiritual director, specialist counsellor for 'hard cases', and giver of retreats. For three successive years he was the man chosen to give the annual retreat to his own community.[1] His books and articles were sought after by priests, nuns, seminarians, and lay people. Remorselessly, his correspondence grew. In another man, such attention might have gone to his head, but for Tyrrell it was only proof of famine all around. With a growing sense of indignation, he worked to provide in any way that he could. He was the cleverest, the busiest, and, it was said, the ugliest of the London Jesuits. In groups he could be surprisingly moody and silent, and his shyness was a constant handicap, but when he talked with individuals in intellectual or moral difficulties he was transformed. They brought out all his courage in facing hard questions, his quickness of understanding, and his compassion. He was unsettled and at times depressed, but he refused to take himself too seriously. When asked to contribute to a series on 'books that have influenced me', he chose *Alice in Wonderland*, because it has the power to enable us 'to turn intellectual back-somersaults at an age when we should be otherwise corpulent and unbendable'.[2] Only he knew by what internal acrobatics he maintained his position. He was living dangerously, and his outspokenness had been noted in Rome, but nothing he had yet said had in any way brought official censure.

What Tyrrell said in the confessional and in private interviews is not totally a matter of conjecture, as he left many letters of direction and advice. His most fundamental principle was thoroughly Ignatian: never to come between the Holy Spirit and the individual soul. Tyrrell abhorred the cultivation of dependence, what he called the 'Ma chère enfant' style of directors and the 'unauthorised tyranny of the "Père directeur"'. 'If I advise,' he said, 'it is always on a footing of perfect equality, to help people to see and decide for themselves or to read more clearly what their own conscience tells them: but not to dictate or stand to them in place of conscience.'[3] Some of the advice was shocking: 'Go often to communion and seldom to confession.'[4] Some showed a luminous common sense: 'Do try to be yourself, and don't try to be *Père* B. or somebody else.'[5] Always he was compassionate: 'As to the matter of which you write, I am *so* sorry for you, for I know the amount of suffering involved.'[6] When it came to sexual matters, as it frequently did, Tyrrell was conspicuously understanding. He considered no sexual inclination abnormal, though he had strong views against indulgence. He would not censure others for heterosexual or homosexual inclinations that he recognized within himself.[7] Sadly, he discovered that his very respect for the freedom of others led some people to become attached to him personally. He was forced to recognize that the direction he gave was based on different principles from that of others around him, and that those who left him for other directors were sometimes 'puzzled and confused'. He likened himself to a thirteenth-century director operating in the twentieth century. With his liberal approach, which he attributed to Aquinas and Ignatius, he found himself, paradoxically, 'too previous to be of help to people who must eventually and in the main be guided by ordinary twentieth century directors'.[8] He never forgot how 'London souls cry out in pain'. Eventually he was driven to limit his hours in the confessional. For him, London was to be 'deeply associated with irremediable spiritual distresses of one kind or another'.[9]

One of those who knew spiritual distress in abundance, both within himself and in those about him, was André Raffalovich, a minor figure in Oscar Wilde's circle of cultured 'decadents', remembered mostly for Wilde's cutting remark: 'Poor André! He came to London to start a *salon*, and has only succeeded in opening a saloon.'[10] Like Wilde himself, who on his release from prison asked to stay at Farm Street for a six-month retreat and was, not surprisingly, turned down, Raffalovich was attracted to the Jesuits. The son of Russian Jews who had settled in Paris, where his father became a prosperous banker, he was baptized at Farm Street on 3 February 1896.[11] Through Raffalovich, Tyrrell was introduced to a number of Wilde's former friends, still in something of a state of shock from Wilde's imprisonment: John Gray, the model for Wilde's Dorian Gray, who turned to Raffalovich when jilted by Wilde and then left London to train for the Roman Catholic priesthood in Rome;[12] Aubrey Beardsley, who called Raffalovich his 'mentor' and followed him into the fold of the penitent and the faithful; and others. Raffalovich described Tyrrell at this time as 'rather *à la* Aubrey', and went on: 'I suppose there is something quite piquant in sitting in a cell where a sort of middleaged Aubrey sits disguised as an SJ.' Shortly after, he promised Gray: 'You will like Father Tyrrel [*sic*] and feel with him that "conspiracy" which persons of male culture do feel with one another.'[13]

What drew Raffalovich to Tyrrell was a common interest in questions of homosexuality. In 1896 Raffalovich published a remarkable book entitled *Uranisme et unisexualité: Étude sur différentes manifestations de l'instinct sexual*,[14] in which he discussed instances of homosexual attraction from a wide range of literary sources. He argued that there is no dividing line between heterosexuals and homosexuals, but he denied that each man has the right to claim the sexual satisfaction he desires.[15] Appended to the book was a reprint of his bitter memoir of the Oscar Wilde affair. Tyrrell read the book in 1899, finding the conclusion very much in line with that in his *Notes on the Catholic Doctrine of Purity*,[16] published two years earlier 'for private circulation amongst Ours'. 'In my own strivings', he told Raffalovich, 'I recognised, as a consequence of the wavering of the balance between male and female during gestation, that the final result was simply the preponderance (in varying ratios) of one sex-characteristic over the other; not the exclusion of that other.' He charted the various forms of male–female and male–male attraction as he saw them, telling Raffalovich frankly: 'In my own case I have certainly recognised almost all the inclinations (at various times).'[17] There is no evidence to suggest that Tyrrell remained other than a virgin and a dedicated celibate in this period or any other, but his approach to sexuality was as undeceived as that of the sexually experienced coterie with which he now came into contact. Nearly ten years later he told Raffalovich:

As a matter of personal experience in your line it is a curious thing that my unisexual sympathies so almost entirely predominant during my long years of college life ceased so abruptly and entirely about 13 years ago that I can no long [*sic*] even *imagine* that propensity now. Such propensities as I have are entirely normal; but sexual rather than amative. I have never been 'in love' with a woman in my life.[18]

Tyrrell's settled conviction, which he shared with Raffalovich, Gray, and others who had renounced sexual practice on their conversion, was that 'the *power* of sexual self-restraint is the root of all morality; that it is obligatory of all—married or unmarried, uni-, bi-, or hetero-sexual . . . Morality', he said, 'is a crucifixion.'[19]

Raffalovich was 'a brand plucked from the burning', and a gossip. He repeated morsels of Tyrrell's careless conversation for the amusement of Gray:

Fr T was amusing about the demoralising professions: *reviewing* (because one has not time to study the books and because one has to put in a quotable piece of flattery to please Fr. S[ydney] S[mith][20]), *having to pay off a debt* (if you are a religious) on a Church or something analogous, because you have to think more of money than a stockbroker and have to do very queer things, and also being a provincial because 9/10 of your decisions are against your conscience etc.[21]

Raffalovich was amused and supported by Tyrrell, but they were Catholics of a different ilk. The erstwhile aesthete remembered 'shrinking' during his catechism when Father Bampton told him that the Catholic faith was not only beautiful but *true*. 'I was willing to believe anything,' he told Gray, 'but I shrank from Objective Truth being flaunted at me.'[22] The flaunting of 'objective truth' was never Tyrrell's style. (Raffalovich once dreamt of a *Month* ballet with Father Tyrrell as the 'prima assoluta who can go on her toes in any direction'.[23]) Raffalovich had, however, found his salvation in 'objective truth', and their ways were bound to diverge. Nevertheless, they did not lose touch, and just before he died Tyrrell wrote to answer a *cri de cœur* from Raffalovich, who had written to say that his '13 years peace', the peace he had enjoyed since admission to the Catholic Church, was at an end. Tyrrell tore out a copy of a letter written 'long ago'. 'Better', it said, 'seek the positive safety of love than the negative safety of flight. The conflict has already made a man of you; it may yet make a god of you, but at the risk of making a devil of you.'[24] It was characteristic advice.

Friends both within the Mount Street house and outside it were well aware of Tyrrell's tendency to exaggerate and to make unguarded remarks, but they also knew the value of his ministry. Tyrrell was never bothered by fear of misinterpretation or delation, which within a religious society he found beneath contempt. At the end of 1899 he wrote one article, 'A Perverted Devotion', that was to cause really serious trouble. His friend Thurston, who had acted as censor, failed to see the danger it contained, so when it was condemned in Rome his anxiety and guilt knew no bounds. He feared that Tyrrell would leave the Society, and 'If Father Tyrrell goes it will be one of the most serious blows that the Catholic Church and the Society have sustained in England for fifty years.'[25] Tyrrell was quite simply too valuable to be treated in this way. 'In spite of his appearance, in spite of his shyness, he meets with respect and courtesy from intellectual men wherever he goes. Men whose names are known wherever the English language is read are polite and considerate in tone even when they differ from him.'[26] Nuns, scholastics, secular clergy, doubters, and enquirers all looked to him in a special way for help and guidance. He was 'a sort of last resort in desperate cases',[27] and of these there were many.

Tyrrell gained a new respect among his colleagues when in January 1899 he was invited by Wilfrid Ward to join the Synthetic Society, the members of which constituted a roll of the most important religious and philosophical thinkers of that time.[28] Once a month from January to June some forty leading politicians, philosophers, scientists, bishops, and religious thinkers met to dine and hear a paper which would contribute 'towards a working philosophy of religious belief'. Tyrrell was accepted as an equal by men like Wilfrid Ward, Arthur Balfour, Charles Gore, Edward Talbot, Richard Haldane, Friedrich von Hügel, Richard Hutton, and Henry Sidgwick, all thinkers of the highest distinction. When it was proposed that Tyrrell be approached, von Hügel wrote to Ward: 'I really think he will turn out, at least on paper, one of the very best members . . . My only uncertainty is whether his shyness and usual reticence may not prevent his doing justice to himself in speaking.'[29] Tyrrell was a little hesitant about the offer, and in replying to Ward told him: 'I am not a man of all-round general education owing chiefly to my wilful perversity in youth; nor am I easy and expansive in society; nor am I ready of tongue in debate and discussion.' However, if Ward thought his 'wit sufficient to atone for [his] ignorance', he would be glad to accept on an experimental basis.[30] Ward took him to the February meeting as a guest, and at the March meeting he was unanimously elected a member.

Membership of the Synthetic Society reinforced Tyrrell's deep conviction that Catholics had nothing to fear and much to contribute if they joined the agitated debates of the intellectual market-place. But the 'synthetic' process affected all parties. Only those who were themselves open to its influence could participate in it fully. Of the six or so Catholic members, the only out-and-out conservative was

Robert F. Clarke SJ, who was described by Ward with appreciation as 'a learned theologian and a man of science'. Tyrrell rejoiced impishly in 'the haunting thought of the mirth there must be in heaven before the angels of God at the spectacle of a grave assembly of creatures discussing the existence of their Creator, and trying to make out a case for Him—not very successfully'.[31] Initially he found the discussion 'desultory and vague', and he 'sighed for some of the formalism of the schools'.[32] Still, he enjoyed the friendliness of what the Carlton Club waiters called 'The Sympathetic Club'. A rare 'sense of thunder in the atmosphere' considerably distressed him.[33] The only member of the Society he actively disliked was Frederick Myers, who succeeded in irritating others as well.

In May 1899 von Hügel was due to give a paper, but he cried off as he was going through a bout of insomnia. Late in April Tyrrell agreed to act as a substitute, and on 9 June he gave a paper which has now been lost in its original form.[34] In it he considered the argument that:

If a given religion or religious belief suggests itself more readily, or when suggested commends itself more cordially, in the measure that men's spiritual needs are more highly developed; if, furthermore, it tends to make men still better and to raise their desires still higher so as to prepare the way for a yet fuller conception of religious truth, it may be said to be adapted to human needs; and it is from such adaptability that we argue its approach to the truth.[35]

For the purposes of discussion in the Society, he bypassed the question of revelation. When he finally rejected, as unhistorical and rationalistic, the understanding of revelation taught by contemporary theologians, he returned to this argument from 'adaptation' to justify his belief in Christian doctrine. On this occasion, however, he was using the argument to attack the cruder forms of evolutionism and to justify a basic theism, which was common ground in the Society. As a newcomer, he was playing safe. 'Willie' Williams, a liberal fellow Catholic, found the paper, which in its expanded form is uncharacteristically turgid, 'most remarkable for its lucidity, directness, brevity and depth'.[36] It probably was.

When Tyrrell and von Hügel saw one another at the Synthetic Society it was the first time they had met that year. Throughout the late winter and spring von Hügel had been in France, and Tyrrell had heard virtually nothing from him. He could not know that the Baron already spoke of him to his philosopher friend Laberthonnière as 'my closest living English Catholic friend', telling him that 'this fine Jesuit is almost as modern as us and will become quite as much so'.[37] Tyrrell was much impressed by the Baron's learning, and he respected his liberal attitudes and critical ability, but when it came to detailed discussion of the philosopher Blondel, whom Tyrrell thought to be saying much that he himself wanted to say, but to be saying it in language of impenetrable obscurity, he found 'the dear Baron . . . too deaf and too transcendental to understand my questions on the subject'.[38] Instances of non-communication (as Tyrrell particularly perceived it) would recur. Nevertheless, the Baron was profoundly grateful to his new-found friend for all the help he had given Gertrud. Von Hügel never ceased to admire Tyrrell's quick-witted intuition and spirituality. The point at which the two men truly met was a common concern for what von Hügel called a 'living, mystical way of taking religion'.[39] Both were pained by inner loneliness; both saw the religious situation in dark yet hopeful terms; both were in need of profound and affectionate friendship. In almost every other way they were opposite personalities.

Shortly after this 'long and interesting' conversation on 11 June, Tyrrell wrote to Bremond, who had met the Baron for the first time that February. His letter spoke of the general religious situation in just the sort of terms that troubled and excited all three men. Tyrrell saw

the new wine straining the bottles into which it is poured—some will burst; others will stretch albeit not without pain and danger. One thing is certain that Time will not go back; nor will any word of new knowledge that has left God's lips return to Him empty, but will accomplish all whereunto it is sent. I think it is just a crisis where hope can shine most brightly. With the Baron I resent all attempts at premature and crude solutions of difficulties which are profound and immense; and still more, the reckless pessimism engendered in minds of the same 'optimistic' class because things will not at once yield to their endeavours to explain.[40]

Only now did Tyrrell let the Baron see how isolated he really felt among the Jesuits, many of whom did not see any crisis of 'new knowledge' at all, though to him it was all around. Sadly, he told his friend: 'I never felt my position more incongruous', and he consoled himself, as he was often to do, with the thought that 'it is to the principles of an institution and not to their misapplication or denial that one is pledged in joining it'.[41] Shortly afterwards von Hügel wrote a letter of delicate comfort and encouragement, talking of the constant discipline he himself encountered in that 'isolation and

interior loneliness' which marked all his close friends—amongst
whom Tyrrell now had a special place:

Like these great large-hearted lonely ones,—Huvelin, Blondel, Laberthonnière, Duchesne, Eucken, and one or two more abroad,—I have so far found
amongst our now living English Catholics but one,—yourself . . . There is,
amongst the Catholic English men I now know, somehow no other one
whom I feel and see to be one of those self-spending children of the dawn and
of Christ's ampler day.[42]

Von Hügel's image of the suffering and isolated elect contained an
element of fantasy and more than a hint of superiority, but such
language sounded a chord that Tyrrell, in his alienation, needed to
hear. He, for his part, acknowledged to the Baron 'the strong
developing influence your friendship has exerted upon my mind'.[43]
Von Hügel continued to keep Tyrrell supplied with the latest material from Loisy, Blondel, and Laberthonnière, and he also provided
a photograph of himself. Tyrrell, who disliked having his picture
taken, sent no photograph, but kept von Hügel up to date with all
that he was writing.

    Two of the pieces that Tyrrell gave to von Hügel in 1899 were of
particular importance. On 7 October he went to lunch with the
Baron, and left him a proof copy of his latest article for *The Month*,
'The Relation of Theology to Devotion'.[44] Von Hügel read it twice
that evening, and the next day he wrote that it is 'the finest thing you
have yet done,—at least of those that I have read. It is really splendid.
I thank God for it with all my heart.' He was heartened to find his
Jesuit friend giving 'such crystal-clear expression to my dearest
certainties'.[45] The article is brilliantly clear; it is also penetrating and
cheeky. Tyrrell was aiming to cut scholastic theology and philosophy
down to size. His central presupposition is that what has been
revealed in Christianity is 'not merely a symbol or creed, but it is a
concrete religion left by Christ to his Church'. The tenets of this
religion were first expressed in the vivid, concrete, and totally
unphilosophical language of fishermen and peasants. God 'has
spoken their language, leaving it to the others to translate it (at their
own risk) into forms more acceptable to their taste'. (It would not be
long before Tyrrell would be writing less uncritically about the
question of revelation.) There is a fundamental and obvious distinction between this immediate, concrete language of revelation and
devotion, and the reflexive, abstract language of philosophy and
theology. The second is of inestimable value in clarifying the muddles

and misunderstandings arising from the naïvety of the first. Nevertheless, the teachers of nineteenth-century scholasticism had all but forgotten that in one important respect the second sort of language is no better than the first. However philosophically or theologically precise its expression, it still has, quite as much as the language of devotion, to speak of God analogically. More than this, it is actually inferior to devotional language in its ability to promote charity, to move rather than to inform. Tyrrell claimed that 'Neither the metaphysical nor the vulgar idea is adequate, though taken together they correct one another; but taken apart, it may be said that the vulgar is the less unreal of the two.' This powerful deflation of theological hubris was bound to be unpopular. When Tyrrell argued that 'Devotion and religion existed before theology, in the way that art existed before art-criticism; reasoning, before logic; speech, before grammar,' he was echoing the very words and thoughts of Newman, but he applied the point with his own polemical deftness. All his fellow Jesuits would agree that 'the use of philosophy lies in its insisting on the inadequacy of the vulgar statement'. Not all would thank him for reminding them that its abuse lay 'in forgetting the inadequacy of its own'.

As soon as von Hügel had read the article he asked for six copies, as he was now recommending Tyrrell to all his friends. Tyrrell himself received a complimentary note from the eminent French scholar Duchesne which he passed on to von Hügel, who showed it to friends in Paris and Genoa as 'the best reinforcement of my propaganda in favour of your writings'.[46] Thus Tyrrell's ideas began to attain a European circulation. Tyrrell saw this article, 'The Relation of Theology to Devotion', as fundamental to his life's work. Eight years later he included it under the title 'Lex Orandi, Lex Credendi' in *Through Scylla and Charybdis.* He then said: 'On re-reading it carefully I am amazed to see how little I have really advanced since I wrote it; how I have simply eddied round and round the same point. It is all here—all that follows—not in germ but in explicit statement—as it were in a brief compendium or analytical index.'[47]

Von Hügel left for the Continent in late November, taking with him an unread copy of *External Religion*,[48] a small book of addresses Tyrrell had given to Oxford undergraduates the previous Lent. At the first opportunity he settled to read it 'most carefully, mostly twice and three times', and then immediately wrote to tell

Tyrrell how impressed he was: 'I accept and subscribe to the whole of your argument with glad and grateful readiness.'[49]

The fact that Tyrrell had been invited to give the lectures at all was a demonstration of trust in his orthodoxy. It was only four years previously that permission had first been granted by the Roman Catholic authorities for Catholic students to study at Oxford and Cambridge, and there were still considerable fears in some quarters that they would be corrupted 'in faith and morals' by university life. Tyrrell, however, put his finger on the real danger to students with typical sharpness:

If there were any real danger to our faith at a University like this, it would lie not in any supposed wickedness or general moral inferiority of the professors of an alien creed—that, indeed, would rather confirm us in our own—but in seeing the genuine goodness, the evident attractiveness of numbers whose religious opinions are not only different from, but in many cases antagonistic to the beliefs of the Catholic Church.

Tyrrell's addresses were in part a veiled attack on the controversial spirit that had corrupted the moral vision of the Church, so that goodness and truth, when they appeared in unlikely or inconvenient places, were not recognized as such. For Tyrrell, to be blind to goodness and truth in any form was to be blind to God. So he wrote to Bremond, with whom he shared a common interest in the liberal and literary English religious tradition that stemmed ultimately from Coleridge: 'All you say of the genuine goodness and implicit godliness of [George] Eliot, Jowett etc. is painfully true. They denied, not the true God or the faith, but the idolatrous form in which they conceived it; so that there was more faith and reverence in their denial, than in the reckless confession of many a Christian.'[50] Tyrrell abhorred religious know-alls 'to whom everything is clear, and common-sense, and obvious; who can define a mystery, but have never felt one'.

As in 'The Relation of Theology to Devotion' Tyrrell was concerned to argue that theology must always be the servant and not the mistress of devotion, so in *External Religion* his main point, repeatedly emphasized, is that 'this development of interior religion is the whole end and purpose of that which is exterior'. To put it in terms of revealed religion: 'The external and visible Christ, the Word Incarnate, reveals and makes plain to our earthly minds, all, and immeasurably more, that the internal Christ of our conscience, the Light which lightens every man that comes into this world, would teach us, did we not harden our hearts by infidelity to grace.' By 'the external and visible Christ', Tyrrell meant, of course, not only the historic, incarnate Christ, but the whole contemporary apparatus of the Catholic Church, for to him the Church was 'the extension of the incarnation'. The 'internal Christ of our conscience'—present in every man, unacknowledged in many, recognized explicitly only by Christians—was absolutely central for Tyrrell. It was the way he correlated the two manifestations of the one Christ that appealed to von Hügel, that and the stress on practical rather than theoretical religion:

I think that in what strikes me as its two main doctrines,—the unconscious or variously obscure, but most real and, when favoured, powerful presence within us of an inward Christ pushing us upwards and outwards with a view to join hands with the outward Christ who is pressing inwards, these two as necessary conditions for the apprehensions of Faith and Love; and the illuminative character of action, which makes the Christianity of the individual soul continually to re-begin with an experiment, and re-conclude by an experience,—that in these two main points it is entirely Blondel and Laberthonnierian, but of course with all the sound and sane mystics generally.[51]

Ironically, in view of later events, he then added: 'How nobly and rightly modern these doctrines are,—modern only, after all, in the sense of being *also* modern, for they are at bottom of and for all times, indestructible as Life and Love themselves.'

A far less sympathetic reader of *External Religion* was Merry del Val, consultor of the Sacred Congregation of the Index, and later Secretary of State to Pius X. His attention was drawn to some particularly daring statements in chapter 5, where Tyrrell wrote about the 'abuse of external means of grace', and seemed all too ready to admit that Catholic teaching about the transmission of grace in the sacraments could lead, and often did lead, to spiritual coasting: 'When we think of the stupendous offering of Himself which God makes to the soul in the Blessed Eucharist, it cannot but astonish us . . . how those who communicate almost daily, such as priests and religious and many devout lay-folk, are so little different from others; so little like what we should have been led to expect.' Tyrrell found them 'very often painfully ordinary people, as mediocre in virtue as the rest'. When he went on to acknowledge openly that there are 'some who, after abandoning the religious practices and even the faith of the Church, have attained to continence, or industry, or sobriety, or self-control, or some other virtue which they had in vain sought to secure by means of the sacraments or of ascetical practices', this sounded to Merry del Val as if he were commending their apostasy. 'Even if not pronounced to be explicitly unsound theology,' he wrote, '. . . the teaching is so confusedly and incompletely expressed as to leave an unsound impression upon the reader's mind.'[52] Tyrrell had made a powerful enemy.

External Religion is filled with pregnant remarks, illustrating most of the themes with which Tyrrell was permanently concerned. From the first he wanted to sketch the whole of Catholic doctrine in its integrated completion, 'for it is our mode of conceiving the whole that determines our mode of conceiving the parts, rather than inversely'. Intellectual and symbolic systems like those of Dante, Aquinas, and the Catholic Church itself always appealed to him. The gentleness of God and the desperation of man are portrayed by means of a characteristically vivid image: 'When man struck against God by sin, he was as a bird in the tempest that flings itself against the face of a cliff, and had been dashed to pieces had not God in His pity become soft and yielding, and taken to Himself a suffering nature, that the hurt of the shock might be His and not ours.' This God is utterly different from the Calvinist God that dominated the Church of Ireland, with his stern demand for propitiation. The image is gentle and maternal rather than judicial and paternal. By taking to himself the pain of sin, he becomes the model or archetype for Tyrrell's inexhaustible sympathy with the weak and the outcast. Tyrrell's abiding conviction of what the Church was for was expressed with perfect and painful clarity: 'As the vine lives only to produce grapes, so the Church exists and labours only to produce good men, that is, to reproduce the life of Christ as fully as possible in each particular soul; to bring minds into conformity with the mind of Christ; and hearts into conformity with the heart of Christ.' Once more the life comes before the doctrine, so that when the doctrine begins to look threadbare or untrue, the life can still be relied on as a guide to truth. If Tyrrell did not yet draw out this implication of what he was saying, or if he failed to point out his exact meaning for a Church caught up with concern about externals, that was understandable. Circumstances would soon force him to be clearer. For now, he concentrated on the inadequacy of religious language to speak about its object, and the inevitable recourse to analogy, as when a blind man tries to understand colour. He re-emphasized that the proper controversial method in matters of religion is to get men to *wish* to believe, 'to make them know and love the idea of the Church and wish it to be true'—just as he had done at Grangegorman.

In talking like this, Tyrrell was taking the arguments of a man like Newman, who realized that religious belief is not solely, nor even primarily, a matter of the intellect, and pushing them to an unbalanced, anti-intellectualist conclusion. When he stressed that 'it is by *doing*, and not by *thinking* or reasoning that we apprehend God and His truth in this life', he had in mind the words of St Ambrose quoted by Newman as an epigraph for the *Grammar of Assent*: 'Not by argument was God pleased to save his people.' For Tyrrell this was a call to action that should be heeded by the whole Church. There could be no question in the Church of a first- and second-class response to God. All are called equally to a life of discipleship:

> Some would almost seem to think that as we distinguish the *Ecclesia docens* from the *Ecclesia discens*, the Church teaching from the Church taught; so we should distinguish the Church active and militant, from the Church passive and quiescent; the former body being identical with the clergy and the latter with the laity—the clergy labouring and rowing; the laity simply paying their fare and sitting idly as so much ballast in the bark of Peter. Plainly this is a most false and pernicious analogy.

Tyrrell's thoughtful commitment to this ecclesiology of the whole body was shortly to be tested in the painful struggle that followed the joint pastoral letter of the English Bishops.

External Religion sets out some of Tyrrell's most fundamental convictions. He still believed that his religious philosophy could be contained within the church structures, as it was in continuity with the deepest roots of the Catholic tradition, but there was already about this thought an arresting radicalism and a tendency to take extreme positions in response to the extremism, as he saw it, of those in authority. He was trying to hold together the dogmatic teaching of the Catholic Church and the disturbing conclusions of nineteenth-century science. As yet he thought mainly in terms of the questions posed by evolution, but he was beginning to realize that the questions of the historians who reconstructed the early history of the Church in terms quite different from church tradition were ultimately far more challenging. When he was so disillusioned with the Jesuits, and felt himself to be a spokesman for theological and mystical truths all too often forgotten or ignored, he survived by concentrating on essentials, and keeping his counsel. He was helped by the tolerance of fellow Jesuits, who respected his ability, put up with his outbursts of temper and savage irony, and refused to pry into his personal concerns, especially since he was so obviously able to communicate with many who would open their hearts to no other priest. Peter Gallwey, another of the Farm Street Jesuits, had to acknowledge that 'Father Tyrrell can see through a stone wall'.[53] Tyrrell, for his part, valued the support he received from his English *confrères*, but he was leading a double life.

With his new-found friend Henri Bremond, who was experiencing many of the same difficulties with the French Jesuits, he was totally honest. Tyrrell's credo was minimal, but firm. He offered it to Bremond, who had asked how someone of his temperament and opinions survived in the Society:

As for my faith, so far as it must necessarily be rooted in some kind of experience and not merely in propositions or principles accepted on hearsay, it rests upon the evidence of a Power in myself and in all men 'making for Righteousness' in spite of all our downward tendencies—that is the basis of my theism which a cumulus of other reasons and experiences only supplement; that is the solid core about which they are all gathered. My Christianism is based on the concrete and intuitive recognition of the full manifestation of that said Power in the man Christ as known to us historically—so full, that I can trust him and take him as a teacher sent by God. Here again this is the core round which all subsidiary arguments from miracles etc. etc. group themselves; and without which they go for nothing with me. I could hardly tell, though I know them, all the concrete impressions that make me feel that the Roman Church is the only authorised representative of Christ on earth; and that whatever truth is revealed is to be found embedded in her general teaching like gold in the matrix.[54]

In the 'present crisis of transition from the old modes of thought to the new', he held on, knowing himself to be in sympathy with St Ignatius, if not with the present-day members of the Society he had founded. 'Were S[anctus] P[ater] N[oster] in my position he would feel all that I feel and yet would stay.'[55] That was the *modus vivendi* of the outstanding man at Farm Street.

Yet he had hope. To Louis Duchesne, the eminent French historian of the early Church, he spoke frankly of the difficulties to be faced in the short term, and of his faith that in the long term the Church could not refuse the light that came both from the teeming intellectual life of the modern world and from Christ:

I have a strong blind unreasoning faith in the conservation of spiritual energy; and in the truth that someday or other, and somehow or other, every effort in the right direction will tell—however futile it seems just now. Even were it not so, I don't think the certainty of failure would exempt one from striving to remove mountains that ought to be removed; and such is the mountain which the theologians, canonists, hagiographers, moralists, pietists, and all the lineal descendants of the scribes, pharisees and lawyers, have heaped up over the remains of Christianity—with reverent intent perhaps, yet with poor judgement. The fact is, these men have no faith. They say Christianity can bear the light of science and history, and the fresh air of modern environment [*sic*], but in their craven hearts they do not believe it; and so they fence it round with their clumsy fences and protect the Light of the World with an extinguisher, and hoard up the salt of the earth in a salt-cellar.[56]

Still, said Tyrrell, like Bunyan's Pilgrim: 'Nothing can fright my faith.'

NOTES

1. Tyrrell to Bremond, 2 Oct. 1899 (BN, Fonds Bremond).
2. *GTL*, p. 297.
3. Ibid., p. 243.
4. Ibid.
5. Ibid., p. 244.
6. Ibid., p. 211.
7. Tyrrell to Raffalovich, 24 July 1899 (Blackfriars Collection).
8. Tyrrell to Raffalovich, 28 Oct. 1900.
9. Ibid.
10. B. Sewell (ed.), *Two Friends* (St Albert's Press, 1963), p. 22; R. Ellmann, *Oscar Wilde* (London, 1987), p. 369.
11. B. Sewell, *Footnote to the Nineties* (London, 1968), pp. 18 ff.
12. Ellmann, *Oscar Wilde*, p. 369; Sewell, *Footnote*, p. 44.
13. Raffalovich to Gray, letters undated (Gray Papers, National Library of Scotland, 372/9).
14. Lyon and Paris, 1896; copies in the National Library of Scotland and the John Rylands Library, Manchester.
15. For an account of the book, see P. Healy, 'Uranisme et unisexualité', *New Blackfriars*, 59 (Feb. 1978), pp. 56–65.
16. Roehampton, 1897; copy in Heythrop College Library.
17. Tyrrell to Raffalovich, 24 July 1899.
18. Tyrrell to Raffalovich, 15 Aug. 1907.
19. Ibid.

20. Sydney Smith was editor of *The Month*.
21. Raffalovich to Gray, undated (372/9).
22. Raffalovich to Gray, 'Friday 20th' (372/12).
23. Raffalovich to Gray, 23 Nov. 1902.
24. Tyrrell to Raffalovich (Blackfriars Collection, encl. 43).
25. Thurston to Chandlery, 20 Feb. 1900 (ARSJ, ANGL. 1021, IC.1).
26. Thurston to Chandlery, 9 Mar. 1900.
27. Thurston to Chandlery, 21 Feb. 1900.
28. On the Synthetic Society, see John Root, 'George Tyrrell and the Synthetic Society', *Downside Review*, 98 (1980), pp. 42–59.
29. Von Hügel to Ward, 30 Jan. 1899 (SAUL, Ward Papers).
30. Tyrrell to Ward, 3 Feb. 1899 (SAUL, Ward Papers).
31. Tyrrell to Ward, 'Monday' (VII 294a (5)).
32. Tyrrell to von Hügel, 10 May 1899 (BL, Petre Papers).
33. Tyrrell to Ward, 2 May 1899.
34. Tyrrell expanded it to become 'A Problem in Apologetic', *The Month*, 93 (1899), pp. 617–26; 'A Point of Apologetic', ibid., 94 (1899), pp. 113–27, 249–60.
35. Ibid., 93 (1899), p. 623.
36. W. J. Williams to Ward, undated (SAUL, VII 318a (4)).
37. Von Hügel to Laberthonnière, 6 Jan. 1899, cited by A. L.-David in her unpublished thesis, 'Lettres de George Tyrrell à Henri Bremond' (Nancy, 1969), p. 53.
38. Tyrrell to Bremond, 11 Jan. 1899.
39. Von Hügel to Tyrrell, 18 June 1899.
40. Tyrrell to Bremond, 13 June 1899.
41. Tyrrell to von Hügel, 10 May 1899.
42. Von Hügel to Tyrrell, 18 June 1899.
43. Tyrrell to von Hügel, 20 Nov. 1899.
44. *The Month*, 94 (1899), pp. 461–73.
45. Von Hügel to Tyrrell, 8 Oct. 1899.
46. Von Hügel to Tyrrell, 4 Dec. 1899.
47. TSC, p. 85.
48. *External Religion: Its Use and Abuse* (London, 1899). Quotations are from pp. 58–9 ('If there were . . .'); 119 ('to whom everything . . .'); 43 ('this development . . .'); 35 ('The external . . .'); 80 ('abuse of . . .'); 93 ('When we think . . .'); ibid. ('very often . . .'); 96 ('some who . . .'); vii ('for it is . . .'); 4 ('When man struck . . .'); 74 ('As the vine . . .'); 139 ('to make them . . .'); 152 ('it is by *doing* . . .'); 123–4 ('Some would almost . . .').
49. Von Hügel to Tyrrell, 4 Dec. 1899.
50. Tyrrell to Bremond, 22 Dec. 1899.
51. Von Hügel to Tyrrell, 4 Dec. 1899.
52. F. A. Forbes, *Rafael, Cardinal Merry del Val* (London, 1932), p. 95.

53. A. L.-David, *Lettres de George Tyrrell à Henri Bremond*, (Paris, 1971), p. 26 n. 1.
54. Tyrrell to Bremond, 20 July 1899.
55. Ibid.
56. Tyrrell to Duchesne, 20 Nov. 1899 (BN, n.a.f. 17263).

8

'A Perverted Devotion'

THROUGHOUT his time in London Tyrrell was identified with the cause of liberal Catholicism. In its late nineteenth-century form this included an urgent quest for intellectual freedom within the limits set by the Church's teaching authority. But what exactly were these limits? After his liberal sympathies were swept away in the revolutionary upheavals of 1848, Pius IX had set himself against the socialism, liberalism, and belief in progress of the nineteenth century. The definition of papal infallibility at the Vatican Council in 1870 represented a victory for the ultramontane party within the Church, and a defeat for liberal Catholics like Döllinger, Acton, and, in his own way, Newman. With the accession of Leo XIII in 1878, the Church seemed to have a Pope who would be much more open to the modern world. Leo was known to be a scholar keen to promote the study of St Thomas. He had the Vatican archives opened to all scholars, Catholic and Protestant alike, and encouraged the historian Pastor in his work on the Popes. By a series of encyclicals on social questions, notably *Rerum Novarum*, he showed himself sympathetic to the aspirations of workers, and set a new direction for Catholic social policy. His encyclical on biblical scholarship, *Providentissimus Deus*, published in 1893, professed to encourage biblical research, but in fact it disappointed Catholic scholars like Loisy by its wholly conservative view of biblical inspiration and authority. Loisy, who had already lost his job at the Institut Catholique through the ineptitude of the Rector, acidly suggested that the real intention behind the encyclical was to strangle Catholic critical work on the Bible.[1] Cardinal Richard of Paris moved to suppress his journal, *Enseignement biblique*, as soon as it was published. He had no option but to submit. Von Hügel tried to maintain a more optimistic interpretation of the encyclical and of the general situation, but his hopes for something less than the outright rejection of Anglican orders were dashed in 1896, when they were declared 'absolutely null and utterly void'. This disappointment for liberals was followed by a declaration from the Holy Office that the *Comma Johanneum*, the verse in 1 John which refers explicitly to the Trinity, was authentic. It was a decision which flew in the face of all the best critical scholarship. Then there came the condemnation of liberal Catholicism in America under the name of 'Americanism'. Leo XIII, now aged and frail, seemed increasingly to have fallen into the hands of his intransigent advisers.

Two of those most concerned for the liberty of scholars were Wilfrid Ward and Baron von Hügel, both slightly older than Tyrrell. Ward, always a keen exponent of Newman, set out his views in a series of articles and essays throughout the 1890s. In the epilogue to *W. G. Ward and the Catholic Revival*, which Tyrrell reviewed in 1893, he looked to Newman as a guide in interpreting the Vatican Council's decree on papal infallibility. He believed that the Council had not committed the Church to an 'unhistorical and uncritical' line, as was commonly supposed. The current intellectual revival was taking place even among ultamontane Catholics, and, inasmuch as it was a revival of historical scholarship, it had the backing of the Pope. Four years later, in the epilogue to *The Life and Times of Cardinal Wiseman*, his tone was more circumspect. He appealed to Newman and Wiseman in defence of the 'ideal combination of intellectual life and freedom with alert obedience to the central religious authority'.[2] Ward made it clear that he was not challenging the power of the Church to define and defend dogmatic truth, or to hold the speculations of scholars in check when this was for the general good. However, with regard to current controversies, both with Anglicans and with modern thinkers in general, he argued for accommodation and assimilation wherever possible, appealing, as Newman had done, to Aquinas's use of Aristotle. 'To show the richness of life which she showed in the Middle Ages,' he concluded, 'the Church must have the same opportunities which she then had. She must be able safely and freely to hold intercourse with secular culture.'[3] When another liberal Catholic, William Gibson, lost patience with Rome and publicly declared in an impassioned article that 'serious scientific investigation in any of the higher branches is impossible, in any Catholic faculty, in cases where the subject matter is likely to be of interest to the ecclesiastical authorities',[4] Ward saw that this kind of intemperate attack could only harm the liberal cause. Tyrrell similarly disapproved of Gibson's 'pranks'. In a speedy reply, Ward carefully set out the relation of theology and biblical criticism as he saw it. 'The critic is the Liberal pioneer, whose privilege it is occasionally to be rash, provided he does not dogmatise; the theologian remains the Conservative make-weight, and sets his remnant of antiquated positions against the critic's overflow of evanescent novelties.'[5] He made a strong case for the conservatism of Rome, and then pleaded, with Newman, for a 'large liberality' in dealing with scholars. In the end, whatever the present impasse, there could be no absolute contradiction between the work of scholars and that of theologians.

Ward was always a moderating influence. Von Hügel, who had schooled himself in critical study of the Bible, was even more painfully aware of the catching-up to be done by the Roman Church in this field. He championed Loisy because he saw in him just that blend of incisive scholarship and fidelity to the Church that he thought was needed. After what he called 'that truly *phenomenal* decision of the H. Office' over the *Comma Johanneum*, he told Ward he 'could not and would not attempt one word' in defence of it.[6] Where Gibson spoke out angrily, and Ward looked for the rationale behind the decision, von Hügel subjected it to measured attack in *The Tablet*. Where Ward was consciously committed to expounding the legacy of Newman, von Hügel was concerned to make space for critical scholars like Loisy and Semeria. For the time being Tyrrell's concerns were closer to those of Ward. In this period he too could be called an exponent of Newman.

In his review of *The Life and Times of Cardinal Wiseman* Tyrrell concentrated on Ward's epilogue, which he welcomed because it said things that he had been saying in *The Month* since 1896. He stressed Newman's view that 'the main bulk of what most men believe is derived from tradition, imitation, blind repetition, and other non-rational sources, which are nevertheless reliable on the whole'.[7] It is the place of analytical reason to curb, test, and order these beliefs, not to argue men into (or away from) the Kingdom. Wiseman is commended for his broad sympathy with the culture of his time, for his concern to make Catholicism attractive to many, and, since Tyrrell was writing in the official journal of the Jesuits, for his unswerving belief in a dogmatic, even exclusive, religion that has the courage of its teaching authority. Tyrrell publicly rejected the label of 'liberal' Catholicism, because he saw all true Catholicism as essentially liberal—open to the best in secular culture and civilization, profiting from it in a spirit of critical, but assimilative, independence. He compared the relationship between the Church and science or

secular culture to that between grace and nature. The one comple-
ments and fulfils the other. When the two come into conflict, patience
and faith will be needed. It may be that for the good of all the Church
will need to pronounce, and perhaps pronounce wrongly, but this is
her prerogative and her duty. In time the truth will become apparent.
Ostensibly, Tyrrell argued that the real danger was impatience in
reaching for a premature synthesis between science and religion. In
fact, he was equally, or more, concerned about the Church's apparent indifference to the sufferings of those who found the teachings of
religion and the conclusions of science incompatible. Ultimately,
men like Ward were prepared, like the Church to which they
belonged, to think in centuries, and this was not Tyrrell's way. He
felt the pressure from the confessional too strongly. Within the
bounds of what could be said in the Jesuit journal, he tried to draw
attention to an impossible situation.

In 1898 Tyrrell told Ward that he had 'been always a devout
disciple of Newman'.[8] This is evident in 'Rationalism in Religion'
and 'The Relation of Theology to Devotion', both of which appeared
in *The Month* in 1899. Even the title of the first is taken from
Newman, and the article does little more than think his thoughts
after him. Tyrrell argues that in speaking about the Trinity we are
speaking about a mystery of which we can have no unmediated
knowledge. All the knowledge we do have is conveyed by means of
inadequate and analogical human language. Precisely because of this
inadequacy, we dare not alter the 'form of sound words' by which
revelation came to us. We must beware of forgetting that this
language of revelation refers not to concepts, but to living realities.
Those who do forget these points fall into the error of *rationalism*, an
absolutely fundamental error responsible for endless religious
casualties. Tyrrell never tired of pleading for a proper understanding
of the nature of religious truth. Heaven and earth are not to be
contained in a syllogism, however subtly expressed. Mysteries,
'truths fringed with darkness', are not riddles, and profane theologians do untold damage when they think they can solve them as
such. All Tyrrell's prophetic indignation was roused by such
enormities.

Although the article was safely directed against the latitudinarian
theologians of the Church of England, it was as much a protest
against similar errors in Roman Catholic teaching. The following
December Tyrrell was stung into a more outspoken protest by the

cheerful certainty with which two Redemptorist writers handled the
doctrine of hell, exhibiting by their alarming enthusiasm 'a perverted
devotion'.[9] As usual he goes to the heart of the matter: 'The real
difficulty proposed to our faith in the doctrine of hell is, that God,
foreseeing that even one soul should be lost eternally, should freely
suffer things to take their course, when He could . . . have hindered
the tragedy.' It is a painful mystery, but faith demands that we hold
on, with Julian of Norwich, to the belief that 'God will save His word
in all things . . . and yet all shall be well'. There can be no question of
falling into the 'pert rationalism' of those who imagine that they
understand these things, when they show by their happy contemplation of everlasting torment that they understand nothing of the
mystery of God's love or, indeed, of his justice. Tyrrell's plea was for
'a certain temperate agnosticism, which is one of the essential
prerequisites of intelligent faith', and the 'purging out of our midst
[of] any remnant of the leaven of rationalism'. This time he had gone
too far. Already he was being closely watched by Monsignor Moyes,
theologian to Cardinal Vaughan. In von Hügel's opinion it was
Moyes, 'a violent-minded and prejudiced man', who delated 'A
Perverted Devotion' to Rome.[10]

Two factors rapidly complicated the situation. The first was that
the writers of the Farm Street scriptorium were already under
suspicion. The General had been told that they were lazy and that
their work was poor. All were rebuked as being 'too anxious to
conciliate the enemies of religion', and were suspected of
liberalism.[11] Amongst those specifically mentioned were Joseph
Rickaby and Tyrrell. More than that, Tyrrell's name was immediately linked with that of St George Mivart, a distinguished Catholic
biologist who, six years previously, had written three articles on
'Happiness in Hell' in which he had tried to give the traditional
doctrine an interpretation that could be accepted by the modern
mind.[12] The articles were placed on the Index. He had recently come
to public notice again when he wrote to *The Times* savagely attacking not only the French Catholic press and the hierarchy, but also the
Pope and the Curia for their behaviour over the Dreyfus case. By the
'amazing and appalling silence' of the Pope, they had lent their
support to the condemnation of Captain Dreyfus for his supposed
espionage, a flagrantly anti-Semitic miscarriage of French justice.[13]
He then published two articles in which he repudiated nothing that
he had written about hell, and challenged a number of basic Catholic

doctrines.[14] By this time he was a dying man. Cardinal Vaughan tried to get him to sign a declaration of faith, but this was obviously quite meaningless to him, as his whole question was about the way in which such declarations could validly be understood. Vaughan referred him to two priests for help, one of whom was Tyrrell.[15] Like Tyrrell, Mivart died excommunicate and was refused a Catholic burial.

This was the background when, on 7 January 1900, Luis Martin, the Jesuit General, wrote, in the absence of John Gerard, the English Provincial, to Alexander Charnley, the Vice-Provincial. He wrote because he was concerned about Tyrrell's article, which was offensive enough to be placed on the Index. He noted that this was not the only example of questionable material being passed by the censors: there had been several complaints about Tyrrell's *Notes on the Catholic Doctrine of Purity*.[16] Charnley was to send the names of Tyrrell's censors, a copy of their judgements on the article, and an explanation of why it had been published in that notorious liberal Catholic journal, the *Weekly Register*. Until further notice, Tyrrell was confined to writing for *The Month*.[17] Meanwhile, the article was subjected to further censorship in Rome—from Joseph Floeck of the Hungarian and German College in Rome, and from Joseph Piccirelli of the Neapolitan Province (neither of whom could possibly have had much understanding of what Tyrrell was trying to do).[18] Floeck was troubled by Tyrrell's use of the word 'agnosticism', thinking that he had no use for reason in expounding the mysteries of the faith. He condemned Tyrrell's handling of the eternity of punishment in hell, and his rejection of the material nature of hell-fire. He found his use of the term *male sonans*, or 'ill-sounding'. Tyrrell's teaching was false, erroneous, discordant, scandalous, and liable to encourage laxity. Piccirelli began his judgement by launching into a tirade against the article, which contained doctrine that was false, temerarious, and erroneous, injurious to the Church, ill-sounding and offensive to pious ears, scandalous, and tending towards heresy if not entirely heretical. He questioned Tyrrell's good faith in writing, and saw here an instance of how ignorance, presumption, and curiosity had combined to lead a man into terrible errors. After 'Happiness in Hell', which had been condemned by the Church, they now had 'Devotion to Hell', which was quite as reprehensible. The substantive points that followed were not greatly different from those made by Floeck.

When Charnley replied to the General's demand for information, he mentioned Cardinal Vaughan's high opinion of the article. The General replied tartly that his own censors had come to a very different conclusion, and in a case like this that was what mattered. The ban on Tyrrell was to be observed to the letter.[19] He then wrote at length to Gerard, reviewing the case.[20] 'A Perverted Devotion' had caused him no end of trouble and deserved to be put on the Index of Forbidden Books. There was, he said, in Tyrrell's work a certain audacity and unclarity which usually leads to serious dangers. He had heard of Tyrrell's outspokenness in giving the Spiritual Exercises. Apparently, Tyrrell had said of 'Americanism' (a current Vatican name for heretical, liberal teaching): 'Americanism can be held; I myself am an Americanist, but I am using words advisedly.' Martin enclosed the reports of his censors so that Tyrrell could use them in writing a piece to repair the damage he had done. He administered a strong rebuke that Tyrrell's article had only been seen by one censor in England—Thurston—and that he had reported verbally. Thurston was never again to be sole censor, nor was anything he had approved to be published against the opinion of other censors. In general, the writers of the English Province were far too accommodating to non-Catholics, and had been infected by the liberalism that Newman called 'profound and specious scepticism' and that Gerard had said, only last year, was not present among them. There was no other remedy, he concluded, echoing Tyrrell's remarks on rationalism, than 'to purge the leaven completely'.

Tyrrell was furious, doubly so when he saw the *censurae*. He was being told that he had put things in a way that was 'offensive to pious ears', that he did not know his Aquinas, and that he did not teach Catholic truth. He also knew that he had the theologians of the English Province behind him, and that all his colleagues thought the *censurae* a disgrace. When the crisis first broke, he wrote to Bremond: 'I wish Rome would either define pious ears, or give a list of them so that one might know. That the popular unauthorised presentation of Hell offends really pious people and either drives or keeps them from the faith seems of no consequence, so long as superstitions are not disturbed.'[21] Two months later he told von Hügel:

These censures, besides a great deal of personality, contain objections founded throughout on the most glaring ignorance of English and a total failure to grasp the motive and totality of the article. I am identified with

Mivart, Huxley, Spencer, and loaded freely with every epithet of theological 'Billingsgate', from 'scandalous' up to 'proximately if not all together heretical', and my 'good faith' is questioned and denied.[22]

For a time he was so angry and hurt that he gave up saying mass. He thought he was being forced by the General to repudiate things he did believe, and write in defence of things he did not, and which were no part of the Catholic faith. Should he not, then, cease to exercise his priesthood?

Tyrrell's predicament was of profound concern to his colleagues at *The Month*, because they too were touched by the criticisms from Rome, and they were amongst the few who knew the value of Tyrrell's work. Sidney Smith, the editor, wrote to Rudolf Meyer, the General's assistant with responsibility for dealing with the affairs of the English Province, in defence of Tyrrell, stressing the value of his work amongst those with intellectual problems:

He is precisely the one amongst us all who is sought out by these earnest enquirers, Catholic and non-Catholic. He holds that they are repelled by the harsh unsympathetic way in which their very real mental difficulties are pooh-poohed by so many of our priests and apologists, in books and conversations, who expect them to be satisfied with solutions taken out of the textbooks which seem to them to explain nothing.[23]

Thurston, who had all too easily passed the article for publication, was thoroughly alarmed by the turn of events. No one was better acquainted with the mercurial and fragile temperament of his friend. He knew the strain Tyrrell was under from the continual demands made upon him, and the depth of his disillusion with the Society. He knew that he would never retract what he had written or comply with demands that he thought to be unjust. He also knew that, if he turned against the Society publicly, Tyrrell had the capacity to inflict very considerable harm. His friend was near the edge of the precipice, and, even if he were not pushed, he might well jump. Moreover, it was Thurston's carelessness that had helped to bring this about. He wrote to Peter Chandlery, secretary to Rudolf Meyer, at great length:

For God's sake, *for God's sake*, FOR GOD'S SAKE persuade Father General somehow or other to withdraw that injunction to Father Tyrrell about his article in the Weekly Register. I am not an alarmist or prone to panics, but I venture to say that no one realises even faintly the harm that may and probably will come of it all, if nothing is done. I know Fr. Tyrrell better than any-one, and I say in all simplicity that I do not believe we shall be able to persuade him to do what he is asked to do.

The letter contains a remarkable testimony to Tyrrell's character:

He is the one man in the Society in England who has really won the respect of thinking men, within and without the Church—men like Professor Sidgwick, Sir Mountstuart Grant Duff, Mr Wyndham and Mr Balfour, members of the Government whom he meets at the Synthetic Society . . . He knows so many scandals. He has been in the thick of all sorts of delicate matters (in giving retreats to Ours etc.), some of which even superiors do not know of . . . Mind I am not saying that Fr. Tyrrell has any formed intention of turning against the Society or of giving up his faith. But I know him so well, I know how things have been preying upon his mind lately, the endless difficulties that have been submitted to him in connexion with this Mivart affair (N.B. He has absolutely no sympathy with Mivart), his depression that has been growing upon him from the sense that everything was going to pieces, that there was no foothold for faith anywhere . . . You see what makes it all so sad, is that Fr. Tyrrell, as you, my dear Father, know very well, is a man *integerrimae vitae*. He has never been in any sort of sense a black sheep. He is observant and mortified and spiritually minded. When he writes, his Catholic imagination and his talent may lead him sometimes too far, may induce him to say things in an exaggerated and sometimes a stinging way, but he writes always honestly and sincerely. What he says he believes, at least at the time, to be true . . . He is the chosen spiritual guide of some of the noblest characters I have ever known both in religion and out of it. He has the confidence of more of our scholastics—I speak especially of the more gifted of these scholastics—than any other father of the Province. His books are literally scrambled for in convents—I know one where they have six copies of *Hard Sayings* and they are always in use—and are read by good people of all classes in the Church and out of it . . . Fr. Tyrrell is always a truthful man but he is not a discreet one and he easily goes further than he means to do.[24]

Thurston was particularly incensed by the report of the second censor, which he called 'simply atrocious'. Two days later he wrote to say that Tyrrell had given up saying mass.[25] Mercifully, the crisis only lasted three days. Unbeknown to his friend, Thurston wrote six letters in just over a fortnight, pleading through Chandlery for Tyrrell and his work, wishing that the opprobrium had fallen on his own head, angered and saddened at the lack of any hint that the Roman censors had made a mistake:

There are thousands and thousands of people here starving for want of bread (intellectually, I mean) but the theologians for all the help that they give them might be in another planet. 'If you don't see the arguments for revelation you are eaten up with intellectual pride, or you keep a mistress', that is practically what they tell them, and when any rash person tries to enter into the difficulties of these agnostics or troubled Catholics, the theologians shut their pious ears and scream 'heresy!'[26]

Meanwhile Tyrrell was working not at an article that would repair the damage done by 'A Perverted Devotion', but at a reply to his censors, which was not at all what the General wanted. He wrote to Gerard that since he saw no reason to change his opinions and could not find the dangerous obscurities that were supposed to exist in his first article, he could only state *as a fact* that certain objections had been found with his article, and then either take issue with the objections or republish 'A Perverted Devotion' with appropriate annotations. Typically, Tyrrell was concerned that his article had not been taken as a whole:

In what follows, it is made evident that my censors have failed altogether to appreciate the purport and spirit of the article *as a whole*, and thus, bring in a wrong key to unlock the meaning of the parts. In dealing severally with those dismembered parts they display a purely destructive and therefore uncritical spirit; and, above all, a patent unfamiliarity with idiomatic and literary English . . . For these, and for other more obvious reasons, I repudiate and protest against these censures in their entirety.[27]

In his typescript[28] Tyrrell dealt with the censors in detail, spending most of his time on the first, because he was 'the more temperate and measured in his judgment and therefore merits more careful hand-ling'. He had nothing but contempt for the second. Point by point he answered their criticisms—of his use of the term 'devotion', of the way that he based his explanation of the doctrine of hell on the divine goodness rather than the divine justice (he actually said precisely the opposite), of his 'fideism', his 'agnosticism' (he quoted St Leo as the source of his ideas), and of his rejection of the physical nature of hell-fire. Gerard, who was in a difficult position, because he thought Tyrrell's protest was amply justified, forwarded both the reply (having 'excised the sarcasms') and the covering letter to Rome.

This drew the strongest response yet from the General—the key letter in the whole exchange. Martin wrote back at length, defending the condemnation of the article, and rejecting Tyrrell's suggested public refutation of criticisms or republication of the article with appended notes. Nothing would suffice but a simple and easily understandable article setting out the Catholic teaching on hell, to be submitted to Rome for approval before publication. Any books that Tyrrell wrote were to be subject to Roman scrutiny after local

censorship. Tyrrell's 'audacity' of expression was shown by: his
behaviour when teaching philosophy; his published articles and
books, which had scandalized some people; the upset he caused to
some of 'Ours' when giving the Spiritual Exercises; the audacious
and sarcastic spirit in which he spoke and wrote of delicate matters;
that dangerous article 'A Perverted Devotion'; his defence against the
censors. Whoever would have believed that a Father of the Society,
writing on a theological matter ('devotion'), would reject the definition of St Thomas and theologians of the Society in favour of a
definition from Webster's Dictionary, and then, because the censors
do not understand or do not permit such a definition, deem them to
be ignorant of English?Tyrrell was not to be permitted to give the
Spiritual Exercises to Jesuits again until he showed himself to have
reformed.[29]

Now Gerard exploded with indignation and frustration. He took
Martin to have put Tyrrell under a total ban and wrote to Meyer to
protest: 'It is ordered that Fr Tyrrell should be inhibited from all
retreats, to Ours, Secular priests, or Nuns, and from Conferences at
the Universities. This means the imposition of total silence upon him
whether in speech or writing.' (Gerard seems to have been exaggerat-
ing a little. Tyrrell was at least free to write for *The Month*, a freedom
that, admittedly, the close supervision he would now experience
made into little more than absolute constraint.) Gerard went on:

He has more power amongst *men* by a long way than any of our Fathers in
London, being sought not only by those whose Faith is weak, many of whom
he alone—as I know—can retain, but by educated Catholics of the old-
fashioned sturdy school who declare that he has done them more good than
any director they ever had. So with the Secular Clergy. He is more sought for
to give their retreats than any one else, it being precisely the better and
sounder men that ask for him, and those who have made retreats under him
declare that they have learnt more from him than from any other.

He was prepared to put his own head on the block to save Tyrrell:
'What I therefore earnestly beg is that the embargo laid upon Fr
Tyrrell be removed, on *condition* that I go bail for him and undertake
that nothing shall occur henceforth to which any just exception can
be taken. I feel sure that I can secure this.'[30] Martin, however,
remained intransigent, simply renewing his demand for an article
that would put the record straight.

Gerard was clearly working to cool the situation. When his
successor as Provincial wrote to ask what exactly he had done, he

told him: 'I did not tell Fr. Tyrrell that he was taboo for retreats, and therefore did not, of course, assign reasons.'[31] He did tell Tyrrell that his 'admonition' was 'but a special section of a rebuke addressed to *all* the writers of the English Province S. J. censuring them for "being too anxious to conciliate the adversaries of the Church and not being sufficiently strong and courageous in their condemnation of heresy and error"'.[32] Gerard's position was clearly impossible. He dared not tell Tyrrell how much pressure he was under from Rome, so all he could do was work on him to provide the article that would satisfy the General. Tyrrell, however, was writing nothing, as he had gone into hospital for an operation on his piles. He followed the tactic he had outlined to Ward: 'I am going to contest the matter to the very last, and am prepared to face any scandal or ill-consequences rather than say the thing which is not. They always modify their terms if they think one will fight; and when I get the price down to its lowest I will see if I can afford it.'[33]

At this point Tyrrell was badly compromised by an intemperate article in the *Nineteenth Century*. Robert Dell was contributing 'A Liberal Catholic View of the Case of Dr Mivart',[34] but in passing he spoke of Tyrrell as 'an English Jesuit father, whose views seem to be as much out of harmony with the spirit of his Society as his abilities are superior to those of his *confrères*'. This was just the sort of compliment Tyrrell did not want. It was noted, inevitably, by the General, who suggested that Tyrrell should write an article repudiating Dell and clarifying his position on the Catholic doctrine of hell.[35] Gerard passed the request on, trying to persuade Tyrrell to be reasonable: 'There is no question of your having to say what you don't believe, but of letting men see the other side of your mind which like the other side of the moon has recently been out of sight.'[36] He then, no doubt from the best of motives but most ill-advisedly, quoted back at Tyrrell some words from 'The Relation of Theology to Devotion': 'Did you not yourself write recently "It is the desire to climb up by some other way, rather than go through the one door of self-denial, that is the source of all corruption?"' The remark was wrenched right out of context. Tyrrell had been talking about purity of heart as the best defence against superstition and the exploitation of religion. However uncertain his temper, he knew that, in this matter, his heart was pure, and that the exploitation of religion lay on the other side.

Accordingly, Tyrrell wrote a stinging letter back to Meyer:

I am informed that His Paternity is impatient at my delay in complying with his commands; and I suppose some explanation is due. In the only definite form in which they reached me they were based on the validity of two accompanying censures which I felt it my painful duty to repudiate as false and calumnious; and for this repudiation I forwarded my reasons through Father Provincial who, together with his consultors and many others, agreed with my estimate in the matter. Since then His Paternity has been kind enough to say that he personally has no suspicion as to my orthodoxy—a statement quite incompatible with his adhesion to the sentiments of the two censors aforesaid who vilify me with various theological 'notes'. Hence I had a right to expect some modification of His Paternity's previous harsh and difficult sentence; and therefore delayed. However for three weeks, previous to the operation I underwent a fortnight ago, I was incapable of literary work; and am writing this from my bed in defiance of doctors and in deference to His Paternity's importunity. Even when I am physically fit to write such an article as is required, there will be moral and mental difficulties that will delay its production indefinitely; for, I have to write an article which no one in the English Province is judged competent to censure, and which has to satisfy such foreign censors as those who have already displayed in their criticism of my work a profound ignorance of literary English, of theology, and of the first principles of truthfulness and candour. I doubt if Christ Himself could satisfy such a request.[37]

Nevertheless, Tyrrell drafted an article and sent it to Rome, discharging the General's request in some measure, but deliberately missing the point of it. His angry and aggressive piece falls far short of the uncritical statement of Catholic doctrine about hell demanded by the General.[38] There also survives from this period a reply to Dell, entitled 'Who Are the Reactionaries?'.[39] In this Tyrrell dissociates himself from Dell and his accusations of Jesuit inflexibility. The spirit of the Society must, a priori, be that of Ignatius, a spirit of elasticity and accommodation. Ignatius was no supporter of 'Chinese inflexibility', so how could the Jesuits be? The article was flagrantly tongue in cheek, but all this activity suggests that Tyrrell was trying to find ways of appeasing his superiors, or at least of justifying himself, without yielding to the General's demands.

By now the General had fallen ill, partly, Meyer thought, because of worry over Tyrrell. Meyer was quite prepared to contemplate Tyrrell's dismissal from the Society, but all would be solved if he would agree to some statement such as the following:

That in the matter which he treated in the article entitled 'A Perverted Devotion', three things must be distinguished, viz. dogmas of faith, Catholic truths and theological opinions; that, as to dogmas and Catholic truths, all loyal sons of the Church are bound to accept them, and that consequently there can be no question as to his position on that score; but that as to theological opinions he wishes to declare that in the matter of which there is question, as well as in others, he subscribes to the common opinion of Catholic theologians, and that in this sense readers must interpret his article in which he meant simply to say that we should not require more than the Church requires through her recognised spokesmen.[40]

Tyrrell had beaten the price down to one he could afford. He agreed to the contorted paragraph, and turned it into an 'absolutely fatuous and unmeaning little letter'.[41] As he told Ward: 'After six months of groaning and labour the seven hills have been delivered of a lean little mouse whose ineffectual squeak will be heard in the Weekly Register of Saturday.'[42]

At the end of May Cardinal Vaughan, Archbishop of Westminster, sent for Tyrrell. He was 'truly cordial and kind', but warned him against the dangers of going too fast. According to Tyrrell, 'he considered the *substance* of what he wrote alright, "but you converts don't put the things as we old Catholics put them. Why don't you honour old Catholics, by adopting their time-honoured way of putting things?"' To that Tyrrell answered:

If a convert's primary object in writing ought to be to honour old Catholics, —then no doubt he had better adopt their way of writing; but that if he wanted to arrest the attention of outsiders, and to gain a hearing for the Church, then he could not do so, for that simple experience, e.g. the entire non-impressiveness of Canon Moyes' writings, showed plainly that, for that purpose, a translation of Church teaching into the current thought and language of the educated, was a *sine qua non*.[43]

Moyes, theologian to Cardinal Vaughan, stood for everything Tyrrell loathed about most theologians. 'It was he', said von Hügel quaintly, 'who by his violent articles in the "Tablet" drove poor old Dr Mivart to fairy at the last.' Commenting on Tyrrell's exchange with Vaughan, von Hügel told Bremond: 'I know well how, with all his admirable devotedness and also kindliness of disposition,—it will never be *our* way of putting things, that he will spontaneously understand.'[44] Von Hügel, in his turn, never really understood Tyrrell's passionate concern, fostered by Dolling, to bring the hope of the Catholic gospel to those lost in the intellectual and moral wastelands of London. Unlike von Hügel, Tyrrell felt no need to defend a reputation for orthodoxy; most of the time he simply wrote or spoke from the heart. It was precisely this that made him both attractive and dangerous, so that the Cardinal wanted him moved from London.

The whole affair over 'A Perverted Devotion' left Tyrrell saddened, angry, and very tired. He was outraged by the censures, and outraged by the General's refusal even to consider the possibility that the Roman censors might have misunderstood him and so have come to the wrong decision. He felt that the Roman authorities showed not an iota of sympathy for his ministry to the lost and perplexed, many of whom were lost and perplexed precisely because of this Roman high-handedness and stupidity. He had the English Jesuits behind him, but was now apparently to be treated as a man who could not be trusted: forbidden to write except for *The Month*, subject to double censorship, and, he began to suspect, forbidden to give retreats. He told Maude Petre that he was to give an ordination retreat in Dublin,[45] but then he found that he had been moved to the less prestigious one for the *Filles de Marie* in London.[46] In July he spoke of himself as 'still under interdict as to writing (outside *The Month*); and also as to retreat-giving'.[47] Maude Petre also says that Tyrrell's rights as a confessor were 'a good deal curtailed'. Because he could not expect intelligent or fair censorship, he understood himself to be effectively barred from writing and from much of the speaking that he really cared about. There was the very real danger that his earlier work would be condemned. Worst of all, Gerard, embarrassed by the whole situation, had not been open with him, so none of this was clear.

Tyrrell suggested that he should leave London for a break. Gerard readily agreed; he thought that Tyrrell's departure for the small Jesuit mission at Richmond, Yorkshire would offer a breathing-space all round.

NOTES

1. A. F. Loisy, *Mémoires pour servir à l'histoire religieuse de notre temps*, 3 vols. (Paris, 1930–1), i, p. 297.
2. W. Ward, *The Life and Times of Cardinal Wiseman*, 2 vols. (London, 1897), ii, pp. 574–5.
3. Ibid., p. 581.
4. W. Gibson, 'An Outburst of Activity in the Roman Congregations', *Nineteenth Century*, 45 (1899), p. 789.

5. W. Ward, 'Catholic Apologetics: A Reply', ibid., p. 957.

6. Von Hügel to Ward, 25 May 1897 (SAUL, Ward Papers).

7. *The Month*, 91 (1898), p. 144.

8. Tyrrell to Ward, 22 Sept. 1898 (SAUL, Ward Papers).

9. 'A Perverted Devotion', *Weekly Register*, 100 (16 Dec. 1899), pp. 797–800; repr. *EFI*, pp. 158–71.

10. Von Hügel to Bremond, 15 July 1900 (BN, Fonds Bremond).

11. Martin to Gerard, 30 Aug. 1899 (ARSJ, *RPA*, v).

12. See St G. Mivart, 'Happiness in Hell', *Nineteenth Century*, 32 (1892), pp. 899–919; 'The Happiness in Hell: A Rejoinder', *Nineteenth Century*, 33 (1893), pp. 320–38; 'Last Words on the Happiness in Hell: A Rejoinder', *Nineteenth Century*, 33 (1893), pp. 637–51.

13. *The Times*, 17 Oct. 1899, pp. 13–14.

14. St G. Mivart, 'The Continuity of Catholicism', *Nineteenth Century*, 47 (1900), pp. 51–72; 'Some Recent Catholic Apologists', *Fortnightly Review*, NS 67 (1900), pp. 24–44.

15. Vaughan to Mivart, 21 Jan. 1900 (AAW, Vaughan Papers). See J. W. Gruber, *A Conscience in Conflict: The Life of St George Jackson Mivart* (New York, 1960); John D. Root, 'The Final Apostasy of St George Jackson Mivart', *Catholic Historical Review*, 81 (1985), pp. 1–25.

16. *Notes on the Catholic Doctrine of Purity* (Roehampton, 1897).

17. Martin to Charnley, 7 Jan. 1900 (ARSJ, *RPA*, v).

18. ARSJ, ANGL. 1021, IB, contains these censures. See *AL*2, pp. 451–8, for an edited version.

19. Martin to Charnley, 5 Feb. 1900.

20. Martin to Gerard, 12 Feb. 1900.

21. Tyrrell to Bremond, 18 Jan. 1900.

22. Tyrrell to von Hügel, 10 Mar. 1900 (BL, Petre Papers).

23. Smith to Meyer, 2 Feb. 1900 (ARSJ, ANGL. 1021, 1B.5).

24. Thurston to Chandlery, 18 Feb. 1900 (ARSJ, ANGL. 1021, IB.7).

25. Thurston to Chandlery, 20 Feb. 1900.

26. Thurston to Chandlery, 9 Mar. 1900.

27. Tyrrell to Gerard, 14 Mar. 1900 (ARSJ, ANGL. 1021, IB.8).

28. ARSJ, ANGL. 1021, IB.9; excerpts in *AL*2, pp. 121–5.

29. Martin to Gerard, 27 Mar. 1900 (ARSJ, *Registrum Epistolarum ad Missiones Assistentiae Angliae*, ii (1891–1912), into which volume it was wrongly transcribed).

30. Gerard to Meyer, 9 Apr. 1900 (ARSJ, ANGL. 1021, IB.13).

31. Gerard to Colley, 23 Nov. 1901 (AEPSJ).

32. Tyrrell to Ward, 'Friday' (VII 294a (20)).

33. Tyrrell to Ward, 'Thursday' (VII 294a (14)).

34. *The Nineteenth Century*, 47 (1900), pp. 669–84.

35. Martin to Gerard, 12 Apr. 1900.

36. Gerard to Tyrrell, 19 Apr. 1900 (AEPSJ).

37. Tyrrell to Meyer, 22 Apr. 1900 (ARSJ, ANGL. 1021, IB.14).
38. ARSJ, ANGL. 1021, IB.18. An edited version of Tyrrell's earlier 'Reply to My Censors' survives in AEPSJ. See G. Tyrrell, with an introd. by R. Butterworth, 'A Perverted Devotion (II)', *Heythrop Journal*, 24 (1983), pp. 379–90. Butterworth also gives a good account of the row over 'A Perverted Devotion' in R. Butterworth (ed.), *A Jesuit Friendship* (London, 1988), pp. 68–81.
39. 'Who are the Reactionaries?' (SAUL, Ward Papers).
40. Meyer to Gerard, 17 May 1900 (ARSJ, *RPA*, v).
41. Tyrrell to von Hügel, 6 June 1900.
42. Tyrrell to Ward, 31 May 1900.
43. Von Hügel to Bremond, 15 July 1900.
44. Ibid.
45. Tyrrell to Maude Petre, 28 May 1900 (BL, Petre Papers).
46. *AL2*, p. 130.
47. Tyrrell to Bremond, 26 July 1900.

9

The Move to Richmond

WITH the crisis over 'A Perverted Devotion', Tyrrell's life moved on to a new plane. As a Jesuit, he was on his death-bed. The blatant misrepresentation of the Roman censures, and the General's inflexibility had turned secret and long-standing disillusion with the Society into unconcealed contempt for 'Jesuitism'. The outcome was inevitable, but it was postponed for five years, partly by Tyrrell's removal from the public eye and his retreat into pseudonymous writing, partly by the continuing support he received from English Jesuit friends, and partly by his natural shrinking from a step so painful. 'Odd as it may sound,' he told Ward at the height of the crisis, 'I have no wish and should have much reluctance to split with the Society where my personal friends are so many and my affections consequently entangled—and I am a slave of habits and customs and would find a change as painful as being flayed alive.'[1] If he left, there was little likelihood of peaceful employment as a secular priest. 'They will never forget or forgive', he told von Hügel.[2] Not to be a priest at all would be to pass into a shadowy world of failed vocations, with the suspicion of moral disgrace, and exclusion from all he held dear. Few would understand why he had effectively torn up his life's work. Still less would they understand that the Church was still his Beatrice, the *donna gentile* who had stolen his heart. But what future could there be for him in the Society when the best efforts of his mind and of his pen were misrepresented and misunderstood, when he was practically debarred from giving retreats and from writing in the way that came naturally to him, and when the counsel he gave all too often led to increased frustration and alienation from the Church?

Any passing identification with the liberal Catholicism of Wilfrid Ward was now finished. Ward misunderstood Tyrrell, in that he thought him a 'wise liberal' like himself. As he told von Hügel:

The only solution *I* can see is that, if wise liberals are very careful *not* to shock, wise rulers should be brought to see that in a most difficult time of transition they are our only hope for the future. But self-restraint on the one

side is the only *possible* means of securing a tolerant attitude on the other . . .
Now the man who seemed to me to have most thoroughly got hold of this
principle was Tyrrell. Have you heard of his troubles? He spoke to me quite
calmly of going into *schism*. This has been far the greatest blow I have had.[3]

Tyrrell tried to explain to Ward that he did not want to be thought of
as either a 'liberal' or a 'conservative', because he did not want to see
a victory for either party within the Church. From his first infatua-
tion with Aquinas, what he wanted was a revolution of presuppositions that would dethrone developed and rationalistic scholasticism,
restore the place of mystery and of the will in Christian understanding, and throw the emphasis back on Christianity as a life of heroic,
self-sacrificial charity, open to all. Such a revolution would undercut
both 'liberal' and 'conservative' positions. It would bring a new
openness to scholarship. It would demonstrate afresh the indispensable role of 'external religion' in promoting the all-important devotion of the heart. At the moment, the parties of right and left were
pulling in opposite directions, threatening to pull the Church to
pieces:

The Extreme Right hopes weakly in violent methods of repression; and
strives to pitchfork back the incoming tide. The Extreme Left calls on them
to surrender and cry *peccavimus* or demands what is not so much a reform as
a revolution . . . If there is not a mediating party; these two will tug till the
rope breaks and each is thrown backwards with disaster.[4]

The mediation that Tyrrell looked for was not so much between right
and left, though it had that aspect to it, but between old and new.
Those concerned with true mediation are those who see the revolution that will come when the results and methods of historical and
biblical scholarship are so much part of the intellectual climate that
even the Church can no longer ignore them:

The Church may *try* Chinese isolation: but it *cannot* succeed. Inevitably
from below upwards the leaven of progress spreads; and the rapid current
that swept the world along in the nineteenth century will most likely make
itself felt in the Church in the twentieth by a similarly sudden change of
conditions. It is the sense of this impending crisis that makes those who see
further than the end of their own noses anxious that the gale may not strike
the vessel unawares; that the Extreme Right may not, by a lazy policy of
inflexible rigidity, be responsible for the wholesale defection of the Extreme
Left. My difference then from both extremes is not one of degree; but of
kind. My position is not a half-way house. My aim or programme is,
whatever *unknown* issue may come forth from the working of the opposed

but complementary tendencies, Right and Left; and [sic] to prevent the catastrophe of the exclusive predominance of either which would result from a schism.[5]

Tyrrell may have been seen for a time as a liberal Catholic, but he could never find in himself the essential deference towards authority that was implied by the position. In the face of the coming storm, not even Newman, the classic 'mediating' liberal, could help. More and more Tyrrell wanted to transcend what he saw as a sterile debate between wooden conservatives and iconoclast liberals, sharing the same medieval presuppositions. To plead for the liberty of scholars was one thing. It was quite another to accept their conclusions, and make these the basis for a new understanding of the Church and the Catholic faith. Strength and imagination for this essential task could only come from the saints and the mystics, not the theologians. The crisis over 'A Perverted Devotion' did not change Tyrrell's fundamental views, but it destroyed the hope that his faltering attempts at mediation between the Church and the modern world would be understood or accepted. Like Nietzsche's madman, who lit a lantern in the morning and ran into the market-place looking for the God who was dead, he would be an outcast, but he would not be silent.

In committing himself to this thankless but essential task, Tyrrell was partly drawn by compassion for his 'London souls', for men of the Synthetic Society like Sidgwick, of the *fin de siècle* arts world like Raffalovich, or of the scientific establishment like Mivart. Partly, he was driven by a paradoxical urge towards self-destruction. Bringing these together, he told a friend:

I do not 'fight down' my doubts, as I should in some cases advise others to do. Rather I go deliberately in search of every difficulty in that line lest I be haunted by the thought that new revelations might rob me of my faith, or that those who deny have reasons for their denial that I have not *felt*. Hence I really do go through stages of spiritual depression and blankness to the extent of being pressed by the great fear; but not of admitting it.[6]

Unfortunately, we cannot *choose* in the end whether to admit 'the great fear' or not. The nearer Tyrrell came to the abyss of doubt, of absolute emptiness, the more he felt the weariness of his struggles with authority, and the inadequacy of traditional apologetic. He could not live with the Church, and he could not live without it:

What a relief if one could consciously wash one's hands of the whole concern and stand aside as a curious but unconcerned spectator; but then there is that strange man on his cross who drives one back again and again . . . My dominant conviction is that what Christ had to say to man is embedded in the Roman system as gold in the ore; and as I cannot sever them I take them in the lump.[7]

As yet Tyrrell was far from clear in what sense he could 'take them in the lump'. But his heart led him in that direction, and the next five years were spent in the seclusion of Richmond working out how his intellect could follow.

Soon after his arrival Tyrrell told Thurston: 'I am *tout à fait ravi* with Richmond and feel like Peter on Thabor.'[8] After the strain and the constant demands of London, here at last was utter and over-whelming peace. Here he could walk for hours on his own, fill his pipe and read undisturbed, listen to the wind in the tops of the trees, or gaze at the stars in the silence of the night, thankful to have escaped from the frenzy of the city,

> *Come quei che con lena affannata*
> *uscito fuor del pelago alla riva*
> *si volge all' acqua perigliosa e guata.*

(As he who with labouring breath has escaped from the deep to the shore turns to the perilous waters and gazes.)[9]

It may . . . be that the graveyard tranquillity of Richmond would drive you mad after a week,' he told Bremond. 'It has saved me from insanity.'[10]

Something of that 'graveyard tranquillity' still persists in the back streets of Richmond. The central square with the old parish church, the castle dominating the wooded slopes above the river, the dark inns, farriers, and ironmongers still retain their old charm. Newbiggin, the cobbled street on which stands the small Catholic church of St Joseph and St Francis Xavier, is practically unchanged in eighty years. 'My affections are twined round every cobble-stone',[11] wrote Tyrrell when he left. The dale, the woods, the open moor delighted him. 'I am on the tramp all day; and am spacing out my congested thoughts, sweet and bitter,' he told Raffalovich.[12] The easy going life of the house under the tolerant regime of Henry Farmer was just what he needed. 'This is the "Domus impossibilium nostrorum"' ('the house of our impossibles'), Tyrrell told Bremond. 'We are all mad, the Superior included. Come, and be happy. You and I will make a *petite église* of our own—very fallible and with no religious orders . . . I hope you will see everybody worth seeing in

London before the season ends; and then you will come and try our baths of quiet and fresh air.'[13]

By the time this letter was written, Tyrrell had in effect become a permanent resident, but initially he only went to Richmond for a short holiday. After an alarming episode of 'now bloody, now milky micturition' that probably represented the first indication of kidney disease, he stayed to wait for a medical opinion, but he then returned to London early in July. Here there was work to be done, including the retreat for the *Filles de Marie* that became *The Soul's Orbit*, but his soul longed for Richmond. When he suggested a longer stay there, Gerard, the Provincial, readily agreed, as he knew that Cardinal Vaughan wanted Tyrrell out of London so he could no longer act as a visible focus for liberal Catholics. It must have seemed an attractive solution to an awkward problem. Presumably Tyrrell could not cause much trouble at Richmond.

Quite apart from the row over 'A Perverted Devotion', Tyrrell had a great deal on his mind. He was beginning to see whole new tracts of intellectual terrain that had to be traversed. Von Hügel was calling him on to deeper and more demanding endeavour, urging him to learn German, to feed his mind on new writers and new ideas. 'What should I read of Loisy—short of everything?',[14] Tyrrell had asked. After Loisy it was Harnack, and then Blondel, whose *L'Action* he found 'a splendid but miserably obscure apologia for faith and mystical religion',[15] and then Bergson. Blondel took up a considerable amount of his time and energy, as, once he had penetrated the contorted and unfamiliar style, he realized that he was being provided with a philosophical grounding for many of his own most pressing thoughts. In October he wrote an anonymous letter to *The Pilot*,[16] defending Blondel against the charge of being a Kantian and an abstract thinker. Tyrrell stressed his originality and the concrete basis of his thought in action. Blondel stood in direct opposition to 'a religion that worships God indirectly through the mediation of abstract ideas', and for one that experiences him 'directly, with the true mystics, as a will, an action, a life, mingling with our own will, action and life'. Blondel, like Newman, was 'conscious of the infinite inability of our mental conceptions to cope with the inexhaustible reality of the concrete'. Tyrrell was struggling to sort out his ideas on mysticism, revelation, doctrine, and the Bible. He was involved in a lively correspondence with Ward on the meaning of doctrinal development and the 'deposit of faith'. He was working hard at the devotional material which was to become *Oil and Wine,* while all the time, in the background, the failing health of the Pope threw dark shadows. Leo, though no friend to liberals, was at least a man of intellect and culture who refrained from punitive measures. There were rumours that his successor might be far more of an obscurantist.

Aspects of Tyrrell's personal life also needed sorting out. For some time he had been working on a project particularly close to his heart—a commentary on the *Spiritual Exercises,* which was nearly complete by the early months of 1900. It fell victim to the crisis. If the Society no longer trusted him to give retreats, what chance was there that he would be allowed to publish the things he really wanted to say about the *Exercises?* The manuscript was burnt. Maude Petre probably knew this when she arranged for some of the *Filles de Marie* to take notes from the talks at their retreat in July, and then to use these notes to reconstruct what had been said. This labour of love, and the retreat itself, brought Tyrrell and Maude Petre much closer. It was followed by a letter, to which Tyrrell replied:

My dear Miss Petre,
   I was almost certain of what you told me; but not being quite certain I had to speak in general terms in my letter; and I do not therefore wish to unsay but simply to emphasise what I said there. We must simply help one another in this matter never to deviate from the highest standard of what such a relationship should be and may be.[17]

The relationship Maude Petre desired was one of spiritual commitment, and her declaration of affection came at just the right moment to unlock a heartfelt response in Tyrrell. He would never have denied the existence of love where it was truly present, but he feared deception on his own part because he believed himself to be essentially unlovable. This was at the root of many of the contradictions in his character. He also believed that the rejection and denial of human emotion was a fundamental cause of the dessication in many Jesuit lives. The proper course for celibates was a chastity that acknowledged human love and human frailty. As it happened, his feelings for Maude Petre oscillated between affection and gratitude based mainly on the sense of intellectual companionship, and irritation and boredom caused by her intensity and her at times pathetic devotion to him. His first instinct was to test, probably (as he thought) to destruction, a love based on a false picture of himself:

It would be a great happiness to me if when you get to know me better with all my fearful limitations and weaknesses you could still extend to me the regard you now entertain for me; but until I feel that you know me more intimately I could never rest in your affection as having a right to it. I feel that in the great interests of life we are in full intellectual sympathy; but I am also convinced that you mistake my clearness of moral perception for a strength and purity of character in which you are immeasurably beyond me, and which would make your intelligent regard so valuable a possession. I dare not let myself think that God is going to break down the cold walls of my isolation and to give me the solace and support I have never had yet, because I have never deserved it. Still I will hope and pray.[18]

This was more than enough encouragement to a woman who had fallen passionately in love. After a holiday alone at Engelberg working on the notes of the retreat and wrestling with her feelings, Maude Petre feared she was close to breakdown.[19] In Paris she opened her heart to Bremond, who looked 'ill and fearfully sad'. He was very close to breaking with the Jesuits. At a chapter meeting of the *Filles de Marie* the following month, Maude Petre asked leave to take a perpetual vow of chastity, wishing it could be taken with Father Tyrrell. Her diaries now speak of a 'contract' between them: she spoke to him of it being 'for better, for worse. Amen'. Awed by what she had done, tormented by letters from him of alternating tenderness and cruelty, she knew she had 'embarked on a stormy sea'. On 8 November she received a batch of retreat notes back from him: 'Poor notes. They took me time and trouble . . . but he has nothing but scathing contempt for them . . . This letter, as usual, a torture to me, and yet so much desired.' All the time there was the struggle with physical longing that had to be sublimated: 'I pray that God may give him those spiritual embraces, that spiritual closeness, which I desire, not perhaps carnally, but tangible and sensibly.' Pathetically, heroically, she struggled with herself, longing to love him unselfishly, to help him by her prayers in the difficulties he now poured out to her. His bitterness and self-laceration were an open wound in her heart.

Nevertheless, something deep within Tyrrell had been unlocked, and he responded. Just at the time when the Society, to whom he had given his first love, seemed to have rejected him, love had now been offered from another quarter. By the end of the year, having advised a fellow Jesuit to leave, he was turning to Maude Petre to help him sort out his own position:

I wonder Maude what you would think were I to take my own advice; for now it is really becoming what W. James calls a 'living hypothesis'. My position as an SJ is becoming such a *lie*; and, bound as I am, there is no way out, but by an act of schism . . . One would submit gladly to the occasional mistakes of a government one respected and felt to be in the main on God's side; but the Society everywhere puts itself before the Church and I have no belief in its corporate sincerity of purpose; in fact I regard it as the chief obstacle to the progress of the Church for whose sake I originally entered it . . . I tell you all this Maude because your heart is mine, and I want at least one confessor to whom [*sic*] I can trust. You just prevent me turning into stone, and then when I think how inaccessible you must always be, I feel harder than ever and put you out of my mind lest you should weaken my ruthlessness to no purpose.[20]

In this spirit, touched by love and yet hardly daring to respond, Tyrrell used the following winter to write his *Autobiography*— precisely to show Maude Petre that he was not worth loving. The circumstances in which it was written undoubtedly contributed to its unforgettable blend of nostalgia, self-mockery, and disillusion.

A major factor in Tyrrell's thought was always his enthusiasm for the saints. Shortly before he wrote 'A Perverted Devotion', he discovered the fourteenth-century mystic, Julian of Norwich. From then on she became a constant inspiration. Tyrrell delighted in Julian because of her luminous honesty and faith, as well as the intriguing psychological and theological problems set by her 'shewings'. He found in her an openness to difficulties that was stifled by the more complex and rationalistic church teaching of later ages. 'It cannot but startle us', he wrote, 'to find doubts that we hastily look upon as peculiarly "modern", set forth in their full strength and wrestled with and overthrown by an unlettered recluse of the fourteenth century.'[21] The particular problem she conspicuously faced was 'the apparent discord between the truths of faith and the facts of human life'—a problem he saw as epidemic in London at the end of the nineteenth century. Tyrrell intended to develop his commentary on Julian in a number of essays, but the trouble over 'A Perverted Devotion' forced him to abandon the series after only two, an introduction and a somewhat technical discussion of revelation. He accepted that the term 'revelation' could be used of Julian's 'shewings', but stressed that what was revealed was not violently imposed upon her, but was 'harmonious with the previous "content" of her mind, being, as it were, a congruous development of the same—not violently thrust into the soul, but set down softly in the appointed place already hollowed for it and, so to say, clamouring for it as for its natural fulfilment'. This point about the supernatural, that it is the fulfilment not the annihilation of the natural, was of central importance for Tyrrell. Practically, it made for an increased attention to nature, including science, as the arena of God's supernatural activity, to man as he is in the world, a creature of doubts, fears, and limitations, all of which hint at his transcendent capacities.

The thought of Julian had begun to make its impact when Tyrrell wrote 'The Relation of Theology to Devotion'. When he spoke of 'devotion' he had Julian very much in mind. Her vivid appreciation of God's 'thirst and longing', his 'moaning and mourning', is described as 'no mere concession to devout fancy, but a far nearer, though still defective, approach to the truth than the metaphysics of theology can pretend to arrive at'.[22] The whole point of 'A Perverted Devotion', too, was an honest facing of a difficulty—that of the existence of hell—in the spirit of Julian, knowing that 'God will save His word in all things; no particle of the Church's accredited teaching but shall be found true in some higher and grander sense than our poor muddled wits ever dreamt of; and yet all shall be well'.[23] Two years later Tyrrell wrote the introduction for a new edition of Julian's *Revelations*.[24] He found in her unforgettable words the key to the whole Christian revelation: 'Wit it well: Love was His meaning. Who shewed it thee? Love. Wherefore shewed He it thee? For Love.' Tyrrell commented:

It is precisely by love and its dependent affections that we are brought into conscious and active relation with the whole world of personalities outside our own, so as to make therewith in some sort one many-membered spiritual organism. It is love which at once saves and yet overcomes that separateness and individual distinction which is of the very essence of personality, and thereby welds the several grains of corn into one living bread. Loveless, self-centred, torn altogether from its connection with the whole, the soul may still live the surface-life of sense or thought or reason, but its grasp on reality is relaxed, as it were, in spiritual death.

Characteristically, he then quotes a favourite saying from Augustine, *Nihil aliud sumus quam voluntates* ('We are nothing else but wills'). Here, in the unity of wills held together by love, we have the heart of the philosophy he developed at Richmond. Christianity, at root, is a life of love, and those who have entered most fully into this mystery are not the theologians but the saints. They are the real teachers of the Church. Doctrinal systems are essential, but it must never be forgotten that their real purpose is to move the will rather than to inform the intellect. Christianity

identifies itself with a certain body of statements—philosophical, ethical, historical—not directly in the interests of the mind, but in those of the heart; not because they are coherent with current conceptions of the order of phenomena, but because they are practically true to the facts of the real order, and guide us into closer will-union with God and man.[25]

This line of thought was helped forward by Julian, who encouraged Tyrrell to pursue his thoughts in a dangerous direction. He seemed to be replacing the rationalism he attacked with an equally flawed pragmatism. Julian's thought was undeveloped. Tyrrell fell on her emphasis on *love* as the meaning of all things, and developed this so powerfully in an anti-rationalist direction that he seemed at times to have no place at all for the intellect in the human approach to God.

Another major influence at this time, of whom Tyrrell made even greater tactical use, was Ignatius Loyola. Late in 1899 he was hard at work on the preface, notes, and epilogue to *The Testament of Ignatius Loyola*,[26] a brief autobiography dictated shortly before Ignatius's death. Tyrrell's first concern was to present Ignatius as a real man rather than as an emasculated saint. He warmed to this early and unadorned account, because he wanted to get as close as he could to the historical truth, because 'in theology, in scriptural criticism, in asceticism, in hagiology, in every department of the study of the Christian religion, history must and will have its say, and those who resist its legitimate authority will deservedly be crushed by it'. Tyrrell believed that the true saintliness of Ignatius (a character whose 'elastic' and adaptable spirit he consistently idealized) would prove all the more compelling if he were depicted as a real human being, learning by his mistakes in the spiritual life. He also believed that close attention to the life and spirit of Ignatius would enable the Society he had founded to bring its life more into line with his imaginative and flexible intentions. The preface to *The Testament* compares Ignatius with Bunyan, and presents him as belonging to a human type that only develops towards sainthood with the illumination of full Catholic faith. The epilogue identifies Ignatius's sovereign genius as an ability to concentrate on 'one end', that is to say 'the greater glory of God in the salvation and perfection of the human soul'. Hence the Jesuit motto, *Ad Maiorem Dei Gloriam*. Ignatius had to contend with a Church that had exalted the means above the end. His life provided the perfect medium for Tyrrell's attack on the Church and the Jesuits of his own day:

Standing on the threshold of the modern world, at one of those crises when the Christian idea seemed to have outgrown its earlier clothing beyond all hope of patching or piecing; when a narrow adherence to non-essentials of form and fashion was equivalently an attempt to pour new wine into already over-stretched skins, Ignatius instinctively divined the source of the Church's danger to lie in the neglect of his favourite maxim; in the tyranny of habit over reason; in the exaltation of what had originally been means, into ends, to the detriment of the very ends to which they had been directed. Rule, precedent, tradition, privilege, immemorial custom, had everywhere clogged the wheels of ecclesiastical machinery; and the inexorable law of old age, with its ossified cartilages and consolidated joints, had deprived the institutions of former centuries of that flexible elasticity needed to meet the sudden change of environment. Hardly shall a man when he is old enter into his mother's womb and be born again; the reform of antiquated methods if not impossible was too difficult and too slow a remedy for the instant danger; and therefore Ignatius could only hope in a new institution which should be free from all the aforesaid trammels and obstructions; which should sit light in regard to all non-essentials; whose governing principle should be his own, namely unqualified adaptability, the sovereignty of the end over the means, the single rule of God's greater glory in the greater help of souls.[27]

Tyrrell edited *The Testament* as a kind of apologia for his continued life in the Society founded by Ignatius. The book was delated to Rome by a fellow Jesuit, R. F. Clarke of Oxford, who could 'scarcely believe it [had] been written by a member of the Society'.[28] Clarke spoke on behalf of precisely that 'Jesuitism' that Tyrrell abhorred.

However much he affected not to care, the delations and recriminations hurt Tyrrell deeply. It was not enough to comfort himself with the thought of the delation, recrimination, and imprisonment that Ignatius had experienced. He did not have the heart to finish his commentary on the *Exercises*, and burnt it. When Maude Petre brought the collated script of his retreat to the *Filles de Marie*, he was at first dismissive, but gradually he warmed to the task of revision, and *The Soul's Orbit*,[29] as the book eventually became, contains, particularly in the early chapters, some of Tyrrell's finest comments on Ignatian themes. There is an urgency about what he has to say, a blend of realism and compassion, a profound humanity in the way he preaches single-minded devotion to God, which is the heart of the Jesuit vocation. The journey to God is one of 'action, experiment, life

and movement'. He speaks with a shining, Julian-like confidence of
the love of God which sustains us every minute, and without which 'I
should be as a dream when one wakens'. The key that unlocks the
mystery of this love is Christ, 'for He Himself is the central and
concrete object of the Christian Revelation; in Him, in His life, the
Father is shown and declared'. Once more the life comes before the
doctrine, for 'His words were but an explanation of Himself, of what
He was and what He did; an explanation which, couched in human
forms of thought and speech, could never equal nor exhaust the
reality'. These addresses breathe a confident trust, but they also
presage the 'great fear', for Tyrrell knew well how dark the night
would be if ever the light of Christ were lost. He knew how much he
needed the 'kindly light' of Christ:

As at Tenebrae one after another the lights are extinguished, till one
alone—and that the highest of all—is left, so it is often with the soul and her
guiding stars. In our early days there are many—parents, teachers, friends,
books, authorities—but, as life goes on, one by one they fail and leave us in
deepening darkness, with an increasing sense of the mystery and inexplic-
ability of all things, till at last none but the figure of Christ stands out
luminous against the prevailing night.

When one reads that, one sees immediately why the beauty of
Tyrrell's language was compared with that of Newman.

During this period Tyrrell was profoundly engaged with one of
Newman's most important themes: the development of doctrine.
Newman wrote his famous *Essay on the Development of Christian
Doctrine* as 'an hypothesis to account for a difficulty', the difficulty
being the manifest changes in the doctrine and worship of the Roman
Catholic Church over the centuries, when it claimed to be *semper
eadem*, always the same. The focus of Newman's interest was the
continuity between the primitive Church and the Roman Catholic
Church of today. In his hypothesis, which he called 'the theory of
development', he suggested: 'In a higher world it is otherwise; but
here below to live is to change, and to be perfect is to have changed
often.'[30] Tyrrell readily accepted this, but he now came to Newman
with new questions. For him, the term 'development of doctrine'
begged the question of the *depositum fidei*, 'the deposit of faith', that
which has been revealed to man. What exactly is it? Should we think
of it as the Scriptures, or the doctrine of the early Church, or the
developed doctrine of the contemporary Church, or some reality

behind all these? Newman's desire to prove that the *doctrine* of the
Church had developed and yet remained the same concealed an
important, unexplained area. Tyrrell, convinced that the words in
which mysteries are expressed are always inadequate to the truths
they express, was concerned to examine the relation between
changing words and unchanging truth.

Tyrrell's own ideas were sketched out for Ward in a letter of
March 1900. First he outlined the theory of the Roman theologians,
men like Moyes and Richard Clarke. They held that the body of
teaching left by the early Church, 'the deposit', had not really
developed, but had unfolded in the way that a folded cloak is
unfolded. Strictly speaking, this is a process of 'elucidation' rather
than 'development'. 'The only advance is from implicit to explicit;
from confusion to distinction.' On this view, put crudely, 'Father
Clarke asserts the Immaculate Conception (e.g.) to have been known
to every pope since Saint Peter; at least *in confuso* or, as it were, in
small type needing only a closer glance.' Newman argued for something quite different: an organic growth of doctrine whereby our
understanding of revealed truth really does increase. This is what
interested Tyrrell, and he illustrated it by the following parable:

A philanthropist desirous to bring the blessings of British civilisation to a
stone-age tribe in the heart of Africa, betakes himself into their midst and
learns their language . . . With great difficulty and using illustrations from
their own social and material conditions he contrives to convey to a few of
the more intelligent or less brutal some faint and grotesque notion of the
material, social, political and religious conditions of great Britain; he teaches
them to put into practice such civility and morality as is within their present
compass; and finally leaves them a record, in their own language, of all he
has told them. After he has been killed and eaten, his few faithful disciples
begin quietly working on his lines, and the practical benefits are such that
opposition is conquered and the record becomes an oracle, to all future
generations. Plainly, here, as soon as the immediate disciples die off, the
earliest interpreters will be most hopelessly at sea; much of the record will
seem sheer nonsense to them, yet because some is so valuable they will force
interpretations of the rest. As their civilisation grows they will come to
understand many things at first inexplicable; and thus be, in some way, in a
better position than the first disciples to interpret and realise their benefac-
tor's mind. But as living languages change rapidly it will be a great point to
preserve the original meaning of the record—the sense it conveyed to the
first hearers, for that is their *depositum fidei*, the third-hand presentment of
the Reality sc. British Civilisation.[31]

Tyrrell was concerned to put the most positive construction on the process of growth, because he saw it as inevitable that the Church should come to terms with the contemporary way of looking at the world. Only in this way can the meaning of 'the deposit' be preserved. The real guide in this process is the Holy Spirit: *Ille vos docebit omnia, suggeret vobis omnia quaecumque dixero vobis* ('He will teach you all things, and bring to your remembrance all that I have said to you'). He was also concerned to show that, though the Pope may be the arbiter of new understanding, the understanding itself grows not in the individual mind of the Pope, nor in the minds of the hierarchy, but in 'the mind of the Church' as a whole.

Tyrrell wrote two articles on this theme at about the time he moved to Richmond.[32] In the first he examines the transition from the Spirit-inspired teaching of the Apostles to the Spirit-assisted decisions of the Church, deciding what conformed to the apostolic witness. Without defining 'the deposit of faith', Tyrrell insists that it was communicated to the 'mind of the Universal Church, which was discerned, formulated, and declared in ecumenical council'. This 'mind' grows by contemplation of the truth received, by harmonizing it with other growing branches of human knowledge, and by understanding it more deeply as its experience, and so its capacity for understanding, grows in other areas. In all this, Tyrrell retains his emphasis on the unchanging priority of the revelation to the Apostles: 'No new expression of the Christian idea can reveal more truth and fact than Christ intended to reveal to the Apostles, but it may give far clearer expression and illustration to the same facts and truths. What grows and develops and yet retains its identity is the expression of the Christian idea.' This was where he now located 'the deposit of faith', by which 'we do not mean any primitive document, nor yet that expression which the faith received in the mind of its first hearers; but the present-day expression of the faith, in which that former expression is at once lost and preserved as the child is in the man'.[33]

He was only satisfied with this formulation for a short time, and he soon shifted his idea of 'the deposit' away from *expression* of the faith in any form. Ward spotted the fact that his mind was on the move, and when he asked about this, Tyrrell told him that in writing about 'the deposit' he should have said:

nor yet that expression which the faith received in the mind of its first hearers, *nor yet* the present day expression of the faith in which that former expression is at once lost and preserved as the child is in the man, *but rather those identical truths and realities which were expressed and seen less perfectly* (relatively to us) *through the earlier forms, more perfectly through the later and more transparent forms.*[34]

This is a radical and important move. In the same letter Tyrrell pointed out to Ward the advantages of his new position. 'This view relieves us of the miracle of a *direct* reading of the mind of the sub-apostolic Church.' That is to say, when the Pope pronounces on a doctrinal matter he does it not by miraculous recall of apostolic truth, but, as Tyrrell would want to argue strongly, by enunciating 'the mind of the Church'. The new view of 'the deposit' also 'shakes us more free of the criterion of primitiveness'. This means that for its claim to authoritative teaching the Church no longer depends upon biblical and historical evidence which hangs upon the increasingly threatening conclusions of the critics. Lastly, 'it excludes "finalism" of dogmatic expression as effectively as the other view, and involves less of a separation from the natural laws of mental progress'. Tyrrell respected these 'laws' as that through which, not in despite of which, God spoke. He wanted to link this conviction with that of a living Church, growing in understanding of the truth, able to speak articulately through the voice of the Pope.

Tyrrell's articles were actually a veiled attack on the definition of papal infallibility. In June of that year he had worked through all the documents he could lay his hands on about the Vatican Council, looking for a way out of the difficulties created by the 1870 definition of papal infallibility. By September he told Ward that 'the articles were but part of a train of thought whose fuller development should lead to a clear sundering of two absolutely incompatible understandings of the Papal infallibility'. He went on:

The test question is: If the Scriptures and the Fathers and all written documents were destroyed (all allow that these are contingent), where lies the *depositum fidei*? In the pope's single brain, or in the collective brain of Christendom? If in the former, then the pope may say *L'Église c'est moi*; the spirit works directly on his mind; and only through it on the Church. If in the latter then the Pope is infallible in declaring the general mind in cases of sufficient magnitude to threaten unity; in such matters as formerly justified an ecumenical council; when he publicly and notoriously does investigate the *depositum fidei* contained in the general mind; when, as the Catechism says, he speaks as Head and Teacher of the Universal Church, in functional union with it; and not severed from it, as a local bishop.[35]

Tyrrell had clarified his position just in time, as it happened, to turn his fury on an official ecclesiastical document that depended on a very different, and dangerous, ecclesiology: the joint pastoral letter of the Bishops of England and Wales, published on 31 December 1900. We shall return to this in the next chapter.

Tyrrell continued to work at his parable of 'the philanthropist'. In August von Hügel read and returned a manuscript about the 'Walla-Washee tribe', which Tyrrell then sent to Alfred Waller, editor of the Duckworth '*Saints*' series for which he had written nine of the prefaces. He explained that he could not get the manuscript past the censors, but very much wanted it published. He was not allowed to publish anonymously, so as to receive profit, but he could give the manuscript away unconditionally! He was now offering it to Waller in the hope that 'some one could take the ideas and reproduce them in his own way, not scrupling to take whole chunks of my text when desirable; or otherwise so modify the M.S. as to be able to claim authorship, or at least enable me to repudiate authorship'. Tyrrell further offered 'to look over the *conflatus* and tinker it up'.[36] Waller accepted the idea, and so, in effect, enabled Tyrrell to publish pseudonymously. The Walla-Washees became first the Cimmerians and then the Matafanus. *The Civilizing of the Matafanus* appeared under Waller's name in 1902.[37]

It was quite likely that Tyrrell would be caught: von Hügel had read Tyrrell's manuscript; Ward had read the outline of the story, and so, presumably, had other friends. But Tyrrell was in a reckless frame of mind. He merely held to the letter of his vow of obedience, feeling that the misbehaviour of the religious authorities robbed it of any meaning. More important than the minute keeping of vows was obedience to the truth. His fable was intended to help those, like Waller himself, who found Catholicism attractive but intellectually impossible. Just as with 'The Mind of the Church', the essay aims to show that, given an original revelation of the type claimed by Christianity, it is reasonable to suppose that the Church's understanding of the truth has grown in the way that the story shows. In *The Civilizing of the Matafanus* Tyrrell's original sketch is improved by the introduction of Alpuca, one of the Matafanus, who is taught the meaning of 'civilization' under hypnosis. He thus shares the experience of two worlds: that of the philanthropical society, as 'the philanthropist' had now become, and that of his own people. Tyrrell works out the christological allegory in terms of Alpuca's painful struggle to communicate ideas quite beyond the capacity of the language of the Matafanus before, inevitably, he is murdered. There can be none but the most inadequate and misleading way of doing this. The hope is that as the tribe grows in 'civilization', so they will understand more of what Alpuca, lovingly remembered through a carefully preserved written record, tried to communicate to them.

As the story unfolds, Tyrrell introduces a whole range of import-ant points: the inability of Alpuca to communicate except by metaphor and analogy; the importance of understanding 'civiliz-ation' as a living whole; the apparent miracles performed by Alpuca through his knowledge of a more advanced society; the triviality of this demonstration of his good faith compared with that afforded by his moral integrity; the importance of maintaining the written record he left behind; the slow growth in understanding the meaning of what he had to say; the temptation to take it too literally; and the need to understand 'the spirit' of his faltering utterance. Tyrrell told Waller he wanted to give 'a wipe' to the 'theo-logicians', who misunderstood the whole nature of Christian doctrine.[38] In delivering his record of 'civilization', Alpuca stressed that it was

not merely an idea or notion to be developed and defined, but a life to be lived; that life was the criterion by which the true development of the notion was to be criticised; that those who strove most to live the life, would be the most apt to apprehend the notion; and that, in so far as they in their corporate capacity would endeavour to lead the way into practical culture, they would in the same capacity be qualified to act as guides and leaders to others; their 'collective' experience would represent the highest rule for the general mind—a rule which would infallibly lead those, who should submit to it, in the right direction from darkness to light.[39]

As far as Tyrrell was concerned, the real darkness was not in the land of the Matafanus, but in the minds of the 'theo-logicians' of Rome.

NOTES

1. Tyrrell to Ward, 'Tuesday' (SAUL, VII 294a (19)).
2. Tyrrell to von Hügel, 6 June 1900 (BL, Petre Papers).
3. Ward to von Hügel, 27 Feb. 1900 (SAUL, MS 3146).
4. Tyrrell to Ward, 18 June 1900.
5. Ibid.
6. Tyrrell to 'Laurence' Housman, 30 June 1900 (AL2, pp. 26–7).

7. Tyrrell to von Hügel, 14 Feb. 1900.
8. Tyrrell to Thurston, 'Saturday' (AEPSJ, 0025).
9. Dante, *Inferno*, I. 22–5 (trans. J. D. Sinclair).
10. Tyrrell to Bremond, 23 June 1901 (BN, Fonds Bremond).
11. Tyrrell to Maude Petre, 30 Dec. 1905 (BL, Petre Papers).
12. Tyrrell to Raffalovich, 3 July 1900 (Blackfriars Collection).
13. Tyrrell to Bremond, 23 June 1901.
14. Tyrrell to von Hügel, 2 Apr. 1900.
15. Tyrrell to Raffalovich, 18 Aug. 1900.
16. *The Pilot*, 27 Oct. 1900, p. 534. The letter is signed 'E. F. G'.
17. Tyrrell to Maude Petre, 3 Sept. 1900.
18. Ibid.
19. The account that follows is based on Maude Petre's diaries for 1900 (BL, Add. MS 52372).
20. Tyrrell to Maude Petre, 18 Dec. 1900.
21. 'A Light from the Past', *The Month*, 95 (1900), pp. 12–23, 250–8; repr. *FM2*, pp. 1–39.
22. 'The Relation of Theology to Devotion', *The Month*, 94 (1899), p. 472.
23. 'A Perverted Devotion', *Weekly Register*, 100 (16 Dec. 1899); repr. *EFI*, p. 170.
24. *XVI Revelations of Divine Love Shewed to Mother Juliana of Norwich 1373* (London, 1902).
25. Ibid., p. xi.
26. *The Testament of Ignatius Loyola*, trans. E. M. Rix (London, 1900).
27. Ibid., pp. 201–2.
28. Clarke to Meyer, 3 May 1900 (ARSJ, ANGL. 1021, IB.21).
29. M. D. Petre, *The Soul's Orbit* (London, 1904). Quotations are from pp. 9 ('action, experiment . . .'); 27 ('I should be . . .'); 54 ('for He Himself . . .'); ibid. ('His words . . .'); 23 ('As at Tenebrae . . .').
30. J. H. Newman, *An Essay on the Development of Christian Doctrine*, ed. J. M. Cameron (Harmondsworth, 1973), p. 100.
31. Tyrrell to Ward, 13 Mar. 1900.
32. 'The Mind of the Church', *The Month*, 96 (1900), pp. 125–42, 233–40.
33. Ibid., p. 237.
34. Tyrrell to Ward, 2 Oct. 1900 (Tyrrell's underlining).
35. Tyrrell to Ward, 10 Sept. 1900.
36. Tyrrell to Waller, 5 Oct. 1900 (BL, Waller Papers).
37. A. R. Waller, *The Civilizing of the Matafanus* (London, 1902).
38. Tyrrell to Waller, 22 Oct. 1900.
39. *CM*, p. 58.

10

'A l'école de Jack'

In Richmond Tyrrell was free from London's 'bondage of the parlour'. He had time to read, to reflect, and to write, at times writing under his own name, but turning increasingly to clandestine authorship. Most of the time he felt that his continued membership of the Society of Jesus was little more than an acted lie, but he was no longer called upon to parade that lie in sermons, conferences, retreats, and articles, intended as much to conceal as to proclaim what he really believed about the Society and the Church. In a more important sense he felt that the Jesuits, dishing out pre-packaged spiritual advice amongst the teacups and the hansom cabs, ministering security to the pampered souls of Mayfair, were living a lie. When anyone really cultured, intelligent, or questioning came into their orbit, they had nothing to say. All around, the crisis of modernity was whipping up an intellectual ferment that only the dead or the wilfully blind could ignore. However much Father Bernard Vaughan, SJ might preach eloquent sermons against 'the sins of society', however much the prosperous and successful citizens of London listened and admired, echoing condemnations of avarice and pride would never roll back the intellectual tide. As the old certainties were pounded to bits, where were the followers of Ignatius who could do something for the human flotsam drifting in the storm? These London priests were as much at sea as anyone else.

In every generation there are a few sensitive individuals who respond instinctively to atmospheric hints and suggestions which others find nonsensical or insignificant. For this tiny minority the new pattern presents itself with irresistible clarity. That is how Tyrrell felt: driven to distraction by needs and dangers that those about him swore did not exist. Troubled souls were drawn to him, sharing questions and difficulties that could not be expressed to priests who were neither questioning nor in difficulties themselves. Some of the most needy cases were priests themselves.

Obviously, much of what was said to Tyrrell has been lost, but occasional fragments have been preserved. In November 1900 he wrote a long letter to the Provincial, John Gerard, explaining why he would not engage in popular controversial writing. In a passion, he pointed to the need for adventurous intellectual work of the highest order, not point-scoring braggadocio. He quoted to Gerard a letter he had recently received from a priest in difficulties:

May I speak quite openly to you. I was born a Catholic, and hope to die one. But I stagger like a drunkard under the theological difficulties that weigh upon my mind. It has been my lot to be thrown among intellectual men for many years now, and I need not conceal from you—I cannot conceal from myself—that to their clear-stated objections my replies have been taken as 'Chinese'. Why? . . . It seems to me the Church is in an evil case. She has lost the intellect of Europe; she is fast losing the intelligence. She may, like a pool, continue to hold water. But it will become stagnant water, of which men will decline to drink . . . I have grown afraid even to undertake a defence of her. I enter a labyrinth with no clue in my fingers. I cannot find my way even among her own teachers. They are hopelessly entangled, ravelled like a wind-tossed skein of silk. What is wrong? If we have a deposit of revealed truth 'once communicated to the saints', in God's name, what is it & where is it?[1]

These were precisely the questions that Tyrrell was trying to answer from his room on the top floor of the clergy-house at Richmond. To the others there—usually about six priests who were convalescent, or semi-retired, or in need of a rest—his presence was an enigma. He did not share with them the strains or the inner details of the controversy that had brought him to live in semi-retirement amongst them. They did not know what he did in the long hours he spent in his room—beyond the fact that he read and wrote endlessly—or precisely what it was about him that involved him in such a herculean correspondence, and began to bring a steady stream of well-to-do guests and friends to Richmond. Each day, except when headaches kept him confined to a darkened room, he walked for several hours with his dog, first 'Spy', then 'Jack'. He was usually affable, often witty, but at any moment he might burst into a lightning rage. He was not conventionally devout, carefully distancing himself from much of the devotional life of the place. He was quick to see a joke, but equally given to remarks of scything cynicism. Those who got on with him best, like Father Farmer, the Superior, were those who did not pry into his private concerns, and knew how to leave well alone.

Tyrrell's superiors clearly did not know what to do with him. More than anything, they wanted him out of the way. John Gerard, who sympathized with Tyrrell in his clash with the Roman censors, ineptly proposed that he should write some popular, controversial 'Tracts for the Million'. Tyrrell's response was an article in *The Month* that was heavy with irony.[2] Only after a full discussion of the 'tidal wave of unbelief' that was engulfing all classes in society, a frank admission that 'the public opinion of the modern world has ceased to be Christian', and an urgent call to work at influencing the opinion-formers, did he reluctantly concede that there might be a place for the proposed popular tracts. They might, he allowed, be a necessity, but they were also an impossibility, 'for what self-respecting man will sit down to weave that tissue of sophistry, special-pleading, violence and vulgarity, which alone will serve the practical purpose with those to whom trenchancy is everything and subtlety nothing?' Archly concluding that there may be *others* who have the gifts of the half-educated that would be needed for this unenviable task, he himself begged to be excused. To Tyrrell's amazement, the article misfired, and people began to ask when he planned to begin work on the new tracts. Very few, it seemed, had a sense, or at least Tyrrell's sense, of irony. Speaking plainly to Maude Petre, he told her: 'The way to "convert" England is to educate our priests and make them sober and pure, and to look after the spiritual wants of our perishing millions; and to leave Protestants alone until we are in a position to set them an example.'[3] He learnt his lesson. When he wrote a preface to *The Faith of the Millions* the following year, he spoke out on the same theme as directly as he could.

So Gerard had his answer. Privately, Tyrrell was even more outspoken. He wrote him a long letter of extraordinary ferocity, after which there could be no shadow of a doubt about his views on apologetics, theology, 'Jesuitism', and the rising tide of unbelief. He would not write cheap tracts, because

the great *scandalum pusillorum* here, today, is the unbelief not of the irreligious but of the religious, the sincere; and those who disbelieve, as every modern seminarian does, in the possibility of honest doubt, are incompetent to go to the root of the evil. We need never hope to win the irreligious intelligence of the country; but if we fail to get hold of the intelligently religious minds the rest of our success is but forking out the waves. But to deal with these best minds, needs a sympathy, a breadth, a subtlety, which the coarse-minded dogmatism of foreign theologians would not tolerate for a moment, and it is they eventually who rule us and prescribe for countries of whose condition they are as ignorant as they are of Christian charity and truthfulness; they are the veritable descendents of those who kept the key of knowledge and would neither enter themselves, nor suffer others to enter.

The hopelessness of his own situation boiled over in bitter recrimination:

Even if I had the fullest liberty I am not at all sure that I should know what to do with it; I should know the right direction but not much more. Therefore I don't want any of my liberties back again. I will write for the Month till the next delation; and then I will throw down the cards, and turn to some other game. But what other? Even preaching, retreat-giving and such publicly exposed work, unless it is to be a mere useless reverberation of 'that which was from the beginning', is rendered impossible where the supreme government is controlled by the secret delations of the stupid, the envious, and the place-hunters, with the old and inevitable result of 'art made tongue-tied by authority; and Folly, doctor-like, controlling skill'.

He quoted from priests in intellectual difficulties, and sharply criticized the inability of the Church to help them:

There is not a single priest at Farm Street or, I fancy, in all London to whom I could recommend an *educated* agnostic to go with any hope, I do not say of being satisfied but even, of being understood. I should without hesitation send such a one to Gore, or to Scott-Holland, or to James Ward; or to Baron von Hügel; or I myself in difficulties would go to them; but if I turn to the Church, who ought to be my first support, 'I ask for bread and she gives me a stone'—a farrago of medievalism warmed up.[4]

These are only brief extracts from a letter of extraordinary, aggressive eloquence. It says a great deal for Gerard's Christian forbearance that he could receive such a blast and still obviously care for Tyrrell. He recognized that much of what was being said—intemperately, exaggeratedly, angrily—was, at least partially, true.

Soon after Tyrrell had written this letter, Gerard, patient, embarrassed, and playing for time, was replaced as Provincial after only one three-year term rather than the usual two, by the 'safer' Reginald Colley, who had been ordered by the General to clamp down on liberalism from the start of his term of office.[5] Tyrrell guessed as much: 'Things might have dragged on under Fr. Gerard but now I must look out for squalls,'[6] he told Maude Petre. His future with the Jesuits hung in the balance as the new Provincial tried, naïvely, to resolve the stalemate.

Colley suggested, as Cardinal Vaughan had done, that Tyrrell return to the sort of mission work he had done in St Helens, that he bury himself in a parish. Tyrrell retorted that if he was not fit to give retreats, he was not fit to preach or to direct souls in the confessional. His hurt and fury at the way he had been treated had not diminished one whit: unless the General fully and publicly exonerated him, there could be no *rapprochement*, however Colley coaxed and persuaded. Things were made worse when Colley's assistant, who had read the correspondence, sent Tyrrell a letter of meddlesome exhortation: 'Is your vocation in danger? Make our Blessed Lady keep you from running away from her, for it could mean that if you take that false step you will immediately be glorified by men whom in your heart you despise. *Pray* hard.'[7] To Tyrrell the only 'false step' conceivable would be submission. He dispatched the note to Colley by return, with a few choice comments about Knight's interference. Colley tried as hard as he could, with his hands tied behind his back, to reach out. Tyrrell called him a 'simple-hearted, pious, schoolboy with [a] naïve faith in the Society as God's chosen paradise in the desert of the Catholic Church'.[8] He thought Tyrrell's problem was wounded pride. It was not, Tyrrell told him, a question of a wound that time would heal, but of *facts* that time cannot alter.

There were further complications. On 16 January 1901 *La Rassegna Nationale*, a 'liberal' Catholic paper, carried a translated extract from *External Religion*. The General was under the impression that the Pope himself had forbidden priests to write for the paper, and so Meyer, his assistant, promptly wrote to Colley insisting that something be done. Colley had already asked whether Tyrrell's works could now be censored in England. 'My only hope', he told Meyer, 'is that an apparent concession may cheer him up, and that I may be able to get him to work in some busy mission, where he will forget other things in hard work for souls.' On the whole he was pessimistic, writing that Tyrrell was 'morbidly sensitive and self-willed', and suggesting that there might even be 'a touch of insanity in his great talent'.[9] When Tyrrell immediately wrote to say that the offending article had been printed without his consent, Colley tried yet again for permission to censor his works in England. Above all, he wanted peace.

Tyrrell, however, wanted justice. He noticed a report in the *Weekly Register* that the Archbishop of Genoa had contributed to *La Rassegna*, and wrote to the editor of *La Rassegna* to enquire about the ban on priests' contributions. When the editor wrote back saying he knew nothing of such an edict, Tyrrell sent his letter on to Colley.

He also wrote to Rome suggesting that the General was misinformed about the papal prohibition. This was not well received. Martin wrote an extremely firm letter to Colley: never mind which bishop had or had not contributed to that periodical, the express will of the Supreme Pontiff, communicated to a Father of the Society by his superiors, should be enough. And if they are wrong about the prohibition, no matter. Superiors do not have to give reasons. Tyrrell should write his disclaimer at once.[10] Tyrrell had already asked the editor to explain that the piece had been included without the author's permission. The storm died away, amid the General's many complaints about the inadequacies of The Month and fears of 'something like a liberal clique in the house of writers at Farm Street'.[11] The strain was telling on Colley, and the General warned him to take care. A good man, out of his depth and in failing health, he had just over three years to live.

To Tyrrell these arguments were an irritating side-show. For the first six months of 1901 the aggravating joint pastoral letter of the English and Welsh Bishops was his main concern. Essentially, the letter was Cardinal Vaughan's response to the storms over Mivart, Dell, and other outspoken 'liberal' Catholics. Vaughan had consulted Monsignor Merry del Val in Rome, who took the matter to the Pope. Leo agreed that there should be a full doctrinal pronouncement, one to which he could give his personal backing. To ensure that the statement was 'unassailable in its force' and that Vaughan could publish it 'with the certainty that every word of it will be supported here as expressing the teaching and mind of the Church', Merry del Val offered to co-operate in the drafting of the document. 'Of course it would be your declaration and none of the cooperators would appear at all. Your task would thus be facilitated and you would speak with the assurance that the Holy See was entirely with you.'[12] This authoritative pronouncement from the Bishops of England and Wales, 'A Joint Pastoral Letter on the Church and Liberal Catholicism', appeared on 29 December 1900.[13]

From Tyrrell's point of view it could not have been worse. The 'liberal' Catholic is mercilessly pilloried for ignorance of the true character of the Church of Christ, because he pits himself against the authorized teachers who stand in the place of the Apostles. He doubts the wisdom, patience, and ability of the Church in dealing with mankind, 'and he flatters himself that his own opinions are the outcome of a strong-minded, impartial and philosophical spirit'.

The Bishops' clarion call to obedience was based upon a two-tier ecclesiology that Tyrrell cordially loathed:

Two orders of persons, therefore, constitute, by the design of Christ, the visible Church. The small body of chosen men, assisted by the Holy Ghost, who represent the authority of Jesus Christ; and the large body of the faithful taught, guided and guarded by the Divine Teacher, speaking through the audible voice of the smaller body. Theologians call the one the *Ecclesia docens*, the other the *Ecclesia discens*.

The *Ecclesia docens* originally consisted of Peter and the Apostles, succeeded by the Pope and the bishops in communion with him. They are 'in supreme command of the flock'. The *Ecclesia discens* consists not only of the laity, but also of the ecclesiastics, and even the bishops, in their private capacity. The Church as a divine teacher speaks through the Pope and the bishops. What is not clear is how the Pope and the bishops arrive at their authoritative teaching—but the faithful are not encouraged to ask.

Tyrrell believed that infallibility, or indefectibility, was a property of the whole Church, not of the Pope or the Pope and bishops. In the summer of 1900 he had 'saddened himself' by going over the story of the Vatican Council of 1870, looking for a way of taking the definition of papal infallibility in this broader sense. If that was hard, it was impossible to see anything but a 'two-tier ecclesiology' in the joint pastoral letter. As he told von Hügel:

The bishops have mounted on metaphors, as witches on broomsticks, and have ridden to the Devil. It is the 'sheep and shepherd' metaphor that does the trick. The sheep are brainless, passive; their part is to be led, fed, fleeced and slain for the profit of the shepherd for whose benefit solely they exist. Apply this to the constitution of the Church and where are you to stop.[14]

To Tyrrell's disgust, Leo XIII specifically congratulated Cardinal Vaughan and the Bishops on the letter.

He was well placed for resistance. When he wrote 'The Mind of the Church' he thought the issue through minutely. As soon as he could spare the time from fencing with his superiors, he mounted an offensive. His general sense of outrage and preoccupation with covert resistance made him even more intransigent and harder to handle than ever. He told Frank Rooke Ley, editor of the *Weekly Register*, that he had been making himself ill over the joint pastoral: '"Authority" is their one note—their whole tune.'[15] He was infuriated by the total lack of understanding for everything liberal

Catholics were trying to do. If he protested publicly, he would of course be finished. Anything he wrote anonymously would immediately be recognized. The expedient with Waller and his 'Walla-Washee' manuscript looked hopeful, so he turned to it again.

This time Tyrrell approached a man of outstanding prominence in ecumenical circles, Viscount Halifax, President of the English Church Union, with whom he had corresponded at the time of the condemnation of Anglican orders, and who had expressed his sympathy over the condemnation of 'A Perverted Devotion'. Tyrrell put to him a number of questions about the limits of papal infallibility that he thought an Anglican like himself ought to be asking after the publication of such a letter. Ten days later, without waiting for a reply, he sent the draft of an article that Halifax might like to use in posing these questions. He suggested, somewhat archly, that the Roman authorities, thinking that Halifax spoke for the whole Church of England—indeed, for England—would listen to his questions far more readily than to the 'smothered protests' of men like Tyrrell or Ward.[16] Halifax took the bait, but he was slow to act because of illness. Tyrrell pressed the importance of the issue. It was a question of 'the very constitution of the Church—of the very nature of the rule of faith . . . We must settle what it is the Pope claims, before we discuss the validity of that claim.'[17] When the article finally appeared in the May issue of the *Nineteenth Century*,[18] the voice was Tyrrell's, but the hand was supposedly that of Halifax.

Meanwhile, Tyrrell assumed a number of other disguises for the fray. There had been a lively controversy about the 'joint pastoral' in the pages of the *Pilot*, in which Tyrrell, as 'a conservative Catholic', was given the last word. A letter of perfect, aggressive clarity put his case:

As an analysis of facts the current theological doctrine of the functions of the *Ecclesia docens* involves at first sight a theory which could in no way be regarded as a legitimate development of earlier teaching, or escape the charge of an almost abrupt innovation, nor could it be defended as a necessary or even valid deduction from the Vatican decrees. It would cleave the Church into two bodies, the one all active, the other all passive, related literally as sheep and shepherds—as beings of a different order with conflicting interests; it would destroy the organic unity of the Church by putting the Pope (or the *Ecclesia docens*) outside and over the Church, not a part of her, but her partner, spouse, and Lord, in a sense proper to Christ alone.[19]

Tyrrell's whole concern was to contrast the two views as sharply as possible, distinguishing between 'the Pope as the voice of a theological clique and the Pope as the voice of the universal Church, past and present', attacking what he called in the 'Halifax' article the 'unqualified vicariate' of the Pope. He attempted to expose the apparently unbridled papal power of the 'joint pastoral' by enquiring about the limits to papal infallibility, and the limits to the obedience required for non-infallible decisions. When he was asked by Frank Rooke Ley to write an editorial on the 'Halifax' article for the *Weekly Register*, he feigned enthusiastic support for the 'joint pastoral' as 'the badge of orthodoxy', but his real concern was to contrast the attitude of the Bishops with the 'amended Gallicanism' that he had learnt from Newman.[20] Writing to Rooke Ley, Tyrrell told him that the Pope's attitude amounted to '*L'Église c'est moi*': he was the steam-engine; the episcopate the carriages; the faithful the passengers.[21] Ahead lay nothing but disaster.

Tyrrell's apparent support of the 'joint pastoral' had been intended ironically. He hoped to draw some comment from its extremist defenders, who could then be mercilessly pilloried. The ruse failed. Those who did respond were H. I. D. Ryder of the Birmingham Oratory, and Wilfrid Ward, two moderates searching for a middle way between the contrasted alternatives posed in the editorial. Tyrrell forced the issue in a series of anonymous letters. It was one or the other: there was no 'middle way'; either there were considerable limits to the Pope's infallibility, or there were none at all. He was now secretly defending his own editorial in response to his own article, something any lover of *Alice* would have enjoyed. Actually, he was disappointed not to have drawn a real defender of papal absolutism into the open. 'I made this view as absurd as was compatible with the show of defending it against the other,' he told von Hügel. 'On the whole I managed to give away the Joint Pastoral pretty well; though I am satisfied that neither Ryder nor Ward are clear about their own position and are trying to blow hot and cold at once.'[22] Ward wrote a full article in *The Pilot* attempting to minimize the damage done by the 'joint pastoral', but Tyrrell attacked again. This controversy drove deeper the wedge between Tyrrell the radical, who would never hold back on an issue of conscience, whatever the cost, and Ward the liberal, for whom respect towards authority was a religious axiom. Ward guessed the identity of the mystery correspondent, 'S. T. L.', in the *Weekly Register*. Under the cover of anonymity, Tyrrell was thinking his most radical thoughts about the nature of the Church. Clearly, the Church as it stood had no place for liberals of his type. Ward, it seemed, refused to face the painful divide. He saw the Church of the future as emerging, not without pain, from the Church of the present. For Tyrrell the only hope lay with a reborn Church of the future.

This was the Church for which Tyrrell was working, to which he felt he truly belonged, though it seemed to have little or nothing to do with the Church of the present. Typical of the irritations in this period was a well-meant, but misplaced, letter of condolence when it was rumoured that he had been summoned by the Cardinal to sign a profession of faith drawn up by Vaughan and his secretary, and had refused, avowing that he would only sign one proposed by the Holy Father. In a letter to Vaughan, Tyrrell called the story 'only one of many equally preposterous rumours created by busy-bodies to explain the simple fact that I have taken refuge in Richmond from the mostly worthless interruptions of London, in order to do my work in peace and keep pious gossips at a distance'.[23] He was now too angry and hurt to be reasonable about any approaches that might come from the Jesuit authorities. Clearly, the presuppositions of men like 'Father General Martin S.J. and a handful of Roman or Spanish Jesuits whose knowledge of England is as defective as their knowledge of English'[24] were quite different from his own, and every fresh clash drove him farther away. His continued existence as a Jesuit posed problems to all concerned, not least himself.

In an effort to budge him, Gerard had suggested that he produce a collection of his past articles for *The Month*. That at least would need no further censorship and could surely do nothing but good. Tyrrell saw that if the project went ahead it would look as though he were free to write when he was not, but he contented himself with the thought that the collection would act as 'litmus paper' with which to test the atmosphere. 'If the air will support life at all I will endure semi-suffocation and loss of self-respect for the sake of many of our common friends and of others,' he wrote to Thurston.[25] By the end of January he had made a selection, but the enterprise alarmed Sidney Smith, who was about to be replaced by Gerard as editor of *The Month*. Not until June was an imprimatur granted, and even then there was a fuss over the title. 'A More Excellent Way' was rejected at the last moment, because it sounded dangerously liberal. Tyrrell facetiously suggested 'The Travails of an Irish Gentleman in Search of a Religion'. Gerard thought 'The Faith of the Millions' suitably safe and affirmative, so the first copies appeared with this pasted over 'A More Excellent Way' on the spine. Tyrrell could not have failed to spot the irony.

The essays he selected were incisive yet moderate, but by the time they were republished Tyrrell had moved well beyond their moderate liberalism. With minor tinkering he managed to shift some of the emphasis so as to bring them into line with his current thinking, but the two volumes were of little interest to him except to re-establish his credibility within the Society, something he cared about passionately but regarded as a weakness. His preface continued the line he had taken in 'Tracts for the Million', though after the 'joint pastoral' he had effectively bidden farewell to the moderate optimism of the essays. He took the opportunity to reiterate his concern for an attractive presentation of Catholicism rather than 'sledgehammer controversy', the rootedness of the supernatural in the natural, and the 'relation of organic unity subsisting between the truth of Christ and all other truth'. His object was to speak to an intelligent, modern audience in language they could understand. As he summed it up afterwards, he tried 'rather to read a wider meaning into the old system and its formulae than to jeopardise [his] ecclesiastical reputation by attempting a new construction'.[26] The books were just 'dry bones', because it was now clear to him that only a 'new construction' would suffice.

Intellectually, Tyrrell was isolated, except for the support of a few close friends: Bremond, Maude Petre, and von Hügel. Von Hügel wrote rarely, as he was weighed down with family problems. His wife was ill and his sister was slowly dying. Just occasionally he found the time to send long, nourishing letters to his hungry friend. Ward offered intellectual companionship of a sort, but Tyrrell was constantly frustrated by his docility before authority. The others in the clergy-house at Richmond were pleasant enough, but at root he was horrified by them, and pitied them as the casualties of an inhuman system. Thoughts like these could only be shared with Bremond, whom he had barely met, and with Maude Petre, who was passionately—over-passionately—involved with everything he thought and did.

For six months she had been pouring out her soul, praying for him, longing for him, suffering with him. She knew the viciousness of his anger and despair. By her determined attempts to love him however much he hurt her, she intended to draw the poison from him. She, too, looked for great, new things in the Church. At the turn of the year she noted in her diary:

A new century. There was a great midnight service in all the churches, mass, communion and exposition of the Blessed Sacrament. I went to Farm Street . . . prayed hard for the victory of *faith*—light for the rigid, conservative and narrow—humility for the more enlightened. How different all will be in a hundred years! What changes in the Church! *Adveniat regnum tuum!*[27]

Tyrrell's prayer on the same night, made under the silent stars of the North Yorkshire sky, may well have been for the victory of truth, his fear that all too little would have changed in a hundred years. His letters to Maude Petre swung between tenderness and savagery. She told him that she thought von Hügel, with whom she had discussed Eucken on Boxing Day, was wonderful, but not human enough for her. Tyrrell commented that the remark might be 'justly retorted' on her. She wrote to him 'very lovingly, I hope not too much so'. If only he would be less bitter—but the bitterness, she recognized, sprang from disappointed love for the Society. She was afraid that when his heart 'came to life again' it would not be for her. She could not 'get at any unity in him', and feared he might break into ten pieces that walked off in different ways, so that she would not know which to follow. No sacrifice would be too great to save his soul.

At last, at the end of January, he invited her to Richmond. Even while she hesitated, he sent her the first instalment of his autobiography, taking himself to the age of 3. 'Very caustic', it gave her nightmares. Further episodes lacerated her: 'I have such a shrinking from seeing in him anything but what is noble.' He sensed this, and became yet more cruel. On 18 February she wrote in her diary: 'I must pray the more. Yesterday after Benediction the children were singing my beloved hymn, "Jesus the very thought of thee"—and I seemed to see F. T. and myself standing before Our Lord in Heaven, and he gave me such a look of love for having helped him to get there. The vision has stayed with me.' She was making him her life, her vocation, and friends seemed only to encourage her in this. With Bremond she was entirely open, and he sent the advice of Abbé Huvelin, von Hügel's revered confessor: 'Dites-lui que c'est Dieu qui l'envoie à cette âme—qu'elle aura beaucoup à souffrir.' It is hardly surprising that when she visited Richmond, there was shyness and constraint on both sides. They walked together in the woods and by the river, talked in her rooms, and in the evening she kissed Tyrrell's hand as they parted. When he clasped her hand and said 'God bless you', she knew he meant it. However, he begged her not to let herself become identified with him, though he wanted her to visit again. The visit, she wrote, was 'a joy and a help to both of us'.

In April there was a second visit of a fortnight. Every evening Tyrrell came to see her in her rooms, but she experienced only desolation and despair. One night they broke through the awkwardness and talked out the whole situation. She wanted to love him because he lacked any love for himself. He swore he was not worth it. 'I nearly cried,' she wrote in her journal, 'but I think there were tears in his eyes too. It ended as it must end—we go on as before . . . How I love him!' Shortly afterwards she made a ten-day retreat in Paris, where she could talk to Bremond. There seemed to be no resolution of the situation. When a Miss Gossage visited Tyrrell in Richmond, Maude was beside herself with jealousy. This was the most damaging element in her relationship with Tyrrell. The more she wanted to possess him, the more he hated her. When she left him free, he could almost believe he loved her.

In June 1901 Bremond came to England, mainly to visit Tyrrell. Although he had taken his final vows little more than a year before, he was now undergoing a long crisis of depression and disenchantment that ended in his dismissal from the Society. He was deeply unsettled, longing for love, for family life, for children, disgusted with himself, choked and repressed as a Jesuit. The fact that two younger brothers had followed his example in joining the Society, and would be bitterly hurt if he left, weighed upon him constantly. From the time that he first met Maude Petre the previous September she had opened her heart to him about her feelings for Tyrrell, and he had turned to her in his need for a woman's comfort and understanding. When he came to London he pained her by his unremitting low spirits. He waited a month before he found the courage to face Tyrrell at Richmond. Yet he needed his friend, as his friend needed him, and on 10 July Tyrrell gladly came to Richmond Station to meet him. The next day both wrote to Maude Petre with their first impressions of the other. Tyrrell found Bremond 'altogether unlike in manner appearance and everything to my preconceptions'.[28] He guessed that Bremond was surprised by his apparent frivolity, by the few books in his room, by the lack of seriousness about things that to him were matters of life and death. Bremond, however, found Tyrrell exactly as he had expected. Their immediate rapport, so much closer than he had dared to expect, was a tonic, though still he despaired of Tyrrell ever knowing and facing what he called 'the worst of me'.[29] It would not be long before they were writing to each other about Maude Petre.

For ten days the two Jesuits, both of them disenchanted with the Society, talked furiously, 'en plein sympathie, d'idées, de sentiments'. Bremond wrote to tell von Hügel that he and St Catherine had been there with them too—'and the good saint had not been too shocked'.[30] Tyrrell was trying to restrain Bremond in his desire to leave the Society, counselling him to hold on to that which was 'substantial' in the Church. He felt that Bremond opened himself to disappointment by his high expectations. Had he expected less of the other priests in the house, he would have been less shocked at the company Tyrrell kept. He could have delighted in his 'fellow-impossibles' as he delighted in children and animals. 'If he did not expect Jesuits,' Tyrrell wrote, 'he would find us a very interesting assortment of oddities.'[31] If he expected less of the Society as a whole, he could live with it more happily, or more patiently, until all affection was dead and he could go without remorse. This was the cold comfort Tyrrell applied to others as well as to himself. The ten-day visit cemented Bremond's friendship with the one Jesuit equipped to support him in his crisis of personal vocation. For Tyrrell, it breached the isolation caused by his intellectual difficulties and his retirement. He needed such friendships as he entered on yet another clash with the authorities.

The *Rassegna* affair had been a minor skirmish. When Tyrrell tried to push past the censors another book in the style of *Nova et Vetera* and *Hard Sayings*, there was a major collision. Throughout 1900 he was working on scraps of material that had accumulated from retreats, sermons, and his incessant jottings. At Easter he added a preface, and by the end of the year the collection that was to become *Oil and Wine* was complete. Early the following year Colley fought for, and won, the concession that Tyrrell's books were to be censored in England not in Rome, but Tyrrell had no confidence in the panel of censors. Of thirty-two, he dismissed twenty-seven as 'no better than pious, raw Stonyhurst schoolboys'.[32] The ruse with Halifax had worked, and that with Waller over *The Civilizing of the Matafanus* looked promising. He now tried something similar with his old friend Robert Dolling, who was working himself to death in what he called 'the dullest, grayest parish in East London'.

Tyrrell gave the manuscript copy of his book to Dolling. This was a carefully calculated move. Then, when the time was ripe, he warned Colley that Dolling wanted to publish it as an anonymous manuscript. To anyone who knew Tyrrell's writings, the authorship of the book would of course be transparent. When, understandably and predictably, Colley jibbed at the proposal, Tyrrell began to threaten, as he frequently did in this period, that he would make his whole case public. He argued that the Institute of the Society forbade him to publish anonymously, or to get others to publish in his name, but it did not forbid him to give away manuscripts that others might publish in their name. Having intimated that Dolling would publish the book anyway, he let Colley know he was prepared to see 'how far the censors would be disposed to go'. He reckoned that as the book would be published anyway, and the authorship was transparent, they would make minimal demands. When Colley wrote back accusing Tyrrell of 'disregard for solemn obligations', Tyrrell told him that he regarded himself as free of obligation to 'your Society', because the Society had not kept to the terms of the bargain that had been made when he first bound himself to its rules.[33] Colley, good-hearted and straight, had not the first idea how to handle such behaviour. The manuscript went to the censors, 'as it were a little mouse to four cats'.[34]

Colley, caught between Tyrrell and Rome, worked for peace as best he could. A routine visit to Richmond, during which Tyrrell chose to be out, reassured him that Father Farmer could handle the situation, and that the best thing to do was to leave well alone. Tyrrell did not know that the censors who were reading his manuscript (Fathers Charnley and Gerard—according to Colley, 'our two safest men'[35]) had actually been appointed by the General. Colley clearly hoped for, though he did not expect, a favourable report because Tyrrell was happy and quiet at Richmond. As far as possible, he left things alone. He reminded Meyer that the book would be published anonymously, not by Longmans, who had published Tyrrell's best-known works, and with a name that did not recall *Nova et Vetera*.[36] Tyrrell had Colley exactly where he wanted him. He was prepared to wait, and to growl if Colley put pressure on him. Not until mid-October did he begin to ask why the censors were taking so long. He also complained of 'wild and malicious gossip' circulating in London about his having left, or being on the point of leaving, the Society. To counter these rumours he had asked to preach at the Farm Street church, and had received no reply. Was there some ban on his preaching about which he had not been told? He warned that he was thinking of justifying himself by an open letter:

I think this is *most* undesirable from many points of view; but I will not let my name be dragged in the gutter through consideration for those who have shown no consideration for me. Your General failed ludicrously to justify his charge of heterodoxy against my article; while he gave no reason whatever for stopping my ministerial work—a species of justice unknown among civilised men who refuse to punish a criminal without first connecting the punishment with some fault and allowing the condemned a chance of explaining and defending himself.[37]

Colley replied by return with the censors' reports—it is not clear how long he had had them—and told Tyrrell that his request to preach was under consideration. Tyrrell responded to the '*definite* objections' of the censors by making alterations, and he offered to change the preface to meet more general criticisms. When he had completed 'a list of alterations and repairs', the censors were satisfied and the book was sent to the press.

So far, all had gone well for him. He expected any day to be invited to Farm Street, and he wanted to go freed from the shadow of disapproval. Once more he took the initiative, writing direct to Meyer, the General's assistant in Rome:

Will you kindly, in my name, ask His Paternity if he realises that it is now close on two years since, *without assigning any reason* for his somewhat drastic sentence, he forbade me to give the Spiritual Exercises . . . I want now to know definitively whether his Paternity feels himself any way bound in conscience to take steps to check the flood of slander to which his action has, I presume unintentionally, given rise: or whether at least, he considers it *due* to one who is condemned, to know the reasons of his condemnation.[38]

Tyrrell gave the General a fortnight to reply. Meyer wrote back immediately to say that the General was on retreat, but he would bring the matter to his attention as soon as he returned to his desk, and he then wrote to Colley asking what had precipitated Tyrrell's latest outburst.

The answer was that he had simply become tired of waiting. He told Bremond that he was dreaming about an open letter to the

General in *The Tablet*, publicly asking to be released from his connection with the Jesuits. (He was joking: they would never have published.) He expected nothing from Rome, and did not think he would be allowed to preach in London. Early in November he exploded to Thurston: 'Why the Devil won't they speak out and tell a man what they have got against him and not leave him to guess and conjecture? Surely it is the most contemptible system of government ever devised and had better be swept off the face of the earth, like the dirt that it is.'[39] The invitation came from Farm Street almost immediatley after this, and Tyrrell went down to London for a fortnight.

Maude Petre was amazed to see Tyrrell saying mass at Farm Street. His appearance in London, without any prior warning, seemed quite unreal. The lack of communication only made her feel how little she was to him. As she had written on her last visit to Richmond: 'The reserve, the coldness of our intercourse almost madden me.'[40] For Tyrrell the trip was a moderate success. Being a skilled practitioner of conversational provocation, he quickly found out what was being said about him, and introduced to 'the chief centres of gossip' the story of his retreat to Richmond as he wanted it told. It was easier to open himself to Maude Petre by letter, on his return: 'Maud [*sic*], I *could* not live in London; it seemed a lower, poisoned air, and God went from me for all those days. A famine-stricken city, and I a poor wretch with a false repute of bread in my pocket and everyone tearing after me for a bite.'[41] In the event, he was not able to deliver his sermon as he was in bed with a chill. This suited all parties—except Maude Petre, who longed to nurse him, and worried that he would be too cold on the journey back to Richmond.

The crisis was now upon him. He was within an ace of leaving the Society and publishing his open letter. He had staked everything on reinstatement to an obedience that he now despised. As he saw the situation, it all depended on how much the Society feared him. Undoubtedly, many English Jesuits who knew him well were exasperated with him, but they were also outraged by the way he had been treated and wanted him to stay. Tyrrell's tactical brilliance was shown by what happened over the next two months. On 19 November Meyer wrote to him with the General's reply. As to Tyrrell's removal from London, the General had had nothing to do with it. On the question of retreats, 'the action taken by Fr. Gerard was desired by Fr. General, though even in this respect, he later on allowed the Provincial some latitude'. Three reasons were given:

a) That, apart from the question of orthodoxy—Fr. General never once impugned your personal orthodoxy nor your good intention—several of your writings were imprudent, and were so regarded by Englishmen of high standing, in the Society and out of it;

b) That these writings were turned against the Society and the Church, *at least outside of England*—as, for example, here in Italy—by men whose doctrine is more than suspect, and who evidently understood you somewhat in the same sense, as did some very sound and intelligent Catholics, who took exception to your manner of expressing yourself on various delicate subjects;

c) That these writings and, still more, things said by you in Retreats and at other times, disturbed the consciences of not a few of 'Ours' and outsiders; and that they gave rise to grave complaints on the part of persons whose authority we cannot ignore.

All this the General had communicated to the Provincial, and assigned as the reason for his action; nevertheless, he did allow the Provincial some latitude later on. Father General, who could not understand what Tyrrell meant by his words about not delaying 'those steps which I have resolved to take for the vindication of my character', hoped Tyrrell would not commit himself to anything 'against our Institute' which would compel him to take 'steps that he would much dislike to take'.[42]

At the same time Colley was told to contact Gerard to find out exactly what he had said to Tyrrell. He was also 'kindly, clearly but firmly' to warn Tyrrell in no way to transgress the Institute of the Jesuits, for, if he did, no Cardinal or bishop would want to employ him in their diocese.[43] When Gerard replied to Colley he made it clear that he had not told Tyrrell he was 'taboo for retreats', because he wanted 'to avoid driving him to extremity', and because he felt he 'could offer no reason which would hold water for a moment with so acute a man as Father Tyrrell'. He thought the censures on 'A Perverted Devotion' were 'simply outrageous, considerably more deserving of blame than the article censured'. With misplaced charity, he had made nothing clear to Tyrrell, but had welcomed his suggestion about moving to Richmond. 'If Tyrrell knew this it would make him wild.' Nothing had been said to him about a prohibition from the General. Gerard had spoken to him 'as from myself alone, seeing that the mention of Fr. General is as a red rag to a bull'.[44] Colley took the way out that Gerard offered. He wrote to Tyrrell to tell him that he thought he was right in saying that the General 'never forbad your giving any retreats'. This was a downright lie from a man caught between the upper and the nether millstone. 'I did not think of asking you to give any Retreat as the reasons assigned by you against undertaking any spiritual work seemed to apply a fortiori to retreats.'[45] In reply to this 'admission', Tyrrell did not mince his words. Did Colley really mean to tell him, after all the distress he had been through, that there had been no general prohibition on his giving retreats?

Why then was not this made plain from the first? Surely I made it clear enough to you and to Fr. Gerard that it was the existence of such a general prohibition, on no assigned reason and with no opportunity of self-defence, that made my relation to the Society one of irreconcilable hostility! It was as inconsistent with such a prohibition, which I am now told, was non-existent, that I refused all spiritual work of a like nature. I had rather fancied that home authorities were more friendly to me than foreign, and had tempered the severity of His Paternity's judgment. It now seems to have been just the contrary—so little can one understand or follow these crooked methods of government by secret delation! Frankly, I never liked giving retreats or preaching; and now, least of all since I have learnt how slanderous delation is encouraged and protected by His Paternity. Still, I think you owe it to my reputation to appoint me to give some one, more or less public retreat which may be well advertised, and I on my part will engage to back out at the last moment, as I did with regard to the sermon the other Sunday.[46]

In the same letter he angrily refuted current gossip that he was responsible for the departure of a number of scholastics, Jesuits in training, and he attacked those who would not see the sexual problems that many of these young men had. Tyrrell's openness and realism had indeed drawn some of them to him, but he always upheld the most rigorous standards of sexual morality, and was particularly hurt by the accusation that he had taught them 'sodomy and self-abuse'. Perhaps a questioner such as he should not have been surprised at being charged with corrupting Jesuit youth. Colley simply absorbed the tirade, and reported to Rome that everything was proceeding 'satisfactorily'. He then wrote to Tyrrell to ask him to give the ordination retreat for diocesan clergy at Oscott the following Lent. Tyrrell accepted, making it clear that he only wanted to do the minimum of such work to protect his good name, but he had made his point, and he later withdrew.

The withdrawal was precipitated by a final twist in the *Oil and Wine* affair. Cardinal Vaughan had given his imprimatur to *The Faith of the Millions* on the recommendation of the Jesuit censors.

He then read a discussion of the book in the *Church Review*, entitled 'Liberalism Again'. Asked to accept the decision of the Jesuit censors on this new manuscript, he was determined not to make the same mistake twice, and insisted on replacing one Jesuit censor by his own man. Tyrrell protested that the manuscript was now illegible after the emendations to suit the Jesuit censors. Thinking that this would be one step nearer publication, he offered to send the book at proof stage. This Vaughan accepted, reading the sheets himself. On 20 March he wrote to Tyrrell: 'I read through the greater part of them: but found myself in such conscientious difficulty that I sent them to be revised by censorship in Rome.'[47] Thus the book went to Merry del Val. Within five days Vaughan was writing to tell Tyrrell that two of the Roman censors had rejected the book, and he had only to hear from the third.

Tyrrell's answer was a masterpiece of insolence. He told Vaughan that 'Whatever the verdict of your Italian censor, it is plain to me on reflection that a book which puzzles Your Eminence will puzzle the average Catholic intelligence of this country.'[48] For this reason *he* would not publish, but he would leave it with Dolling to publish if ever he wanted to—under his own name, making it clear that it had been repudiated by its anonymous author. Vaughan thanked Tyrrell for this response, which fully justified the 'high opinion' which he had formed of his loyalty and virtue.[49] Colley and Gerard (who was also consulted) saw with horror that Vaughan had allowed himself to sanction the pseudonymous publication of a book doubted by himself and condemned by Rome. Tyrrell reminded them that the Jesuit censors had passed it, but he left the issue up to Dolling. He did not, however, lose the opportunity of reminding Vaughan that the points censured in *Oil and Wine* were scattered throughout his other books. Would it, he wondered archly, help the cause of Catholicism if he repudiated them all? 'No', said Vaughan and Colley in unison. Tyrrell withdrew, again satisfied that he had scored his point.

The prospect of double censorship seemed to rule out any more writing of this type, leaving only the possibility of clandestine publication. That was a loss. However, he had won all along the line with regard to the interdict. He had extorted his freedom to preach, write, and give retreats under the same conditions as any other Jesuit (in theory if not in practice), though actually to do so was the last thing he wanted. There had been no apology or admission of error from the authorities; the change in the wind was as near as the

Society would ever come to that. He had proved how much they feared him, and, provided he kept his head, he should now be left well alone. The moral was, as he told Bremond: 'When dealing with cowards you must growl and show your teeth. This also I have learnt 'à l'école de Jack'[50] He did not even have to bear the strain of dissembling, as he could not have been more forthright with his superiors about his contempt for this 'government by prying, keyhole-listening, letter-opening, secret delation, unexplained punishments, suppressions etc.'[51] It was only his vision of what the Church and the Society might be that kept him at Richmond, the belief that he had a *right* to be there because he was serving the true spirit of these bodies. It had been a long, hard struggle, and for three years he and his Jesuit superiors left each other alone until Tyrrell began the moves that ended with his dismissal.

As for *Oil and Wine*, Dolling honoured a personal plea from Colley that the book should not be published, but to Tyrrell's great sorrow Dolling died that same year, 1902. Tyrrell had, however, taken good care to see that the type was already set up, and he quietly arranged for copies to be printed at his own expense. These were marked 'for private circulation only', and were passed out to friends. Only in 1906, after he had left the Jesuits, did the book become generally available. The following year it was republished by Longmans with a new preface in which Tyrrell disingenuously announced that he wished 'to label the book "Dangerous" in the largest type possible'. He might as well have written 'Drink me' on the cover.

Oil and Wine[52] looks like a collection of devotional meditations, a sequel to *Nova et Vetera* and *Hard Sayings*. Actually it contains a strong vein of religious philosophy. More confidently than ever, Tyrrell entered the fray against the theological rationalism that his experience in the confessional had taught him was doing so much damage to souls. Against the exaltation of the intellect and neglect of the heart, the exaltation of the clergy and neglect of the laity, the exaltation of the Church and neglect of humanity, he stressed the organic unity of man in his apprehension of God, the organic unity of Catholic doctrine, the Church, the human race, and the whole 'sentient creation'. He wavered between stressing 'not only the mind but the whole soul' as 'the organ of truth', and an admission of the priority of heart over head: 'In this life God presents Himself to us as the object of the heart and will rather than as an object of the mind and intelligence.' This was a dangerous challenge to Vatican orthodoxy. Only thirty years before the Vatican Council had declared: 'If any one shall say that the One true God, our Creator and Lord, cannot be certainly known by the natural light of human reason through created things, let him be anathema.'[53] Tyrrell now described 'the whole principle of faith' as 'a holding on *by the will* to truths which for the moment the mind does not see, or is incapable of seeing'. Instructed by Newman, von Hügel, and Blondel, he knew that he stood in a tradition broader and deeper than that of his Roman censors. His position was based upon a confidence in religious progress and the immanent activity of God, 'that divine and universal Will, which works in us and in all creatures'. To this he gave primacy over human doctrinal formulations, which he described as 'the effort of religion to find utterance and embodiment'. He was working to put the life before the doctrine, the heart before the mind, the activity of God before the activity of man. According to his critics, he was guilty of neglect or misunderstanding of revelation, of 'voluntarism', 'pantheism', 'immanentism'. By the time the book finally reached the public, the Vatican was ready to pronounce in precisely these terms.

NOTES

1. Tyrrell to Gerard, 17 Nov. 1900 (AEPSJ).
2. 'Tracts for the Million', *The Month*, 96 (1900), pp. 449–60; *FM*2, pp. 136–57.
3. Tyrrell to Maude Petre, 12 Jan. 1901 (*AL*2, p. 166).
4. Tyrrell to Gerard, 17 Nov. 1900.
5. Martin to Colley, 2 Nov. 1900 (ARSJ, *RPA*, v).
6. Tyrrell to Maude Petre, 18 Dec. 1900 (BL, Petre Papers).
7. Knight to Tyrrell, 13 Jan. 1901 (AEPSJ).
8. Tyrrell to Maude Petre, 29 Jan. 1901.
9. Colley to Meyer, 22 Jan. 1901 (ARSJ, ANGL. 1021, IC.9).
10. Martin to Colley, 3 Mar. 1901.
11. Martin to Colley, 13 Mar. 1901.
12. Merry del Val to Vaughan, 30 June 1900 (AAW, Vaughan Papers, VI/14).
13. *The Tablet*, 5 Jan. 1901, pp. 8–12; 12 Jan. 1901, pp. 50–2.
14. Tyrrell to von Hügel, 20 Feb. 1901 (BL, Petre Papers).
15. Tyrrell to Frank Rooke Ley, 5 Jan. 1901 (*AL*2, p. 152).
16. Tyrrell to Halifax, 28 Jan. 1901 (Borthwick Institute, Halifax Papers).

17. Tyrrell to Halifax, 17 Feb. 1901.
18. 'The Recent Anglo-Roman Pastoral', *Nineteenth Century*, 49 (May 1901), pp. 736–54.
19. *The Pilot*, 2 Mar. 1901, p. 282.
20. 'Lord Halifax Demurs', *Weekly Register*, 103 (3 May 1901), pp. 549–50.
21. Tyrrell to Rooke Ley, 27 Apr. 1901 (*AL2*, p. 160).
22. Tyrrell to von Hügel, 17 June 1901.
23. Tyrrell to Vaughan, 26 Aug. 1902 (AAW, Vaughan Papers, VI/12).
24. Ibid.
25. Tyrrell to Thurston, undated (AEPSJ, 0015).
26. Tyrrell to Dimnet, undated (*AL2*, p. 165).
27. The account that follows is based on Maude Petre's diaries for Jan.–Apr. 1901 (BL Add. MS 52372).
28. Tyrrell to Maude Petre, 11 July 1901.
29. Bremond to Maude Petre, 14 July 1901 (BL, Petre Papers).
30. Bremond to von Hügel, 15 Aug. 1901 (SAUL, MS 2315).
31. Tyrrell to Maude Petre, 16 July 1901.
32. Tyrrell to von Hügel, 20 Feb. 1901.
33. Tyrrell to Colley, 27 June, 1 July 1901 (AEPSJ).
34. Tyrrell to Raffalovich, 30 July 1901 (Blackfriars Collection).
35. Colley to Meyer, 11 Apr. 1902.
36. Colley to Meyer, 25 Aug. 1901.
37. Tyrrell to Colley, 15 Oct. 1901.
38. Tyrrell to Meyer, 1 Nov. 1901 (ARSJ, ANGL. 1021, IC.16).
39. Tyrrell to Thurston, 6 Nov. 1901.
40. Maude Petre diaries, 7 Sept. 1901.
41. Tyrrell to Maude Petre, 20 Nov. 1901.
42. Meyer to Tyrrell, 19 Nov. 1901 (BL, Add. MS 52368; ARSJ, ANGL. 1021, IC.18).
43. Martin to Colley, 19 Nov. 1901.
44. Gerard to Colley, 23 Nov. 1901 (AEPSJ).
45. Colley to Tyrrell, 24 Nov. 1901 (AEPSJ).
46. Tyrrell to Colley, 25 Nov. 1901.
47. Vaughan to Tyrrell, 20 Mar. 1902 (AAW, Vaughan Papers, VI/12).
48. Tyrrell to Vaughan, 27 Mar. 1902.
49. Vaughan to Tyrrell, 28 Mar. 1902; copies by Gerard for Colley (AEPSJ).
50. Tyrrell to Bremond, 3 Dec. 1901 (BN, Fonds Bremond).
51. Tyrrell to von Hügel, 12 Nov. 1900.
52. *Oil and Wine* (London, 1907). Quotations are from pp. 39 ('not only the mind . . .'); 206 ('In this life . . .'); 45 ('the whole principle . . .'); 315 ('that divine . . .'); 5 ('the effort . . .').
53. DS, 3026.

11

'A Painful Process of Necessary Readjustment'

FROM 1901 to 1903, despite the outward calm of Richmond, the threads of Tyrrell's life became ever more entangled. After the embarrassed and dishonest avowal on the part of his superiors that there had been no 'ban', Tyrrell, now totally disaffected, contributed occasional articles to *The Month*, but effectively withdrew from Jesuit affairs. All his energy, however, was poured into intellectual work. In this period he wrote two pseudonymous seminal books of religious philosophy. He applied himself to the biblical question, with von Hügel and Loisy as his tutors. He was a constant resource to those in trouble or need, especially Henri Bremond, whose Jesuit vocation was in ruins. The ambiguous relationship with Maude Petre deepened when she moved into lodgings in Richmond. Endless correspondents turned to him for his unique brand of witty, penetrating, ironical advice. In June 1903, when he had finished *The Church and the Future*, he wrote: 'In my own inward history the book ends a painful process of necessary readjustment, and I feel as one who, after much uncertainty, has at last chosen a path that is clear, however difficult and uninviting in many ways.'[1] Three years had been spent at Richmond in reaching this point.

The correspondence between Tyrrell and von Hügel runs to hundreds of letters, but during 1901 Tyrrell received only three letters from the Baron, all of great length, all packed with interesting news. Von Hügel wrote about his travels and the progress of criticism, which meant the doings of men like Loisy, Eucken, Semeria, Mignot, all his friends. Alone in Richmond, Tyrrell devoured these letters avidly. 'My very dear friend,' he wrote, 'your letter is simply bewildering in the multiplicity and intensity of its interests.'[2] Such letters brought much-needed support when he fought in isolation against the infamous joint pastoral letter, and laboured under the silently imposed, unacknowledged Jesuit ban. For his part, Tyrrell sent von Hügel copies of all the most important things he wrote. The Baron was often preoccupied—with his health, his work on St Catherine, and his enormous correspondence—but he read Tyrrell's work with the closest attention, and wrote back offering careful, constructive criticism. At this stage he was very much the master and Tyrrell the eager pupil, but there were technical theological points on which he turned to Tyrrell for help. Steadily, Tyrrell was drawn into the world of critical thought, into contact with the international circle of scholars that revolved around the Baron. 'Every time I meet you or hear from you', he told von Hügel in February 1901, 'I am poked on a little further; but like a wheelbarrow I am not susceptible of sustained impetus, but stick where I am dropped.'[3] In September 1901 von Hügel at last 'poked' him into learning German. 'Work, work, work at your German', he told him.[4]

Von Hügel's letters were only infrequent because he had so much else on his mind. His sister Pauline was slowly dying that winter, and after her death at the end of March 1901 he set off for the Continent to see his friends and have a holiday with his family. In Paris he visited Bremond ('that astonishingly sensitive, quick and exquisite mind') and Loisy ('as witty and as astonishingly master of his great subjects as ever').[5] Shortly after the Baron's visit Loisy learnt that he was under renewed threat of condemnation. From May 1901, not for the first time, von Hügel devoted a great deal of time and energy to supporting his friend. He feared the condemnation of Loisy would be a complete disaster. The Church was in grave danger of disowning the one Catholic biblical scholar who had truly understood the challenge of contemporary critical scholarship and had the skill to produce a creative response, a provisional reconciliation between his faith and his scholarship. Loisy's condemnation would be more than a personal tragedy. It would be a tragedy for the whole cause of free intellectual enquiry in the Catholic Church. Von Hügel went on fighting to avert this until December 1903, when five of Loisy's books were placed on the Index. This campaign remained a major drain on his time and energy for nearly two years.

Loisy knew that his work was being denounced in Rome by Cardinal Richard, the Archbishop of Paris, and that his books were under investigation by the Holy Office. When von Hügel heard about this he wrote, after due consideration, to Cardinal Rampolla, the Secretary of State, pointing out the disastrous consequences that would follow in English intellectual circles if Loisy were condemned. The Roman Church would appear in the worst, most reactionary, light. Later that year he pressed the point in interviews with Rampolla and with Padre Lepidi, Master of the Sacred Palace. Tyrrell received a full account of all these manœuvres, including von Hügel's examination by Lepidi on 'Inspiration, Inerrancy, Development, Relativity, Scandal, Pious Ears, German Rationalism, French fougue'.[6] The Baron was deeply worried about the future:

All the symptoms of what is coming are bad; and, without bitterness be it spoken, I think one has to fear most that the coming action will be something just narrow enough to hamper, still further hamper, solid methods for years to come, and yet not sufficiently clearly unworkable (at least in the eyes of the large majority of our even quasi-educated public) to help bring on a reform and relaxation of our present system of denunciation and censorship.[7]

Like the Baron, Tyrrell agonized over the whole situation; more than the Baron, he raged. He accepted von Hügel's estimate that Loisy was the most skilled, as well as the most daring, of Catholic critics. 'We shall find ourselves with no modus vivendi', he wrote to von Hügel, 'if we now burn the boats that Loisy has prepared for our escape.'

Loisy was important to Tyrrell because he offered a way of understanding Christianity that was rooted in the history of the faith itself, in the very gospels and the life of Jesus, and that was entirely open to critical scholarship, as it had to be in the contemporary world. Tyrrell took from Loisy the principle that 'inspiration means the progressive spiritualising and refining of those gross embodiments in which man expresses his own ideas and sentiments about God . . . Christ's whole "revelation" was little else but a further correction of the better sort of religion which he found in Israel.'[8] On this principle, a revitalized Christianity would be a 'spiritualized' and 'refined' version of the 'materialistic' Catholicism with which he, even more than Loisy, was locked in bitter combat. For both of them, this belief in man's progress from a cruder to a more 'spiritual' form of religion was axiomatic. It was, in large part, what made them 'modernists'. Loisy argued that modern Catholic critics, with their rationalistic presuppositions, were blind to this process in the very gospels. They were blind to the difference between the first three gospels and the fourth, which was so clearly mystical and symbolic in character.[9] Tyrrell applauded Loisy's 'luminous treatment of the Fourth Gospel which deserves the honour of the Index more than anything I have seen for a long time'.[10]

Like Loisy, but moving about five years behind him, with far less knowledge of biblical studies, but a clear understanding of what their more radical conclusions would mean for the self-understanding of the Catholic faith, Tyrrell was working out a programme for the survival of Catholicism. Like Loisy, he saw that the Church could no longer present its teaching about Christ as though it had been taken from Christ's own words, or its teaching about Christian dogma as though it could be read off from the Bible, or the Bible as a book which, because supernaturally inspired, was miraculously free from error. Like Loisy, he had to prove to himself how he could stay in the Church he loved, when the Church seemed to regard any acceptance of the 'assured results of criticism' (about the 'assurance' of which, it must be said, Tyrrell at times showed considerable naïvety) as a lapse of faith. His constant theme now was the change that the Church would have to undergo in order to be true to the Gospel and to the needs of the modern world.

About Christmas 1901 he wrote a short paper diagnosing the 'whole situation'. He was savagely critical of the Roman education system, and described Roman Catholic theology as standing 'in the world of present-day thought like a well-preserved ruin in the midst of London—the dead in the midst of the living'.[11] He called the paper 'Rome's Opportunity'. It is important as a first sketch for *The Church and the Future* a year later, but it is dull. Tyrrell abandoned it, as he told Bremond, because he found 'G. T. writ large over every page, in the style and the matter', and he knew 'it would be suicide to publish it in its present form'.[12] He turned his attention to an attack upon the roots of the religious problem. Within a few weeks he had drafted *Religion as a Factor of Life*,[13] a major statement of his reworked religious philosophy.

This short essay has a place in the development of Tyrrell's religious thought that is out of all proportion to its length. For nearly two years he had been intermittently at work on a study of Christian ethics, arising from a second series of addresses given at Oxford during Lent 1900. *Religion as a Factor of Life* was probably intended as a philosophical introduction to this larger work. In the event, it was published separately and Tyrrell lost interest in the major project. He thought the *Ethical Preludes* 'incoherent, dry and dreary',[14] but pressed on to finish an 87,000-word manuscript two years later.[15] This he used as a quarry for a number of articles.[16] However, the important work was done in *Religion as a Factor of*

Life, which was first announced to Bremond as a work 'utterly unfit for publication this century'.[17] He told Wilfrid Ward that he wanted to see 'how far religion can be preserved and yet severed from its present troublesome entanglement with positive [i.e. scientific] knowledge'. So much had been conceded to 'physics, biology, history etc.', that it was difficult to see where the concessions would end. This was why he was now asking: 'Is there then some new orientation which will make it possible to be almost indifferent not merely to what criticism has done, but to anything it could conceivably do? I suppose', he went on, 'at present, we should have to say: "No: Christianity would fall with the denial of certain facts of the positive order." Yet, for hypothesis' sake, I have endeavoured to find a way.'[18]

Tyrrell would never have been permitted to publish an essay like this under his own name. Now that he was subject to censorship from both the Jesuits and Cardinal Vaughan, as had been shown by the fate of *Oil and Wine*, George Tyrrell, SJ was effectively silenced. He knew he could 'get *nothing* through two iron walls—not even the Pater Noster if it were in my own hand-writing'.[19] Some other way had to be found. As far as Tyrrell was concerned, the printing of *The Civilizing of the Matafanus*, and its publication under the name of A. R. Waller, had been a great success. The presentation had been adequate and the cost reasonable. So he turned to Waller again for help. He reconciled his conscience to the subterfuge by brooding on the way he had been treated: 'Now that my muzzle has been so unfairly tightened I feel no scruple in biting in any way that a chance offers.'[20] Waller arranged for the typescript to be printed, and Tyrrell had the proofs, which he thought 'deadly dull', at the end of May 1902. He gave the author as Dr Ernest Engels, and in July he began to send 'Engels' to selected friends.

Tyrrell claimed no originality for his essay. He told von Hügel that he should not expect to find in it 'anything that I have not derived from you directly or indirectly—saving blunders and paralogisms'.[21] He described his theory as 'an amalgam of Loisy, Blondel, Munsterberg, Eucken, etc.' (he might well have added Bergson), 'nothing being my own but the amalgamation'.[22] The work is untidy—it consists of an essay with extended notes and an appendix nearly as long as the main text—but it carries the conviction of Tyrrell's clear exposition, and was well received by the select group who received a copy.

What he tried to do was to show that religious life takes place upon a plane of human existence completely different from that of scientific and intellectual endeavour. Human beings are not just articulated minds. Early in the essay he quotes Augustine: '*Nihil aliud quam voluntates*' ('We are nothing else but wills'). Tyrrell does not go into what is meant by 'wills', but he uses the term decisively to shift attention from what human beings *think* to what they *do*. From the beginning it is clear that Tyrrell wishes to attack the 'intellectualism' that misconstrues religion as first and foremost a matter of the intellect. Basing what he says upon the *Spiritual Exercises* of Saint Ignatius, he asserts that 'thoughts are created by feelings rather than feelings by thoughts'. A religion, then, is a dynamic system and not a static ideology: 'a feeling, or group of feelings, determined by certain perceptions, and giving birth to certain actions.' Within the religious system, the role of the understanding is crucial but secondary. It is in part 'to map out in small, and by aid of symbols, the wilderness of our experience for the better guidance of our conduct'. Religious dogma is thus created by the mind's attempts to give systematic expression to what is felt, or experienced, at a far deeper level.

The provisional and practical nature of dogma raises crucial questions about revelation. Tyrrell begins to approach these by stressing a favourite point: the inadequacy of our conceptions of God. 'No one pretends that our conceptions of God, as an object, are adequate or more than analogous and symbolic; yet they possess an equivalent or practical truth in the measure that they guide our conduct more or less surely in the right direction.' The understanding deals only with 'the divine manifestations and effects'; it is the will that knows direct contact with God. (This is pure Kantianism.) All the externals of a religion, its dogma and its institutions, exist for the sake of the will and its union with 'that supreme, eternal, eventually irresistible Will, which we call God'. The tests of a religion, and in particular of its dogma, are therefore practical: it is to be judged by the extent to which it promotes spiritual life or union with God. 'A religion is an attempt of the understanding to systematise a certain element of our manifold life, to find a theory of it, and thence to deduce practical rules for our guidance.' It is to be judged by practical criteria. Its truth is its 'utility for eternal life'. Thus, there are two aspects to a religion: the human and the divine. By perfectly normal human endeavour, accessible to scientific or historical enquiry, doctrine is constructed from the intellectual material to hand.

Through this construction, in a supernatural manner, the divine life is revealed to the soul. New intellectual expressions that promote the soul's union with God can be called 'inspired', the experience of that union 'revelation'. Thus, 'It was by revelation that Peter apprehended; it was by inspiration that he formulated and confessed, the Divinity of Christ.'

In developing his account of religion Tyrrell stresses this crucial point: every religious doctrine, as a construct of the imagination or understanding, has both a 'religious' and a 'historical' aspect, and these must be clearly distinguished. In its historical aspect it is a particular human expression articulated at a particular time, and it can be studied as such. It may be judged true or false, but the judgement that is passed according to these criteria will have no bearing upon its religious truth. Just as 'what is historically false may be poetically true', so what is scientifically false (say, the creation of the world in six days) may be true in the sphere of religion. The relation between language and truth is sacramental, so 'each ethical or theological statement ... belongs at once to the world of the natural understanding, and to the world of faith and spiritual reality'. The 'scientific' truth or falsity of the statement is immaterial for the function it has to perform. If it brings souls closer to God, it is 'true'.

Religion as a Factor of Life is fundamental to everything that Tyrrell wrote subsequently.[23] A lengthy appendix sketched out the application of the philosophy Tyrrell now held to the doctrines of the creed. This material was later reworked for *Lex Orandi*, and we shall consider it in the next chapter. It is sufficient to note here how Tyrrell's thinking had undergone a decisive and permanent shift away from those points that Rome most passionately defended: the objectivity of revelation; the transcendence of God; and the uniqueness of Christianity. Tyrrell did not consider himself to be denying what these doctrines asserted. He simply took the Roman understanding of Christianity to be impossible in an age that had turned radically to man as the agent of all knowledge. This radical anthropocentricity, which is the hallmark of the modern mind, led Tyrrell to stress the subjectivity of revelation, the immanence of God, and, as yet only by implication, the relative value of all religions. The theologians of Rome, imprisoned within scholastic categories, were blind to the need for a Copernican revolution of the intellect, and rested their case for Christianity on a classic—and to Tyrrell chimerical—objectivity. For Tyrrell the 'turn to the subject', which is what his new philosophy was all about, amounted to a rediscovery of the spirit of the Gospel, its liberation from the letter of an outmoded intellectual law. Having made his great leap, at the cost of so much he held dear, he knew that his difficulty now would be to show that he had not landed on ground that would forever shift beneath his feet. 'I am quite aware', he told Ward, 'that I have come close to two heresies against which I have written': against 'rationalism in religion' he thought he had erected 'a firm wall of partition'—he was not just offering a new intellectual system, but a concrete *modus agendi*; but he thought he might have fallen into Sabatier's view of dogma as an ever-developing system in which meaning and truth were reduced to perennially emergent expressions of an immanent reality.[24] What he had done with the faith, only time would tell.

Throughout his five years at Richmond Tyrrell fought against isolation—if not physical, for he lived in a house with other Jesuit fathers, isolation of the spirit and the mind. He had ended up at *Domus impossibilium nostrorum*, 'the house of our impossibles', the Jesuit equivalent of 'the cancer ward'. He loved Father Farmer, the Superior, because he was a man of simple goodness who had the sense to leave him alone. He pitied his 'fellow-impossibles', victims, as he saw it, of a system which chafed his wild spirit like bit and bridle. He salved his depression by long walks with Jack, his undemanding terrier friend, and worked out savage indignation in seemingly unending letter-writing. Maude Petre suggested a visit to Richmond at Christmas 1901. He told her he did not want to see her, and her protest brought from him 'the hardest, most cruel letter he has ever written . . . He wishes no further mention in my letters of my affection for him . . . He is sometimes so sore and angry that he needs to hurt somebody and why not me.'[25] The autobiographical letters were discontinued as 'too harrowing'. Maude Petre read a life of Swift, and found that the parallels tore her in pieces: 'How like in many of the external circumstances of life and how many characteristics in common. In spite of all his trying faults Swift was deeply loved and so also is he.'[26] Early in 1903 Tyrrell wrote to Bremond —in whose lot there was nothing to envy: 'You have been seeing beautiful things and places, and I almost envy you—I, who have seen nothing and nowhere; and have been dead all my life.'[27]

Bremond's visit to Richmond had cemented the one friendship since Willie's death in which Tyrrell experienced pure, fraternal *philia*. His letters to Bremond begin 'Carissime', and are unique in their frankness about Jesuit life. At this time Bremond felt unconverted, abandoned, reprobate. Tyrrell alone of his friends knew the ambiguities of the Jesuit life from the inside:

Our whole life, in the pulpit, the confessional, the chair, the parlour, forces us to play a part; to speak in the name of the Church, or of the Society, or of a system and tradition which is *ours*, as our clothes are: but is not *we*. At most we are defending a thesis proposed to us by another. I begin to think the only real sin is suicide, or not being one's self.[28]

Truth to oneself, to the light one has been given when the light of God and of religion is extinguished, simple integrity, is a recurrent theme in these letters. It was the only remedy for the sickness in Bremond's soul and in his own, the only remedy for this nausea. In one marvellous vignette Tyrrell captures the essence of this tragicomic theme, and gives us the authentic tone of his own voice:

Only yesterday Father Cary-Elwes—one of our Angers tertians—was telling me with reverent awe and admiration how P. Coubé rehearsed his sermons in detail over and over, practising each gesture emphasis etc. etc.; and how P. Somebody else had formed himself on Bourdaloue or on Segneri—till at last the Methodist devil broke loose in me and got control of my tongue: 'Good God!' said I suddenly, so that C.-E. jumped and turned pale:—'Good God! Fancy Jesus Christ or Peter or Paul, or any man not sodden through and through with artificiality and untruthfulness, mincing before a mirror, prinking and preening his peacock feathers; practising sighs and grimaces, in order to what? To cover the hollowness of his heart, the non-existence of his own faith and love, and to excite faith and love in others by a make-believe display of the same in himself.' Pulpit rhetoric, I went on to explain, is the surest symptom of religious decadence and death; of the subjection of faith to form. 'But the Society's custom etc. etc.' 'Rotten', said I, 'rotten to the core!' Nothing could have been more indiscreet, and indeed a little excessive and exaggerated. But C.-E. is such a perfect S. J. product— a man by nature bright, artistic, attractive and human, but, by docile submission to the system, dreary, uninteresting, self-centred, emasculated. Could I but excite a spark of rebellion in his heart he might be saved so as by fire! How far better, from a spirit and character point of view, if such a man could be thoroughly shaken in his faith and pass through a crisis ending in the so-called loss, but really the salvation, of his soul! His passivity goaded me on and on till Jack looked up at me in perplexity at my unwonted vehemence, as though he thought I must have seen a rabbit.[29]

This might have made Bremond smile in agreement for a moment, but it would not have healed his soul, for he was passing through a time of utter desolation, tormented by the demands of his Jesuit vocation and by what he felt to be his moral ruin in failing to live up to it. He longed to leave the Society, he craved the love of a wife and family, he dreaded the effect of his behaviour on his two younger brothers, both Jesuits like himself. Turmoil in the life of the French Jesuits contributed to his unsettlement. The government was applying with renewed ferocity an anti-clerical law of 1901, so that the Jesuit community at the Rue Monsieur (including the scriptorium to which Bremond belonged) was scattered, and Bremond (surprised to find that he was 'more of a Jesuit than he thought') found himself moving into a flat. Through the autumn of 1901 he followed Loisy's course on the parables 'with passionate attention', telling von Hügel that there was 'not one of his lectures from which he did not emerge more of a believer'.[30] A month later he was writing to Blondel: 'I am lower than ever—sour, sullen—and I no longer smile, except at little children. Pray for me.'[31] About February 1902 his superior on *Études* (the French equivalent of *The Month*) submitted a worrying report to the General, and Bremond's Provincial was told to warn him that he should produce 'better fruit' or he would be recalled from Paris.[32] Tyrrell advised his friend to 'ask for more detailed instructions as to how much more often and how much more religiously you should write'.[33] Bremond, deeply wounded by the situation, poured out his heart to Tyrrell, who wrote to restrain him from precipitate action, urging him to hurry up and public more of his essays in book form to demonstrate the quality of his work. Bremond wanted to throw up everything and follow his heart. Tyrrell faced him with what that would mean:

None knows better than the undersigned the temptation to take the wings of a dove and fly away to the desert and be at rest. Nay, have I not made a certain compromise with it? The Yorkshire shepherdesses are however too beefy to form a suitable complement of the tableau, and so I have taken Jack to my bosom as a *pis aller*. My cold reason tells me that this longing for simpler conditions, when life has grown complicated beyond endurance, enfolds an illusion similar to that which makes us often wish to be children again. But a man *cannot* when he is 40 crawl back into his mother's womb; its limitations would stifle him as soon as the first novelty of the situation had worn off.[34]

Tyrrell's letters to Bremond are all in this vein: mordant, compassionate, full of common sense, humanity, and wit. Bremond respected him for the quality of his religious life and for the advice that he offered, but he could never accept that Tyrrell knew, still more that he accepted, the mess that represented the life of Henri Bremond.

George Tyrrell was not Bremond's only confidant in these years. He remained closely in touch with Maude Petre, who, as Superior of the English *Filles de Marie*, had reason to visit Paris from time to time. Bremond shared with her the desperation of his feelings about the Society; she shared with him the pain she felt over Tyrrell. 'If you had remained, you would have perhaps converted me,' he told her.[35] 'Pray for me,' he wrote. 'It seems to me that God wants to use me for His work, but I cannot understand why He is not yet disgusted with me.' 'Forgive my utter *unsettlement*. Nothing is of any use to me so long as I drag this chain. For fourteen days I have been through a crisis of disgust, profound disgust for this burden of convention, craving for liberty.' 'Always the same veil over the eyes of my friends, the same difficulty in knowing the *worst of me*.'[36] In April 1902 Maude Petre suggested that Bremond should come to England for a year. She could look after him, and he would recover his peace. 'For sheer audacity', commented Tyrrell, 'your Bremond-scheme licks creation.'[37] Bremond did come to England in May, visiting his brothers in Canterbury, but he refused to visit Richmond. If Tyrrell wanted him, he did not know him. To Bremond's desperate entreaties about the silence of God, the absence of grace, the lack of peace, the failure of his vocation, Tyrrell wrote back exposing his own inner travail with trenchant frankness:

I should have to write you my autobiography (I once tried to do so in order to disabuse M. P. of her ideas about me) in order to make you see that I have really no *personal* interest in religious questions but purely a public interest; that I groan under the inevitable necessity of having to live the life myself in order to prescribe for others; that the thought of heaven or hell or my own 'perfection' (odious word) has never, even in childhood, influenced me in the smallest degree; and hence that I would not give 6d for a personal *paix* that could not be communised. The idea of *grace* as a special favour—a piece of Divine favouritism—is to me utterly repulsive. I would not accept salvation on such iniquitous terms. If the '*massa*' is to be '*damnata*', be my soul with the masses and not with the Saints! This is a pretty piece of blasphemy and heresy; the more, as being *ex corde* and *very* deliberate. This too is at the root of my impatience with the contradiction of a sectarian or exclusive Catholicism, of a Catholicism that needs so much explaining, defending, darning, patching-up, as to be immeasurably worse than the complications of the

Law from which Christ—the first liberal Catholic—came to deliver us . . .
So do not speak as though there could ever be a 'great gulf' fixed between
us—you on one side, I on the other. We shall both look up from our place of
torment to a greater than Abraham who will send us a better than Lazarus to
satisfy the thirst after Himself which he has given us, not for nothing.[38]

While Tyrrell rusticated in Richmond, Bremond journeyed dis-
tractedly: Bavaria, the Tyrol, Aix, the Jura, Clermont, cobbling up
reasons to keep moving. Meanwhile Maude Petre, who had accepted
the guardianship of two small nephews while their parents were
abroad, moved up to lodgings in Richmond. After June 1902, letters
from Bremond to one friend at Richmond were in effect letters to
both; advice offered by one was advice that came from both. In
September Tyrrell wrote:

One thing is *quite* clear: that you cannot go on as S. J. Even could your
temperament stand the monotonous solitude, there is no Richmond and no
Farmer in your province. It is equally clear that the kind of moral suicide you
contemplate is as impracticable as the wish to be a child again. We *cannot* go
backwards and the attempt is always disastrous . . . Pippa is all right for a
week but Pippa year in and year out, Pippa reeking of garlic, Pippa rabid
with animal jealousy, Pippa . . . I needn't go on; you know the appalling
failure it is in 99 cases out of 100 . . . You really *must* break with the S. J. *at
once*; but for Heavens sake not in the way you propose—not so as to put
them in the right.[39]

Still Bremond could not abandon the longing for home and family. It
drove him to Italy, where he met a string of von Hügel's cultured,
aristocratic, and scholarly friends, many of whom were admirers of
Loisy; men like Semeria and Minocchi. He was captivated by the
home life of Antonio Fogazzaro, soon to achieve fame and a place on
the Index for his novel, *Il Santo*. Such a vision only plunged Bremond
into renewed despair: 'It is so evident that I was made for that life and
not for mine . . . I look back at the expression of Fogazzaro's little girl
(14 years) as I was speaking to her father, and nothing can surpass
that pleasure. It is the awful solitude that I see now and foresee to
come—the impossibility of ever possessing the *casa mia* for which I
was made.[40] During his stay in Italy Bremond tried the life of a
secularized priest. When he returned to Paris his 'indolence' had
again been reported to Rome. Waiting for him was a letter which, on
the express orders of the General, forbade his residence in Paris.
'May God have pity on that unhappy father and avert from us a
serious scandal.'[41]

Tyrrell was quick to invite Bremond to Richmond, but permission was refused. He was to go to Farm Street instead. 'How ludicrous', wrote Tyrrell, 'that London should be the refuge from the worldliness of Paris! They seem to [think] all the pomps and vanities of London less dangerous for you than to be alone with the Devil in the desert of Richmond.' From 'the desert' came warnings about the moral perils of London: 'F[lorence] B[ishop] will want you to sit in chairs *tête-à-tête* in Kensington Gardens or to change hats on the top of a 'bus; or to waltz down Piccadilly in tights. Please don't!— at least, not at first; for the gendarmerie will be very vigilant for a full month or even five weeks.'[42] Not only the General, but also Bremond's close friends lived in daily expectation of some scandal. It almost happened. The 'gendarmerie' had indeed been very vigilant, prying into Bremond's affairs. The General had agreeed that a young Jesuit should be sent from France to make secret enquiries about him.[43] Thus, by January 1904 he was in a position to give Bremond's Provincial full, and entirely credible, details of compromising behaviour in Italy and a long-standing *affaire* in Paris.[44] Tyrrell had guessed that that was how it would be: he knew, and despised, the mentality of those who read private letters, noting down dates, addresses, and postmarks. On 6 February 1904 Bremond was dismissed from the Society.[45] He became a secular priest, incardinated to the Archbishop of Aix. Had Tyrrell been dismissed for similar sexual indiscretions, and not for something far more dangerous —insubordination—he too might have continued to stand at the altar.

Maude Petre always regretted Tyrrell's belated attempts to master biblical criticism. It was a field for which he was supremely ill-equipped. He did not have the patient temperament and cautious judgement of the biblical scholar; as he said himself, he was 'weak in facts, strong only in fancy and fiction'.[46] As a young man he had wisely turned from critical study. Now the Baron, who had precisely the temperament needed for scholarly work, but a kind of lumbering myopia in personal relations, was urging him on as he had urged on his own daughter until Tyrrell rescued her. As a cradle Catholic, von Hügel could not see the abyss that opened out before his convert friend. Tyrrell saw the abyss and refused to turn from it. He was in a frenzy, breaking his head on whatever literature the Baron cared to send him. Everything that was recommended he devoured, regardless of the intellectual or spiritual cost. The year 1902 was one of unremitting toil: of immersion in German critical writing; in *'la question biblique'*, where Loisy was the master; in working out the implications of what he had written in *Religion as a Factor of Life.* Around Christmas 1902 the strain brought him close to breakdown.

He had foreseen it a year before. A visit from Giovanni Semeria, an Italian Scripture scholar and friend of von Hügel, was 'like a sudden burst of sunshine', but Semeria's cheerfulness merely sprang from a cheerful temperament. Tyrrell described him as 'wonderfully buoyant in the midst of the ruins he is creating'.[47] His own temperament, and his own situation, were entirely different:

> For one who begins life with the fullness of popular Catholicism the disillusionments of criticism are not so costing as for one who has climbed up somewhat laboriously to that position at the cost of a good deal of needless intellectual torture and is now forced step by step down to the level of sane Christianity. I feel that Semeria does not, perhaps cannot, know experimentally the horrors of pure negation; that his sense of the extremest possible issue of honest criticism is more 'notional' than 'real'.[48]

Tyrrell knew precisely 'the horrors of pure negation'. Von Hügel, to whom he was writing, did not.

The Baron was in hopeful mood. At the beginning of 1902 the Vatican announced a new, permanent Biblical Commission to which the problems raised by scholars like Loisy would be referred. When *The Tablet* declared that 'Catholic scholars all the world over will have the fullest opportunity of stating their views and difficulties, and bringing them to the direct notice of the Holy See',[49] Tyrrell dismissed the plan out of hand. 'It is a foregone conclusion that the *Providentissimus* will be extolled as all-sufficient, and the liberty of discussion will be like that at the Vatican Council; and the issue will [be] the contemptuous toleration of the Batiffols [Batiffol was a moderate, in von Hügel's opinion 'not to be trusted'] purchased by the sacrifice of Loisy.'[50] Von Hügel, however, was full of faith and hope and not a little charity. He was jubilant over the names of the twelve consultors, 'not one of whom, with the exception of Vigouroux, belong to the strictly narrow set', and believed that the appointment of the Biblical Commission could be regarded as a delaying tactic. It would take its time and would act 'as a substitute for condemnation and restrictions'.[51] To Tyrrell he described its object as being 'to form a breakwater behind which we might work in tolerable comfort and fair security', and he went on:

When one realises at all vividly, in its astonishing depth strength and breadth, the revolution, almost invisible because of its substantial swiftness and silence, through which our religious categories are passing, when one clearly grasps what it means that we should have been examined here in detail and under the pressure of relentless foes, pressure exercised upon people without a spark of enthusiasm or of real comprehension for and of such questions: and that after *years* of denunciations (for this thing has hardly ever stopped for the last 8 years) we have still no condemnation, but a Commission with not one of [Loisy's] denouncers, and with several of his warm friends on it, a Commission which, from its very constitution, will be largely passive and 'break-water' in its character: I think it would be wrong not to take a little cheerful, hopeful rest, of thankfulness and of reconstitutive hope, getting thus ready for such fast battles, or, please God, strenuous labours, as God, in slow self-manifestation, may demand of our poor wills, rendered, we pray, indomitable by his mysterious strength.[52]

There fine, trusting words, which had a solid grain of truth in them, were uttered at the beginning of a year-long power struggle behind the scenes, at the end of which the membership of the Commission was enlarged to forty, with hardly one more name friendly to Loisy, and many blind to critical issues. Throughout 1902, when no official announcement about the membership of the Commission was forthcoming, it gradually became clear that the conservatives were gaining ground. Tyrrell's jaundiced prognostications would, after all, prove correct.

Tyrrell's view was further confirmed when in April 1902 he read Albert Houtin's *La Question biblique chez les catholiques de France au XIXème siècle*. It was, he said, 'a strange revelation'. As he told Ward: 'If authority were *occasionally* on the wrong side in that matter, it would be no difficulty; but that it should be so always and systematically makes one pause.'[53] For Tyrrell the 'biblical question' raised the whole question of church authority in its acutest form.

For three weeks in August and September von Hügel came to stay. Maude Petre was at Richmond with her nephews, and W. J. Williams was on holiday there with his wife. For Tyrrell and the Baron there were walks to the abbey ruins and to the Swale, and an encounter in which they were forbidden entry to some private grounds. From the conversation during one of these walks, 'climbing down the green bank by the old bridge', came the germ of 'Mysteries a Necessity of Life', which Tyrrell later submitted to *The Month*.[54] The Baron was reading *Religion as a Factor of Life* and *Oil and Wine* with appreciation. On his departure he left behind six books, all in German

(Eucken, Fichte, Duhm, and three by Troeltsch), and then followed this with a letter containing further recommendations. Of all these books, the most significant for Tyrrell was Weiss's *Die Predigt Jesu vom Reiche Gottes* ('extraordinarily original and vivid', said von Hügel), which decisively established the importance of apocalyptic for the understanding of Jesus' ministry. Von Hügel was, as usual, full of enthusiasm for all Tyrrell's writing and study. He had no idea of the strain it cost him, nor of the state of exhaustion and confusion in which he left his friend after that summer visit. To Bremond Tyrrell wrote:

The Baron has come and gone, and left me, as usual, with more to think of than I can digest. I wish he would draw up a list, not of what he doesn't believe but of what he does. A few months ago Dr Engels seemed to me an ultra-liberal; now he seems an ultra-montane. Were it not for men like Caird and Eucken I don't know where I should be, but these men have touched what Jesus Christ touched.[55]

Through the autumn Tyrrell laboured on: he read Falckenberg on Nicolas Cusanus, Wobbermin's *Theologie und Metaphysik*, Gunkel on Genesis. Then, in November 1902, Loisy sent him a copy of his new book, *L'Évangile et l'Église*. Tyrrell's letter of thanks was the first time he had corresponded direct with Loisy:

What especially pleased me in *L'Église et l'Évangile* [sic] is the manner in which you have assimilated and rendered helpful instead of harmful the somewhat disconcerting position of Weiss' *Predigt Jesu vom Reich* [sic] *Gottes*—a book which had given me considerable pause. As perhaps the only adequate reply to Harnack's *Wesen des Xm.* your book may I trust escape the envious attacks of those who keep the key of knowledge and will neither enter themselves nor suffer others to enter.[56]

Over a year before, Tyrrell had read Harnack 'with feelings of great disgust and contempt', admiring his historical criticism but finding his philosophy of religion 'silly and inadequate': Harnack made Christ 'a glorified Sunday-school teacher, and no more'.[57] It was typical of Tyrrell to direct his criticism at the religious value of the book.

Harnack, whose book was a transcript of lectures given at Berlin University in 1900, argued forcefully that dogma was a necessary evil in the development of the Church which he sought to get behind to the teachings of Jesus that comprised the 'essence of Christianity': the Kingdom of God and its coming, the fatherhood of God and the infinite value of the human soul, the 'higher righteousness' showing itself in love. In a typically sweeping, intuitive response, Tyrrell dismissed the attempt as 'morality divorced from mysticism', which makes for 'a lean sorry religion'. Loisy was more measured and more effective. He spotted in Harnack a central, exegetical weakness, but this was only part of his case. In contrast to Harnack, Loisy followed Weiss in stressing the apocalyptic background to the teaching of Jesus and the corporate nature of the life he engendered. Loisy would not allow Harnack's radical divide between the teaching of Jesus and the inevitable declension into the life of the Church. His positive rejoinder, 'Jesus proclaimed the kingdom and it was the church that came',[58] contains the seed of the best modernist apologetic. As he later expressed his purpose: 'M. Harnack maintained that the fact of the church is alien, heterogeneous, adventitious to the fact of the gospel; Firmin [i.e. Loisy] wanted to show that the two facts are connected, homogeneous, intimately bound, or rather that they are the same fact in its lasting unity.'[59] Loisy's book delighted Tyrrell because it embraced critical scholarship as radically as Harnack—in places more radically than Harnack—but to completely different ends. Loisy offered his tract as a defence of the Catholic Church, but in depicting the Church, including its sacraments and its institutional structure, as the dynamic, ever-changing vessel of the life of Christ, he backhandedly criticized everything that was static and defensive about Rome. It took Cardinal Richard, Archbishop of Paris, two months to formulate his verdict: he banned the book.

That was after Christmas, in January 1903. Meanwhile, Tyrrell, over-strained and overtired, had passed through an appalling crisis of faith. Sensing that something was wrong, von Hügel, who was waiting to hear how Tyrrell reacted to Weiss, wrote a letter of tender concern at the beginning of December: 'My very dear Friend,—I hardly know exactly *how* or *why*,—unless it be in part your, after all not long silence,—I come to have a strong and abiding, unreasoned and, so far, irrepressible impression that you are in interior trouble and trial,—of a specially strong kind or degree: but I know that I *have* this impression.'[60] He felt he was at fault because he had 'urged too much or too rapidly upon you the Wernle–Troeltsch–Weiss–Loisy contention as to the large element of Hereafter and Non-Morality in the First Form of Christianity', and recognized that 'it has been the merciful condescension of God, which has generally given me my spiritual and mental food so piece-meal in such manageable and far-between fragments, which has also, by this, enabled me to keep and improve and add to, I hope and think, my convictions (and their centre and life-giving power) as to Him, and Our Lord, and His Church'. He wrote to express his conviction (to himself, one feels, as much as to Tyrrell) that 'at bottom, and in the long run, all is well'. At the end of the letter he added a postscript: 'And now I will sink back into my own work, but with my poor heart prayerfully and affectionately full of you my intensely alive, immensely impulsive and hence astonishingly, most meritoriously and fruitfully balanced Friend!' Only von Hügel could have found a sense in which to call Tyrrell 'balanced', but the letter had discerned his friend's need. Tyrrell wrote back immediately, with a courage and a calm he did not really feel.

My very best of friends, I cannot thank you too much for this last mark of your affection. My letter of yesterday will show that your telepathy was not altogether at fault. . . Still the temporary bouleversement of my ideas did not in any appreciable way affect my general faith or hope or even good spirits. Indeed I am too accustomed to such crises of alternating night and day to doubt but that the sun will appear again, and that seeming loss of truth is the condition of fuller gain. We get our food in blocks and periodically like the lions in the Zoo, and not like babes in a continual stream from our mother's breast; and I am not sure that I don't sometimes long for a good tough block and rejoice when it comes . . . And then, my dear kind friend, as to your 'economizing' with me for my own peace sake, I don't think you understand how absolutely, and indeed culpably, little I have ever cared about my own soul, my present or future peace, except as a condition of helpfulness to others. It is a natural affection that has been left out of my composition for some strong purpose. Like Moses I had rather be damned with the mass of humanity than saved alone or even with a minority; and so I could not bear to think that there were faith- or moral difficulties pressing on others of which I knew nothing; and that I owed my stability to any sort of ignorance or half-view. All the vast help you have given me—and surely I have grown from a boy to a man since I knew you—has been in opening up my eyes to an ever fuller and deeper knowledge of the data of the great problem of life.[61]

He added a rider at the end which gave a glimpse of his true state: 'I have never troubled you or anyone with my inward autobiography' (this was a half-truth: the autobiographical letters to Maude Petre were deeply introspective); 'but I feel sure if you knew all you would have no anxiety for so non-personal a being as myself.' This was precisely the sentiment that should have sounded the alarm. No one can be 'non-personal' and healthy.

Christmas 1902 was the lowest point: 'no worst, there is none.' With Bremond Tyrrell was entirely honest. Together with emptiness went ferocious anger:

It has been a bad Xmas for me and '*lampades nostrae extinguuntur*' has been on the tip of my tongue all the while. Saying the Midnight Mass for the nuns for whom it was all so real, life-giving, factual and tangible I could fain have cried out '*date nobis de oleo vestro*', hankering after the flesh-pots of Egypt and loathing the thin and windy manna of criticism and truth. And then appealing to my emotional feebleness, round came the Waits [carol-singers] at 2 a.m. with their 'Glad tidings of great joy' till I could have damned all the critics into hell, if they had but left me such a receptacle. However they wound up with a somewhat dolorous rendering of 'So long thy power hath blessed me' etc. and so I went asleep with a vague hope that in some, as yet unguessable, way we should find the synthesis and that the angel-faces of the beliefs, loved long since and lost awhile, would shine out on us again glorified and eternalised. After all, it is the fault of the official guardians, and not ours, that the said lamps have burnt so low, tho' it [is] we who suffer the darkness.[62]

Shortly after this Tyrrell heard that Cardinal Richard had banned *L'Évangile et l'Église*.

For much of the winter Tyrrell had been reading. Now the shock of Loisy's condemnation stirred him to furious action. As he told von Hügel, the *Daimonion* was crying 'Write! Write! anent a certain difficulty that must be faced'.[63] On 1 February 1903 he told Maude Petre: 'Am writing all day like mad . . . I am now summing up the *whole* situation as seen from my chink in the door of eternity. "Am I solvent" is the question I have been choking down for years. Now others put it to me and I must answer it.'[64] In March he sent the typescript of ' "Catholicism Re-stated" by an Evangelical' to Waller, and in April the proofs were ready, Loisy's name having been prudently removed. By the middle of June Tyrrell had begun to distribute copies of the book, now renamed *The Church and the Future* and supposedly by 'Hilaire Bourdon',[65] to carefully selected friends.

This short book is one of Tyrrell's most successful pieces of work. In it he draws on all that has gone before, bringing together his critique of 'officialism' and his restatement of Catholicism. He sets out to show why the Church has reached a crisis: quite simply because the doctrine of inerrancy upon which church teaching —specifically teaching about her own authority—is based, has been demolished by critical study. The authorities do nothing. They refuse to recognize that there is a case to answer, and so are 'blind guides'. Meanwhile the people cry for bread and are not fed. Tyrrell offers an alternative account of church authority that is not vulnerable to the critics' most radical questions about Christian origins. In the process, he also offers an alternative account of the nature of Christian truth and the authority of the Church, calling the first 'prophetic' rather than 'theological' or, still worse, 'scientific', and showing how the second is no longer the prerogative of charismatic individuals, Popes, or bishops, or even theologians, but of 'the entire Christian people'. The Catholicism of the future will be a new creation of the same Spirit that inspired Christ and the Church, but has so signally departed from the Vatican.

As Tyrrell told von Hügel: 'The Church is being driven fast to what you Germans call an Entweder-Oder.'[66] There could be no middle way between 'officialism' and some version of the 'liberalism' he proposed if a general collapse into Protestantism was to be avoided. 'Officialism' was impossible, because it read the New Testament in a pre-critical manner, 'proving' Christ to be God incarnate, and the Church his 'vice-gerent' from the miracles and the fulfilment of prophecy in the New Testament. The Bible was taken to be 'a miraculous book, dictated by the Holy Ghost; free from error in all its original parts'. 'The *consensus* of current criticism of even the more moderate sort makes the Bible an insufficient basis for the scientific establishment of a single indisputable miracle or of a single clear fulfilment of prophecy.' Not only that: it also made impossible the notion of an original 'deposit of faith' which was simply explicated down the years. According to the 'official' theory, Socratic questioning of St Linus, the second Bishop of Rome, about any of the dogmas or sacraments should have elicited answers substantially the same as those of a 'D.D. of the Gregorian University'. This was nonsense. Doctrine had manifestly undergone changes in the course of its development as it interrelated with the language and concepts of various cultures. What, then, was the unchanging element, the 'deposit of faith'?

These questions Tyrrell attempted to answer. His handling of them is sure, because there was little that was new in his fundamental position. He argued that the officials of the Church misunderstood the teaching of Christ, which was not 'doctrinal' or 'theological', but 'prophetic': 'Directly, explicitly, and in aim, this teaching is altogether practical and not intellectual; prophetic and not theological.' Christ was not offering a series of premises for theological deductions, but a call to a new kind of life, the life of charity and of the Kingdom. The continuity between Christ and the Church is in the Spirit that inspires the life, not in the intellectual content of the doctrine: 'It is not then precisely as a creation of Christ that Catholicism can claim to be divinely instituted, but as the creation of that Spirit which created both Christ and the Church to be different and complementary organs of its own expression, adapted to different phases of the same movement.' Tyrrell uses this supposed continuity to marvellous polemical effect:

I do not suppose that any 'official', from the Cardinal Secretary downwards, nor any theologian would care to dispute the proposition that the Church is before all else a school of Sanctity and Charity; that her sole *raison d'être* is to reproduce the pattern of Christ as exactly as possible, in as many as possible; that this simple end is professedly the ultimate justification of all her institutions, her hierarchy, her sacramental system, her dogmatic system, of all her battlings and diplomacy in defence of the temporal power; of all the pomp and parade of the Court of Rome in its palmiest days; of all the ceremonial, the purple and scarlet and fine-twined linen of bishops and prelates and cardinals; of all that is mere worldliness, if not sanctified by that end, and mere fraud and hypocrisy if it only pretends to be so sanctified. Pass through the courts and halls of the Vatican Palace amidst the outward semblances of earthly vanity and secular power, and ask yourself the ultimate *Why* and *Wherefore* of all that you see and hear going on around you; or ask the first Monsignore or Cardinal who will deign to notice you, and he will have to answer you, as gravely as he can, 'Our sole thought and aim is, that men may love God and love one another as much as possible in the Spirit of Christ. We do not care about temporal power for its own sake, or for money, nor even for spiritual power over men's minds and wills; nor for our own dignity and position; nor for the system and institution which we defend; but we desire purely and simply to make men holy and Christlike, and we are convinced that these are lawful and expeditious means to that end.

Not only did Tyrrell think he had seized the nub of the issue; he also thought he had found a criterion by which true and false development in the life of the Church could be distinguished:

No conception whatsoever of the order of Nature or of the order of Grace can conduce, widely and regularly, to the development of the natural or spiritual life, except in virtue of a certain approximative agreement with ontological reality. Life is the very test and measure of its truth; or, in other words, its practical truth is grounded in its speculative truth.

By 'life', Tyrrell meant, of course, the sort of life manifested by Christ and the saints, the life of love. He saw in this some sort of 'experimental' basis for the truth of Catholic Christianity. The problem is proving that one brand of Christianity produces more 'saints' than another, or even than another religion. After all, Catholicism had produced the Curia, and Protestantism had produced the critics, who were, in Tyrrell's eyes, far more honest men. Still, Tyrrell maintained that truths of religion operate on a higher level. However misguided the teaching at the historical level, however rotten the institution, the spirit of Catholicism would survive, and when one form in which it had found expression died, as it inevitably would, another would be born.

Tyrrell believed he was offering an argument that could be heard in the 'scientific' world. In fact, what he offered was a vision. This became patently clear when he dealt with 'the ethics of conformity'. How could he, with views like these, stay in the Church as it was? His answer was that 'as long . . . as the liberal Catholic believes himself to be in communion with the spirit of the whole Church, he need not trouble himself about the views of her officers for the time being, unless in some matter obedience to them would put him in a false position'. The problem was that *all* obedience put him in a false position, because it was always tinged with equivocation: he fully accepted the words in which the Church expressed Christian truth, but he took them in a different sense. Paradoxically, in appealing to the consensus of Catholicism against the institution, he was forced back on his own private judgement. Who was to judge whether George Tyrrell was in communion with 'the spirit of the whole Church', if the Pope and the bishops said not? And if they said not, in what sense was he still a Catholic? *In spe*, in hope, was his answer, an answer to which he adhered for the rest of his life.

One of the subsidiary themes within the book is that of Christology. Tyrrell had long ago dismissed 'the Christ of the cardinals', with his knowledge of himself as divine, a knowledge accommodated to the limited perspective of his hearers, but disclosed through miracles and the fulfilment of prophecies. Loisy and Weiss had taught him how much Jesus was a man of his own time, with the apocalyptic expectation of a first-century Jew looking for God to put a rapid and decisive end to the world. Jesus and the early Church clearly expected the end at any time. When, in April 1902, Maude Petre asked Tyrrell about his view on the Incarnation, he replied: 'You are right in feeling I am working down to that root gradually, instead of beginning there. But, odd as it may sound to you, I have been afraid to touch the basis of all lest I should find myself houseless and homeless in the wilderness.'[67] By emphasizing the apocalyptic outlook of Jesus, together with his mistaken expectations about the *Parousia*, Loisy and Weiss had indeed 'touched the basis of all', and left Tyrrell feeling 'houseless and homeless'. *The Church and the Future* was his response to that situation, a situation in which Christmas, the feast of the Incarnation, was an empty revel. He now thought of Christ as fallible (he had been wrong in expecting the imminent return of 'the Son of Man'), just as the Bible, doctrine, and the Church were fallible—all being, none the less, in their own way, vehicles of the Spirit. In fact, he now argued that Christ's fallibility was essential to his humanity.

All this was spelt out to von Hügel. On 8 April 1903 Tyrrell sent the Baron a statement of his own position:

I am anti-Fawkes in regarding the 'catholicising' of Christianity as a *per se* result of the spirit of Christ, and not as a perversion or accident; but I perceive in that 'catholicising' process (as in the Scriptures) a divine and a human; an inspired and an uninspired, element; and I apply the '*quod semper* etc.' test in a *practical* way sc. Beliefs and institutions which are universally proved, experimentally, to foster the Christian spirit *ipso facto* are proved to be true to that spirit. And by the Christian Spirit I mean that spirit which spoke from the beginning in the prophets and men of faith and found its most docile organ in Christ and which still speaks in the corporate life of the Church so far as holiness is found there. i.e. I make the Saints and not the theologians the teachers of Christianity. The Spirit of Christ rather than Christ himself is the creator of the Church—or rather of the whole organism of the pre- and post-Christian Church of which Christ is the bond, and of which no part, not even Christ, exhausts the potentialities of that spirit.[68]

As for Christ himself, since he was fallible, Tyrrell's understanding 'leaves his human sanctity in the same category as ours, while allowing room for a mysterious relation between his humanity and that spirit of which it was the most perfect, *but infinitely inadequate*, utterance, and whose utterance (as the spirit of *human* sanctity) needs *all* humanity for its organ'.[69] What this amounts to is a bringing-together of three things: the historical Jesus as portrayed by the biblical critics; the vision of the mystical body that always attracted Tyrrell; and the belief in immanent spirit which was axiomatic to his understanding of development. To minds imbued with scholasticism, or any Trinitarian understanding of God, his synthesis raises as many questions as it answers, because he seems to have subordinated Christ to spirit, and to talk about spirit in ways that do, and do not, suggest the Holy Spirit of Christian orthodoxy. Tyrrell, it is almost true to say, was not interested in orthodoxy, but truth, and nowhere was his hold upon truth stronger than in his thought about Christ. The historical Christ, for him, 'shared all our groping and darkness and uncertainty and blameless ignorances—to me, that were more than his sharing mere physical pain and weariness. The theological Christ lived in a blaze of certainty about everything—like a Roman Cardinal.'[70]

The Church and the Future was Tyrrell's most outspoken critique of the whole Roman system, and was intended only for '*very* private circulation'. Discovery would have meant the heaviest penalties, so he took pains to see that it fell only into the right hands. Von Hügel finished reading it on 15 June, and sent a detailed analysis. He found 'five closely interconnected theses' in the book, two of which he thought were argued 'with an extraordinary force and consistency', but three of which left something to be desired.[71] Von Hügel added a list of those to whom the book might be sent, and some to whom it might not. Those he principally recommended were: Christian van den Biesen, Professor of Scripture at St Joseph's College, Mill Hill; Dom Cuthbert Butler, a gifted Benedictine, later Abbot of Downside; Alfred Loisy; Albert Houtin, author of *La Question biblique*; Archbishop Mignot of Albi ('relatively a giant among pygmies'); Rudolf Eucken; and Ernst Troeltsch. To this was later added the name of Don Brizio Casciola. Von Hügel's list was a preliminary roll-call of 'the modernists' and their friends.

While the Baron was reading the book, Tyrrell came to London to hear him read a paper on 'Experience and Transcendence' at a meeting of the Synthetic Society. The discussion he found 'very dreary', but the paper 'excellent'. For ten days he lingered, hoping to see Bremond when he finally arrived at Farm Street, but on 9 June he bolted back to Richmond to write a preface for *The Imitation of Christ*, which he had promised Waller for 20 June. On his return there was a disturbing bout of illness, probably migraine, that sent him to bed for a week, but then his senses felt less 'beclouded' and he could catch up on correspondence. To Alfred Lilley, a fellow Irishman, now Vicar of St Mary's, Paddington Green, he sent copies of *Religion as a Factor of Life* and *The Church and the Future*.[72] From this time the two men corresponded regularly and became fast friends. To Raffalovich, who had rebuked him for his sojourn at Richmond, he replied:

London means for me a life of superficiality. I could not live on so little thought and reflection as suffices those good priests at Mount St. who never open a book from years end to years end; and who by posing as oracles to crowds of uncritical admirers lose their sense of proportion in another very disastrous way. Here I have no followers or admirers [Maude Petre was in London]; but some excellent books that convince me of sin and of ignorance every hour and keep me so low and discouraged that I am fain to run up to London once a year to inhale the sea-breezes of mild flattery.[73]

To Waller he wrote begging for more time to 'tinker up' the preface, which had been written when he was only 'half alive'.[74] To Albert Houtin, now deprived of his right to celebrate mass, who had sent Tyrrell a copy of *Mes difficultés avec mon évêque*, he sent a sympathetic acknowledgment 'as one who has already tasted a little of your chalice and may yet have to taste a great deal of it'.[75] To a lady who was thinking of becoming a Catholic he wrote:

Though the reserves under which alone you ought to make such a submission are in themselves right, and would be approved by the great saints of the past, who knew that the Church was a means and not an end, yet, as things are at present, ninety-nine priests out of a hundred, and the whole Roman Curia to boot, would hold you no true Catholic were you to join us in the only spirit that I could justify.

She could regard herself 'as belonging in spirit to the Church; as excluded from its outward communion by circumstances for which none of us are directly responsible; as a Catholic in hope and desire'[76]—the position he had prepared for himself when the deluge came.

Leo XIII was dying. Within narrow limits he had shown himself to be a friend to scholarship and historical enquiry. Loisy had as yet eluded the Index, but who could tell what a new papacy would bring? On the day after the election of Pius X, a relatively unknown quantity, Tyrrell wrote to Waller: 'I will praise Pius X when he is dead.

Meantime I will watch. I think he is a really good and unworldly man; more human-hearted than Leo, less diplomatic. But goodness can be very narrow, very irritating and even very fierce.'[77] To von Hügel he wrote: 'I do hope he is not a Jesuit.'[78]

NOTES

1. Tyrrell to von Hügel, 27 June 1903 (BL, Petre Papers).
2. Tyrrell to von Hügel, 3 Jan. 1902.
3. Tyrrell to von Hügel, 20 Feb. 1901.
4. Von Hügel to Tyrrell, 10 July 1902 (*AL2*, p. 94).
5. Von Hügel to Tyrrell, 28 May 1901 (BL, Petre Papers).
6. Von Hügel to Tyrrell, 18–20 Dec. 1901.
7. Von Hügel to Tyrrell, 28 May 1901.
8. Tyrrell to von Hügel, 3 Jan. 1902.
9. 'L'Évangile selon Saint Jean', *Études bibliques*, 3rd edn. (Paris, 1903), pp. 290–335.
10. Tyrrell to von Hügel, 22 Sept. 1901.
11. 'Rome's Opportunity', p. 17 (CP).
12. Tyrrell to Bremond, 26 Jan. 1902 (BN, Fonds Bremond).
13. 'Dr Ernest Engels', *Religion as a Factor of Life* (Exeter, 1902). Quotations are from pp. 2 ('*Nihil aliud . . .*'); 47 ('thoughts are created . . .'); 5 ('a feeling . . .'); 6 ('to map out . . .'); ibid. ('No one pretends . . .'); 11 ('that supreme . . .'); 13 ('A religion is . . .'); 14 ('It was by revelation . . .'); 57 ('each ethical . . .').
14. Tyrrell to Maude Petre, 13 May 1902 (*AL2*, p. 192).
15. Tyrrell to von Hügel, 25 Sept. 1904.
16. Maude Petre lists (*AL2*, pp. 192–3): 'Christianity and the Natural Virtues', *International Journal of Ethics* (Jan. 1903), pp. 285–97; 'Religion and Ethics', *The Month*, 101 (Feb. 1903), pp. 130–45; 'A Chapter in Christian Ethics', refused by *The Month*; but there were probably others.
17. Tyrrell to Bremond, 17 Feb. 1902.
18. Tyrrell to Ward, 21 Feb. 1902 (SAUL, Ward Papers).
19. Tyrrell to Waller, 2 May 1902 (BL, Waller Papers).
20. Tyrrell to Waller, 23 Apr. 1902.
21. Tyrrell to von Hügel, 3 Jan. 1902.
22. Tyrrell to von Hügel, 12 Apr. 1902.
23. Throughout this section and that which discusses *The Church and the Future*, I am much indebted to David Schultenover's careful study, *George Tyrrell: In Search of Catholicism* (Shepherdstown, 1981), chaps. 6 and 7, pp. 188–317.

24. Tyrrell to Ward, 21 Feb. 1902.
25. Maude Petre diaries, 9 Jan. 1902 (BL, Add. MS 52372).
26. Ibid., 7 Feb. 1902.
27. Tyrrell to Bremond, 16 Mar. 1903.
28. Tyrrell to Bremond, 16 Sept. 1901.
29. Tyrrell to Bremond, 7 Mar. 1902.
30. Bremond to von Hügel, Dec. 1901, quoted in A. Blanchet, *Henri Bremond* (Paris, 1975), p. 164.
31. Quoted in Blanchet, *Henri Bremond*, p. 216.
32. Martin to Bouillon, 16 Feb. 1902 (ARSJ, Reg. Prov. Lugdun. VIII).
33. Tyrrell to Bremond, 12 Mar. 1902.
34. Tyrrell to Bremond, 14 Apr. 1902.
35. Bremond to Maude Petre, 3 Nov. 1900 (BL, Petre Papers).
36. Bremond to Maude Petre, 2 Dec. 1900, 29 May 1901, 20 October 1902, quoted in M. D. Petre, *My Way of Faith* (London, 1937), pp. 262–4.
37. Tyrrell to Maude Petre, 3 May 1902 (BL, Petre Papers).
38. Tyrrell to Bremond, 2 Aug. 1902.
39. Tyrrell to Bremond, 22 Sept. 1902.
40. Bremond to Maude Petre, 10 Jan. 1903, quoted in Petre, *My Way of Faith*, p. 265.
41. Martin to Labrosse, 30 Jan. 1903 (ARSJ, Reg. Prov. Franc. VIII); Martin to Bouillon, 12 Feb. 1903.
42. Tyrrell to Bremond, 25 Apr. 1903.
43. Martin to Bouillon, 15 Dec. 1903.
44. Martin to Bouillon, 19 Jan. 1904.
45. Martin to Bremond, 6 Feb. 1904 (ARSJ, Reg. Prov. Lugdun. VIII).
46. Tyrrell to Waller, 21 Apr. 1904.
47. Tyrrell to Bremond, 3 Nov. 1901.
48. Tyrrell to von Hügel, 3 Jan. 1902.
49. *The Tablet*, 4 Jan. 1902, p. 10.
50. Tyrrell to von Hügel, 3 Jan. 1902.
51. Von Hügel to Ward, 11 Jan. 1902 (SAUL, Ward Papers).
52. Von Hügel to Tyrrell, 8 Jan. 1902.
53. Tyrrell to Ward, 8 Apr. 1902.
54. 'Mysteries a Necessity of Life', *The Month*, 100 (1902), pp. 449–59, 568–80; repr. in TSC, pp. 155–90. Cf. Tyrrell to von Hügel, 14 Oct. 1902.
55. Tyrrell to Bremond, 18 Sept. 1902.
56. Tyrrell to Loisy, 20 Nov. 1902 (BN, Fonds Loisy).
57. Tyrrell to Maude Petre, 18 Aug. 1901.
58. A. Loisy, *L'Évangile et l'Église*, 3rd edn. (Bellevue, 1904), p. 155. Cf. *Autour d'un petit livre*, 2nd edn. (Paris, 1903), p. xxvii.
59. Loisy, *Autour*, p. 12.

60. Von Hügel to Tyrrell, 4 Dec. 1902.
61. Tyrrell to von Hügel, 5 Dec. 1902.
62. Tyrrell to Bremond, 29 Dec. 1902.
63. Tyrrell to von Hügel, 26 Jan. 1903.
64. Tyrrell to Maude Petre, 1 Feb. 1903.
65. *The Church and the Future* (republ. naming Tyrrell as author, London, 1910). Quotations are from pp. 17 ('a miraculous book . . .'); 20 ('The *consensus* . . .'); 27 ('D.D. of . . .'); 45 ('Directly, explicitly . . .'); 64 ('It is not . . .'); 71–2 ('I do not suppose . . .'); 85 ('No conception . . .'); 142–3 ('as long . . .').
66. Tyrrell to von Hügel, 2 Feb. 1903.
67. Tyrrell to Maude Petre, 27 Apr. 1902.
68. Tyrrell to von Hügel, 8 Apr. 1903.
69. Ibid.
70. Tyrrell to Maude Petre, 21 June 1903.
71. Von Hügel to Tyrrell, 22 June 1903.
72. Tyrrell to Lilley, 14 June 1903 (SAUL, Lilley Papers).
73. Tyrrell to Raffalovich, 16 June 1903 (Blackfriars Collection).
74. Tyrrell to Waller, 22 June, 6 July 1903.
75. Tyrrell to Houtin, 24 June 1903 (BN, Fonds Houtin).
76. *GTL*, pp. 268–9.
77. Tyrrell to Waller, 9 Aug. 1903.
78. Tyrrell to von Hügel, 9 Aug. 1903.

12

An 'Apostleship of Protest'

ANY equilibrium in Tyrrell's situation was, by 1903, profoundly unstable. One small change in the ecclesiastical atmosphere, and it would be destroyed. Such a change occurred in August of that year when Guiseppe Sarto was elected Pope Pius X. As so often with papal elections, the new Pope was a total contrast to his predecessor. Leo XIII was aristocratic in background, scholarly (Tyrrell mocked his penchant for composing Latin verse), diplomatic, and remote. Not one of Loisy's or Tyrrell's books was placed on the Index during his time. Pius, on the other hand, was a 'peasant-pope' who won hearts by his unaffected warmth and simplicity. Even as Pope he delighted to teach the Catechism on Sunday afternoons.[1] In his first encyclical he set the tone for the new pontificate: 'to re-establish all things in Christ'.[2] Like Pius IX, whose name he had taken, he saw the Church as under threat, and from the start he went on the offensive. He was responsible for extensive devotional reforms: the promotion of Gregorian plainchant, more frequent Communion, Communion at an earlier age. He set in hand the codification of canon law, the reform of the Curia, and the improvement of discipline in the seminaries. From the first he took an aggressive line against the snare of 'a certain new and fallacious science, which doth not savour of Christ'.[3] To Pius, the work of men like Loisy was undermining the faith of which the Roman Church was the divinely appointed guardian. From the beginning of his pontificate he set about their extirpation.[4]

Questions and rebukes about liberalism and slackness in the English Province of the Society of Jesus were nothing new. The teaching at St Beuno's was being closely watched in Rome. It was reported that Ernest Hull, a fourth-year scholastic, had been saying that the Gospel of John contained many interpolations, that Christ could not have spoken as reported in the Gospel, and that the encyclical *Providentissimus Deus* should be abandoned.[5] Such opinions reflected badly on the Professor of Sacred Scripture, Father Lucas, who was said to favour higher criticism, and not to have contradicted a student who argued that the Book of Judith was not history but 'a pious, poetic story'.[6] Lucas lost his teaching post. The following year John Rickaby made a stand against those who wanted to discontinue subscriptions to some journals that contained the writings of 'half-Catholics' like Loisy. Rickaby was reported to have said that 'The heterodoxy of today will be the orthodoxy of tomorrow,' thus implying—so the complaint went—that the Church changed her doctrine.[7] In writing to the English Provincial, the General quoted a letter he had received:

I have reason to fear that the young Jesuits who pass through St. Beuno's will be what are called *Liberal Catholics*. I do not think that Fr Rickaby gives a *solid, scientific* theological training. He hardly explains the text book. He *reads* much, gathers a vast amount of erudition *from history and all kinds of sources*, and at times gives very interesting lectures which captivate his audience but there is no *systematic training*.[8]

John Rickaby was relieved of his teaching at St Beuno's.

Farm Street was also infected with the taint of liberalism. Tyrrell was only one of a group who gave cause for official concern. Sidney Smith, editor of *The Month*, was accused of being too conciliatory to Anglicans. Thurston was accused of wasting his talent exposing historical errors in devotional books in a way that was neither useful nor edifying.[9] Lucas, who had been moved from St Beuno's to Farm Street, was considered a danger to the scholastics with whom he still kept in close contact, telling them that Loisy's *L'Évangile et l'Église* made safe and harmless reading.[10] For all these writers, who had so far faced nothing more serious than a rebuke or a change of job, the summer of 1903 marked the end of an era. On 19 June 1903 Cardinal Vaughan had died; the death of Leo XIII had come only a month later.

As soon as Pius X began his reign, assisted by Merry del Val, his talented young Secretary of State, repressive policies began to be prosecuted with much more vigour. At the end of September the General wrote to Reginald Colley, the English Provincial, expressing his hope that the new Archbishop of Westminster, Archbishop Bourne, would handle Tyrrell 'with greater severity than Cardinal Vaughan', and that he would continue to keep a close eye on Tyrrell's writing. In October he wrote again, forbidding the appointment of Tyrrell's old teacher, Thomas Rigby, to St Beuno's because of his dangerously liberal opinions. Rigby was known to have said: 'I think the Divinity of Christ just as much of a mystery and incapable of proof as the Blessed Trinity.' In closing his letter, the General told Colley that he had been called *again* (and this was only two months after Pius's election) by the Holy Father, who had spoken 'most severely against those who pursue new ways of this type and others of the same sort, declaring that he would act most severely against such men'. As a final spur to action, he reminded Colley how their rule bound them in obedience to the Pope.[11]

None of this took Tyrrell by surprise. Not so long before, he had advised Bremond to prepare his 'apologia' in case he needed to defend himself publicly. Now, with the new pontificate barely a week old, he began work on his own.[12] The detail of what he wrote we do not know, but the substance is clear from a letter he sent to the General six months later,[13] and from the major letter that he wrote four months after that.[14] To his detailed statement we shall return. At this point he needed to clear his conscience of duplicity or infidelity. He explained that one of the reasons he had come to Richmond had been to consider his position as a member of the Society. His increasing conviction had been that, since the Society was 'essentially false to its original spirit and aims', his 'disillusion-ments were such as to make that contract null and void *in foro conscientiæ* (as e.g. if a man were to take passage in a ship for the West and to find she was going East)'. He had told the General that he felt 'no *inward* obligation whatsoever towards the Society', he needed 'no dispensation from her claims . . . and could, if challenged, justify this conclusion in the eyes of all right-thinking men'. He now believed that the Society was 'leagued with those who are doing everything to make faith impossible for whole multitudes of the most sincerely religious-minded intelligences of these difficult days; and who (in all good faith and misguided zeal) are preparing disaster for the Church in the social, political, moral and intellectual order'.

After this letter, the General could not be under any illusions about Tyrrell's position. Why, then, did Tyrrell not yet ask for release? In the first place, he still remained loyal to the vision of the Society he had embraced with such enthusiasm as a young convert. In all his clashes with authority, in all his doubt and disappointment, this vision never left him. He believed that the Society was where he still belonged; he shrank from the pain of a separation which would tear him away from many who would not understand why this had to happen, and who would only be hurt and confused by his fate. Moreover, he retained a shrewd appreciation of the influence he wielded by remaining an SJ, and revelled in the positive advantages of his peaceful life at Richmond: time to read and write, the lack of responsibility, the solace of the countryside, freedom from the worst chafing of ecclesiasticism. He had never known adult life as anything other than a Jesuit, so it was virtually impossible for him to conceive of a life outside the Society. Clearly, all this had to end. His position was impossible. It says a great deal for the patience and humanity of the English Jesuits that for so long they tolerated a man who made no secret of his bitter alienation. Many admired Tyrrell, though he was known to hold dangerous opinions. It suited Colley to leave him alone—when Tyrrell was so gifted at making trouble, when he was widely thought to have been unjustly treated, and when Colley himself had not the first idea what to do with him.

Tyrrell was still nominally a staff writer on *The Month*, though his contributions were sometimes leaden and increasingly infrequent. Five of his books had been published with the imprimatur: two major works of devotion, one of apologetic, and two of essays, enough to establish him as one of the most popular Catholic writers. Amongst friends he was now known for four more works, three of them pseudonymous and one clandestine. All his life he wrote relentlessly, testing out ideas in letters and jottings, searching his own heart and the hearts of others, probing spiritual pathways like a mountaineer painfully pressing forward because he cannot go back. Tyrrell wrote with exhilaration, with anger, with consummate ease of expression. No one expressed as he did the pain and perplexity and the unyielding demand of faith in the modern world. It was not enough to offer 'strong meat' privately to friends, and to babes the sort of pap that the censors would accept. He had to see how much of 'Engels' could be made public. In doing that, he could minister to genuine need and perplexity, and have the added satisfaction of defeating the authorities at their own game.

In April 1903 Tyrrell told von Hügel that he was working on 'a sort of expurgated and amplified "Engels" for the orthodox multitude'.[15] This became *Lex Orandi*.[16] By the end of July the text was finished, and, after some 'very troublesome' work on the proofs to meet the demands of the censors, it was published with the imprimatur of Cardinal Bourne at the end of 1903. It was only then that the Cardinal, who cannot have known Tyrrell all that well, read the work. Immediately, he wrote to the Jesuit Provincial, Father Colley, to express his disagreement with the chapter in which Tyrrell discussed the virgin birth.[17] Tyrrell offered to write a preface to meet the Cardinal's objections, but not to change the text. Bourne wisely saw that this could only draw attention to the theological deficiencies of the book, and withdrew.

Tyrrell had hoped that *Lex Orandi* would be a *tour de force*, showing how the central doctrines of the faith could, in the face of critical questioning, be established on a completely new basis. For this he was much indebted to Loisy, who was a trained biblical critic, where he was at home with philosophy and devotion. *Lex Orandi* hovers uncomfortably between the two, too slight to satisfy those whose questions would have been better answered by the unexpurgated *Religion as a Factor of Life*, too abstract to satisfy as devotion. It is really an essay in religious epistemology that points out a new direction, one that is still fruitful today. Tyrrell's aim was to combat that 'confusion between the intellectual and the religious values of the Christian creed; between the embodiment and the spirit embodied; between the outward sign and the inward power and significance'. His book is about the sacramental nature of all religious knowledge. Tyrrell repeatedly emphasizes that beliefs which 'universally and perpetually' foster the life of religion 'must be true to the ultimate nature of things'. He works through the doctrines of the creed, showing how they are a *lex orandi*, with a 'prayer-value' for the sanctification of souls, before they are a *lex credendi* to be analysed and built upon by the theologians. Ostensibly he is restoring a lost perspective, that which he had been stressing for years: devotion before theology, charity before creeds. At another level he is showing how none of the doctrines of the creed depend upon historical proof or are vulnerable to historical disproof. Even if shown to be historically 'untrue', they are 'true' in another and a higher sense. Bourne had good reason to be disturbed when he read:

That God reveals Himself by preference to the simple; that the glory of God and the redemption of man is the meaning of Christ's earthly mission; that the Messiah was to be sought, not as worldly materialism had hoped, in the palaces of the great, but wrapt in swaddling clothes and laid in a manger —all this constitutes the religious value, the faith-matter, underlying the inspired narrative of the Evangelist. Were it merely a legend inspired, or selected and shaped, by some prophet full of the spirit of Christ, this religious value would not be affected; the only difference would be in the mode of expression—the difference between the language of facts and that of words and images; between an enacted and a spoken allegory.

This, in a passage discussing the appearance of the angels to the shepherds. Any attentive reader who knew something of Tyrrell's supposed liberalism might well have guessed that his real views were veiled under the thinnest disguise. Of course, he no longer believed in the historicity of 'the enacted allegory'. When he sent Bremond a postcard depicting an angel, he apologized for it.[18]

Lex Orandi is a brave attempt to 'save the appearance' of Catholic doctrine, in the belief that 'there can ... be no ultimate conflict between what is true for the religious life and what is true for the understanding—philosophical or historical'. However intense the historical battle might be in the short term, it was wrong of the Church to make her stand upon history. She could confidently abandon the field, knowing that the struggle for hearts and lives, for communion with God, did not take place there. Further—and this was a point he did not stress in *Lex Orandi*—he believed that the Church would make her own return upon the field of history sooner or later. Early in 1905 he responded to a shrewd critique by the Abbé Venard with the substance of a chapter that he would have added to the book 'had I any hope of making myself intelligible to my censors'.[19] In the letter to Venard he suggested that, although no individual dogmatic assertion might serve as the basis for an assertion on the field of history, taken together they might. He spoke of a 'religious reading' of history which is 'related to the truth, as a dramatist's reading of history might be', and of 'prophetic truth' which is 'analogous with poetic, artistic, dramatic truth'. Such truth does not, in an immediate sense, depend on correspondence to known facts, but rather on 'the sympathy of man's spirit with the Divine spirit immanent in man's spirit'. It operates by discernment: 'this sympathetic divination of prophecy reaches the truth of what *is* in the divine or eternal order of reality; and the truth of what *ought to be* but *is* not, or is only in process of becoming, in the order of finite reality.' Christianity, as a religion of the Incarnation, could not abandon all claim upon history. However much, in the short term, the historical critique threw Christianity on to the defensive, in the long term the doctrine provided a framework for the interpretation of history.

Tyrrell believed that the critics should be listened to, and if the Church, through misplaced fear, would not listen, the world would listen anyway. Through her fear the Church was making things worse, and the impasse between criticism and Catholicism was forcing people to a wholly unnecessary, and desperately painful, choice. They had either to remain loyal to a Catholicism which affronted their understanding but satisfied their souls, or to abandon the Church and Christianity in order to retain their mental integrity. For many of those who wrote to Tyrrell, there was no middle way, no way by which adherence to the teaching of the Church could be distinguished and distanced from fundamental belief in God. All sense of the Church as sacrament had been lost. Tyrrell strove to recover it.

This is why he wrote his *Letter to a University Professor*[20] late in 1903. It was the composite fruit of many such letters to intellectuals in difficulties, 'a medicine for extreme cases'. It was also a practical attempt to express 'the essence of Christianity' as both Harnack and Loisy had done, showing with Loisy how the fullness of Catholic doctrine could be retained, and stressing with Harnack the fundamental simplicity of Christianity. Tyrrell's strategy consisted in 'finding out what a man does believe, and building on that'. Given that a man is 'absolutely and practically sincere to whatever little measure of religious and moral truth he still holds', he believed that he is 'bound to advance to whatever fuller measure of truth may be necessary for him'. In the first place, he may advance from an unspoken and implicit faith in God to a faith that is explicit, where faith means 'a *seeing* of God, not face to face but through a glass darkly'. In the second, he may recognize the link between this and Catholic doctrine as the expression of such a vision:

The Trinity, the Creation, the Fall, the Incarnation, the Atonement, the Resurrection, Heaven and Hell, Angels and Devils, the Madonna and the Saints, all are pieces of one mosaic, all, closer determinations of one and the same presentment of the Eternal Goodness in the light of which man must shape his will and affections and actions if he is to live the life of religion, of self-adaptation to the ultimate realities.

It was in terms such as these that he described the basis of his own faith to Bremond in 1899,[21] moving from belief in God to 'Christianism', to Catholicism. At that time he made Christ 'known to us historically' the pivot of his 'Christianity'. Now the historical Christ, as depicted by the critics, seemed a much more credible figure, but hardly one on whom to found the religion of the Incarnation. The 'extreme case' for which Tyrrell's 'medicine' was developed was, of course, his own.

At this time he could see no middle way between the new and the old, between acceptance of historical method, wherever it might lead, and acceptance of church teaching and church theology, whatever the intellectual cost. 'Mediating liberalism' he felt was a sham. Anything short of revolution was capitulation to the age-old tyranny of dogma. He believed passionately that science, including historical science, and religion would be reconciled in the long run, but at the moment he could not see how. What he did see with absolute clarity was the need to resist any facile, timorous, or premature solution of the problem.

Foremost among those who worked for reconciliation without revolution was Wilfrid Ward, who in 1903 published a book of essays called *Problems and Persons*.[22] Tyrrell had never been that close to Ward, whose obedient accommodation to the Roman authorities was so unlike his own careless radicalism, but he knew him well enough through the meetings of the Synthetic Society, and had been visited by the Wards at Richmond. By 1903 he had decided that Ward—and Newman, to whose ideas Ward remained unswervingly loyal—had nothing to offer in the present crisis. He used a review of Ward's book[23] ('a long question-clearing, muddle-dissipating article'[24] to set up as sharply as possible the opposition between what he called 'scholastic' and 'liberal' theology. As he told Ward: 'In my article I have laid them side by side like two snakes eyeing one another.'[25]

Tyrrell's sharpest contrast was between the notion of revelation in the two schools. He claimed that 'Catholic theology' (for which he later wrote 'scholastic theology') believed the Church to have received 'a certain body of divine knowledge revealed supernaturally to the Apostles and delivered by them under the form of certain categories, ideas, and images to their immediate successors'. This apostolic deposit is, for the 'Catholic theologian', *semper idem*. For the 'liberal theologian' (here Tyrrell was careful to mention the names of three non-Catholics, Caird, Gardner, and Sabatier), that which is *semper idem* is not the representation of a transcendent reality, but the reality itself, known in present religious experience. For 'Catholic theology', revelation is the record of an experience, for 'liberal theology' it is the experience itself. Tyrrell contrasted these positions further by examining their notion of development. For conservatives, Christian doctrine is the growing explication of an unchanging deposit. For liberals it is the developing science of religious experience in which 'each stage of development dies in the next'. Ward attempted to follow Newman, who, in his *Essay on Development*, used the liberal notion of development without criticizing the conservative notion of the deposit. Tyrrell's article was intended to show that the two could never mix, but not yet to resolve the dilemma. He left his readers to conclude that Ward, though dressed as a 'liberal' Catholic, was really a conservative.

The article misfired badly. Few, if any, of the readers of *The Month* can have guessed that a Jesuit staff writer had not set out to pillory 'liberal theology'. Congratulations flowed in from those who assumed that, by his clear statement of the conservative position, Tyrrell was exposing the perils of liberalism and of a 'liberal' like Ward. 'Your article has given great satisfaction here,' he heard from St Beuno's. 'The Provincial, and Father Gerard and the rest are perfectly delighted with your article,' he heard from London.[26] 'The reactionaries', Tyrrell told Lilley, 'like the Babylonian dragon have swallowed my cake of pitch and fat and hair. I really feared I had exaggerated the grotesque impossibility of their position, but the letters of congratulation that pour in assure me that I have not done so at all.'[27] When Tyrrell told Ward that his apparent defence of 'Catholic theology' was only a pose, Ward was astonished; and when Gerard, the editor of *The Month*, understood the truth, he refused to take a second article explaining Tyrrell's placing of Ward among the conservatives in terms of a comparison between Newman's last University Sermon (which Tyrrell thought 'liberal theology') and his *Essay on Development* (which he thought fudged the issue, and so could be counted as 'conservative'). Tyrrell argued that neither Ward nor Newman had, in principle, departed from the conservative position. What was needed, he would go on to say in other places, was not capitulation to the liberals, but a subtler kind of theological revolution. It was not individual articles of the creed, but the very word *credo* that was at issue, and here neither Newman nor Ward offered any help at all.[28]

This incident brought to an end two relationships that were hangovers from the past. Apart from one further disagreement about Bremond's interpretation of Newman, Tyrrell's correspondence with Ward, which had never been intimate, dwindled to almost nothing; and he never wrote for *The Month* again.

The skirmish over his review of Ward's book was for Tyrrell only a minor incident in a long campaign. At this time Loisy was involved in a major battle. After Cardinal Richard's condemnation of *L'Évangile et l'Église* in January 1903, he had made a limited submission condemning and reproving 'all the errors that others have been able to deduce from my book by placing themselves, for purposes of interpretation, at a totally different viewpoint from that at which I must have placed myself, and actually did place myself, in composing it'.[29] Loisy defended himself by arguing that he had written purely as a historian to refute the historical arguments of Harnack, but that he was being judged by the theologians as though he had written a book of theology. He developed his position in a second book, *Autour d'un petit livre*, which spelt out the basic position of *L'Évangile et l'Église* in seven letters of compelling clarity. This appeared in October 1903, together with Loisy's major study of the fourth gospel, *Le Quatrième Évangile*. Within a week Tyrrell had read the copy of *Autour d'un petit livre* that Loisy had sent him, and wrote to tell him that, 'as an objectively valid defence of *L'Évangile et l'Église* it seems, in my poor judgement, absolutely convincing and un-answerable'. He also took the opportunity to encourage Loisy by telling him of the way in which his work was received among young English Jesuits: 'Only two days ago one of our ablest men, to whom your name was anathema, took your Études from my room in a spirit of hostile curiosity. Being fundamentally honest-minded the result has been a complete bouleversement of his whole attitude.'[30]

Loisy had already noted in his diary: 'The most pressing duty of the new Pope will be to put my books upon the Index.'[31] That is precisely what happened. On 16 December 1903 five of Loisy's books, *La Religion d'Israel*, *Études évangeliques*, *L'Évangile et l'Église*, *Autour d'un petit livre*, and *Le Quatrième Évangile*, were placed on the Index. So began three months of agony in which Loisy sought wretchedly to find a formula that would enable him to accept the decree, but preserve his critical integrity.[32] Merry del Val, as Secretary of State, had notified Cardinal Richard of Paris that the errors in Loisy's book concerned 'the primitive revelation, the authority of the facts and teaching of the gospels, the divinity and perfect knowledge of Christ, the resurrection, the divine institution of the Church, and the sacraments'.[33] By the end of the year the condemnation was public knowledge. Tyrrell wrote immediately, calling it 'blindly suicidal' on the part of the Roman authorities. As he told Loisy a year earlier: '*Eppur si muove*; Facts are stronger than Cardinals; nor will the whole Curia be able to prevent the tide of history coming in and sweeping down all barriers that are of sand instead of rock.'[34] He encouraged him in his one consistent defence: 'It seems to me that you must hold fast to your distinction between the religious and the scientific aspects and approaches of the same questions, allowing the Church's jurisdiction over the former; firmly denying it over the latter.'[35]

This Loisy did, sending a guarded statement of submission to Merry del Val on 11 January 1904. When he made it plain that his submission was 'purely disciplinary in character', and that he did not intend 'either to abandon or to retract the opinions which I have uttered in my capacity of historian and of critical exegete',[36] he cannot seriously have expected Rome to be satisfied. Merry del Val responded, through Cardinal Richard, with strong words and thinly veiled threats of excommunication. Further letters brought no change in the situation on either side. In this extremity Loisy appealed directly to the Pope:

Most Holy Father:
I well know Your Holiness's goodness of heart, and it is to your heart that I now address myself.
I wish to live and die in the communion of the Catholic Church. I do not wish to contribute to the ruin of the faith in my country.
It is beyond my power to destroy in myself the result of my labours.
So far as in me lies, I submit myself to the judgement brought against my writings by the Congregation of the Holy Office.
To give evidence of my good faith, and for the pacification of spirits, I am prepared to abandon my teaching in Paris, and at the same time to suspend my scientific publications now under way.[37]

On 12 March Cardinal Richard summoned Loisy to hear the Pope's answer. The Pope declared that Loisy's letter, addressed to the heart, did not come from the heart, as it did not contain the required act of submission. He should 'burn what he once adored, and adore what he once burned'.[38] Loisy's reaction is best described in his own words:

When the opening words greeted my ears, something gave way within me. The head of that Church to which I had devoted my life, for which I had so abundantly laboured for thirty years past, which I had loved and could not help loving still, outside of which I had neither ambition nor hope of any kind, when I had responded to absurd demands by offering a supreme sacrifice, could find nothing else to say to me than the harsh words: 'That letter, addressed to my heart, was not written from the heart.'[39]

That evening Loisy wrote one more brief note of submission to Cardinal Richard: 'Monsignor, I declare to Your Eminence that, out of a spirit of obedience to the Holy See, I condemn the errors which the Congregation of the Holy Office has condemned in my writings.'[40] He later commented: 'I have never forgiven myself for this absurd and seemingly dishonest declaration.'[41] Loisy's 'submission' was greeted with silence.

Throughout the crisis Loisy stayed closely in touch with von Hügel, who kept Tyrrell informed of developments. Both were distracted—Tyrrell with work on his 'Wilfrid Ward review' and its sequel; von Hügel with work on his book—but both responded by writing articles about Loisy's work. Tyrrell had a piece published in *The Pilot* in which he argued that the condemnation of Loisy would rebound against the Church just as that of Galileo had done, and that the quarrel was not 'between criticism and authority but between criticism and a certain theological *theory* of authority'.[42] His two main concerns now were the exposure of 'the theological conspiracy', and the search for a new theological theory of authority which would replace that of the 'Catholic theologians' without collapsing into the morass of Sabatier's liberalism. A signed article by von Hügel followed a week later.[43] He also wrote to *The Pilot* when an erroneous report gave the impression that Loisy had submitted totally. 'No act of submission', wrote von Hügel, 'was made by him to the Archbishop; and the act which he has now made in Rome will, no doubt, have been thoroughly respectful and sincere, and cannot therefore have been without some reasonable and necessary reservation in the matter of his historian's conscience and method.'[44] After Merry del Val's violent response to Loisy's qualified submission, von Hügel wrote to him directly, warning of the harm that would be done in English intellectual circles if Loisy were condemned outright.[45] At the end of January he told Tyrrell that he was 'on the verge of breaking down',[46] but that he was hard at work on a letter to *The Times* in answer to one setting out the Roman case against Loisy. Using letters from Loisy to von Hügel which the Baron had sent on to him, Tyrrell prepared a summary of the case for the defence. Von Hügel's letter, signed 'Romanus', appeared in early March. It reviewed with great power the critical evidence for the positions Loisy had taken on controversial questions of New Testament interpretation, and concluded with a statement of faith in 'that uniquely great cause, sincere Science linked hand in hand with the sincerest Faith'.[47] 'This way our group has taken to writing in the papers, is, of course,' wrote von Hügel, 'an indication of how largely, at this turn of the long road at least, we have been defeated.'[48]

In the bleak months of February and March 1904 Bremond was dismissed from the Jesuits; Colley, the English Provincial, suddenly died; and Tyrrell sent the General the first letter to broach the question of his own departure from the Society.[49] As he waited for the axe to fall on Loisy, he wrote to von Hügel:

I do wish some committee of three *unimpeded* laymen would undertake to receive protests against the condemnation *in strict secrecy*, and then publish them in classified form from time to time e.g. 25 bishops; 250 university professors; 339 canons; 10,000 priests; 1½ Jesuits etc. They would have to take an oath before a notary as to the genuineness of the cases; in short a sort of 'Apostleship of Protest' on the lines of the 'Apostleship of Prayer'.[50]

Now that the atmosphere was heavy with thunder, Tyrrell swung between elation and despair. At one moment he told Waller: 'I am really *wanted* at present, which one so seldom feels in one's work. All my friends are in trouble; the bishops are furiously raging together and the Cardinals are imagining a vain thing. Further, I hear my own name is on the black list—as well it deserves to be.'[51] A month later, in a whimsical letter to Florence Bishop, with whom he maintained a light-hearted friendship from his days in London, he quoted what he called his 'well-known oad':

> Tho' povertee my porshun be
>   And tho' I walk in tatters,
> Exposed and bare to wintry air
>   I know that nothing matters.
>
> When in disgrace I hide my face
>   And Fame no longer flatters,
> My eyes I'll wipe and smoke my pipe,
>   And think that nothing matters.
>
> And when with pain that racks my brain
>   I'm mad as twenty hatters,
> I'll just pretend it suits my end
>   And say that nothing matters.
>
> And if the wife who plagues my life
>   For ever nags and chatters,

> When at my Club or in my pub
> I feel that nothing matters.
>
> When problems deep do murder sleep
> And doubt my portal batters,
> I say, oh well, just go to H___,
> For nothing really matters.
> Etc., etc.[52]

He had to tell himself that nothing mattered, because it all mattered so very much.

It mattered very much to Tyrrell that he might at any moment be challenged to disown the views of 'Engels' or 'Bourdon', and that when he refused, like Loisy, he would face excommunication. In May 1904 he wrote a paper entitled 'Beati Excommunicati' which discussed the meaning of excommunication for those Catholics like himself who felt themselves driven to a position that set them at odds with the institutional Church. 'However spiritually harmless or even helpful . . . excommunication may be,' he wrote,

> yet is still retains enough of the bitterness of the cross to make it in many ways terrible to human frailty and to cause weaker souls sometimes to shrink from the stern duty of perfect sincerity and candour. The parting with friends, the breaking up of old associations, the bewilderment of new conditions, the forfeiture of confidence, the perplexity of the simple, the triumph of detractors, the slanders of the offended, the frustration of a career, and in many cases poverty and temporal embarrassment and a painful struggle for existence—some or all of these trials are the price that must be paid for the peace of a good conscience.[53]

This was the practical cost of exclusion from the sacraments, but exclusion from the sacraments need not mean exclusion from the communion of the saints, especially the *beati excommunicati*. For those who no longer saw the Church as 'a sharp-edged sphere of light walled round with abrupt and impenetrable darkness but rather as a centre or focus from which the light of religion spread over all ages and nations shades away indefinitely and is mingled in varying degrees with that darkness which can never wholly conquer it', there cannot ultimately be 'complete, inward, spiritual excommunication'. The piece is dated 18 May 1904, twenty-five years from the day of Tyrrell's reception into the Catholic Church.

For Tyrrell the price of a good conscience was plain-spokenness with the General. His February letter, written *ad petendum consilium* ('to seek advice'), was received politely but firmly, and answered in Martin's own hand. In reply to that, Tyrrell put his finger on the trouble-spot: 'The real question concerns the actual spirit and principles now governing the corporate action of the Society on the minds and consciences and characters of those who are brought within the sphere of her influence.'[54] Here there could never be agreement between him and the authorities. Nevertheless, he agreed to reconsider the question of his relations with the Society.

Just at this delicate stage in his negotiations with the General, the *Giornale d'Italia* carried a report that a Jesuit was about to leave the Society, and in England Tyrrell's name was linked with the rumour. Tyrrell immediately suspected the General as the source of the leak, and wrote a letter of accusation.[55] The General promptly replied denying the allegation, and pointing out that the *Giornale* had named Bremond a few days later.[56] Matters might have rested at this impasse had not Tyrrell discovered that his authorship of *Religion as a Factor of Life* was now known in Rome.[57] The only thing protecting him from the Index was Bourne's imprimatur on *Lex Orandi*, for the Cardinal had thereby unwittingly given his approval to the work of 'Dr Engels'.

Tyrrell now wrote a letter to the General that explains the later attempt by the authorities—an attempt which antagonized Tyrrell deeply—to censor his private correspondence. Tyrrell told the General:

> Some two years ago I had a lengthy correspondence with an agnostic who was enquiring about Catholicism. The substance of the correspondence I showed to another agnostic, or at least non-Catholic, friend now at Cambridge University in an official position. He was anxious that it should be published for the sake of others of his own sort, saying that it opened a possible ground of discussion. This was, of course, out of the question for every reason. Later, on the clear understanding that it should fall into no hands but theirs who were educationally fit to criticise it, I allowed him to arrange and print the correspondence for strictly private use among those whom it could not hurt; with the express stipulation that I should be referred to in every case of donation; also that it should be copyrighted to protect it from any risk of unauthorised publication. It bore the title: *Religion as a Factor of Life*; by Dr Ernest Engels.[58]

Tyrrell went on to acknowledge that 'Dr Engels' brochure' had 'fallen into mischievous hands'. Since it was Tyrrell who had approached Waller (his Cambridge friend) about publication in the first place, his letter is, to say the least, a bending of the truth. After reading it one understands the attempt at a ban on his 'epistolary correspondence'.

Shortly after this, when the General wrote a letter to Sykes, the new English Provincial, he urged him to show himself 'severe and inflexible', and briefly reviewed past problems with Tyrrell, Thurston, Lucas, Joseph Rickaby, John Rickaby, Rigby, and others. In speaking of the row over 'A Perverted Devotion', Martin referred to the letter in which he had ordered Tyrrell to be prohibited from giving the Spiritual Exercises to 'Ours' or to others.[59] Here is further evidence of the ban that Tyrrell suspected, Gerard could not bring himself to impose, and Colley denied.

The following month Tyrrell set about writing a lengthy letter to the General.[60] First he contrasted the spirit of the Society as he thought it to be when he joined it (one of 'elasticity and accommodation') with that of the Society as he found it ('reaction and intransigence'). Then, in answering the points put to him the previous February, he developed a searing critique of 'Jesuitism', the whole Jesuit system, tracing it back to a distorted and absolute notion of authority that had departed totally from the open spirit of Ignatius. Tyrrell's most savage words were reserved for the training of Jesuits, which protected their young men as much as possible from the moral and intellectual struggles that go with life in the world:

> As far as your system goes it can only result in crippling the mind and character. After three years of exclusively ascetical training, after all your annual retreats and semestral triduos, after all your daily meditations and examinations of conscience and your periodical spiritual directions, manifestations, exhortations, your multiplied Masses, Confessions, Communions, what have you to show as an average in the way of character and of independent morality? How far can you or do you *trust* your men? Dare you take away the props and splints and crutches with which you have held them in position for so long, and not feel certain that they would tumble to pieces for lack of those protections, because your system ignores the fundamental law of life; because it demands instruments and not men; blindly passive and not intelligently active obedience; the destruction not the development of personality and character?[60]

Tyrrell felt that the average Jesuit remained 'a schoolboy all his life'. He called the Society 'a man-trap, a dangerous snare set for young souls in the early paths of life, resulting in the ruin of their happiness and spiritual health'. No less savage were his words about the lot of the lay brothers, kept in 'holy ignorance', forced to meditate for a solid hour and two more quarter-hours each day, without the education or training to benefit from the dreary silence. All in all, Tyrrell set out to show 'why, for me, subjectively, the Society has ceased to exist; and to justify my assertion that she is travelling against the sun and not with it, as I had believed, and that therefore my contract with her is null and void'. The letter was finished on 26 June 1904, and lay waiting for fourteen months until the day that it was needed, 2 September 1905.

Throughout this time, in which he had in some sense already parted from the Jesuits, and might well have been excommunicated, Tyrrell hardly moved from Richmond. When von Hügel's wife was ill, the Baron asked if his friend would come to him in Scotland. He later suggested a trip to London so that they could have some good talks about the general situation. When Archbishop Mignot was to visit England for ten days, von Hügel very much wanted Tyrrell to come south and meet him. All these requests were firmly refused. Technically, Tyrrell would have needed the permission of Gerard, the editor of The Month, for which he was still nominally a staff writer, but since the Wilfrid Ward review, Gerard had virtually cut him. More importantly, Tyrrell loathed London, and would not now stay at Farm Street at any price. The longer he was away, the more violent and unreasonable became his language about London and London Jesuits. He did not want to be prised from the Dales, from his books and his dark thoughts. Already he had distanced himself as far as possible from former ties. If he would not go to friends, they must come to him.

This they did, in great numbers. Maude Petre was living in lodgings with her two nephews, Arthur and Billy Clutton, while their parents were in China. There was a constant flow of her friends from Farm Street, including Florence Bishop. The Baron came each summer for about three weeks. The Wards visited in 1903. Bremond came three times, staying about a month in the early summer of 1904. W. J. Williams came with his sister Dora, and 'dumped' the manuscript of his book on Pascal, Newman, and Loisy on Tyrrell's desk for comment. In August 1904 Tyrrell wrote to Bremond: 'Baron here; and Gertrud; and Abbé Guillaume of Bourges; all the Petres in existence (150) all the Cluttons (150); L. Thompson; Miss Gossage —et alibi aliorum; and many of ours. Hence I am sick and silent.'[61]

Relations with Maude Petre, who was still passionately attached to him, were far from easy. She was seriously depressed and troubled with obsessive thoughts about death. When she and Tyrrell read together in the evenings, she was too passive, too serious, she did not stimulate. He told Bremond in January that he was 'a little wearied with the Vescovina—very kind and good, but certainly childish-minded; and, as you say, not too discreet or secretive'.[62] He prevailed on her to take a holiday in Italy, where she met Bremond, newly dismissed from the Jesuits, with a little group of ladies, including Florence Duff Baker. She was distressed and noted in her diary: 'I am *very* sad. I can see he is enslaved by Mrs D. B. and is not free in mind or will to follow the course that may seem best to him . . . I cannot but feel, as I have indeed felt for a long time, that I am not quite the same to him since this other influence came in.'[63] She left Bremond the next day. Although she had given him £50 when he left the Society, there had been an occasion when she thought she had not paid her share of expenses: 'Ne craignez pas,' Bremond had said, 'C'est toujours vous qui perdrez.' In her diary she added: 'This is what I want, and he knows it.'[64]

After Bremond returned from Italy he stayed with the Baron for a week, working on the translation into French of an article von Hügel had written in response to a critique of Loisy by Blondel.[65] He then went on to Richmond, where Tyrrell compared himself and his friend to 'the two disheartened travellers to Emmaus, walking, and sadly talking of all these things which have happened: "*sperabamus*".'[66] They had indeed hoped, particularly in Loisy. In a letter written from Richmond, Bremond called him 'a true Noah', of whose ark the Church would in time be thankful.[67] He was dipping into works of biblical criticism and reading the *Tracts for the Times*. Out of this, he and Tyrrell began to plan a series of 'New Tracts for New Times'. Tyrrell described their aim as 'a sort of Tractarianism *à rebours* for the Protestantising of Romanism'.[68] They ran into problems because the group of Roman writers they could call upon was too small, so they turned to Lilley, with his contacts in Anglican liberalism. Tyrrell's first effort in this line was entitled 'A Plea for Candour'.

At the end of August Maude Petre went to London for a retreat. In her absence Tyrrell decided that she should leave Richmond permanently. There had been too much gossip. In her diary Maude Petre attributed the calamity to Miss Gossage and Miss Thompson, 'and perhaps others'. The prime mover was, in fact, her relation by marriage Kitty Clutton, whose hatred of Maude Petre is all too evident in later letters. In a letter to Bremond Tyrrell attributed the situation to 'Cluttonian malice reaching hence to London'. Kitty Clutton, who had visited Richmond, was spreading the rumour that Maude Petre was 'overtly and palpably in love' with him, and 'practically besieging' him in his 'unprotected solitude'. 'In a word,' he went on, 'the hypothesis of a Platonic relationship had broken down; and her intention of settling here after the departure of the children was interpreted as a proof . . . It was absolutely imperative to cut slander's throat as promptly and effectively as possible.' For all his hardness towards Maude Petre, he had come to depend upon her friendship a very great deal:

I never felt anything more deeply than the pain of telling her; and still more, of insisting on my decision which is even still contrary to her own conviction of what is right and prudent; nor did I ever realise before how much I really cared for her and depended on her companionship and sympathy . . . I am almost afraid the separation will kill her. For me it will [be] almost intolerable; but I have less passionate need of happiness, more patience of drab monotony than she.[69]

Maude Petre's departure was followed by days of sickness and depression. A few fragments of a diary written by Tyrrell survive from this time:

October 6th.—Storm all night and till about noon, but clear blue through rolling cloud masses. Sick. Two letters; tried to read but gave up at about 11 p.m. Half alive; tried to read and even to write a little. Finished the minor prophets (R. version) to-day . . .
October 8th.—Nausea all day; no Mass, no meals. Animation enough just for office and for *Brand*, which I got through . . .
October 9th—Nausea still. *Heard* Mass at 8, tried breakfast in vain; tried to write sermon after but had to give up . . . Managed office and visit . . . Went to dinner in despair from sheer starvation . . .
October 10th.—Returning vitality, etc . . .
October 11th.—Normal . . .[70]

At last he decided to consult a doctor. On 21 October he had 'an hour of catechising, weighing, testing, inspection . . . *Verdict*—sound as a bell everywhere, even stomach and liver; but three stone under due weight; *migraine* and nerve-storm resulting from over-fatigue and under-nutrition.'[71] He was ordered to change his diet to fattening foods, cutting out tea, alcohol, and 'baccy', and his health began to improve.

Some of the visitors at this time were particularly welcome. There was his old friend Edward Lawless ('rightly so called'), and Norah Shelley, who, lacking Maude Petre's intensity, became the kind of friend that she could never be. After Tyrrell's death, she wrote: 'We were such "chums" . . . ; he used to tell me he was always *himself* with me—never had the feeling he was playing a part as happens so often even involuntarily when one is with one's friends. That he could say anything he liked; and he so loved the real rest it gave him.'[72] Clearly, she did not relate to him as Jesuit, or priest, or theologian, or thinker, but as a friend. From the time he went to Richmond he corresponded both with her and with her mother. She was probably with him for Christmas 1904, and he wrote to her mother: 'Aren't you afraid to trust your giddy daughter down here all alone? I confess I don't like being left at her mercy unprotected. For my sake, if not for her own, you ought to be more careful. You know how she used to pursue me over the hills and dales and lay traps for me like Kathleen and St Kevin.'[73] One thing they shared was the same sense of humour.

Friends like this could give respite for a time, but it was a time of prolonged agony and anger. He told Maude Petre:

I have the horrors on me, and feel tangled in the arms of some marine polypus or giant octopus. The Church sits on my soul like a night-mare, and the oppression is maddening . . . I do not wonder that to Savanarola and the medieval mystics Rome seemed anti-Christ. The misery is that she is both Christ and anti-Christ; wheat and tares; a double-faced Janus looking heavenwards and hellwards . . . The grotesque insincerity of my position as a Jesuit appals me at times. During Mass this morning I was planning advertisements: 'A Roman Catholic Priest, retiring from the exercise of his ministry for reasons of conscience, desires temporary occupation, literary, secretarial, or even tutorial, which will leave him leisure for writing. Country much preferred. Address XYZ, office of *The Guardian*.' And then something says: No, wait till you are driven. Initiate nothing. Yet if an opening offered I think my prudence would prove frail against the temptation.[74]

Work was still a narcotic, and, hardly surprisingly, Tyrrell's thoughts turned on the problem of authority.

Early in the year he read with immense enthusiasm Sabatier's *The Religions of Authority and The Religion of the Spirit*. This had left him wondering yet again where their positions differed, if they differed at all. He told Lilley that the 'religion of the spirit' does need 'an external pedagogic religion as its protection; that their relation should be somewhat that of the earliest Church in the bosom of Judaism'. He now saw the authority of the Church's doctrinal system as the same kind of authority that Sabatier claimed for the Bible: 'a certain moral, *inwardly binding* authority—consistent with perfect intellectual sincerity and freedom'.[75] His thoughts were further clarified when he read Andrew White's account of the *History of the Warfare of Science with Theology*, showing how, again and again, scientific advance had been opposed by the theologians, who were then forced, bit by bit, into retreat.

In the first fortnight of October Tyrrell developed a review of White's book into an important essay on 'The Rights and Limits of Theology'.[76] He argued strongly that the original expression of Christian revelation 'was altogether apocalyptic, prophetic, visionary in character', and so any later dogmatic expression will also be in 'prophetic' language. It is quite wrong to treat revelation as 'a miraculously communicated science'. The purpose of the creed is practical: to promote religious life rather than to inform curious minds. However, theologians in particular have continually failed to appreciate this fundamental point. White showed how 'the very conception of a divinely revealed doctrinal system, ramifying out into the field of knowledge, held the Christian intelligence for centuries captive to the Christian conscience'. Once the difference between the 'prophetic' and the 'scientific' functions of language is clearly understood, there need no longer be any confusion between the 'prophetic' expression of revelation in dogma and the 'scientific' language of theology. Each can be left to develop in its own way. As far as 'revelation' is concerned, there will be a certain priority for the language in which it is first expressed, as being closest to the event, but expression cannot stand still, and other ways of expressing revelatory experience will grow up. On the other hand, the language of theology, which seeks to place Christian truth in the universe of knowledge, must draw upon the changing language and concepts of 'science' in its broadest sense. As these change, it too will develop. Some kind of control is exercised over development by the interdependence of revelation and theology: 'A revelation that ignores the check of theology, that speaks in a dead language, that uses an obsolete and unintelligible thought-system; a theology that ignores the check of revelation, the continual progressive self-manifestation of God in the religious life of humanity . . . both these are alike fruitless.'[77] Between the two there will always be tension, due to 'the shock and clash of their interests in the soul of man'. At that stage in the life of the Church it is not the rights, but the *limits*, of theology that need defining. This is best done by curbing its inflated claims, which come about through the confusion of theology with revelation. Tyrrell had more work to do on revelation, but he professed himself satisfied with the article. 'That, with a revision of Bourdon,' he told the Baron, 'ought about to complete my attempt at a synthesis. I feel somehow that I have got my idea out at last.'[78] In so doing, he had completed his major intellectual task at Richmond. His other task was, one way or another, to sort out his relations with the Jesuits.

Obviously, he would leave. It was remarkable that he had held on for so long. The question was when he would go. In November 1904 he was discovered to be the author of the apparently conservative 'S. T. L.' articles in the *Weekly Register* apropos of the joint pastoral letter. Nothing more came of this. There was a visit from Sykes 'in pacific mood', and from Thurston 'to open *pourparlers*'. Exhausted by continual migraines, Tyrrell dreamt of ending the uncertainty: 'I have now resolved on a slow and deliberate ecclesiastical suicide,' he told Bremond, 'i.e. I will work out my whole synthesis and publish it under my name without censorship; and bide the consequences. Else I shall be stifled morally. I must purge my life of all pretence and duplicity.'[79]

Tyrrell's 'apostleship of protest' was developing apace. It was at one and the same time a protest against 'Jesuitism', against 'the dogmatic fallacy', against authoritarianism, against all the suffering, distortion, and inhumanity by which he felt himself surrounded. In letters to Dora Williams he discussed the 'cat-theory' of the universe:

The mixture of good and evil, kindness and cruelty, in the world (prescinding from the human soul) is far better explained by an all-governing Cat than by Paley's 'good man in the skies'; for puss allows the mouse little runs and counterfeit liberties and escapes; and smiles at his gambols and dandles him lovingly in velvet paws, but all with a view to a final grab and crunch. It is easier to suppose that an evil agency would do good for evil ends than that a good agency would do evil for good ends—so that, if we leave inward human goodness out of account, as the old apologists so often did, the argument from design makes for the Cat-theory.[80]

When life was bleak it became all too easy to take a tragic view of Christianity as one more futile attempt to escape from the 'Cat', 'the ruthless "wheel of things"': 'Give me the faith of the mouse', wrote

Tyrrell, 'who dies squeaking out: "O lovely Pussy! O Pussy, my love! What a lovely Pussy you are, you are; what a lovely Pussy you are!"[81] In dark days he likened Jesus to the mouse. Disgusted by 'the parochialism of Christianity . . . its ridiculous little world-scheme and its fussy little god, and above all its deplorable history', he found himself driven back in a new sense to the lonely figure of Jesus, to 'the religion of Jesus and away from that *about* Jesus'.[82] In February 1905, immersed in Schopenhauer, he wrote to Bremond: 'It becomes harder and harder to say: *Pater Noster*, as the darkness deepens. Was the Kindly Light a Will o' the Wisp after all?'[83] A month later he said he had 'arrived at Flat-Land, at the end of all things, at *Vanitas Vanitatum* and Nothingmatterdamn'.[84]

Tyrrell was also pursuing the 'apostleship of protest' in another sense. When he and Bremond planned the 'New Tracts for New Times', they intended 'a restatement of Catholicism in relation to criticism', as 'Bourdon' had attempted in *The Church and the Future*. Realizing that they could not rally enough Catholic support, they had widened the scheme to include Lilley and his liberal Anglican friends, such as Inge and Henson. Before the condemnation of Loisy, Don Brizio Casciola, an old friend of von Hügel, had proposed something similar, and in March 1905 Tyrrell wanted to go back to a plan for 'a sort of "Synthetic Society" without any meetings'.[85] Members would circulate brief tracts or letters, signed only with a *nom de plume*. There would be no organization for Rome to break, but the tracts would be made available to the public. It was a good scheme, but the interests of those who might have contributed to it were too diverse. Von Hügel wanted an international, polyglot venture. Lilley's Anglican friends were not all sufficiently interested in the Catholic dimension. In the end the plan came to nothing.

Tyrrell had also been planning with Maude Petre for his departure from the Society. She was near to breaking under the strain of separation and uncertainty, and pinned her hopes on a plan to renew the former life of Richmond in the tranquillity of Assisi. To Tyrrell it offered 'all the scandal of an elopement without the fun',[86] but for once Maude Petre's wishes prevailed. Tyrrell repeated to Bremond her plea for 'the Italian scheme', which she called 'a prospect literally of *life*, as opposed to the state of inanition to which continual uncertainty and disappointments have reduced me'. She went on: 'For some time I have felt life simply ebbing away from me . . . and the continual strain [to] conceal one's weariness and depression has been more than anyone can know—I tell you all this because I want you to know how much it all means to me; that it would save me, even more than you.' 'Could any *man*, not to say an impulsive Paddy,' Tyrrell asked Bremond, 'do less than [act] at once to end her suspense?'[87] He wrote immediately to the Provincial and then to the General* asking for release. When the General replied that an approach to the Sacred Congregation of Bishops and Regulars would be necessary if Tyrrell were to avoid a suspension from which he might be restored only by the Pope, Tyrrell readily supplied the material that the General needed to make his case: on 2 September 1905 he sent the letter he had written more than a year before.

NOTES

1. C. Falconi, *The Popes in the Twentieth Century* (London, 1967), p. 19.
2. *Encyclical Letter of our Holy Father Pius X on his Accession to the Chair of St Peter* (London, 1903), p. 5.
3. Ibid., p. 11.
4. Falconi, *The Popes*, pp. 42 ff.
5. Martin to Colley, 13 Mar. 1901 (ARSJ, *RPA*, v).
6. Ibid.
7. Martin to Colley, 1 Feb. 1902.
8. Martin to Colley, 25 Aug. 1902.
9. Martin to Colley, 13 Mar. 1901.
10. Martin to Colley, 28 Mar. 1903.
11. Martin to Colley, 30 Sept., 18 Oct. 1903.
12. Tyrrell to Bremond, 20 Aug. 1903 (BN, Fonds Bremond).
13. Tyrrell to Martin, 8 Feb. 1904 (ARSJ, ANGL. 1021, II.1; *AL2*, pp. 228 –30).
14. Tyrrell to Martin, dated 11 June 1904, sent 2 Sept. 1905 (see *AL2*, pp. 458–99).
15. Tyrrell to von Hügel, 8 Apr. 1903 (BL, Petre Papers).
16. *Lex Orandi: Or Prayer and Creed* (London, 1903). Quotations are from pp. 207 ('confusion between . . .'); xxvi ('universally and . . .'); 177 ('That God reveals . . .'); 167 ('there can . . . be').
17. Tyrrell to von Hügel, 6 Feb. 1904, referring to chap. 23.
18. Tyrrell to Bremond, 1 Feb. 1903.
19. Tyrrell to Venard, 15 Jan. 1905 (see N. Sagovsky, *Between Two Worlds* (Cambridge, 1983), p. 149).
20. Printed anonymously in 1903–4; then published as G. Tyrrell, *A Much-Abused Letter* (London, 1906). Quotations are from pp. 7

('a medicine for . . .'); 28 ('finding out . . .'); ibid. ('absolutely and practically . . .'); 69 ('a *seeing* of God . . .'); 78–9 ('The Trinity . . .').

21. Tyrrell to Bremond, 20 July 1899.
22. W. Ward, *Problems and Persons* (London, 1903).
23. 'Semper Eadem', *The Month*, 103 (Jan. 1904), pp. 1–17; repr. as 'Semper Eadem I', in *TSC*, pp. 106–32.
24. Tyrrell to von Hügel, 5 Dec. 1903.
25. Tyrrell to Ward, 11 Dec. 1903 (*AL2*, p. 216).
26. Tyrrell to Ward, 4 Jan. 1904 (SAUL, Ward Papers).
27. Tyrrell to Lilley, 4 Jan. 1904 (SAUL, Lilley Papers).
28. Tyrrell to von Hügel, 19 Feb. 1905.
29. A. F. Loisy, *Mémoires pour servir à l'histoire religieuse de notre temps.* 3 vols. (Paris, 1930–1), ii, p. 207 (translation adapted from *My Duel with the Vatican* (New York, 1924; trans. of *Choses passées* (Paris, 1918), p. 232).
30. Tyrrell to Loisy, 12 Oct. 1903 (BN, Fonds Loisy).
31. Loisy, *Mémoires*, ii, p. 259.
32. Ibid., pp. 299 ff.
33. Ibid.
34. Tyrrell to Loisy, 27 Jan. 1903.
35. Tyrrell to Loisy, 27 Jan. 1904.
36. Loisy, *Mémoires*, ii, p. 313.
37. Ibid., p. 351.
38. Ibid., pp. 360–1.
39. Ibid., pp. 362–3.
40. Ibid., p. 367.
41. Ibid., p. 369.
42. 'L'Affaire Loisy', *The Pilot*, 9 (2 Jan. 1904), pp. 10–11, signed 'From a Correspondent'; Tyrrell to von Hügel, 17 Dec. 1903.
43. 'The Case of the Abbé Loisy', *The Pilot*, 9 (9 Jan. 1904), pp. 30–1.
44. *The Pilot*, 9 (23 Jan. 1904), p. 94.
45. Loisy, *Mémoires*, ii, p. 324.
46. Von Hügel to Tyrrell, 28 Jan. 1904 (BL, Petre Papers).
47. *The Times*, 2 Mar. 1904.
48. Von Hügel to Tyrrell, 23 Mar. 1904.
49. Tyrrell to Martin, 8 Feb. 1904.
50. Tyrrell to von Hügel, 12 Feb. 1904.
51. Tyrrell to Waller, 8 Feb. 1904 (BL, Waller Papers).
52. Tyrrell to Florence Bishop, 7 Mar. 1904 (*GTL*, p. 166).
53. 'Beati Excommunicati' (BL, Add. MS 52369).
54. Tyrrell to Martin, 22 Feb. 1904 (*AL2*, p. 233).
55. Tyrrell to Martin, 9 Apr. 1904.
56. Martin to Tyrrell, 24 Apr. 1904 (ARSJ, ANGL. 1021, II.5).

57. In fact, it had been known from Aug. 1903 (Martin to Colley, 30 Aug. 1903).
58. Tyrrell to Martin, 30 Apr. 1904.
59. Martin to Sykes, 21 May 1904 (ARSJ, *RPA*, v).
60. *AL*2, pp. 487–8.
61. Tyrrell to Bremond, 19 Aug. 1904.
62. Tyrrell to Bremond, 3 Jan. 1904.
63. Maude Petre diaries, 24 Mar. 1904 (BL, Add. MS 52373).
64. Ibid., 25 Mar. 1904.
65. Blondel's *Histoire et dogme* appeared in 3 parts in *La Quinzaine* (16 Jan., 1 and 16 Feb. 1904.); trans. by A. Dru and I. Trethowan in M. Blondel, *The Letter on Apologetics and History and Dogma* (London, 1964). Von Hügel's response, 'Du Christ éternel et de nos christologies successives', appeared in *La Quinzaine*, 58 (1 June 1904), pp. 285–312.
66. Tyrrell to Lilley, 20 May 1904.
67. Bremond to Blondel, in A. Blanchet, *Henri Bremond 1865–1904* (Paris, 1975), p. 184.
68. Tyrrell to Lilley, 25 Mar. 1905.
69. Tyrrell to Bremond, 18 Sept. 1904.
70. *AL*2, pp. 18–19.
71. Ibid.
72. Norah Shelley to Lilley, 16 July 1909 (SAUL, MS 30754).
73. Tyrrell to R. M. Shelley, 25 Dec. 1904 (*GTL*, p. 186).
74. Tyrrell to Maude Petre, 5 Nov. 1904 (*GTL*, p. 109).
75. Tyrrell to Lilley, 7 Mar. 1904.
76. 'The Rights and Limits of Theology', *Quarterly Review*, 203 (Oct. 1905), pp. 461–91, review of A. White, *A History of the Warfare of Science with Theology in Christendom* (New York, 1903), repr., with alterations, in *TSC*, pp. 200–41.
77. Ibid., pp. 488–9.
78. Tyrrell to von Hügel, 13 Oct. 1904.
79. Tyrrell to Bremond, 27 Dec. 1904.
80. Tyrrell to Dora Williams, 12 Jan. 1905 (*GTL*, pp. 285–6).
81. Tyrrell to Dora Williams, 6 Mar. 1905 (*GTL*, p. 289).
82. Tyrrell to Maude Petre, 1 Jan. 1905 (*GTL*, p. 25).
83. Tyrrell to Bremond, 5 Feb. 1905.
84. Tyrrell to Bremond, 15 Mar. 1905.
85. Tyrrell to Lilley, 25 Mar. 1905.
86. Tyrrell to Bremond, 2 Aug. 1905.
87. Tyrrell to Bremond, 22 Aug. 1905.

13

The 'Conservative Left'

WITHIN three days of sending the fateful letter to the General, Tyrrell would gladly have changed his mind. After years of waiting, the final step had been taken on the spur of the moment, in answer to Maude Petre's *cri de cœur*; or so he afterwards claimed when he was filled with hesitations and regrets. Three days after pleading for 'life' with him, she wrote again: 'You shall not through me have the old jibe of "*Cherchez la femme*" cast at you . . . I can be happy about you whether you stay in the Society or whether you leave.' Tyrrell was furious, as 'it was only for her sake that I had determined to cut my cables at once'.[1] He flatly turned down any idea of living with her in Assisi as likely to leave him '*tête à tête* in a little Umbrian village away from all my friends and from all life, in a most ridiculous, uncomfortable and scandalous position'. Aix, with Bremond, was a possibility. London, which he loathed, was the only place where he and Maude Petre could live close to one another without giving rise to comment. Wretchedly, he counted the cost:

Of course, it is a vile melancholy climate; it is very expensive for one lodging alone; besides which, if alone, I shall certainly contract syphilis in a week. Still I would be near my other girls; near the Baron; near life of a sort; near libraries; near Lilley and Co; near Anglican Churches; and M. D. P. could come once a week and send my clothes to the wash. But Oh! how I *hate* the place; and long for the country; and for a dog and a decent climate; and the refinement and distinction of old-world feudal surroundings! So I spend my days like a caged canary hopping from the Aix-perch to the London-perch and back again *sine fine*![2]

Meanwhile, the wheels were slowly turning in the Jesuit Curia.

When the General first wrote back agreeing to put Tyrrell's case to the Sacred Congregation of Bishops and Regulars, he warned him that the Congregation was in its summer recess, and also that he thought Tyrrell's reasons for wanting to leave the Society inadequate.[3] Tyrrell, who was in a very suspicious mood, took this to mean that he would deliberately give a lame account of his case, pleading that he was merely a liberal Catholic out of tune with the way things were done, and, when the request was refused, provoking him into taking precipitate action and damning himself. This is why he sent his long letter to Rome, and asked for it to be translated and presented to the Congregation.[4] This Martin duly acknowledged, telling Tyrrell that these moves were already in hand.[5]

Late in September Martin approached Cardinal Ferrata, Prefect of the Sacred Congregation, sending him excerpts from Tyrrell's letters, and offering to send the whole text if Ferrata wanted to see it. He pointed out that Tyrrell was a skilled trouble-maker who, with or without permission, was likely to leave the Society and lead a liberal faction. On balance he thought it better if he were granted secularization (that is, allowed to become a secular priest), provided that an *episcopus benevolus*, a bishop who would take him into his diocese, could be found.[6] Ferrata told Martin that Tyrrell should present his own case to the Sacred Congregation, but that it could be done for him in Rome.[7] Martin simply told Tyrrell to present the petition himself, mentioning nothing about an *episcopus benevolus*, nor about the possibility that the petition could be made for him.[8]

Tyrrell was impatient; he had already written to Martin complaining that no specific guidance was ever given by those in authority as to which erroneous opinions in an author's work were to be censored, and asking him to point to any errors in his long letter to the General. If no errors were pointed out to him, and the Sacred Congregation granted him secularization, he would take it that they found nothing wrong in what he was saying.[9] The General saw the obvious danger—that Tyrrell might split the Jesuits from the Sacred Congregation—and wrote back directly. One specific error in Tyrrell's letter, he said, was the accusation of a Jesuit conspiracy against 'Americanism', the Catholic University, and the Abbé Loisy. If the Sacred Congregation granted secularization it would be for the reason Tyrrell himself suggested: *ne scandalum gravius eveniat* ('lest worse scandal ensue'). Tyrrell had expressed concern lest his departure 'trouble many in their vocation'. He need not worry. *Qui enim hac de causa Societatem relinquerent, ipsi non haberent veram et solidam vocationem* ('for those who might leave the Society for this reason would not have had a true and solid vocation').[10]

Tyrrell was tempted to throw caution to the winds, and approach the Sacred Congregation without a bishop. Von Hügel and other friends repeatedly warned against this. It incensed Tyrrell that the onus of finding a bishop had been thrown upon him by Martin's silence about the matter, that he was having to beg for something which was his baptismal birthright, and that in looking for a bishop he was actually looking for *restraint* upon his liberty. Every Christian has a right to a bishop, but not, it seemed, a Jesuit, known to be a liberal and a dangerous man, who now wanted to leave the Society. Von Hügel could see how easy it would be for Tyrrell to put himself in the wrong. He reminded him that he was 'a sensitive, very sensitive man, a Celt of poor health, and profound depressibleness', and wrote with anguished affection:

I love you,—can you doubt it?—as I love at most some four or five souls now living our poor earthly life throughout many a country, race, position, sex, and religion. And I feel saddened and benumbed when the vivid and ever-recurring impression seizes me that what looks like a coming deliverance is, at bottom, a diminution of your utility in and for the Church, and through it, for religion at large.[11]

Von Hügel wanted Tyrrell to retain his credibility as a Catholic writer. Even though he knew that he was 'being heroic vicariously', he encouraged Tyrrell to think again. Certainly, Tyrrell still loved the Society, expressing his love in a bitter parody of Catullus:

> Whatever joy may yet be won
> From consciousness of duty done
> Of loyal faith, of truth unstained
> Of oaths by no deceit profaned
> All this in after years for thee
> Fruit of this fruitless love shall be.
> For when was costly word or deed
> Too costly so it served her need?
> All squandered on a thankless w——!
> Why worry about her any more? . . .
> 'For my own health alone I pray:
> God purge this loathsome love away!'[12]

Such bitterness was as yet confined to private papers. Tyrrell still hoped that the General would try to patch things up, but he did not seriously expect it. As he told the Baron:

The balance of expediency is nearly *all* against my moving. In such cases one should be very very certain that there is a matter of principle in the opposite scale. When that is so, one has to take the scandal, disappointment and flight of innumerable friends as the price of one's manhood—not to speak about a broken career; and more personal matters. I do not see how I could with

self-respect have done *less* than I have done. About *more*, I still hesitate . . .
But I take the divorce (and the Provincial who was here 3 days ago takes it) as
virtually a *fait accompli*; and our only wonder is why Rome delays. I am
resolute that for all I am worth there shall be no sign of bitterness or
ungenerosity.[13]

The immediate problem remained that of a bishop.

First Tyrrell approached Bourne, who told him he made a rule of
refusing ex-regulars. Then, on Maude Petre's suggestion, he wrote to
Archbishop Walsh of Dublin, where he was born, but he received the
same response. For a short while he hoped for a chaplaincy in the
Diocese of Southwark, but that came to nothing. After this he began
to think about possibilities abroad—Aix or San Francisco. He was
chafing under the delay, and wanted more and more to apply to the
Sacred Congregation without a bishop. As he told Bremond: 'If the
worst comes to the worst there is the Archbishop of Canterbury.'[14]
The Baron remained deeply concerned:

Grieved as I am to think it, I cannot but fear that this matter of a Bishop may
easily turn out *the* stumbling-block in the way of the whole movement. I
know well how determined you were to keep yourself unattached; and see
too how difficult, even apart from any such wish of yours, it would be or will
be to find, under the precise combination of circumstances in question, a
Bishop who would take you, under conditions that would not more or less
nullify the objects of your move.[15]

It was more than difficult; it was impossible.

On 14 November Tyrrell wrote to the General admitting his
position, and taking up with him a comment about his influence on
the juniors. He was now thoroughly incensed, and took the General's
implication to be that he was 'a corrupter of Jesuit youth'.[16] Martin
responded promptly, approving Tyrrell's search for a bishop, but
suggesting that he might be wiser to approach the Sacred Congregation anyway, while also looking for a bishop. He defended himself
against Tyrrell's charges of prosecuting his case in a half-hearted
manner. Finally, he suggested that the difficulties Tyrrell was now
experiencing in finding a bishop were only the first of those that
would follow his secularization. He gave warning *de aliis molestiis
moralibus* ('of other moral vexations').[17] Whether he liked it or not,
Tyrrell was going to find himself in the wrong, and this was sure to be
painful.

Meanwhile, some diplomatic manœuvres of comic ineptitude had
been made on Tyrrell's behalf. The Baron had taken advantage of a

visit from Semeria, who was skilled in Roman procedure, to ask advice about the way in which Tyrrell's case should be presented. Semeria's opinion was that the maximum pressure should be put on Ferrata, the Prefect of the Sacred Congregation, to facilitate Tyrrell's departure. Von Hügel also asked his prospective son-in-law, Count Salimei, who was a canon lawyer, to find out the correct procedure for an application by Tyrrell to the Sacred Congregation. His intention was that the British Ambassador in Rome should approach Ferrata to impress upon him Tyrrell's standing in England, and the importance of smoothing his path to secularization. Von Hügel hoped to contact the Ambassador through Tyrrell's cousin William, who had been a secretary in the Rome embassy. William Tyrrell, however, did not write to the Ambassador himself, but to a former colleague, E. W. Howard, who had worked in the embassy more recently and was close to the Ambassador. Howard happened to be on holiday in Crete, and thought it better to pass William's letter on to his own close friend, Merry del Val, writing: 'I know of no better man to go to in any case of trouble: there is no one more large-minded or more ready with sympathy.'[18] When Tyrrell heard about this from the Baron, who was chastened but none the less trying to make the best of the situation, he spent the morning 'in gusts of laughter', for 'Merry del Val and the General are as identical as any two persons of the Trinity'.[19] Maude Petre thought the incident accounted for a distinctly cooler tone in the General's next letter.

By December, although the outcome of his case still hung in the balance, Tyrrell had decided to leave Richmond. One reason for slipping away from the presbytery quietly was that he dreaded the pain his departure from the Society would cause Father Farmer. He was still smarting from what he took to be the General's accusations and threats, and from the injustice of a situation in which he was denied episcopal care. On 9 December he wrote to Maude Petre:

I screwed myself up yesterday to finish the draft of my reply to the General. Till then I felt too full to trust myself to expression. I have no doubt at all that I must purge my soul. There is no coming to terms with the S.J. and to accept secularization under the circs. would be only to defer, for a worse *denouement* later, and to open a new era of worries and anxieties . . . I think it wiser to send the letter—and also a brief line indicating the lie of the situation to the Provincial—as soon as I have got away, *permissu superiorum*, for a change.[20]

Just then he heard that the Archbishop of San Francisco was willing to take him, but he rejected San Francisco as 'too far'. He asked Maude Petre to look for temporary rooms in Askrigg or Bainbridge, villages about twenty miles from Richmond. This she loyally did, sending addresses and charges. She had recently conferred an annuity of £100 a year on Tyrrell, making him, as he put it, 'a rich man for life', so at least he had enough money to live on, which many suspended priests did not. His needs were modest. Nine months before, he had written to Maude Petre: 'I have 30/- at present that I don't know what to do with. Could you say that?'[21]

It was not until 31 December that the letter to the General was sent. In it Tyrrell protested against the tone of Martin's last letter; he had wanted a peaceful separation, and Martin was threatening to make things difficult. 'It seems I am to be released pacifically from the Society but that I am subsequently to be brought into such a collision with ecclesiastical authorities as will redound to the Society's credit.' He would not agree to be secularized on those terms; he withdrew the request. Let the General dismiss him, so that he incurred suspension. He would simply circulate the relevant documents to the few whose opinions mattered most to him. Condemnation of his work would remove the false impression of tolerance for his writing and opinions, and excommunication, when undeserved, would be 'spiritually a gain and not a loss'.[22] He was out of patience, and wanted to be free of the Society at any cost.

Yet he half hoped, and even expected, that it would not come to that. It was not to be. On the very day that he left Richmond, fate gave the General the card that he needed to put Tyrrell in the wrong. The *Corriere della Sera* published an article containing several extracts from the *Letter to a University Professor*, naming the author as 'an English Jesuit'. Immediately, the Archbishop of Milan wrote to the General asking who was responsible for such ideas. Tyrrell was of course the prime suspect. On 7 January the General wrote to him repudiating the accusation that he was intent on making trouble for him, and asking if Tyrrell was responsible for the article in the *Corriere*.[23] Tyrrell replied that his policy was neither to affirm nor to deny authorship of an anonymous or pseudonymous work, but that he agreed with the excerpts except in one minor point (where he had spotted an error of translation). Then he added:

What I do want to know *at once*, and with a view to external arrangements, is whether you will now, on your own initiative, send me out of the Society. I will neither ask for dismissal nor apply for secularisation; but I will throw the whole onus on your Paternity. If you do not dismiss me, then I return to Richmond as before—*liberavi animam meam*. If you dismiss me; then I go to London and begin my life's work.[24]

Three days later, reckoning that an admission of guilt might hasten his dismissal, Tyrrell changed his mind and wrote to the General acknowledging authorship of the original *Letter*, though disclaiming responsibility for the somewhat free translation.[25] The General's next move was to put the article, as he could not obtain a copy of the original booklet, into the hands of three censors, two of whom condemned it strongly, the third being more discriminating. He then wrote to Tyrrell telling him that his authorship of the *Letter* did not make a peaceful departure from the Society any easier, though this was what both of them wanted. He told him that his censors had advised that the article was scandalous and should be publicly repudiated. Yet again he encouraged Tyrrell to present his petition to the Sacred Congregation, as, if he were dismissed on the General's authority, he would not only not be released from his vows, but he would be unable to exercise his priesthood.[26] Tyrrell responded:

You would not, I am sure, wish me to repudiate what I would not have written had I not sincerely believed it. Am I to deny or pretend to deny the existence of the common difficulties enumerated in the first paragraph quoted by 'The Corriere'? Have not the authorities themselves admitted all these things? Am I to say that Religion is primarily theology, and *not* eternal life? Am I to say that Catholicism is *not* something greater and grander than can ever attain adequate expression in its theology or its institutions, however they may progress? I should be contradicting the Scriptures and the greatest saints and doctors of the Church.[27]

He enclosed a letter 'explaining his position' about the private nature of the original *Letter*, his regret that it had been published, his defence of its fundamental ideas, and noting one significant mistranslation. He concluded: 'Needless to say, the Society of Jesus is in no way responsible for correspondences or conversations never destined for publicity and therefore never submitted to its official censorship.'[28] Predictably, such a response was judged inadequate.

Martin spoke to Ferrata about Tyrrell on 16 January.[29] It was probably after this interview that he drafted a letter to him outlining Tyrrell's inability to find an *episcopus benevolus*, and the situation over the *Corriere* article. He commented: 'I do not know what more I could do to restrain and bring back to wiser counsels a man who believes that he is bound by no obligation to the Society of Jesus, and who asserts that he has no fear of ecclesiastical censures.' Now he was asking for permission to dismiss 'such a dangerous man' as soon as possible.[30] On 31 January Martin again wrote to Ferrata, quoting Tyrrell's last letter and his refusal to repudiate the *Letter*. He told Ferrata of an audience with the Pope in which the Pope had a copy of the offending document, and said that if Tyrrell did not retract the doctrine therein he should be dismissed from the Society. So, as Tyrrell had refused to retract, he wanted to see Ferrata the following morning to put in hand the machinery for the dismissal.[31] It is clear from this, and from a letter written three months later by Rudolf Meyer, the General's assistant,[32] that Tyrrell was dismissed on the express orders of the Pope. Ferrata must have seen Martin the following morning, as the letters of dismissal were despatched to Sykes, the English Provincial, on that date.[33] Even while his dismissal was in transit, Sykes still pleaded with Tyrrell to choose secularization 'under the conditions offered' rather than the 'dismissal and perpetual suspension' of which Tyrrell now spoke.[34]

Sykes failed totally. On 7 February he had to inform Tyrrell that the documents from Rome had now arrived.[35] Incredibly, Tyrrell had again begun to hope that he would avoid dismissal, so the letter from Sykes came as a bitter shock. The General had written: 'Since your reverence asserts that he cannot send the declaration which is required, nothing else remains but for me at last to accede to the petition often explicitly and now again implicitly made.'[36] This wording afforded Tyrrell one last chance to wriggle, since he was clear in his own mind that he had not *asked* for dismissal. Was he or was he not being *expelled*? The General was apparently trying to find a formula that would throw the responsibility for departure back on to Tyrrell himself, and this Tyrrell would not have. If he was to go, he wanted it to be clear to all the world that he was *expelled*.

Sykes himself was confused about the situation, and contacted Martin, who now ended all confusion. Tyrrell, he said, was *dismissed* for his failure to obey the ecclesiastical and Jesuit authorities, and to repair the damage done by the article in the *Corriere*. He could not say mass, but he could receive Communion.[37] Only the Pope, through the Sacred Congregation of Bishops and Regulars, could restore his standing as a priest. Whether he ever resumed his membership of the Jesuit order was a matter for the General alone.

On 19 February, shortly after 11.30 a.m., Sykes called at 45

Egerton Gardens, the home of William Tyrrell, with the papers of dismissal. Tyrrell read them, appended a brief protest to make it clear that he had not *asked* for dismissal, and then, while the tears stood in Sykes's eyes, signed the papers.

So ended seven weeks of intense strain which began when Tyrrell left Richmond in desolate mood: 'One must', he wrote, 'practise dying.'[38] He yearned for the sea and solitude, so he asked Maude Petre to book rooms in Tintagel, about as far from Richmond as could be. Here he found nothing to comfort him. The last part of the journey was made in pouring rain, and when he arrived he found Tintagel 'a cruel bleak spot', with 'angry sea, angry wind, merciless cliffs'.[39] Storms of depression and loneliness swept over him. He was only too aware of the difficulties that lay ahead, of the complications in his relations with the Society, with the Church, with Maude Petre. Where, amidst all these entanglements, would he find a home? Worst of all, how could he ever be sure that he had done the right thing:

> Nor have I even the solace of having chosen the best; or of having arrived at the best. I marvel at those who can be so sure what is best, or that their aim is pure. To me it is all a more or less; a probability, a chance, a groping. Life offers us choices of evils; rarely a clear choice of good and evil.[40]

To stay in the Society or to leave the Society, to stay in the Church or to leave the Church: these seemed choices of evils, but by this stage there was no choice. His choice, for good or evil, was made.

After four weeks in Tintagel, alone but for a brief visit from Maude Petre, he went to Clapham for a few days so as to be near the Shelleys, 'never . . . more perplexed or hopeless as to a home'.[41] Then he moved to Eastbourne to stay with 'Willie' and Dora Williams. 'Willie' delighted him by his eccentricity, and Dora by her whimsy. Here he preached his last sermon, and celebrated 'positively the last Mass till the reign of Pope Angelus'. 'It shall be', he told Maude Petre, 'for you.'[42] Though he abused her and railed against her possessiveness, he nevertheless recognized an immense debt to her loyalty and love. The shock of that love drew out the cruelty in him, but also, at times like this, his tenderness. From Eastbourne he returned to London, staying with his cousin William. Though he knew that suspension was inevitable, he wanted to retain all that he could of his priesthood. For a short while he had ceased to say the office, but now he took it up again. When Sykes had contacted him to say that the letters of dismissal had come, all Tyrrell's unreal hopes of reconciliation were dashed. Von Hügel had been with him both the day before and the day after he put his signature to the papers. His next letter to Bremond was signed 'George Tyrrell, Ex-S.J.'.[43]

For a week longer Tyrrell lingered in London as 'a torrent of kindness' began to wash over him. Letters poured in, many from friends in the Society, and from those he had never counted friends. A welcome visitor, who still hoped for reconciliation, was Thurston. At the first opportunity, 'like Abraham from Haran', *nesciens quo iret* ('not knowing whither he went'), Tyrrell left for France, where Bremond, the one friend in the world who could really understand his emotions on being dismissed from the Society, was waiting to greet him.

On 27 February 1906 Tyrrell arrived in Paris. Bremond was there, and there he met Laberthonnière, with whom he 'fell right in love at first sight'.[44] Tyrrell was much amused that Laberthonnière knew only French and Latin, and since they could not converse freely in either, they were 'simply like two sympathetic horses meeting over a fence'.[45] Laberthonnière was equally delighted with Tyrrell,[46] and they met three or four times in as many days. Tyrrell also took to Dimnet, but failed to meet Houtin, who was just finishing his *La Question biblique au vingtième siècle*. Houtin asked Tyrrell for a brief statement of his present position. Tyrrell was at first glad to comply, but then an abusive review of *Lex Orandi* in *Études*, the magazine of the French Jesuits, made him realize that the saga was not yet complete, and that he was not quite ready to give the story to Houtin. He was particularly incensed by the *Études* attack, because it cast a slur on the English Jesuit censors who had passed the book two years earlier. Letters of sympathy and support were still pouring in from English Jesuits, some of whom would have been horrified had they known what Tyrrell really thought. Bernard Vaughan was one such. He was in tears when he spoke about Tyrrell to Maude Petre after mass at Farm Street. Tyrrell was held in affection and respect by many who had not the first idea how radical he really was.

Tyrrell stayed a week in Paris. Bremond vacillated endlessly about whether they should go to Aix or Freiburg. Finally Tyrrell forced a decision by threatening to go home. They stopped overnight in Strasburg, with 'just time to see the Cathedral in the rose-light of a frosty morning',[47] and then moved on to the Pension Bellevue, Freiburg. Here, on the edge of the Black Forest, looking out on 'wooded hills-upon-hills soft and beautiful in their varying lights beyond description', Tyrrell was able to re-establish a routine of prayer and work in the company of his restless friend, who planned '12 book[s] and 20 articles and 50 changes of residence every day'. His greatest pain was 'nostalgia for the altar', which was not helped by Bremond's situation. 'The infamy', he wrote to Maude Petre, 'is that HB is just as much suspended as I, but that he never even read his dismissorial form and the Archbishop of Aix assumed that he was secularized—which he isn't.'[48] That simply reduced the difference between the mass-saying priest and the mass-hearer to a nonsense.

Their routine was simple. Bremond said mass at 7.00 a.m., and after breakfast they visited Josef Sauer, a sympathetic church historian ('I expected a torpedo-boat and found a whale, a fat soft German rather encumbered with the multitude of his books and interests; the number of his loquacious friends; the violence of his anti-Jesuitism'[49]). For the rest of the morning they worked. After lunch they walked, and then worked from 4.00 p.m. until dinner at 7.30. In the evening they walked or worked until about 10.00. Tyrrell was under a great deal of strain, so he welcomed the regular routine. He drafted what he thought was an appropriate reply to the review in *Études*, and then, guided by the eirenic spirit of Laberthonnière, moderated his language. He also wrote the preface and corrected the proofs of *Lex Credendi*. Early in April Tyrrell and Bremond heard that Fogazzaro's *Il Santo* and two books by Laberthonnière had been placed on the Index. Anticipating the same fate, Tyrrell wrote to Ferrata, at last making the formal request for secularization.[50] Then he and Bremond lost no time in setting out for Paris to console and encourage Laberthonnière.

Tyrrell was now faced with the prospect of returning to England. He had promised to help von Hügel revise his book on St Catherine before it was sent to the publisher, and as the Baron would not come to Paris, he had to return to London. He dreaded the talk that would be aroused by his failure to celebrate mass, and wrote to ask Thurston's help:

I *think* I shall have to go to London in about a fortnight to do some work with von Hügel that may take some weeks; unless he can come here, which is unlikely. It would save a deal of anger against the S.J. and the Church-authorities if the *purely red-tape* objections to my saying mass could be removed for that period. It is not for immorality or even for heterodoxy that I am suspended; but merely as a vagrant religious. I am sure E. I. P[urbrick] or Colley could have set that matter right in a trice.[51]

There was nothing Thurston could do, however much he and the English Jesuits wanted Tyrrell back. The problem was much more serious than his being a 'vagrant religious', though there was enough confusion about the difference between 'dismissal' (expulsion from the Jesuits without the right to say mass) and 'secularization' (departure from the Jesuits to become a secular priest with the right to say mass) for Tyrrell to play upon it mightily. In the event, Tyrrell returned to England dressed as a priest, unable to celebrate mass, and unable, in a climate where priests were always celebrants, to attend mass without causing gossip. In a letter to Bremond written from Clapham, he said: 'To-day I realise for the first time that I am alone, unattached, one of the loose pebbles on the shore of time which the storm has broken from the rocks. One never means to leave the Church; but what if the Church leaves us—as boats stranded on the beach when the tide goes out?'[52]

Just as Tyrrell arrived back in England, *Lex Credendi*[53] was published. It represented, he believed, the best answer to any wild rumours about the ideas he had been propounding, for it was in one sense considerably more careful and cautious than *Lex Orandi*. He had been taken aback by those who read *Lex Orandi* as an essay in religious pragmatism, and one reason for writing the sequel had been to show that he held very firmly to the place of doctrine in the Christian life. He had expounded the creed as a *lex orandi*, a guide for prayer; now he expounded the Lord's Prayer as a *lex credendi*, a guide for belief. To do this, he added one further point to the distinctions he had so clearly established between revelation and theology: the normative value of the earliest expression of revelation, the 'form of sound words'. He did not retreat from his position that the words of Jesus were in no sense 'scientific', but rather 'prophetic' or even 'poetic'; but he attributed to them 'a derived and secondary sacredness ... as being the first and divinely chosen vehicle of revelation'. In doing this, he clearly distinguished himself from both the liberals and the conservatives that he had criticized in 'Semper Eadem'. He showed that there was another way, 'conservative' about the place within Christianity of the 'primitive forms of religious thought and language', but 'liberal' in the way in which that 'thought and language' was interpreted. The book brought together the best of Tyrrell's theological reasoning and his devotional writing—an astonishing feat, given the conditions under which it was written. In May 1906 it was warmly reviewed in *The Month*, a brave and generous gesture for which the editor, John Gerard, received a severe rebuke from Rome.

On Tyrrell's return to London von Hügel was promising the typescript of his book in about four weeks, and urging him to come and live near him while they worked on it together. Tyrrell still felt dreadfully in need of a settled home, and was perpetually pained by 'nostalgia for the altar'. Having received no answer to his letter to Ferrata, he wrote again, angrily threatening to make public all the relevant correspondence, since nothing had been done about his situation. Despite the General's clear statement that he could receive Communion, he had not been doing so, as he was refused absolution by confessors who thought he had been excommunicated, so now he made an issue of this, asking specifically for 'permission to approach the sacrament of the altar'.[54] Meanwhile, through a nun to whom Tyrrell had given retreats at the English convent in Bruges, Archbishop Mercier of Malines had expressed his willingness to accept Tyrrell in his diocese.[55] On 18 June Ferrata wrote to Mercier giving his permission, on condition that Tyrrell neither published religious works nor engaged in 'epistolary correspondence' without the approval of a censor appointed by the Archbishop.[56] At this point the situation was complicated by the death of Martin, the Jesuit General, pained to the last by the Tyrrell affair; but the fact that Ferrata wrote as he did suggests that Tyrrell was now to be regarded as secularized. Both parties might well feel that this was an acceptable solution to the impasse. No further reference was made to the *Corriere* article; it was enough that a suitable bishop had been found. As yet, however, Tyrrell knew nothing about the outcome of these negotiations.

Tyrrell was still preoccupied with the search for a home. In the middle of May he moved to the small Premonstratensian priory at Storrington, in the lee of the Sussex Downs. 'Hattie' Urquhart, a relative of his cousin by marriage, had taken a house in the priory grounds, and there were plans afoot for what Maude Petre called 'certain philanthropic works'. Tyrrell described the project as 'a sort of *home* for wild street-boys; *nullus ordo*; *sempiternus horror*'.[57] The William Tyrrells had also settled in Storrington, so if he stayed he could count on friends. Excitedly, he described the priory to Bremond, who was in Provence collecting material for a book on Provençal mystics:

These 3 jolly Devil-may-care anti-Jesuit monks of Aix are most anxious to fill their empty priory with paying guests and offer me two good rooms and everything else for 30/- a week. I put all possible ecclesiastical difficulties before the Prior but he only pished and pshawed, and say [sic] he would entertain the Devil if he chose and no bishop should say him nay. He says I can have all my lady friends to dine and visit me as much as I like—the *one* restriction is that '*pour les miserables conveniences*' they must not sleep in the priory. Yesterday he had Hattie, Mrs Tyrrell and Miss Ormsby at lunch; the 2 former have been having meals there for 3 weeks. The food and wine is Provencal. He is longing for you to come over. It is very queer; very medieval. In a sense they are pagan; and yet very truly, because unconsciously, Christian and human.[58]

Here he lived for a month, recommending the priory to Bremond, the hotel to von Hügel, and the social work to Maude Petre.

Unfortunately, Maude Petre took Tyrrell's delight in the place, which was no Richmond, far too seriously. She had been deeply hurt by her exclusion from the plans of Tyrrell and Bremond when they were abroad. Depression, isolation, and bitterness had closed in, but Storrington seemed to offer renewed hope of life with him. Before long she had her eye on Mulberry House, an elegant eighteenth-century house in the centre of the town. She bought it as a convalescent home for needy ladies, where she could also live. It was to be, in more senses than one, her 'Home for the Unhappy'. The expense frightened her, but Tyrrell seemed to like Storrington, he could live at the priory or the hotel, and would be glad of a study overlooking the mulberry tree in the garden.

By the end of June von Hügel's typescript was still not finished, and Tyrrell left for France again. This time he and Bremond made for Brittany, and, after some days' restless wandering 'like two outlaws', they took lodgings in the little fishing village of Damgan, at 'the other end of nowhere'. In a card to Maude Petre he described it as 'a shabby little Irish village' with 'a dingy cheap church'. The beauty, he said, was 'in the interlocked arms of sea and barleyfields, ripe with harvest, the mingling of lighthouses and windmills; also in the archaic simplicity of manners that makes one feel 3000 years old and look on the Church as a raw intruder who has extinguished the fires and cut down the fetishes and altars that were the centre of now centreless mystic dances'.[59] The fishermen of Damgan brought back memories of the fishermen of Howth that he had known as a boy. It was in Damgan that Tyrrell first learnt of Ferrata's condition upon his acceptance by Mercier of Malines.

His reaction was one of uncontained fury. Barely able to cope, Bremond wrote anxiously to Laberthonnière:

Do come; do come—but perhaps you would do better to wait a little. He is still under the first impact of this iniquity and he has great need of silence. You know well that no sympathy touches him more than yours. But, Irishman that he is, he shuts himself up in himself—I am there to ring the bells for meals—to go for walks with him on the beach and play the fool. But I do not intrude on his thoughts. Tell us the day and the hour—and once you are here don't speak of the incident.[60]

Immediately, he began contacting friends in England and France: Dell, who had so embarrassed him by his tactless compliment at the height of the crisis over 'A Perverted Devotion', Lilley, and Houtin, asking them to make known to the press

that Cardinal Ferrata has refused Fr Tyrrell leave to say Mass unless he promises for the future to submit his private correspondence to ecclesiastical censorship. This move is attributed to the Jesuit authorities at Rome who are determined that Fr T. shall be either utterly discredited by permanent suspension, or else absolutely silenced. None of his works have as yet been condemned by the Church but only by the Society of Jesus. Neither Abbé Loisy nor any other priest whose books are on the Index has been thus suspended or subjected to such monstrous conditions.[61]

Neither the Abbé Loisy nor any other priest whose books were on the Index had, of course, used supposedly private correspondence to such subversive effect as Tyrrell. Mercier wrote to reassure him that the condition applied only to letters on the themes of his religious publications, but Tyrrell was not interested. That meant

only the most private parts of all my private correspondence; only my letters to priests, seminarians, professors, religious etc. etc. who write to me about those doubts which they dare not breathe to their confessors—only those letters! But if I write to my nurse or my grandmother about their rheumatism the Church leaves me quite free to say what I like. This is a valuable distinction![62]

Tyrrell's next move was to write a stinging letter to Ferrata in which he reviewed his whole case, accusing the Cardinal of making life difficult by his slowness in answering letters, and driving home the point that none of his works had been placed on the Index. He stressed that his suspension was, as he put it, 'not directly penal', but 'simply indirect and involved in [his] status as a religious dismissed (illegally?) *sine episcopo receptore*' ('with no bishop to receive him').[63] Privately, he acknowledged that this statement of his case was 'more or less a bit of special pleading', and magnified his grievance as much as was 'consistent with perfect truth'.[64] Publicly, he stood by the letter, which he had printed and then distributed to selected friends. He numbered the copies to increase the effect, beginning at sixty-seven. One copy went to Ferrata, and two went to Merry del Val, who was asked to bring the letter to the attention of the Pope.[65]

From Brittany Tyrrell and Bremond moved to Bremond's family house in Provence:

Well here I am. It is a little plain of about a hundred acres, with an old fourteenth-century farm house with seventeenth-century additions, furniture and fittings; very sleep[y] and charming. Shut in by a triangle of hills from whose tops mountains range away *ad infinitum* in all directions, and never a dwelling in sight; all most wild and rugged; and giving gorgeous sunsets and risings.[66]

Here he waited for von Hügel's typescript. On 13 August the Baron at last sent off 'two—alas, very heavy packets', containing 2,000 pages of typescript. Even while the book was in transit, his relationship with Tyrrell came under threat, for Tyrrell accidentally read a letter from Maude Petre containing an allusion to something with which she had already taxed the Baron: that he had 'nearly abandoned' Tyrrell. Certainly, Tyrrell's increasingly wild behaviour had offended von Hügel's diplomatic instincts. As the Baron told Maude Petre, he originally thought that Tyrrell had gone abroad because he needed a change and a rest, but he now realized that his friend had gone '*at least* as much because he wants to be in a position where he can throw bombs without injuring or distressing *directly* those that have grouped themselves about him'.[67] Tyrrell was shocked to think that Maude Petre's charge against the Baron might be true, and that he had no inkling of how near he had come to being dropped by his friend. However, he did not let this affect his attitude as he set to work six hours a day, for six weeks, on von Hügel's book. 'I feel it would take me a year of study to form a really competent judgement on a work of such depth and subtlety,' he wrote in admiration.[68] His contribution was to make it readable.

Tyrrell's work on von Hügel's book was done out of loyalty and admiration. The cracks in their relationship, undoubtedly exploited by Maude Petre, who saw the Baron as standing in the way of her plans for Tyrrell, were beginning to show. Von Hügel deplored

Tyrrell's 'bomb-throwing'; Tyrrell deplored von Hügel's diplomacy. In August he wrote: 'I belong to von Hügel's eleven. I wish I didn't. But every life is tangled with other lives and none of us can do just what we want.'[69] His work on the Baron's *The Mystical Element of Religion* exacerbated a sore difference, because one pillar of the Baron's thought was the need for institutional religion, whereas Tyrrell was locked in mortal combat with the institution:

As to what you say about me it is of course what the author of M. E. is bound to say just because it is his deepest conviction. But is there not just a touch of 'orthodoxy' in the assumption that a scepticism as to the claims of particular institutions connotes a decay of personal religion? . . . I agree . . . about what Churches *ought* to do for one. But for me they don't do it, and the effort to accommodate myself to Rome has been a source of mental untruthfulness and moral cowardice and spiritual sterility. It is the best in me that kicks against it.[70]

Von Hügel told Maude Petre how Tyrrell reminded him of one of 'those beautifully delicate, and *in their own way*, wonderfully strong marine-creatures' that he saw as a child when bathing in the Mediterranean, for 'in water and sunshine, how expansive, how delightful, how happy they were; and out of water and in the bleak winds, how shrunken, limp, mere husks and weeds they were'. Tyrrell, he felt, was too utterly sensitive a human being 'not to get dried-up, embittered, unbalanced' over his conflicts.[71]

All Tyrrell's close relationships were now showing the strain of his situation. Maude Petre knew she had pressurized him about Storrington, and that he was backing off. She was in an agony of suspense in case all her preparations had been made for nothing, and that he would not come, leaving her to run the home, to which she was now irrevocably committed, without him. 'Am very, very anxious,' she wrote in her diary. 'Cannot help thinking he is wanting to shake off Storrington etc. that he is, in his own way "off" with me. I am resolved that all hell shall not take him from me so far as my love and labour for him go.'[72] 'All hell' in this case meant the Shelleys, for Tyrrell had gone to them, precipitating a fierce row with Maude Petre, bitter recriminations ('I shall soon *hate* if she has not sense to stop'[73]), mutual explanations, and the eventual decision that she would continue the Storrington project without him.

When Tyrrell left the Society he did not know that he had so many Jesuit friends. The letters and messages he received were not so much a vote of confidence in him, as a gesture of loyalty to one who had fallen foul of Rome. At the beginning of November Tyrrell's *Much-Abused Letter* appeared, together with an introduction in which Tyrrell told the story of his dismissal, printing all the relevant letters between himself and the General, and explained why he had produced such a 'medicine for extreme cases'. His stated aim was to show that though the *Letter* was 'liberal', it was nothing to be ashamed of. His real aim was to embarrass the authorities. Now that English Jesuit friends were beginning to realize the extent and nature of his secret writings, they were far less sympathetic. Tyrrell told Bremond: 'The English S.J. have been "converted" against me since the Gen. Congregation [at which a successor to Martin was chosen], and the Bourdon disclosures. They are incensed by the impression which the *Much Abused* has made; and talk of telling the *whole* truth. I wrote to Sykes and invited him to do so at once. They are great asses.'[74]

Early in December Tyrrell, who was now suffering continuously from migraines, moved down to Storrington, which he found 'soothing to ruffled tempers'. Maude Petre was away, so one cause of friction was removed. His thoughts were dwelling on the nature of Catholicism. He never lost his faith in, and his love of, the Catholic ideal, but events had shown how little he could live with the institution as it was. As he expressed it to Bremond: 'If I could, in my imagination and not merely in my understanding, dissociate the ideas of religion and Rome I might still find life worth living. But to do that I should have to break externally with "the cause" and bring shame and confusion on so many who have ignorantly trusted me; and so I go on living with a dead heart.'[75] Just before he left Clapham he asked Thurston, who was proving a loyal friend, to bring him a copy of what he miscalled *The Church of the Future*, and tried to explain the import of that tract to his uncomprehending friend. He explained that it was an attempt to find a middle way between the Catholicism that Thurston still embraced and the emaciated 'Protestantism' that many feared would be all that was left for Catholic Christians when the acid of the critics had corroded their faith to nothing. Tyrrell chided Thurston for wasting his historical and critical skills, frittering them on legends of saints when he could have been working on the gospels and the early Church: 'We differ chiefly', he told him,

in that I believe a very radical transformation of Catholicism is both necessary and possible; you believe it is not necessary and would not be possible. Should you ever believe in its necessity I hope you will reconsider its possibility and not fling the haft after the blade as so many are now doing thanks to the All-or-nothing principle which has been drilled into them so long and so assiduously.[76]

All that Tyrrell succeeded in showing Thurston was that he would not come back to the Society.

Von Hügel was as much taken up with the nature of Catholicism as Tyrrell. He was struggling to complete his essay on the fourth gospel for the *Encyclopaedia Britannica*, and working on his paper 'Official Authority and Living Religion'. In the middle of December he sent Tyrrell a long letter discussing some points that he had also put to Loisy. He summed up not only the conflict between 'the ultramontane *Fragestellung*' and that of 'our group', but also the sort of behaviour that could be expected of him and his friends: a willingness 'slowly and deliberately to let drop, to damp down, as far as possible to exterminate, cleverness as distinct from wisdom, clearness as distinct from depth, logic as distinct from operativeness, simplicity as distinct from life'.[77] 'Bomb-throwing' was out. The author of the *Much-Abused Letter* responded warmly to the Baron's panoramic vision for work that would be done in 'this sort of but approximately "logical", obtuse-seeming, costingly wise not brilliantly clever, ruminant, slow, if you will stupid, divinely blest, thorn-crowned, ignored, defeated, yet soul-inspiring, life-creating fashion'. 'A grand letter in every sense,' said Tyrrell. His contribution was a sharp reading of the political situation, in which he distinguished the group around von Hügel—Loisy, Maude Petre, himself, Laberthonnière, Blondel—from a 'radical left' that had lost all faith in the existing Church, and now worked for its destruction. This included the likes of Houtin: 'It cannot be denied', he wrote,

that between us of the ecclesiastical left a line of cleavage is becoming more marked every day analogous to that which divided Erasmus from Luther. The former is, in the deepest and truest sense, conservative: *Non veni solvere sed adimplere* ['I have not come to destroy but to fulfil'] is its guiding principle; it destroys only incidentally in the course of building up and continuing. The latter is of course radical, and as regards the existing structure, pessimistic and hopeless.

Their one point of agreement was 'the negative one of resistance to blind intransigence'.[78]

Von Hügel, however, believed in 'official authority' in a way that Tyrrell did not. In his long letter he had stressed that 'We, i.e.

[Cardinal Ferrata], [Loisy], you, MDP, I—our housemaids too, are true, integral portions of the Church, which in none of its members is simply teaching, in none of its members is simply learning,'[79] but he did not share Tyrrell's total alienation from the actual workings of authority, he did not look to the *consensus fidelium* as a simple counterweight to the aggressions of those in power, he had not lost patience. Von Hügel believed in a restoration of organic unity; Tyrrell believed in the overthrow of an ultramontane clique, animated by the Jesuits, who had wrested control of the Church. In a letter to Dell he expounded this view:

Our work must be to work within the Church for the unravelling of this gigantic papal imposition; for the restoration of the hierarchy; for the inversion of the hierarchic pyramid now unstably poised on its apex and which needs to be planted firmly on its basis; for the recognition of the *regale sacerdotium* of the Christian people as the fount of all order and jurisdiction. The modern mind, especially as saturated with the ideas of divine Immanence, will soon be incapable of any other way of seeing things. The leadership of Rome must be, as primitively, one of example, not one of coercive right. I could not stay in the Roman Communion if I had to accept the new Vaticanism as part of the system. I can endure it as a heresy or disease. One joined the Church to be delivered from the tyranny of individualism, and to live under the rule of a wide and quasi-Catholic consensus, in which the vagaries of individualism are eliminated and the true developments of mind-in-general made manifest. But one finds oneself subjected to the tyranny of a privileged private judgement; the election of the cardinals makes the personal ideas of Guiseppe Sarto a rule of truth, and his will is substituted for the canons and customs shaped by the growth of the Christian people. If this is not a revolution and a heresy I don't know what is.[80]

To attack this heresy Tyrrell was prepared to go 'on the bayonets'. He knew that he was placarded as negative, insidious, destructive, but that is always the way with revolutionaries.

To the end of his life he was captivated by the vision that first drew him to the Catholic Church. In the early part of 1907 he wrote a long essay describing that vision.[81] He spoke of Catholicism as 'a natural and therefore a divine religion', 'a religion of the people', 'a religion of the whole man, body, soul and spirit'. He spoke of the centrality of conscience, of continuity with the past; of the 'collective mind, will and sentiment of the community'. He called Catholicism 'a tendency, a religion at all stages of spiritual development'. In conclusion he wrote: 'Catholicism seems to stand for the widest, the oldest, the

deepest stream of collective experience.' He saw it as 'divine with the
divinity of a natural process'. In all, the essay was a paean of praise to
his love, and an *apologia* for loving her still, while holding to his
ecclesiastically ambiguous position. It was poetry and not history.
He ended by telling this story:

The Fathers have long since discovered an image of the Church in Eve,
drawn from the side of Adam to be a helpmeet for him, albeit a costing one in
many ways. In some respects the Hindu legend of the same event is even
more illustrative. It tells us that when the Creator had taxed a million
contradictory elements of the universe for contributions which he blended
into a new creature and presented to man, the man came to him in eight days
and said: 'My lord, the creature you gave me poisons my existence. She
chatters without rest, she takes all my time, she laments for nothing at all,
and is always ill.'
    And Twashtri received the woman again.
    But eight days later the man came again to the god and said:—
    'My lord, my life is very solitary since I returned this creature.'
    And Twashtri returned the woman to him.
    Three days only passed, and Twashtri saw the man coming to him again.
    'My lord,' said he, 'I do not understand exactly how, but I am sure the
woman causes me more annoyance than pleasure. I beg of you to relieve me
of her.'
    But Twashtri cried: 'Go your way and do your best.'
    And the man cried: 'I cannot live with her!'
    'Neither can you live without her', replied Twashtri.
    And the man was sorrowful, murmuring: 'Woe is me! I can neither live
with her nor without her.'[82]

This was exactly Tyrrell's dilemma. As he expressed it in a letter to
Osborne: 'Institutionalism or externalism is at once essential and
fatal to religion. Every day I feel more of a Catholic (not Roman) and
more of a Quaker than ever.'[83]
    With views like these he could not encourage others to join or to
leave the Roman Church, yet he continued to receive endless letters
asking for help. In January 1907 he sent Maude Petre some typical
letters that made him 'contemplate suicide'. 'These drowning folk',
he lamented, 'little know what a poor straw they are clutching at.'[84]
In one set of letters from this time he gave counsel to a lady who had
been pressurized into conversion from Anglicanism by an over-
zealous priest. Tyrrell had been in touch with her almost ten years
before, warning against precipitate action, encouraging her to take
things at her own pace, and recommending Roman Catholic de-

votional classics with the *caveat*: 'All these books are to be got through Burns and Oates; but unless you get them through some intermediary you will probably find a paragraph in the papers announcing your conversion to Romanism.'[85] In February 1907 Tyrrell wrote kindly about her reception, hoping he had not retarded her progress too much. By March it was clear she had indeed been badly advised, so Tyrrell wrote:

I should say: Communion as often as you like; and confession very rarely and, if possible, never. And, above all, avoid discussing religious questions with traditional Catholics, whether priests or layfolk. For your mind has been built up on a different system altogether, and it will be like a conversation between a dog and a fish. All their machinery is justified solely as a means of getting where you have got already; namely, alone with God.[86]

When she asked him to be her spiritual director, he refused, saying: 'It is a position that I have never taken nor desire to take. I am always willing to give as well as to take suggestions; and to talk matters over as between friend and friend. But I can never feel that I have a right to speak with authority, or to be followed and obeyed.' Nor did he feel that she should throw her responsibility 'on other shoulders' more than she could help. The object of such outward help was to enable her to dispense with it sooner or later, 'and to make God your one great spiritual director'. Finally, he advised: 'Keep to the old books and the old friends and the old thoughts by which God has led and consoled you in the past. Break with your past as little as possible.'[87] In the end he bluntly told her that her over-zealous director 'wanted to land a fish, and, having landed it, he left it'. He told her that she had 'bounced' into Romanism 'uninstructed and unpractised', and was still at heart an Anglican. Therefore, she should take what she could in Romanism, and if that did not work, 'relapse into full Anglican communion, going to their services, first occasionally; then frequently; finally altogether'.[88] She hesitated, and two years later he repeated the same advice: 'Do remember that Churches are only helps to get to God. If you find that one walking stick is too long or too short, you must choose another.'[89] When Wilfrid Blunt, the diarist and explorer, who had long lost his faith, met Tyrrell, he lamented that they had not come into contact years before. 'If there had been any exponent of views like his forty-five years ago,' he wrote, 'it might have made all the difference to me in my spiritual life.'[90]

For Tyrrell 'the only possibility was Roman Catholicism, but not in any narrow, exclusive, ultramontane sense'. It was the very openness of Catholicism to all, the religious expression of humanity, that attracted him. Catholicism was the fulfilment, not the negation, of man's hopes and longings. 'My faith (if it is not too strong a word)', he told Thurston, 'is in the "religious process" throughout the world by which God makes himself known to and loved by man, and in Christ and Christianity and Catholicism as the so far fullest and best fruit of that process.'[91] Alienated from the Jesuits and the Roman authorities, he longed at times to return to the quiet dignity of the Anglicanism in which he had been brought up: 'Church of my baptism! Church of Westcott, Hort, Lightfoot, Church, Liddon, Taylor, Leighton, Coleridge! Church of better-than-saints, why did I ever leave you?'[92] On the first Sunday in September 1907 he went, with Norah Shelley, to hear his old friend Osborne preach at St Paul's. 'Dolling's shade', he said, 'must have been with us last night',[93] and he wondered if he himself would be in that pulpit in twenty years' time. Had he lived to occupy the pulpit of St Paul's, it could only have been as a Roman Catholic. What he saw as the unstable *via media* of Anglicanism was an intellectual impossibility to him now, though it had 'all the illusive attraction of "the haunts of my childhood"'.[94]

The early months of 1907 were months of unsettlement, illness, controversy, and superhuman labour. Still Tyrrell had no permanent home. In January he moved from Storrington to stay with his friend, William Gibson, and then he returned to Clapham for two months. After a month with Willie and Dora Williams he returned to Storrington and another appalling row with Maude Petre, who had returned after three months of nursing her demented brother-in-law, Jack Sweetman-Powell, through his last illness. The atmosphere of hatred emanating from Jack had nearly choked her; now she wanted to re-create the peace of Richmond, but Tyrrell was at his most awkward:

Poor M. D. P. has lived and laboured and hoped for this. Indeed she is completely broken in nerves and the doctors ordered her abroad for some months. But no, she says nothing will rest her so much as to see me perfectly at home here at last! Was there ever a more ridiculous situation? Poor thing; I find her harder to talk to than ever; and as she gets more nervous with me I get more formal and stiff *malgré moi* ... Of course I am elaborately reminded that if I would rather live with the Williamses or with you or at

Clapham I am not to consider myself tied in the least degree to Storrington. To which I only answer that Storrington is the pet ideal of my heart.[95]

In his frustration Tyrrell became dictatorial, and was moderately satisfied with the results:

This menage is more tolerable now. I have had the oldest and ugliest cats dismissed; M. D. P. understands clearly that there is not to be a religious atmosphere, or any suggestion of an 'institution'. I sleep (only) at the Priory and go to my duties regularly just to annoy our enemies. That I can do so is not because I believe more, but because I believe less; or perhaps, because I believe quite differently.'[96]

The fundamental problems in their relationship were alleviated, but not removed: 'She cannot but see that I am alive with my other friends and dead with her. I cannot help it. She has no *light* side—all philosophy, or romping. Community of *humour* is the *sine qua non* for companionship.'[97] What Maude Petre lacked—to her infinite sorrow, and to Tyrrell's infinite frustration—was wit.

Despite the strain, Tyrrell had now completed what he thought would be his last theological work. It was intended to bring together his writings on theology and devotion 'from first to last', with a new chapter on revelation ('very important and conservative'), and 'a terrifically modest and profound Introduction as to why I remain and will remain a Roman'.[98] He included 'The Relation of Theology to Devotion', now called 'Lex Orandi, Lex Credendi', 'Semper Eadem' in two parts (the first printed by *The Month*, the second refused), 'Mysteries a Necessity of Life', 'The Rights and Limits of Theology', an essay on 'Prophetic History', the essay on 'Theologism' from which he wanted the book to take its title, and two important pieces on revelation. Pride of place was given to his 'Reflections on Catholicism'. After some haggling with his publisher, the agreed title became *Through Scylla and Charybdis*.[99] The book represented Tyrrell's most cogent statement of his position on the 'conservative left'. Once it was out, he felt he could turn again to negotiations for his *celebret*.

He could not have chosen a worse moment. For months there had been rumours of a new 'Syllabus of Errors' against the 'liberal Catholics'. *Lamentabili*[100] appeared on 3 July. It was a broadside of sixty-five propositions, mostly drawn from the writings of Loisy, in which the magisterium tried to reassert by force the teaching of Trent and a pre-critical way of looking at the Bible. One of the propositions condemned was that 'Even by dogmatic definitions the Church's magisterium cannot determine the genuine sense of the Sacred Scriptures.' Condemnations ranged through critical positions on revelation, the *ecclesia discens* and the *ecclesia docens*, the interpretation of miracles in the Synoptic Gospels, the view that 'the narratives of John are not properly history, but a mystical contemplation of the Gospel', the nature of revelation, the divinity of Jesus, the Resurrection, the institution of the sacraments, the primacy of Peter, the Apostles' Creed. It was at least clear; it was also utterly devastating, in the way that a blunt instrument is devastating. The only condemnation with which Tyrrell would whole-heartedly have agreed was the last: 'Modern Catholicism cannot be reconciled with true science unless it be transformed into a non-dogmatic Christianity; that is into a broad and liberal Protestantism.' That was a hit at the radical left he would gladly have endorsed.

Tyrrell, of course, held the 'Syllabus' in utter contempt. In so far as it was intended to catch Ward or himself, he thought it failed because it was too loosely worded. Loisy and the critics were merely bludgeoned:

The only tangible part is the direct collision with the inevitable data of scriptural and historical science; and the implied claim to settle such scientific points by official *fiats*. Also; the plain contention that the whole present dogmatic hierarchic and sacramental system dates from A.D. 30, and has never developed one bit. The sane world will laugh and will forget it all in a month; but it will be the rule for seminary teaching *in aeternum* and that is where its poison will enter in and kill the Church.[101]

Things seemed to be moving towards the paradoxical conclusion that Tyrrell, with his love of irony, had long desired: 'If we could get the Pope to say that the Syllabus is *ex cathedra*, we should have a new and decisive situation—for, I assume, that at least 25 of these propositions will prove as evidently false to the next generation as the condemnation of Galileo.'[102] Would the Pope and the Cardinals now declare the moon to be made of green cheese?

At this unpropitious moment Tyrrell asked for help from the Prior of Storrington, who was anxious to regularize the situation of the alienated priest who lodged under his roof. On 20 July Tyrrell wrote to him formally:

Since there has been no charge alleged or proved against me, there must be no question of any condition that would be interpreted as penal; but only of such conditions as are obligatory on every priest in virtue of the common laws of the Church. When the Holy See restores me my rights as a Priest, I will engage faithfully to render the duties dependent on those rights; that is to say, I will not publish any sort of theological teaching, nor will I disseminate such teaching by epistolary correspondence, or in any other way equivalent to publication, without due authorisation. (But till my rights are restored I will regard myself as free from all corresponding duties.)

My principles will not allow of any further concession.[103]

On 29 August the Prior told Tyrrell that he had heard from Ferrata, who was willing to give him permission to celebrate, using the exact words of Tyrrell's letter. Tyrrell immediately sent the desired undertaking. On the same day, however, *The Times* followed the *Giornale* in speaking of Tyrrell's 'submission'. They were joined the next day by the *Daily Chronicle*, though this report expressed doubt about the truth of the rumour, since it would mean Tyrrell giving up his career as a writer and withdrawing into private life. This was not at all what he intended. As he saw it, there was nothing to 'submit' to, except the normal censorship imposed on any Roman priest. He was expecting the appearance any day of 'A Plea for Candour' in the Italian journal *Rinnovamento*. As a result of the reports in the Press, which showed how his letter to Ferrata would be construed, and the fact that he was actually moving *away* from 'submission', his patience snapped. He sent a wire asking Maude Petre to see the Prior and stop dispatch of the documents. It was too late; they were sent. Immediately he wrote to the papers disclaiming 'submission', and to Ferrata retracting his undertaking. 'This inordinate thirst for "submissions",' he told Ferrata, 'this desire to humiliate and degrade, is suicidal and disastrous.'[104]

Eight days later the encyclical *Pascendi*, which comprehensively condemned every form of 'modernism', was published.

NOTES

1. Tyrrell to Bremond, 22 Aug. 1905 (BN, Fonds Bremond).
2. Ibid.
3. Martin to Tyrrell, 29 Aug. 1905 (*AL2*, p. 238; BL).
4. Tyrrell to Martin, 2 Sept. 1905 (ARSJ, ANGL. 1021, IV.4; *AL2*, p. 499; BL).
5. Martin to Tyrrell, 15 Sept. 1905 (ARSJ, *RPA*; BL).

6. Martin to Ferrata, 25 Sept. 1905 (ARSJ, *REEPE*, iv); Oct. 1905 (ARSJ, ANGL. 1021, IV.5).
7. Ferrata to Martin, undated (ARSJ, ANGL. 1021, IV.6).
8. Martin to Tyrrell, 12 Oct. 1905.
9. Tyrrell to Martin, 10 Oct. 1905.
10. Martin to Tyrrell, 14 Oct. 1905.
11. Von Hügel to Tyrrell, 9 Oct. 1905 (BL, Petre Papers).
12. Tyrrell to Bremond, 14 Oct. 1905.
13. Tyrrell to von Hügel, 11 Oct. 1905 (BL, Petre Papers).
14. Tyrrell to Bremond, 10 Nov. 1905.
15. Von Hügel to Tyrrell, 24 Oct. 1905.
16. Tyrrell to Martin, 14 Nov. 1905.
17. Martin to Tyrrell, 25 Nov. 1905
18. Von Hügel to Tyrrell, 18 Nov. 1905.
19. Tyrrell to von Hügel, 19 Nov. 1905.
20. Tyrrell to Maude Petre, 9 Dec. 1905 (BL, Petre Papers).
21. Tyrrell to Maude Petre, 16 Mar. 1905.
22. Tyrrell to Martin, 31 Dec. 1905.
23. Martin to Tyrrell, 7 Jan. 1906.
24. Tyrrell to Martin, 10 Jan. 1905.
25. Tyrrell to Martin, 13 Jan. 1906.
26. Martin to Tyrrell, 20 Jan. 1906.
27. Tyrrell to Martin, 24 Jan. 1906.
28. ARSJ, ANGL. 1021, V.11; *AL*2, p. 252; BL.
29. ARSJ, *REEPE*, 15 Jan. 1906.
30. Martin to Ferrata, undated (IV.11).
31. Martin to Ferrata, 31 Jan. 1906.
32. Meyer to Sykes, 15 May 1906 (ARSJ, *RPA*, v): '*jubente ipso Summo Pontifice*'.
33. Martin to Tyrrell, 1 Feb. 1906.
34. Sykes to Tyrrell, 4 Feb. 1906 (BL, Petre Papers).
35. Sykes to Tyrrell, 7 Feb. 1906.
36. Martin to Tyrrell, 1 Feb. 1906.
37. Martin to Sykes, 13 Feb. 1906 (*AL*2, p. 254); Sykes to Tyrrell, 18 Feb. 1906.
38. Tyrrell to Maude Petre, 30 Dec. 1905.
39. Tyrrell to Bremond, 25 Jan. 1906.
40. Tyrrell to Maude Petre, 22 Jan. 1906.
41. Tyrrell to Bremond, 30 Jan. 1906.
42. Tyrrell to Maude Petre, 12 Feb. 1906.
43. Tyrrell to Bremond, undated.
44. Tyrrell to Maude Petre, 3 Mar. 1906.
45. Tyrrell to von Hügel, 18 Mar. 1906.

46. Laberthonnière to Bremond, 13 Mar. 1906, in M.-T. Perrin (ed.), *Laberthonnière et ses amis* (Paris, 1975), p. 66.
47. Tyrrell to von Hügel, 18 Mar. 1906.
48. Tyrrell to Maude Petre, 9, 21 Mar. 1906.
49. Ibid.
50. Tyrrell to Ferrata, 7 Apr. 1906 (*AL2*, p. 503).
51. Tyrrell to Thurston, 19 Apr. 1906 (AEPSJ).
52. Tyrrell to Bremond, 25 Apr. 1906.
53. *Lex Credendi: A Sequel to Lex Orandi* (London, 1906). Quotation is from p. 5 ('a derived and secondary . . .').
54. Tyrrell to Ferrata, 4 May 1906 (*AL2*, p. 504).
55. *AL2*, p. 299; R. Thibault, *Abbot Columba Marmion* (London and St Louis, 1932), pp. 286–90.
56. Ferrata to Mercier, 18 June 1906 (*AL2*, p. 504).
57. Tyrrell to Bremond, 30 Jan. 1906.
58. Tyrrell to Bremond, 15 May 1906.
59. Tyrrell to Maude Petre, 12 July 1906.
60. Bremond to Laberthonnière, undated, in Perrin, *Laberthonnière*, p. 96.
61. Tyrrell to Lilley, 30 June 1906 (SAUL, Lilley Papers).
62. Tyrrell to Houtin, 23 July 1906 (BN, Fonds Houtin).
63. Open letter from Tyrrell to Ferrata, 4 July 1906 (*AL2*, p. 302).
64. Letter to Mrs Scorer, 11 Oct. 1906.
65. Tyrrell to Merry del Val, 20 July 1906 (ARSJ, ANGL. 1021, V.16).
66. Tyrrell to Maude Petre, 17 Aug. 1906.
67. Von Hügel to Maude Petre, 3 July 1906 (BL, Petre Papers).
68. Tyrrell to von Hügel, 20 Sept. 1906.
69. Tyrrell to Kitty Clutton, 18 Aug. 1906 (C).
70. Tyrrell to von Hügel, 8 Dec. 1906.
71. Von Hügel to Maude Petre, 3 July 1906.
72. Maude Petre diaries, 20 Oct. 1906 (BL, Add. MS 52374).
73. Tyrrell to Bremond, 31 October 1906.
74. Tyrrell to Bremond, 6 Dec. 1906.
75. Tyrrell to Bremond, 27 Dec. 1906.
76. Tyrrell to Thurston, 'Friday' (0028).
77. Von Hügel to Tyrrell, 15 Dec. 1906.
78. Tyrrell to von Hügel, 23 Dec. 1906.
79. Von Hügel to Tyrrell, 15 Dec. 1906.
80. Tyrrell to Dell, 16 Jan. 1907 (*GTL*, pp. 105–6).
81. 'Reflections on Catholicism', *TSC*, pp. 20–84.
82. Ibid., pp. 83–4.
83. Tyrrell to Osborne, 30 Mar. 1907 (SAUL, MSS 37018/10).
84. Tyrrell to Maude Petre, 4 Jan. 1907.

85. Tyrrell to L. R., 9 July 1898 (*GTL*, p. 256).
86. Tyrrell to L. R., 17 Mar. 1907 (*GTL*, p. 258).
87. Tyrrell to L. R., 18 May 1907 (*GTL*, pp. 248–9).
88. Tyrrell to L. R., 26 May 1907 (*GTL*, p. 260).
89. Tyrrell to L. R., 14 Apr. 1909 (*GTL*, p. 261).
90. W. Blunt, *My Diaries*, 2 vols. (London, 1919–20), ii, p. 195.
91. Tyrrell to Thurston, 'Friday' (0028).
92. Tyrrell to Maude Petre, 30 Aug. 1906 (*AL2*, p. 366).
93. Tyrrell to Osborne, undated [2 Sept. 1907].
94. Tyrrell to Maude Petre, 7 May 1905 (*AL2*, p. 368).
95. Tyrrell to Bremond, 26 May 1907.
96. Tyrrell to Bremond, 23 June 1907.
97. Tyrrell to Bremond, 25 July 1907.
98. Tyrrell to Bremond, [?] Apr. 1907.
99. *Through Scylla and Charybdis: Or the Old Theology and the New* (London, 1907).
100. The text of *Lamentabili* is printed in *The Tablet*, 27 July 1907, pp. 138–41.
101. Tyrrell to Bremond, 25 July 1907.
102. Tyrrell to Houtin, 26 July 1907.
103. Tyrrell to de la Fourvière, 20 July 1907 (*AL2*, p. 323).
104. Tyrrell to Ferrata, 31 Aug. 1907 (*AL2*, p. 327).

14

'Modernism'

'MODERNISM' was, in effect, created by Pius X through the encyclical *Pascendi*.[1] Until September 1907, when the encylical was published, there was little coherence and a variety of aims in the liberal Catholic movement, but once *Pascendi* appeared, it was widely accepted that the modernist movement represented nothing less than a conspiracy to undermine the Church. The 'modernist' was unmasked as an insidious operator, out to destroy from within, concealing vicious aims behind a façade of scholarship and piety. The encyclical systematically exposed and condemned the modernist as philosopher, believer, theologian, historian, critic, apologist, and reformer.

Modernism was effective because it was based, according to the Vatican, on a coherent and highly destructive philosophy, and presented with a beguiling display of incoherence. At the philosophical root of modernism lay agnosticism. From the Kantian belief that human reason can deal only in phenomena, things as they appear to us, the move to practical atheism was, said the encyclical, all too easy, since the modernist no longer looks for God in scientific or historical phenomena. For the modernist, knowledge of God is located in 'a certain interior sense', which is to be equated with revelation. Supernatural religion is reduced to the level of natural religious experience. Dogma arises from reflection upon this experience. Religious formulas and dogmas express the truth symbolically, and are by no means fixed. They change and develop. *Pascendi* paints a picture of religious knowledge that is radically open, secularized, and undiscriminating.

For the modernists the consequences of this fundamental stance are allegedly worked out in terms of teaching about the sacraments, the Scriptures, the Church, and ecclesiastical authority that is consistent with their agnostic and immanentist presuppositions. There is no part of the life and teaching of the Church that is not subject to their criticism. Modernism, then, is the 'synthesis of all heresies'. It is rooted in pride and ignorance. The system is 'born of the union between faith and false philosophy'. The encyclical outlined a series of defensive measures: renewed stress on the study of scholastic philosophy; careful screening of teachers and students in seminaries; more vigorous censorship; prohibition of congresses of priests, except under careful supervision; the establishment of vigilance committees; and triennial reports to Rome on progress in the battle against modernism. The sweeping terms of the encyclical make it clear that no aspect of Catholic life and thought was considered safe. By shoring up the old foundations, the Church was hoping to withstand the trembling of the earth.

Undoubtedly, Tyrrell was one of those at whom the encyclical was principally aimed. Shortly after 'the new Roman candle' was published, he went to stay with von Hügel so that they could consider it together. Two copies arrived on 19 September, and that evening Tyrrell read one. Von Hügel worked through his the next morning, and in the afternoon they called on Lilley for tea, leaving a copy with him. Tyrrell's immediate response was pugnacious; von Hügel was more cautious and anxious to restrain the outspokenness of his friend. Tyrrell was being pressed for a reaction to the encyclical, and within a week the *Giornale d'Italia* published a signed letter in which he suggested that the Pope was too simple to understand the theological issues behind the encyclical.[2] This shocked a number of his Italian friends, and left von Hügel 'busy rallying and steadying, for all I am worth'.[3] Making the best of the situation, he pronounced the letter 'very strong, indeed vehement, but I expect, useful'.[4] Tyrrell acknowledged that it had been written in haste and was intemperate.

Tyrrell also contributed two articles to *The Times*.[5] These were more measured in their language, but still savaged the encyclical from end to end. He argued forcefully against the identification of Catholicism with scholasticism, and the portrayal of modernist alternatives as a form of apostasy: 'When the encyclical tries to show the modernist that he is no Catholic,' he wrote, 'it mostly succeeds only in showing him that he is no scholastic—which he knew.' The scholasticism endorsed by the encyclical was precisely what the modernists rejected as implying 'a science-theory and psychology that are as strange as astrology to the modern mind'. In response to *Pascendi*'s presentation of a modernist system, Tyrrell gave a curt summary of the received Thomistic system on which the encyclical was based. As with the most telling caricatures, it is exaggerated but damning:

Religion is derived by deductive reasoning from natural and miraculous phenomena. God is not reached through inward religious experience, but by argument. The divinity of Christ and Christianity can be thus argued so as to coerce the understanding. The Roman Catholic Church, with the Papacy, the sacraments, and all its institutions and dogmas, was, in its entirety, the immediate creation of Christ when upon earth. There has been no vital development, but only mechanical unpacking of what was given from the first. The Scriptures were dictated by God, and are final in questions of science and history. All doctrinal guidance and ecclesiastical authority is mediated through the infallible Pope from God to the Church. The Church is the purely passive recipient of the guidance so received. The Bishops are mere delegates of the Pope; the priests of the Bishops. The laity have no active share of any kind in ecclesiastical concerns; still less in the so-called growth of the Church's mind. Obedience and pecuniary succour are their sole duties. Science is subject to the control of scholastic theology; secular government is subject to the control of ecclesiastical government in mixed matters. Their jurisdiction is in the same order; only in different departments. There has been no true enlightenment and progress in modern times outside the Church. There is no element of truth in any other religious system.[6]

All this Tyrrell thought it self-evidently impossible for any critically educated modern mind to accept. It was not ignorance of the scholastic system, as the encyclical alleged, but a close familiarity with it that had driven him to seek something different. He dismissed *Pascendi* as an attempt, by disciplinary means, to modify ideas that could not and would not be changed, but might well, under the storm of repression, have to go underground for a while. He claimed the lineage of Erasmus and Colet when he presented the modernist as a man of the centre whose spiritual roots are too deep for him to bend before the juridical bullying of the church authorities, for 'to secede would be to allow that his calumniators were in the right'. The encyclical, he concluded, damaged the Church, because, in identifying Catholicism with scholasticism, it debarred from grace and from the sacraments all those who could not and would not make an archaic and unnecessary identification.

Tyrrell had shot his bolt, well knowing that the outcome would be excommunication. The articles in *The Times* were better argued and more measured than the letter to the *Giornale*, but they still carried a note of bitterness that disturbed von Hügel, who consistently called for moderation and an absence of personal rancour. He had found them 'very hot, vehement, and sarcastic', and called for compassion towards the Pope, 'a peasant of simple seminary training and speaking to some 200 million souls of whom, doubtless, a good nine-tenth [sic], at least, are even less cultured than himself, and whom he is sincerely trying to defend against what he considers to be deadly error. We can', he concluded, 'afford to be magnanimous.'[7]

Magnanimous was the last thing Tyrrell wanted to be. An article published in the Vatican-controlled *Corrispondenza Romana* on 24 September and taken up by the *Daily Chronicle*,[8] had fuelled the fire of his indignation. Publishing the story of the secret negotiations for his *celebret*, it accused him of breaking his pledge to accept censorship, both when he wrote to the Press disavowing rumours of 'submission' and when he published, uncensored, *Through Scylla and Charybdis*. All these charges he repudiated. In a letter to the *Daily Chronicle* he pointed out that his pledge had been conditional on receiving a *celebret*, and at the time of writing to the Press this had not been granted. Moreover, *Through Scylla and Charybdis* had been published well before these negotiations were concluded.[9]

In a letter to Cardinal Ferrata that can only be called insolent he demanded that he should either publish their whole correspondence or at least set the record straight in the *Corrispondenza*.[10] He now believed that the promise of a *celebret* had been a snare, intended to silence him before the appearance of *Lamentabili* and *Pascendi*. Even before Rome spoke, he was to be portrayed as having 'submitted'. The scheme had misfired, however: 'In their eagerness to begin at once this work of misrepresenting, they cannot wait till the bird is in their hand. But the bird sees the snare before it is too late; and flies away. That is the whole story; and they are furious at being detected.' As to his articles on *Pascendi*, their meaning was simply '*Quod facis, fac cito* [What you are doing, do quickly]; excommunicate me and be damned to you all for a pack of knaves and fools.'[11] Having so much less to lose than others less prominently opposed to Rome, he had thrown himself on the bayonets. Better, he argued, to be condemned for what he *had* said, than to be silenced and then misrepresented without the right of reply. By his outspoken resistance he intended to shock those in Rome who assumed that religious obedience excluded this right. 'Poor Laberthonnière; poor Blondel; poor Baron, poor everybody—even poor *Ward!*'[12] he wrote, as he contemplated the list of those who could not or would not speak out. Only Buonaiuti, who was as unyielding as Tyrrell in his opposition to *Pascendi*, was 'a man of true steel'.[13] 'If even 10 men would shout "No",' he wrote, 'God might spare Sodom yet.'[14]

Exhausted, Tyrrell retired from Clapham to Storrington. 'I must stay quiet for a bit,' he told von Hügel, 'till my guns are cool—else there may be an explosion.'[15] With typical honesty he admitted to Wilfrid Blunt how he really felt about the fray: 'As you may imagine, the air is full of missiles directed at my head, and I am busy dodging them. It is not pleasant, yet to my Irish blood not wholly unpleasant.'[16] Maude Petre was glad to welcome him as 'at present *quite* the central figure of the modernist movement'.[17] She even deluded herself into thinking that the company of four ladies at Mulberry House would provide agreeable respite.

In the weeks that followed, Tyrrell was rarely without company: Alfred Fawkes, like himself a convert from Anglicanism, and, unlike him, soon to return, took a small house nearby. Standing together in the Anglican church at Storrington with Albert Houtin, now deprived of his *celebret* for writing on the Church's failure to face 'the biblical question', he and Tyrrell jokingly agreed that they should never have left Anglicanism. Houtin, who had given up all hope of a reformation in Catholicism, was on his way back from a conference on religious liberalism in Boston. He struck Tyrrell as 'very dry and grave and sedate and well-informed;—a terrible because a cold enemy'.[18] Where Tyrrell argued that the place of the modernists was within the Church, Houtin believed that attempts to accommodate the Church to modern times were beside the point, as 'Jesus never founded a church'.[19] Houtin later wrote biographical accounts of Tyrrell and Loisy in which he alleged that, as modernists, both had given up their Christian faith. Twice in these weeks the Baron came to sit with Tyrrell under the mulberry tree. After one of these visits in early November, Maude Petre noted that he was 'upset and nervous and overwrought—thought GT was against him etc'.[20] Despite the strain on the relationship, von Hügel, whose friendship had wavered the year before, now proved a faithful friend who gave Tyrrell generous and valued support in time of crisis.

Once more Tyrrell was ready for the offensive. On 11 October he wrote to Ferrata threatening to publish their correspondence himself,[21] but only two weeks later such wrangling ceased to matter. On 23 October the blow at last fell. Bishop Amigo of Southwark informed him that his articles in *The Times* had been referred to Rome, and that he was to be deprived of the sacraments. What

Tyrrell did not know was that the instruction for his exclusion from the sacraments actually came from Cardinal Merry del Val, on the Pope's personal authority.[22] He was simply relieved that the suspense was over. 'It is a relief', he told Lilley, 'to have one's head clean off instead of dangling.'[23] Fearing another explosion from Tyrrell, von Hügel urged a policy of silence and conciliation, advice which, for the time being, Tyrrell was disposed to accept. His reply to Bishop Amigo is a model of aggressive and unyielding penitence:

You speak of 'submission', but your letter in no way defines the precise nature of my offence—since to write to *The Times* in not of itself a canonical offence meriting excommunication. I have rarely or never written anything which after-thought would not have mended in some respects. And therefore it, in defence of the imperilled faith of so many souls inside and outside the Church, I was at moments carried away by indignation into any unbecoming irony or sarcasm; if I forgot myself and the Gospel so far as to answer reproach with reproach, or bitterness with bitterness; if I allowed myself to be drawn down to the level of personal attack, to the detriment of the courtesy and reverence due to the office of the Holy Father, I deeply regret such a defection from what I hope are my habitual instincts and principles, and I cordially apologise to those whom I have unintentionally shocked or offended . . . If, however, my offence lies in having protested publicly, in the name of Catholicism, against a document destructive of the only possible defence of Catholicism and of every reason for submitting, within due limits, to ecclesiastical authority—a document which constitutes the greatest scandal for thousands who, like myself, have been brought into, and kept in, the Church by the influence of Cardinal Newman and of the mystical theology of the Fathers and the Saints—for such a protest I am absolutely and finally impenitent.[24]

Tyrrell challenged Amigo to publish the letter, but Amigo wisely left him to publish it himself. This he did the more readily when Amigo wrote to the Central Press Agency explaining that Tyrrell had not been 'excommunicated', as had been widely reported, but merely 'deprived of the sacraments'. Technically, this meant that he was subject to 'minor' and not 'major' excommunication: he was welcome to be present at mass, though not, of course, to communicate; and he was not, as Loisy was shortly to be, *vitandus*, 'to be shunned' by the faithful. Tyrrell, however, had referred to his 'excommunication' in his letter to Amigo, and he lost no time in writing to *The Times* to say, that, as far as he was concerned, the Bishop's distinction was meaningless: he was excluded from Communion and that was all that mattered to him.[25] In writing to Amigo he asked why, if the distinction was so vital, the Bishop had not immediately corrected his mistake. Actually, he said, he wanted to hear no more of the business. 'If anything is lacking to the process of my defamation,' he told the Bishop, 'let it be done without reference to me.'[26]

Tyrrell was hard put to it not to fire off a stream of letters to the Press, as *Pascendi* had given rise to a lively controversy in the pages of *The Times*. W. J. Williams argued forcibly that Newman was caught by the ignorant and sweeping condemnations of Rome, and if Newman was condemned, then, at a stroke, the encyclical had locked Catholicism into an intellectual ghetto. He maintained that the encyclical had condemned 'every characteristic proposition' of Newman, thereby drawing an assertion from John Norris, the Superior of Newman's old community, and from Abbot Gasquet of Downside, that it had not.[27] Tyrrell watched, and prompted Williams, as the issue was debated. All the while the Baron, in his inimitable way, was restraining him: 'The more rapid-than-light friend will put his beetle-crushers on, won't he? and will walk with brave, browsing, apparently bumbling, determination, these days, especially!'[28] Tyrrell was certainly brave and determined, but he could not have 'bumbled' to save his life.

Relations with the Baron continued to be a major problem, as the two men responded so differently to pressure from Rome. Von Hügel could accept it, defer, and go his own way. Tyrrell felt that bullying and intellectual boorishness should be denounced and resisted, but the fight had embittered him, and this saddened the Baron immensely. With pained affection he wrote to his friend:

Perhaps the ideal, all-round man, should be able to hate and pursue destructively, with the same directness and fulness, with which he would love and construct. *Perhaps*, though I am far from sure even of this. But I am very sure that, in any case, George Tyrrell is not that kind of man. A dominant hatred and determination to destroy even a set of men or an institution predominant[ly] evil; such a disposition would, the writer of this scribble is absolutely certain, shrivel up and evaporate all the true power, all the deep glorious helpfulness of G. T., long before he had done any serious execution upon those his enemies. May G. T. keep realising this, and that we have no opponents who can do us or our cause much harm, except in this our temptation, our weakness, which might drive us into such sterilizing negation and feverish hate.[29]

After one visit Tyrrell wrote to Bremond: 'The Baron was here yesterday; in tears, because he got some idea that I was off on some new line and going to leave him. He is sensitive as a woman.' Irritated by the Baron's habitual caution, he became contrary and outspoken: 'I told him that I would play the game as long as one man was left on the field; that it was only loyalty to my fellow-players that kept me where I am; that when they had all kissed the Pope's toe and disowned me I would return quietly to the Church of my Baptism and die in a country vicarage.'[30] This was not at all what the Baron wanted to hear, nor was Tyrrell capable of doing such a thing. Still, he had been shocked to think that von Hügel would rather see him an atheist than an Anglican. For his part, von Hügel could understand neither how Anglicanism beckoned, nor how, despite Tyrrell's fantasies and his own fears, he would never leave the Church to which he had given his heart. Tyrrell knew perfectly well the depth of the gulf that divided them. He once said to von Hügel: 'We shall go separate ways. You believe in love as the final end, but I believe in love and hate. I believe in the devil, I fight him with hate.' Such combative ferocity was utterly alien to von Hügel's measured and pacific caution. 'I always felt restless after being with him,' he said. 'One is always restless after being with sceptical minds.'[31]

During the last quarter of 1907 Tyrrell was at the centre of the modernist storm. To some extent, he followed the Baron's advice, but he was incapable of remaining silent for long, and in the prevailing climate of repression it was clear to him that there was nothing to be gained by doing so. As the immediate crisis receded he spoke and wrote with more moderation, but he remained a committed leader of the modernist resistance. At times he felt *'infinitely ennuyé* of the whole business'.[32] In November he contributed an article to the *Guardian* in which he reviewed the evidence that the encyclical had blindly and foolishly condemned Newman.[33] He defended his position by letters in the *Guardian* and *The Times*.[34] He also prepared an article on 'The Prospects of Modernism' for the *Hibbert Journal*,[35] and completed a major piece of work in his translation of *The Programme of Modernism*,[36] a fierce riposte to *Pascendi*, mainly by Ernesto Buonaiuti, who was then only 28 and had produced the tract at white heat within days of the encyclical's publication. The previous June Tyrrell had worked over Lilley's translation of a slighter piece by a group of young Italian priests, called *What We Want*.[37] At first he and Lilley thought that they would follow the same procedure with Buonaiuti's tract, but in the end it was agreed that Tyrrell should be the sole translator. He set to work with a will, as he thought the anonymous tract 'masterly'. To Lilley he confided that he was being 'most free and unscrupulous, weaving little comments of my own into the text; but with absolute fidelity, I hope, to the sense and spirit of the writers'.[38]

One of the strengths of *The Programme of Modernism* is the clarity with which it shows that 'modernism' was not, as alleged by *Pascendi*, the product of a union between the faith and a new philosophy, but the outcome of prolonged wrestling with the findings of biblical and historical criticism. Buonaiuti's summary of these findings is still convincing today. By patient and concise exposition of the critical method, he shows how 'everything in the history of Christianity has changed—doctrine, hierarchy, worship'. It was this unavoidable fact that scholasticism could not accommodate. Buonaiuti also expresses his conviction that 'all these changes have been providential means for the preservation of the Gospel-spirit, which has remained unchanged through the ages'. This conviction was near to the heart of modernism: the fact that Christianity has changed, and needs to change, to preserve its identity. Tyrrell delighted in pointing out that, in condemning the modernists, *Pascendi* quoted an encyclical of Gregory IX's which spoke of certain doctors of theology who twisted 'the heavenly pages of the Bible into agreement with philosophical theories', and that these words were actually written against *scholasticism*—the modernism of the thirteenth century. Moreover, three years later Gregory had practically to retract his words. *The Programme of Modernism* goes on to refute the attack of *Pascendi* upon modernist apologetic, showing how it could not be both 'agnostic' and 'atheist'. The 'immanentism' (or stress upon God as found within human consciousness) of the modernists is defended by quotations from Augustine, Aquinas, and others. On other specific matters—the accusation that modernists say 'all religions are true', that they separate science from faith, and make faith subordinate to science, that they desire to separate Church and State—the encyclical is criticized for inaccuracy and ignorance of the tradition. Modernists, it is claimed, see the relation of other religions to Christianity as that of 'the less perfect to the more perfect'; they distinguish between 'the scientific faculty' and 'the faculty of faith', recognizing that each has its part to play in the examination of the Scriptures, but not making one subordinate to the other; in advocating the separation of Church and State, modernists call on the Church to leave the pursuit of power in the political arena, and to 'retire back into the sphere of her spiritual dominion'. Each of these positions, while needing qualification, has been vindicated by time. Finally *The Programme of Modernism* criticized the practical measures that had been called for to stamp out modernism. Like scholasticism, it would not be stamped out by papal fulminations, and, like many of the finest servants of the Church, the modernists themselves would not be discouraged or silenced by the treatment they received. As far as Tyrrell was concerned, *The Programme of Modernism* was his own. He told Bremond that 'The *Programma* is a quite workable religion and will be received by large sections of the Anglican and Protestant religions with open arms; and when the Papacy is thoroughly found out and discredited we shall walk into the Vatican and put the Baron on the chair of Peter as the first lay-Pope.'[39]

Though he was a shrewd observer and an avid reader of biblical criticism, this was an area in which Tyrrell never felt competent to speak. He directed his attack upon *Pascendi* as the canonization of scholasticism and a travesty of modernism, which was 'a method and a spirit rather than a system; a mode of enquiry not a body of results'. In his article on 'The Prospects of Modernism' he claimed that most modernists had attempted to stretch the categories of scholasticism to accommodate the awkward facts with which they were presented by critical study, but the vessel had broken, as it was not designed for the dynamism of modern thought, with its commitment to historical growth, development, and change. They had been forced to find new ways of thinking about the identity of the faith. So how were they to respond when the Church ordered them back into the old mould? 'When the house is in flames should one wait for orders or for leave to cry "Fire"?' Tyrrell was not sanguine about the short-term prospects of modernism, but he had no doubt of the long-term outcome of the Church's attempts to keep the clergy, and thus the laity, in ignorance:

The attempt to create and maintain an uneducated clergy ignorant of real history and of everything except scholasticism and what scholasticism sanctions, is doomed to speedy defeat. With education will come the knowledge of history, and still more, the sense of history, the category of growth and development. It will be utterly impossible to keep from the Catholic clergy of the near future the knowledge of those facts which are fatal to the whole juristico-scholastic conception of Catholicism, to the notion of the Church with all her essential dogmas and institutions, as an abrupt and immediate creation of Christ, and as exercising in His name, not a spiritual, but a juridical authority in intellectual, moral, social, and political matters, which He never exercised.[40]

These words were written at the darkest time of the crisis. In November 1907 a *Motu Proprio* was published which made the doctrinal decisions of the Biblical Commission binding upon the consciences of the faithful. Contradiction of them, or defence of the propositions condemned in *Lamentabili* and *Pascendi*, would entail automatic excommunication.[41] A small sign of the changing climate was a letter from Bremond's housekeeper expressing her unhappiness that Tyrrell was coming to stay. Tyrrell now realized how deeply his presence would compromise his many French friends, and he cancelled plans to visit Bremond in Paris. Meanwhile, the Baron, who needed further help with the typescript of *St Catherine*, was urging him to come and stay in lodgings near Vicarage Gate, an invitation that Tyrrell was disposed to resist. However, he could not stay at Clapham, as there was illness in the family. Early in 1908, when Maude Petre was in Montreux, he spent just over a month in her house, seeing von Hügel virtually every day. On moving to Clapham he retired to bed for three days—'the accumulated result of a month with the Baron'.[42]

Tyrrell hoped that resistance to *Pascendi* would take the form of a series of *affaires*, his own being merely the first. He predicted that Loisy, who had now lost his *celebret* and ceased to say mass, would wake from apparent slumber round about Christmas. He knew Loisy was far from asleep, because he had received a letter from him soon after the publication of *Pascendi* in which he asked Tyrrell to identify any quotations in the encyclical that were taken from his works. Tyrrell replied: 'When I first read the document, I, like others perhaps, found myself in every paragraph; but now I see that, in most cases, it is impossible to say whether I, or Laberthonnière or Ward, or Newman, or Le Roy etc. be the culprit.'[43] He gave four instances in which he thought the reference was to him, complaining that 'in all cases they are *lectiones conflatae* and quite impossible to verify'. He also told Loisy that he would stick to his Catholicism, excommunicate or not. 'The worst that could happen', he claimed, would be 'if their diplomacy got the better of their anger and they were to silence me with a *celebret*.'

All this Loisy absorbed carefully, as he was preparing a volume of *Simples réflexions* on *Lamentabili* and *Pascendi* in which he argued that the modernist 'system' was a fabrication of the systematic, scholastic Roman mind, backed up by selective quotation from modernist works. In January 1908 he was pressed by Cardinal Merry del Val to declare his adherence to the Roman pronouncements. He answered by acknowledging that a large number of the condemned propositions had been taken from his writings, but deploring the way in which their meaning had been twisted. 'My spirit', he said, 'would be as incapable of living in the intellectual atmosphere of the decree *Lamentabili* and of the encyclical *Pascendi* as my lungs would be of breathing at the bottom of the sea.'[44] He knew that his two-volume study of *Les Évangiles synoptiques* and his *Simples réflexions* would be on sale before the end of the month. The first was the fruit of fifteen years' scholarly work; the second an exercise in critical polemic.[45] He knew that in Roman eyes they would merit equal condemnation. In February they were duly condemned by Archbishop Amette of Paris. 'Major excommunication' came from Rome on 7 March not on account of the books, but because he would not declare his adherence to the Roman condemnations of modernism. Loisy was now *vitandus*, to be shunned by the faithful. His response was to give up clerical dress and clerical identity. Unlike Tyrrell, he now felt that, since the Church had put him out, her affairs were no longer any concern of his. As he put it: 'If Tyrrell was in rebellion against Roman absolutism, it was because he was still passionate about the interests of the catholic religion; and if I did not conduct myself like him, it was because the affairs of the church no longer concerned me.'[46]

Tyrrell was not surprised, but he was saddened by Loisy's condemnation. His own quarrel was largely with the injustice, the authoritarianism of the Roman system. Loisy's was with its intellectual darkness. Tyrrell did not feel in the least competent to assess Loisy's critical judgements—here he relied on the Baron—nor was he attracted to Loisy as a personality, but he always defended Loisy's right to exercise his critical judgement with perfect freedom from accusations of heresy. When Loisy offered to send Tyrrell copies of his new books, Tyrrell gladly offered to review the *Simples réflexions*, but demurred from tackling *Les Évangiles synoptiques*. In the event, however, he was persuaded, and, after urgent cries to von Hügel for help, he submitted a review (from which the editor deleted his signature) to *The Nation*.[47] In it he made no substantial criticism of the book, merely noting that as a critic Loisy was 'nearer the

extreme left than the extreme right', and stressing that the judgements he made were purely *historical*: the language of faith and the
judgements of history operated at a different level.

Tyrrell was sure that attempts were being made to prise him and
Loisy apart. On the very day that Loisy was excommunicated,
Tyrrell passed through Paris *en route* for Montreux, where Maude
Petre was recovering from a serious fall, and where he planned to
meet Bremond. Shortly after, *Il Momento*, a right-wing Catholic
paper, carried a story about his strong words in condemnation of
Loisy and Houtin. He was reported to have said that Loisy's latest
works were a disaster for the cause of modernism in England because
of their aridity of spirit, lack of mystical sensitivity, and brutally
negative attitude.[48] It was a shrewd hit, because, even if Tyrrell had
never said this, and he hotly denied it to Loisy, he was certainly
disgusted with him. On 18 March he wrote to the Baron: 'I am
afraid, after you have defended Loisy, he may give you away badly by
some fault of taste and judgment. He never seems to think of other
people, neither his friends, nor the simple.'[49] This was a sharp
assessment, for the Baron does not emerge well from Loisy's
Mémoires. Tyrrell, however, like the Baron, was a publicly loyal
friend, but he was two-faced in private, and he was always indiscreet.
When he wrote to Loisy, indignantly denying that he had ever
criticized him publicly, he gave the following account of events:

I think I have traced the *canard* to a conversation I had in Paris with one of
the *Rev. d'Églises Catholiques* young men whose English was as weak as my
French and who seemed in a fever to get patronage for his ideas. Having
most carefully explained my conviction that no historical event could by any
possibility become a matter of faith, ... that the Virgin birth, on its
phenomenal side, could never be other than a matter of history etc.—I found
to my surprise that he agreed with me and seemed to think I had said
something very important and conservative; especially as I said, that the
principles of physical and historical science were quite different, which
seemed to him very illuminating and original. He said: 'That is not M.
Loisy's view'. I said I thought it was; but anyhow it was mine. However he
was quite confident and happy; and so I did not disturb him. That, I suspect
is the seed of the legend; its development is the work of more practised
hands.[50]

As an exercise in criticism, this was less than impressive. It is much
more likely that Dell was correct when he told Lilley that the basis of
the story was an accurate report of Tyrrell's disapproval of some

remarks made by Houtin in Boston, and his criticism of *Simples réflexions* as egotistical in tone.[51] Three days later Tyrrell wrote to Loisy again with fulsome praise of *Quelques lettres*,[52] a new book in which Loisy had published a dossier of correspondence about the progress of his case, from the placing of his works on the Index to his excommunication. 'It seems to me', said Tyrrell, 'that you have excelled yourself, and may now sing your *Nunc Dimittis*. They were tenfold fools and idiots who persecuted and urged you on and on to such a plain-spoken merciless exposition of the true state of the case.'[53] Loisy had successfully written the self-justifying book that Tyrrell had so often threatened to write.

Tyrrell wrote warmly to Loisy not only because he felt guilty, but because it was essential that the modernists, as they now began to think of themselves, should stay together. It would be all too easy for Rome to break up the movement and make capital out of the victory. Since Loisy's reaction to excommunication was the opposite of his own, it only demonstrated how far apart they were on every issue except opposition to scholasticism, and the need for continued resistance to Rome. Laberthonnière's prompt submission to *Pascendi* had shocked Tyrrell, and again showed, in a different way, how disparate were their convictions. When he joined Tyrrell and Bremond at Bremond's family home in Provence for Holy Week, the two ex-Jesuits teased him mercilessly. Tyrrell found him 'grotesquely ignorant of the contents of Denzinger's Enchiridion' and so of 'the positions of the enemy'.[54] Laberthonnière's saving grace was his gentleness. It was impossible to be angry with him for long.

The real shock to Tyrrell was von Hügel's evident fear of excommunication. After yet more revision, the Baron's great book was at last in the hands of a publisher and due to appear shortly. In view of this, von Hügel wanted to leave unsigned three articles on Loisy that he was about to contribute to the banned periodical *Il Rinnovamento*. Only eight months before, he had been with the editorial group at a secret meeting in the woods near Molveno—ironically not far from Trent. Here they had discussed what they should do if *Il Rinnovamento* were condemned and the Pope demanded submission to *Lamentabili*. Von Hügel had read them his latest letter from Loisy, and had then spoken about the 'necessity of sincere, thorough critical work; of deep, self-renouncing Xtian life; & of careful charity and magnanimity to'rds our opponents'.[55] In mid-November the Archbishop of Milan had forbidden the sacraments to all those in his diocese who were in any way associated with *Il Rinnovamento*. Von Hügel had sent a telegram of support to Alfieri, one of the editors: 'Profonde sympathie—vif désir ne pas changer dispositions —résolutions—Huegel', and had written to Scotti, another editor, who had decided to leave *Il Rinnovamento*, encouraging him to stand firm.[56] Some of the group had been shocked by the tone of Tyrrell's protests against *Pascendi*, and, as an encouragement to them to stand by Tyrrell and Loisy, von Hügel had promised to write openly for their journal. The articles he now proposed to leave unsigned were written to honour that promise. No wonder Tyrrell called the Baron's suggestion that he should leave his articles unsigned 'the worst shock yet to my dwindling faith in human nature'. 'If he does not stand firm now,' he told Maude Petre,

he is a lost man as far as I am concerned; nor do I think he will keep many of his friends ... Von Hügel, with all his preaching of stress and strain and friction, a coward! It only remains to discover that Christ kept a mistress, or that you have been delating me to Rome. The man who has been a sort of conscience to me never existed![57]

It was now Tyrrell who spoke frankly to von Hügel about the need for unity among the modernists, and, for good measure, accused him of inadvertently starting the rumour about his split from Loisy.[58] In the event, von Hügel signed his articles 'H'. He also contributed a signed review of Loisy's *Évangiles synoptiques* to the *Hibbert Journal*.[59]

Tyrrell lived in daily expectation of 'promotion' from minor to major excommunication, to *vitandus*. He also feared the break-up of modernism, because he thought that the movement had been taken over by the mob. 'What should have been a quiet incubation', he told Maude Petre, 'has become a conflagration; the mob has got hold of us. It is exactly the story of 1789.'[60] As in all revolutions, there was no place for moderates. He was sure he would not be heard when he used radical arguments to defend the traditional teaching of the Church. 'Two thousand years ago', he wrote, 'I should have sided with Peter and have had no faith in a breach with the synagogue.'[61] In the heat of the battle, he urgently needed to make space for a clear exposition of his 'modernism'.

This he did in *Medievalism*,[62] a book of white-hot polemic, written in April and May of 1908. In it he took issue with a pastoral letter issued by Cardinal Mercier of Malines the previous Lent.

Tyrrell was hurt and angered that the man who had offered him a home in his diocese only a year before, had so turned against him as to pillory him alone of all the modernists. The explanation of Mercier's conduct was simple. Despite being compromised in Rome by his brief association with Tyrrell, he had received his Cardinal's hat in April 1907. The speech that Pius made on that occasion, in which he had spoken of a sinister attack upon the faith 'which is not a heresy, but the compendium of all heresies', had concluded with an exhortation to the new Cardinals to help by their solemn condemnation of all such teaching. It was this speech that had occasioned the tract *What We Want*, which Tyrrell had helped to translate; and, by his *volte-face*, Mercier was only obeying the Pope's instruction—a prudent thing for a Cardinal to do, especially one who had unwittingly erred. In his pastoral letter he congratulated the Belgians on the absence of modernists in their midst, attributing this to the vigilance of the episcopate ('a reflection not quite complimentary to the French and Italian episcopate', as Tyrrell observed); gave a somewhat *gauche* characterization of modernism, lumping it together with Protestantism; pilloried Tyrrell as one infected with the Protestant spirit; and called for renewed application to the basic teachings of the Church. It was easy for a controversialist as skilled and as angry as Tyrrell to tear the letter apart point by point, pointing out a host of inconsistencies, inaccuracies, and stupid misunderstandings. When the Cardinal read *Medievalism*, he must have wished he had never heard the name Tyrrell.

Tyrrell used his attack on Mercier's 'medievalism' to develop a brilliant, swift-moving apologia for his own modernism. Not for a moment does the tone of ironic reasonableness, nor the intellectual tension, nor the passionate sincerity degenerate into shrill self-justification or rhetorical bludgeoning. As with his attacks on the joint pastoral of 1900, he succeeded because his arguments had been carefully prepared in advance, and because he was given the occasion to marshal them in anger. 'It is necessary for my sincerity', he told von Hügel,

to say why and to what degree I still think it right to belong to so mendacious and immoral an institution as the Roman Church; why I still hesitate to follow Fawkes [who had reverted to Anglicanism]; why I dislike certain schools of Modernism. Because I am exactly *myself* I am sure to please nobody entirely, everybody partly. It is however my farewell to all specifically Catholic writing.[63]

Having dealt with Mercier's ill-advised self-congratulation and his misleading account of modernism, Tyrrell's first major assault was against the ecclesiology of the Vatican Council as commonly interpreted, against 'papolatry' in all its forms. Digging deep into long-prepared positions on the nature of theology as opposed to revelation, the entire Church as the organ of divine tradition, and the distortions occasioned by papolatry, he set out to show not that the Vatican Council had been invalidated by the misbehaviour of the 'dominant faction', but that it had failed to endow the Pope with a personal charism of infallibility: 'My whole position as a Roman Catholic', he declared, 'depends . . . on my being able, if necessary by some *tour de force*, to show that the Vatican Council did not succeed in its efforts to turn the Church upside down and to rest the hierarchical pyramid on its apex.' He argued that, as a theological statement, the definition of papal infallibility could not affect the substance of the Christian revelation, and that this revelation included the infallibility not of the Pope but of the whole Church. 'The Council tells us that the infallibility of the Pope is not other than that which belongs to the whole Church.' Tyrrell was carefully expounding a position that allowed him to stay in the Roman Church, and not to leave it as the Old Catholics had done after the defeat of their position at the Council.

Having justified to his own satisfaction his adherence to a Church that did not want him, Tyrrell turned to an exposition of the meaning of modernism. After disposing of some significant misunderstandings, he set out what modernism meant for him:

'Modernist' as opposed to 'modern' means the insistence on modernity as a principle. It means the acknowledgement on the part of religion of the rights of modern thought; of the need of effecting a synthesis, not between the old and the new indiscriminately, but between what, after due criticism, is found to be valid in the old and in the new. Its opposite is Medievalism, which, as a fact, is only the synthesis effected between the Christian faith and the culture of the late Middle Ages, but which erroneously supposes itself to be of apostolic antiquity . . . Medievalism is an absolute, Modernism a relative term. The former will always stand for the same ideas and institutions; the meaning of the latter slides on with the times. If we must have a sect-name, we might have a worse than one that stands for life and movement as against stagnation and death; for the Catholicism that is of every age as against the sectarianism that is of one.

Later, in a chapter on 'The death-agony of Medievalism', he summed up the contrast between medievalism and modernism: 'On the one side, the category of mechanism—government by machinery; truth by machinery; prayer by machinery; grace and salvation by machinery. On the other, the category of life and growth and spiritual unity.' Tyrrell's conclusion was damning:

How can the world imagine that you have faith in God, that you believe sincerely in the harmony of revelation and science, when it sees you so manifestly afraid of criticism, afraid of the light, afraid of liberty, afraid of outspokenness and moral courage; when it sees the Encyclical placing all its hopes in the repression of knowledge, in the paralysis of mental activity, in the revival of those inquisitorial methods, unchristian and unmanly, that have done more to dishonour religion and scandalise the world than all the enemies of the Church put together?

In a final appeal Tyrrell spoke to the Cardinal directly: 'Your Eminence, will you never take heart of grace and boldly throw open the doors and windows of your great medieval cathedral, and let the light of a new day strike into its darkest corners and the fresh wind of Heaven blow through its mouldy cloisters?'—words that were not forgotten when John XXIII called the Second Vatican Council.

Tyrrell was still with Bremond in Provence when he began work on *Medievalism*. In mid-April he returned to England, staying first at Clapham and then with the monks at Storrington. Maude Petre was also abroad recovering from her near-fatal fall, having been through 'one long nightmare of intermittent pain and agony'. Depressed and heartsick, she was longing to come home and be 'cherished'. 'I am *terribly* down,' she wrote in her diary. 'I want what I cannot have.'[64] In this mood she was ready to throw discretion to the winds. 'Owing . . . to M. D. P.'s grand idea of doing without a chaperon,' wrote Tyrrell to Bremond, 'there is going to be another Storrington crisis . . . My God, what we suffer from the devotion of woman! "Cut *it* off and cast it from thee." It is by that member they hold us. Let us leave it in their hands and fly, like Joseph from Mme. Potiphar, sexless but free.'[65] At the first hint of Maude Petre's return to Mulberry House, Tyrrell fled to Clapham, promising to return in two months. Such vicious rejection caused agonies. 'Intensely sad, desolate, lonely,' she wrote in her diary. 'What this house has cost me God only knows.'[66]

Tyrrell's contracts in London were always broad, and from the time of his excommunication they became even broader. He was continually called on to help and advise ex-Roman priests, many of whom were in severe financial difficulties. Others brought stories of

moral and spiritual ruin, but his compassion never failed. One such
was his old Jesuit friend Edward Lawless, for whom he wrote a
tender letter of recommendation in May 1908, describing him as 'a
dear good affectionate big Irishman with a great love of the people
who has done years and years of hard mission work in slums of
Glasgow Edinburgh and Lancashire and so drugged down the
continual offence of his human and Christian instincts'.[67] Lawless
was now 'immured with the Jesuits at Bournemouth, loathing the
mean, money-grubbing godless business with all his soul and driven
almost mad with "the blindfold sense of wrong", with nothing
before him (he is 51) but a life [of] bitterness and resentment. A fine
man spoilt.' When Lawless 'broke down and cried like a child at the
indignity of his position', Tyrrell approached Lilley for help.

Another who received Tyrrell's help was the former 'Father
Angelo' of the Capuchins.[68] William Blunt recorded that when he
had become a monk at 15, as a result of the influence of his parents,
he was still innocent of the 'facts of life'. Tyrrell advised 'Angelo',
whose real name was de Bary, that his vow of chastity was not
binding under the circumstances, and put him in touch with the
editor of *L'Exode*, a journal founded to help ex-priests. De Bary
subsequently became chaplain to Lord Shaftesbury.

Yet another ex-Roman priest who approached Tyrrell was Arnold
Mathew.[69] He had left the priesthood in 1889, and got married three
years later. What he really wanted was an Anglican living, but this
was refused, so he turned to the non-Roman, but Catholic, Church of
Holland for help. It so happened that the Archbishop of Utrecht had
just been approached by another ex-Roman priest, who guaranteed
to a non-Roman, but Catholic, bishop seventeen English congregations with ex-Roman priests at that time in need of episcopal
guidance. After consultation with Bishop Herzog, the Old Catholic
Bishop of Bern, the Dutch Catholics agreed to create an English
bishopric for Mathew. He was, in effect, to be the bishop for those
disaffected English Roman Catholics who could not find a home in
Anglicanism. After a short delay, during which the Dutch decided
that his married status was no bar to clerical orders, he was duly
consecrated on 28 April 1908 by three Dutch bishops and the Old
Catholic Bishop of Bonn. To Mathew's embarrassment, it then
became clear that there were nothing like seventeen congregations
willing to recognize him. Nevertheless, he was validly consecrated,
and he represented what Tyrrell called 'a Catholicism without

papolatry'. It was Tyrrell's hope that Mathew would provide a focus for an *entente* between Old Catholics and non-Romanist Anglo-Catholics. The following year the Anglican bishops, meeting at the Lambeth Conference, predictably deplored the setting up of 'a new organised body in regions where a Church with Apostolic ministry and Catholic doctrine offered religious privileges without the imposition of un-Catholic terms of communion'. Shortly after, the whole project foundered.

As a newly consecrated bishop without a territorial diocese, Mathew, coached and encouraged by Tyrrell, proved himself an energetic and effective publicist for the non-Roman, Catholic movement. Tyrrell made it quite clear that he himself would stay with Rome, to which he was 'unilaterally united as a bull-dog to the calf of a man's leg',[70] but since he regarded the disagreements between Dutch Catholics, Old Catholics, and Roman Catholics as a series of theological squalls that did not trouble the deep waters of the Catholic faith, there was no inconsistency in supporting Mathew. He hoped that Mathew might inaugurate 'a return to the primitive household church', in which the meaning of authority and ministry could be thought out from first principles. If Tyrrell were Pope, he would make the Christian notion of authority the theme of his first encyclical:

Georgius, gratia Dei et populi Romani voluntate, urbis Romae episcopus, co-episcopus [sic] *et confratribus paribus in Domino, salutem et obsequium,* etc., etc . . . My first encyclical would remind my brethren that as all my authority derives from the *populus Romanus*; so theirs from the faithful of their several dioceses; that each diocese in a *societas perfecta* and only of its own free and reversible choice federated with any other; that the bond of any bigger aggregate is free and spiritual; in no sense juridical; that Masses etc. are valid because they are the acts of a community ('when two or three, etc.') that 'orders' are simply delegation and can take any form the community chooses, e.g. Tom, Dick or Harry *might* be told off to say Mass just for one occasion, and possess orders for half-an-hour; that orders are only indelible because and when the community so will it.[71]

Tyrrell knew that, as a married man, Mathew would be accused of concubinage and of having invalidated his orders, but 'Why should not sober married men be empowered to preach and say Mass?' he asked. With Mathew he planned a new edition of H. C. Lea's *History of Sacerdotal Celibacy*,[72] which, if made 'watertight' (Thurton was said to have wagered, and to have won the wager, that he could find ten mistakes in any chapter by the notoriously inaccurate Lea[73]) and given a preface by Tyrrell, would 'shake [a] column of the Devil's temple'.[74] More important than issues of sexuality, he thought, were those of payment for priestly services. 'Cut off the pecuniary advantage', wrote Tyrrell, 'and you cut off the root of sacerdotalism and all the doctrinal and other corruption it entails.'[75] Like Mathew and the other Old Catholics, he was opposed to the territorial principle by which in England they would have to defer to Anglicanism, and on the Continent to Rome. In the letters he wrote to Mathew Tyrrell pointed the way towards a radical, but deeply Catholic, reinterpretation of church structures. Unfortunately, Mathew proved to be an unstable eccentric, quite unequal to the task that Tyrrell planned for him. When, in 1915, having split from the Dutch bishops, he offered to re-ordain the Bishop of London, so 'validating' that bishop's orders, he simply brought ridicule upon himself and his whole, unsupported enterprise.[76]

In letters to Mathew, written 'in shirt sleeves', Tyrrell allowed himself to think some of his most radical thoughts. These ideas, when published, caused considerable shock. Shortly after Tyrrell's death, Bishop Herzog, who had approved Mathew's consecration, published a letter in which Tyrrell had taken a far more radical line on the Vatican Council than he had done in *Medievalism* less than six months before. In November 1908 he told Herzog:

Needless to say that I entirely deny the ecumenical authority of the exclusively Western Councils of Trent and the Vatican and the whole medieval development of the Papacy so far as claiming more than a primacy of honour for the Bishop of Rome; and this, I suppose, is exactly the Old Catholic position. Also I hold to the inherent autonomy of each diocesan Church, subject only to the authority of a truly ecumenical Council. Nor do I believe that the Pope can validly or lawfully sterilise the sacramental life of such Churches; or that their bishops derive their jurisdiction from him either by divine institution or by the decree of any truly ecumenical Council.[77]

For Tyrrell to hold such views and call himself a *Roman* Catholic was, in the climate of his day, an astonishing paradox. It would be easy to dismiss them as wild posturings, but they were not. They were carefully thought-out positions that Tyrrell well knew had a place within the *Roman* Catholic tradition, however much the authorities might try to bar the doors against them. Certainly Tyrrell was in full reaction against the aggressive and ignorant application of ecclesiastical authority within the Church, but he was no anarchist. He believed that true Christian authority was moral and spiritual. For this reason he denounced Roman hegemony and ecclesiastical co-ercion, including the weapon of excommunication. He loathed 'papolatry', and was glad of any chance to expose it.

Such a chance was given him at the end of 1908. Throughout the year, he had supported Mathew, who was a frequent contributor to the *Guardian*, by a series of notes signed 'Lux'.[78] Writing as 'one who knows', he mocked the Anglo-Catholics of the Society of St Thomas of Canterbury for a congratulatory letter they had written to the Pope on the occasion of his jubilee. Why, he asked, did they 'drag their church's honour in the gutter by kissing the foot that kicks her'?[79] His one signed contribution was a short article on 'The Eucharist and the Papacy',[80] a topical subject, as a great and controversial Roman Catholic Eucharistic Congress had just taken place in Westminster. He noted how the Duke of Norfolk had spoken of the Eucharist and the papacy as 'the two *foci* of Roman Catholic life and movement', and went on first to show how it was that inessentials became taken for essentials, since the *focus* of Roman Catholicism was not the papacy, nor even the Eucharist, but *God*, and then to quote a tract that had recently appeared, in which devotion to the papacy was expounded in the same terms as devotion to the Eucharist: 'As the Tabernacle is the home of Jesus the Victim so the Palace of the Vatican at Rome is the home of Jesus the Teacher . . . it is from this Palace, or rather Sanctuary, that since His Ascension our Lord Jesus Christ, the Divine Word, speaks to the world by the mouth of His Vicar, whether he be called Peter, or Pius IX, or Leo XIII, or Pius X.'[81] So, 'All the devotion to Jesus as Priest, Shepherd, and Father that enlightened faith can inspire is summed up practically and effectively in devotion to the Pope.' Tyrrell concluded his attack by pointing out that Cardinal Merry del Val had written to the author expressing the Pope's satisfaction with the tract as 'a work of "intelligent piety" worthy of a devout priest'.

As far as Tyrrell's writing was concerned, 1908 was a year of prolonged controversy. Not only did he answer Mercier in round terms, but he continued to promote modernist resistance wherever he could. This involved him in much correspondence, giving support and ammunition to those who were coming under pressure from their bishops and from Rome. He was continually under threat of 'major excommunication', and there was the daily danger that the modernist movement would break up. Indeed, it had already begun to do so with the secession of Loisy and the capitulation of Blondel and Laberthonnière. 'If only one could live on a spiritual mountain-top and above all these storms', wrote Tyrrell, there might be peace.[82]

Von Hügel was trying to draw Tyrrell back to spiritual writing, as he felt that controversy was bad for his soul. Tyrrell was unable to take a long view of things: 'Successive atmospheres simply suck you up for the time,' wrote von Hügel.[83] Plain-spokenness, with affec-tion, marked their correspondence throughout the year, though Tyrrell became increasingly irritated with his demanding friend. When the Baron sent him the typescript of St Catherine for final revision, he called it 'a hopeless book; a battery of heavy artillery to bring down a flea'.[84] 'I sometimes wonder', wrote Tyrrell, 'whether you are not driven to value complexity for its own sake.'[85] When Fawkes relapsed to Anglicanism, von Hügel wanted to have nothing more to do with him. Tyrrell thought this pharisaical and unchrist-ian, and told him so. This the Baron took with extreme seriousness, so much so that Tyrrell in turn felt considerably humbled. Von Hügel, however, wanted to balance charity, of whose prior claim he was well aware, against the principle that 'not only bigotry but also indifference is to be fought and daily overcome'.[86] He told Tyrrell he was worried about the effect of Medievalism, and advised a delay in publication. Tyrrell merely responded: 'I think you had equally sombre presentiments about poor Lex Credendi [from] which you have never recovered.'[87] What irritated him about von Hügel, especially in this period, was his intensity, his carefulness, his strategic planning. He lacked wit, so Tyrrell teased him:

You have no protective vices: you don't even smoke. The lack of a play-instinct in Christ is no doubt due to Docetan suppressions, and represents a blemished and imperfect humanity. Christian ethics allows play merely as a medicine and means to labour. Surely that is all wrong; and play ceases to be play the moment it is poisoned by utilitarian motives. The irrational is more than half our nature and our highest action is that which is good for nothing but itself. Please buy a diavolo and a pipe.[88]

In his turn, von Hügel was just as worried that Tyrrell would suppress aspects of his humanity for the sake of the battle. Several times during the year he recalled him to what he considered his true vocation:

You are a mystic: you have never found, you will never find, either Church, or Christ, or just simply God, or even the vaguest spiritual presence and conviction, except in deep recollection, purification, quietness, intuition, love. Lose these and you lose God; regain these, and you could as soon doubt Him as you could deny that you have hands and feet. And your helping others, *any soul alive*, depends upon your keeping or regaining those convictions, hence these dispositions; not all the wit, vehemence, subtlety, criticism, learning that you can muster (and *how* great they are!) will ever, without those, be other than ruinous to others as well as to yourself.[89]

Tyrrell knew that to some extent the Baron was right. He had himself confessed to von Hügel: 'All this controversial, church-political, newspaper writing makes one empty and bitter. I long to get back to mystical ways and mystical subjects, and yet I cannot. I am out of tune for them.'[90] The trouble was that, for Tyrrell, fighting, which usually meant writing, was always easier than praying.

In early August 1908 the Baron joined Tyrrell and Bremond for ten days at Storrington. By now he had read *Medievalism*, which meant, as Tyrrell said, that he 'had it to his fingers' ends—scored analysed numbered'. He was totally converted, and surprised Tyrrell by his enthusiasm for it. Perhaps feeling guilty about his earlier premonitions, von Hügel even paid for extra copies to be distributed. 'I believe he would listen to the Devil and give him a perfectly fair hearing', commented his friend. Nevertheless, Tyrrell was confused, as he had often been before, by the apparent inconsistencies of the Baron's faith:

Wonderful man! Nothing is true; but the sum total of nothings is sublime! Christ was not merely ignorant but a *tête brulé*; Mary was not merely not a virgin, but an unbeliever and a rather unnatural mother; the Eucharist was a Pauline invention—yet he makes his daily visit to the Blessed Sacrament and for all I know tells his beads devoutly. Bremond's french logic finds it all very perplexing.[91]

So did Tyrrell's Irish faith. Faith and theology he was well used to separating, but faith and history was another matter.

Until the summer of 1908 Tyrrell's relations with the monks of the Premonstratensian priory had been very good. He stayed with them, even as an excommunicate, ate with them, continued wearing clerical dress and attending Sunday mass. In August, when he received von Hügel, Bremond, and other friends, he was living in two rather dark rooms annexed to Mulberry House, giving on to the garden. Unknown to him, the Prior had been asked to report to Bishop Amigo the names of priests present at Mulberry House, but the only name he knew was Bremond's.[92] By the beginning of September Tyrrell sensed a change in the wind: 'The monks here, formerly very kind and civil,' he wrote, 'have suddenly cut me dead.'[93] In October the Prior confronted Maude Petre, asking her not to walk openly with, nor to associate with, modernists like Tyrrell and Fawkes.[94] He also bluntly asked Tyrrell to leave Storrington. Nothing could have been better calculated to make him stay. He fired off a furious letter to Bishop Amigo:

Even were Miss Petre and her sister to defer to the Prior's insolence and leave Storrington, I should remain there and the place would still be a rendezvous for all those who are suffering from the same infamous treatment as myself. You will gain nothing by tormenting Miss Petre. You will only bring upon yourself an open letter that will make you wish you had never been born. Storrington is not a fief of the Church or the Priory. Any peaceful citizen has more right to be there than these foreign monks . . .[95]

In January 1909 Maude Petre followed this up with a letter complaining of the Bishop's 'mischievous' talk, and threatening legal action if she were slandered.[96] However, the situation was temporarily resolved when she left for Rome at the end of the month. She never knew that on 16 November Merry del Val authorized Amigo to excommunicate her: 'If your endeavours to bring home to her how very wrong and sinful is her conduct in protecting and defending one who has acted as Father Tyrrell has, are not successful, she cannot be allowed to receive the Sacraments.'[97]

Tyrrell had already returned to London. Von Hügel made a point of once more inviting him to spend a week with him at Vicarage Gate. He was careful to state that, though his wife had to be away while Tyrrell stayed, she would be there to welcome him before she left, and she was delighted that he should stay under their roof.[98] Tyrrell declined, choosing to remain with the Shelleys in Clapham.

Having just spent the best part of six months in Storrington, he now remained in Clapham almost as long, enjoying the ready access to friends, libraries, and interested audiences, and the anonymity which meant that he could attend church services, both Catholic and Anglican, without causing a stir. At Clapham he was able to work without the emotional tension generated by his relationship with Maude Petre. He was accepted by the Shelleys as one of the family, something he found nowhere else. Here, if he was prostrated with migraine, he was neither pestered nor ignored, something that became increasingly important as his health deteriorated. He was never strong, but at 47 he was increasingly prone to bouts of illness, physically and emotionally exhausted. He was thin to the point of emaciation, by turns caustic and affectionate, and always ready to burst out with flashes of wit. Long hours were given to writing, standing at his desk, the room thick with pipe-smoke, but there was also time for the garden, walks on Clapham Common, and expeditions to the churches of London. Time was what he needed, because he was continuing to think radical, new thoughts about the whole basis of his undeviatingly Christ-centred Catholicism. Such time as he had, he used to extraordinary effect, but little now remained.

NOTES

1. See *The Tablet*, 28 Sept. 1907, pp. 501–15 (English); 5 Oct., pp. 549–54, 12 Oct. 1907, pp. 589–94 (Latin).
2. *Giornale d'Italia*, 26 Sept. 1907.
3. Von Hügel to Lilley, 3 Oct. 1907 (SAUL, MS 30537).
4. Von Hügel diaries, 29 Sept. 1907 (SAUL).
5. *The Times*, 30 Sept., 1 Oct. 1907.
6. Ibid., 1 Oct. 1907.
7. Von Hügel to Tyrrell, 1 Oct. 1907 (BL, Petre Papers).
8. *Daily Chronicle*, 24 Sept. 1907.
9. AL2, pp. 329–30.
10. Tyrrell to von Hügel, 5 Oct. 1907 (BL, Petre Papers).
11. Tyrrell to Bremond, 30 Sept. 1907 (BN, Fonds Bremond).
12. Ibid.
13. Tyrrell to von Hügel, 17 Oct. 1907.
14. Tyrrell to Bremond, 9 Oct. 1907.
15. Tyrrell to von Hügel, 30 Sept. 1907.
16. W. S. Blunt, *My Diaries*, 2 vols. (London, 1919–20), ii, p. 196, entry for 16 Oct. 1907.
17. Maude Petre diaries, 6 Oct. 1907 (BL, Add. MS 52374).
18. Tyrrell to Kitty Clutton, 21 Oct. 1907 (Clutton Papers).
19. A. Houtin, manuscript life of Tyrrell (BN, Fonds Houtin, n.a.f. 15743) p. 216.
20. Maude Petre diaries, 5 Nov. 1907.
21. AL2, p. 330.
22. Merry del Val to Amigo, 17 Oct. 1907 (SDA).
23. Tyrrell to Lilley, 23 Oct. 1907 (SAUL, Lilley Papers).
24. AL2, pp. 341–2; original in SDA.

25. *The Times*, 2 Nov. 1908.
26. Tyrrell to Amigo, 1 Nov. 1907 (SDA).
27. *The Times*, 2, 3, 4 Nov. 1907.
28. Von Hügel to Tyrrell, 24 Oct. 1907.
29. Von Hügel to Tyrrell, 15 Nov. 1907.
30. Tyrrell to Bremond, 6 Nov. 1907.
31. G. Greene (ed.), *Letters from Baron Friedrich von Hügel to a Niece* (London, 1928), p. xxxvi.
32. Tyrrell to Bremond, 29 Dec. 1907.
33. 'The Condemnation of Newman', the *Guardian*, 20 Nov. 1907.
34. The *Guardian*, 27 Nov. 1907; *The Times*, 2 Dec. 1907; the *Guardian*, 11 Dec. 1907.
35. 'The Prospects of Modernism', *Hibbert Journal*, 6 (Jan. 1908), pp. 241–55.
36. *The Programme of Modernism* (London, 1908); see C. Nelson and N. Pittenger (eds.), *Pilgrim of Rome* (Welwyn, 1969), p. 12, and von Hügel to Tyrrell, 19 Apr. 1909, for Buonaiuti's authorship of the *Programme*.
37. *What We Want: An Open Letter to Pius X from a Group of Priests* (London, 1907).
38. Tyrrell to Lilley, 23 Nov. 1907.
39. Tyrrell to Bremond, undated [late 1907].
40. *Hibbert Journal*, 6 (Jan. 1908), pp. 254–5.
41. See *The Tablet*, 30 Nov. 1907, pp. 843–4.
42. Tyrrell to Kitty Clutton, 8 Feb. 1908.
43. Tyrrell to Loisy, 20 Oct. 1907 (BN, Fonds Loisy).
44. A. F. Loisy, *Mémoires pour servir à l'histoire religieuse de notre temps*, 3 vols. (Paris, 1930–1), ii, p. 610.
45. A. F. Loisy, *Les Évangiles synoptiques*, 2 vols. (Ceffonds, 1907–8); *Simples réflexions sur le décret du saint-office Lamentabili sane exitu et sur l'encyclique Pascendi dominici gregis* (Ceffonds, 1908).
46. Loisy, *Mémoires*, ii, p. 611.
47. The *Nation*, 7 Mar. 1908, pp. 829–30.
48. Houtin, manuscript life of Tyrrell, pp. 225–7.
49. Tyrrell to von Hügel, 18 Mar. 1908.
50. Tyrrell to Loisy, 1 Apr. 1908.
51. Dell to Lilley, 17 Apr. 1908 (SAUL, MS 30611).
52. A. F. Loisy, *Quelques lettres sur des questions actuelles et sur des événements recents* (Ceffonds, 1908).
53. Tyrrell to Loisy, 6 Apr. 1908.
54. Tyrrell to von Hügel, 23 Apr. 1908.
55. Von Hügel diaries, 29 Aug. 1907.
56. L. F. Barmann, *Baron Friedrich von Hügel and the Modernist Crisis in England* (Cambridge, 1972), p. 208.
57. Tyrrell to Maude Petre, 1 Apr. 1908.

58. Tyrrell to von Hügel, 23 Apr. 1908.
59. *Hibbert Journal*, 6 (July 1908), pp. 926–30.
60. Tyrrell to Maude Petre, 21 Apr. 1908.
61. Tyrrell to Maude Petre, 3 May 1908 (*AL2*, p. 350).
62. *Medievalism: A Reply to Cardinal Mercier* (London, 1908). Quotations are from pp. 79–80 ('My whole position . . .'); 86 ('The Council tells us . . .'); 143–44 ('"Modernist" as opposed . . .'); 175 ('On the one side . . .'); 178 ('How can the world . . .'); 183 ('Your Eminence . . .'). See also G. Daly, 'Tyrrell's "Medievalism"', *The Month*, NS 42 (July–Aug. 1969), pp. 15–22.
63. Tyrrell to von Hügel, 27 Jun. 1908.
64. Maude Petre diaries, 8 Mar., 11, 17 May 1908.
65. Tyrrell to Bremond, 12 May 1908.
66. Maude Petre diaries, 17 June 1908.
67. Tyrrell to Lilley, 22 May 1908.
68. Blunt, *My Diaries*, ii, p. 282; Tyrrell to editor of *L'Exode*, 15 Mar. 1909 (BN, n.a.f. 15743, pp. 373 ff).
69. For Mathew, see P. F. Anson, *Bishops at Large* (London, 1964), pp. 156–215.
70. Tyrrell to Mathew, 15 Dec. 1907 (AEPSJ).
71. Tyrrell to Mathew, 15 Dec. 1908.
72. H. C. Lea, *An Historical Sketch of Sacerdotal Celibacy in the Christian Church* (Philadelphia, 1867); 3rd edn. rev., 2 vols. (London, 1907).
73. A. L.-David (ed.), *Lettres de George Tyrrell à Henri Bremond* (Paris, 1971), p. 227.
74. Tyrrell to Bremond, 9 Nov. 1906.
75. Tyrrell to Mathew, 25 July 1908.
76. See A. H. Mathew, *'An Episcopal Odyssey': An Open Letter to His Grace the Rt. Hon. and Most Rev. Randall Thomas Davidson D.D.* (Kingsdown, 1915), p. 5.
77. Tyrrell to Herzog, 4 Nov. 1908 (*AL2*, p. 383).
78. The *Guardian*, 20 May, 3 June, 12 Aug. 1908.
79. The *Guardian*, 30 Dec. 1908.
80. 'The Eucharist and the Papacy', the *Guardian*, 16 Dec. 1908.
81. Ibid.
82. Tyrrell to Maude Petre, 8 Feb. 1908 (*AL2*, p. 348).
83. Von Hügel to Tyrrell, 25 Mar. 1908.
84. Tyrrell to Maude Petre, 1 Apr. 1908.
85. Tyrrell to von Hügel, 22 June 1908.
86. Von Hügel to Tyrrell, 23 June 1908.
87. Tyrrell to von Hügel, 27 June 1908.
88. Tyrrell to von Hügel, 23 July 1908.
89. Von Hügel to Tyrrell, 7 Dec. 1908.
90. Von Hügel to Maude Petre, 20 Feb. 1908.

91. Tyrrell to Lilley, 14 Aug. 1908.
92. De la Fourvière to Amigo, 14 Aug. 1908 (SDA).
93. Tyrrell to Dell, 2 Sept. 1908 (*AL*2, p. 363).
94. De la Fourvière to Amigo, 20 Oct. 1908.
95. Tyrrell to Amigo, 14 Nov. 1908.
96. Maude Petre to Amigo, 24 Jan. 1909 (SDA).
97. Merry del Val to Amigo, 16 Nov. 1908.
98. Von Hügel to Tyrrell, 9 Jan. 1909.

15

'So Utter an Ending'

NOT long before Tyrrell died, his former pupil, Joseph Thorp, who never completed his Jesuit training and became a writer, asked him what now remained of the beliefs he had once so enthusiastically taught to the philosophers at Stonyhurst. Tyrrell thought for a few moments and then replied: 'Nearly all the detail's gone. But every day it becomes more clear that the only thing that matters at all is—to find God and Truth.'[1]

He was convinced that the best of the modernist resistance had been spent in the year after *Pascendi*. The disciplinary measures of the Church had proved too strong for the modernists; their time had not yet come. Since it was sure to come sooner or later, continued battering at the iron gates would only be hurtful to the modernists themselves. For some, like himself, the path of undeviating adherence to a Church that rejected them had to be followed whatever the cost. 'I cannot say I have found it spiritually beneficial in my case,' wrote Tyrrell, 'nor would I ever conscientiously advise it to any ordinary mortal.' For those who had lost all hope or belief in the Church, it would be necessary to found some new sect, as the Old Catholics had done. Better that 'than that they should drift away one by one and be, mostly, lost to all religion'—the path which Loisy was to follow. These might be the very people to show how modernism would work out in practice, 'as to sacraments, dogma, priesthood etc.'.[2]

This was for others to explore. Tyrrell himself was turning back to basics. He complained to Wilfrid Blunt that Newman had never really argued out the fundamentals on which Christianity is based: the existence of God and the reality of a revelation.[3] He was determined not to be guilty of the same failure. In the last months of his life he was hard at work on these questions. When in November 1908 Lilley proposed that he write something about his 'religious philosophy', he declined, because it was 'at present pulled down for repairs and alterations' of which he did not see the end.[4]

At times he lost hope. He talked with Hensley Henson about the

Church of England, and came away saying he agreed with Houtin and Loisy: 'The Christianity of the future will consist of mysticism and charity, and possibly the Eucharist in its primitive form as the outward bond. I desire no better.'[5] This might seem adequate in practice, but he knew it was a counsel of last resort: it would not satisfy the questioning mind. Tyrrell had to convince himself once more that it was reasonable to believe in God:

I am sure it is a mistake to try to prove the existence of God. What I try to prove is that every man, honest or dishonest, does at least subconsciously believe in God by the mere fact that he believes in truth and right and disbelieves in falsehood and wrong. God, for me, is the creative Power that pushes everything on towards its higher development; the principle of life and health and growth and truth and goodness. I know It, as I know electricity—in its effects, not in itself . . . What he is in himself we cannot know owing to the fact that our minds are made for the physical, finite, material order of things.[6]

Houtin concluded from this passage that Tyrrell had ceased to be a Christian. Tyrrell thought that a grotesque misjudgement, based upon an identification of Christianity with dogmatic orthodoxy. It indicated an underlying 'rationalism' in Houtin's mind, the very rationalism that Tyrrell had resisted all his life by stressing what we do *not* know about God as much, or even more, than what we do know. In August 1908 he wrote a long letter to a fellow modernist in which he stressed the 'economy' of revelation:

We do not know nothing about God; but we know infinitely little. We can have no word of God, no revelation, except the ideal or eternal Man; the Christ. That is as much of God as we can ever *see*; but we can have the sense of the infinitely more and other that God is. It is only because He presents Himself to us as the Christ, with a human spirit, face, voice and hands, that we can speak to Him or deal with Him at all.[7]

Tyrrell would have been the first to acknowledge that this view of revelation raised as many questions as it answered. Does it not concentrate too exclusively upon Christ? To what extent does revelation depend upon a knowledge of Jesus 'as he really was'? Does it matter if many of the reported words of Jesus were not spoken by him at all? To what extent do the words of Jesus, or the words of Scripture about Jesus, matter at all? What if the 'Jesus of history' was radically different from the Jesus of the Bible? What of those who have never heard of Jesus? Is the revelation of Jesus one to the heart or to the intellect, or both? How do we recognize God in Jesus? To each of these questions the dogmatic teaching of the Roman Church had an answer, but such answers appeared increasingly threadbare in the light of advancing historical knowledge. Tyrrell pressed the issue. 'My own work', he told Arthur Boutwood, 'has been to raise a question which I have failed to answer. I am not so conceited as to conclude that it is therefore unanswerable.'[8]

Tyrrell was in touch with Boutwood, an intelligent Anglo-Catholic, because Boutwood had written a lengthy critique of *Through Scylla and Charybdis* that pressed the question of revelation.[9] Tyrrell was always ready to answer those who criticized him in an open search for truth. His response to Boutwood was 'Revelation as Experience', a paper delivered at King's College Hostel, London on 26 March 1909.[10] In this he argued that revelation is not a matter of speech or of propositions, but of experiences which give rise to speech. A truer view focuses upon a revelation 'written in the heart and consisting in the indwelling spirit of Christ, present to all men at all times'. Tyrrell explained what he meant 'if I say Christ is God and mean that He is Conscience incarnate':

I do not mean that He is omnipotent or omniscient but that He has the words of eternal life; that He makes Himself felt in me as a Power that makes for Righteousness—a redeeming strengthening power; that his words have a sacramental spiritual efficacy beyond their merely intellectual value; that I owe Him the same worship of obedience and self-sacrifice that I accord to my Conscience. The Church's doctrine of His Godhead but formulates her collective and progressive experience of His power over the heart and will.

Boutwood argued that Tyrrell's idea of revelation would rob the creeds of all truth-value for ordinary believers. Tyrrell tried to show a different way by which their unchanging truth-value might be computed. If Boutwood's view smacked of 'rationalism', Tyrrell's smacked of 'pragmatism'. Tyrrell was trying to show how revelation 'worked'. Essentially it worked because Tyrrell remained captivated, as he had been all his life, by the enigmatic but arresting figure of Jesus.

In the last months of his life, however, Tyrrell radically rethought his Christology. Not that he felt he had made much progress. When asked for a contribution to a collection of essays on the contemporary Christological debate, he complained that he had no Christology of his own to offer, but submitted an essay that reviewed the state of the question.[11] Since his time at Richmond he had been aware of

Johannes Weiss's little book on *Jesus' Proclamation of the Kingdom of God*. Weiss stressed that Jesus was a first-century Jewish prophet, with radical, apocalyptic expectations about the Kingdom of God. Jesus expected the Kingdom of God to supplant the political kingdoms of the world in a violent cataclysm that would mark the end of the age. Nineteenth-century theologians had turned this into a benign message about moral progress and the inward, spiritual transformation of individuals. Weiss was followed by Schweitzer, who showed how nineteenth-century theologians had consistently created Jesus in their own image. For him, Jesus 'comes to us as one unknown', a radical visionary, whose last attempt to inaugurate the Apocalypse was his own virtual suicide. Tyrrell was convinced, at least to the extent that he believed Jesus's inspiration and enthusiasm to have been 'entirely religious, mystical, and transcendent, but in no sense liberal or modern-minded'.[12] When he had finished reading Schweitzer and rereading Weiss, he wrote to the Baron:

I am satisfied that the Liberal Protestant Sunday-School-teacher Christ is as mythical as the miraculous Christ . . . I feel that my past work has been dominated by the liberal-Prot. Christ and doubt whether I am not bankrupt . . . If we cannot save huge chunks of transcendentalism, Christianity must go. Civilisation can do (and has done) all that the purely immanentist Christ of Matthew Arnold is credited with. The other-world emphasis; the doctrine of immortality was what gave Christianity its original impulse and sent martyrs to the lions. If that is accidental we only owe to Jesus in a great measure what we owe to all good men in some measure. In the sense of survival and immortality the Resurrection is our critical and central dogma.[13]

These were the ideas that Tyrrell worked out in his last book, *Christianity at the Cross-Roads*,[14] which he finished only days before the onset of his final illness.

In terms of constructive theology, it is his masterpiece, drawing fully on the New Testament work he had so carefully imbibed, and putting it to good use in the service of Catholicism. In doing this, he was following Loisy's *L'Évangile et l'Église*, but he took a more radical line than Loisy. 'Former heresies', he proclaimed, 'have questioned this or that dogma, this or that ecclesiastical institution. Modernism criticizes the very idea of dogma, of ecclesiasticism, of revelation, of faith, of heresy, of theology, of sacramentalism.' Loisy had struggled to make his work acceptable to Catholic theologians; Tyrrell no longer saw the need to make his work acceptable to anyone. Weiss and his followers, he concluded, had destroyed 'the hope of smoothing away the friction between Christianity and the present age'. In understanding Christianity, with its claims to revelation, dogmatic teaching, and an unbroken tradition of ecclesiastical life, the modernist employs all the critical tools of modernity. In accepting Christianity, he turns his back on the intellectual idols of the modern world for the images and symbols of another world. What Tyrrell called for now was 'a frank admission of the principle of symbolism'. 'With this admission,' he said,

we have no need to abolish the Apocalypse, which, as the form in which Jesus embodied His religious 'idea', is classical and normative for all subsequent interpretations of the same. In the long series of translations the original sense may be easily perverted if the original text be lost. What each age has to do is to interpret the apocalyptic symbolism into terms of its own symbolism.

In these words, so clearly marking the centrality of hermeneutics for an understanding of Christianity, Tyrrell put his finger on a major concern of twentieth-century theology. His own hermeneutical test remained obstinately simple and practical: 'Any construction of the transcendent that yields the same fruits as the apocalyptic construction is true to the "idea" of Jesus.' The Catholic Church, in her preaching of resurrection, judgement, heaven, and hell, had remained true to that 'idea', and Tyrrell had no wish to move away from the language and images that had proved fruitful of sainthood for 2,000 years. When he tried to explain this to Houtin, Houtin thought that he detected a fatal Jesuitical equivocation. Tyrrell had written:

I think it important to insist that we hold the *faith* though not the theology of the Church. Of course it is not what *they* mean by faith; but it is a tenable meaning. I would never deny the divinity of Christ, or the Atonement, or the Real Presence etc. etc. partly because they symbolise real religious experiences; partly because it would enlist protestant sympathy on the side of Rome. Other symbols might do as well; but these are in possession.[14]

Houtin, and the Church, thought Tyrrell was equivocating. Tyrrell thought he was defending the faith of the saints.

In the final section of *Christianity at the Cross-Roads* Tyrrell made yet another prescient leap. He now considered Christianity as one of the religions of the world, subject to 'the laws of religion in general'. He believed that the study of such 'laws' would promote the development of a universal religion that would transcend the Christianity of his day. This would involve no contradiction to, but rather an extension of, the process that had produced contemporary Christianity, for 'Christianity has but brought the universal principle of salvation to its highest degree of force and explicitness'. This development is sure to continue, and the modernist, who trusts in the immanent working of the Spirit, has nothing to fear in promoting it. Again foreshadowing later theological developments, Tyrrell called the Church 'not merely a society or school . . . but a mystery and sacrament; like the humanity of Christ of which it is an extension'. Where else but in the transcendent and inclusive Church of the future, asked Tyrrell, will the modernist find 'the true Catholicism of which he dreams'?

When Tyrrell wrote these words he was a dying man, but neither he nor his friends realized how ill he really was. He had been subject to prostrating headaches and bouts of sickness for so long. At the beginning of March 1909 he was seriously ill for ten days. The local doctor gave him 'a scare', but a specialist was more reassuring, attributing the episode to migraine and a bad cold. Tyrrell recovered rapidly, and by the 15th he had produced a draft of 'Revelation as Experience' which he sent to Lilley for comment. In Kensington Town Hall ten days later he delivered a newly written paper, much indebted to Bergson, entitled 'Divine Fecundity'.[15] The following day he delivered his response to 'Hakluyt Egerton' to 'a very alert crowd of young men and their professors' at King's College Hostel. On his way back to Clapham Tyrrell happened to take the same tram as Albert Cock, a young lecturer from King's College, who recorded his memories of that evening's conversation.[16] Tyrrell struck Cock as 'a very tired, a very wistful, and a very determined man'. Although he had just delivered a paper and participated in a taxing discussion, he still had energy for 'a long and restless walk' round Clapham Common late into the night. On that walk Cock came to understand for the first time 'the spiritual anguish of a priest without an altar'. He opened his heart about his own sense of spiritual need, and Tyrrell took care to introduce him to the Baron shortly afterwards. Still depressed, Tyrrell moved down to Storrington in time for Easter.

Here he worked furiously on *Christianity at the Cross-Roads*. His mood remained black and unsociable. At table he was virtually silent, and when the Baron visited Mulberry House the intensity of his conversation with Maude Petre drove Tyrrell further into himself. Writing to Kitty Clutton, he described how his two companions '"soared" mid the silence of a depressed and blighted auditory'. Fortunately, said Tyrrell, there was a dog there 'who needed massage'.[17] To Norah Shelley he complained: 'The Baron is here for five days and I am ill able to bear it. A sort of chronic depression seems to have settled upon me. Perhaps it is just lack of ordinary human conversation—a loathing of the world of talk and ideas.'[18] Still, in mid-June Tyrrell was able to visit Oxford, where he delivered a reworked version of his paper on 'Divine Fecundity'. For a time he moved back to Clapham, finding solace in the garden. He collected the stones to make a rockery, but, in a fit of restlessness, he returned to Storrington before the project was finished.

At Storrington, on 6 July, he was taken ill.[19] For three hours in the afternoon he had talked with his friend, Arthur Bell, and when he came to table he was tired. Wanting nothing to eat, he retired to his room again, saying he did not feel well. Here he walked up and down agitatedly, was violently sick, and complained of pains in his head. At first it seemed like yet another migraine attack, but that evening Maude Petre was worried enough to call the local doctor, who was not unduly alarmed. All that night and all the next day she stayed with him. He now began to vomit blood, his left side was becoming paralysed, and his speech was indistinct. Seriously alarmed, Maude Petre insisted on a second opinion. A specialist arrived from Worthing and immediately commented that Tyrrell was too old for his years. He was worn out, and probably had kidney trouble. That night Maude Petre recorded in her diary her 'first kiss' with the semi-delirious, dying man. The next morning she was told he had advanced Bright's disease, and she sent for von Hügel.

The Baron arrived on the evening of 9 July and stayed at The White Horse, opposite Mulberry House. The next morning he and Maude Petre took a walk, during which he confessed that he was afraid Tyrrell would live, but remain mentally incapacitated. The likelihood, however, was that he would die, and this had raised the urgent question of sending for a priest. Any priest who came to the death-bed of the excommunicate modernist would need to be exceptional, a man of courage and sensitivity who could both appreciate Tyrrell's disdain for attempts at a 'death-bed reconciliation', and his longing for the sacraments which he considered his right. Bremond was due shortly, but it would take time for a message to reach him. So

Charles Dessoulavy, a secular priest from the Southwark diocese, a friend who had been helped by Tyrrell when he expressed his doubts and difficulties, was urgently summoned. When he arrived on 10 July Tyrrell was drowsy, so after a brief visit to the sick-bed, 'merely looking at him', he spoke to von Hügel outside. It is a moot point how much Tyrrell was able to take in of the situation, and to be understood. Certainly there were lucid intervals, but he was in no state to make his confession to Dessoulavy. Von Hügel took the line that

Father Tyrrell would certainly wish to receive the sacraments and would certainly be willing and eager to confess, and to express penitence for, any and all excesses of speech or of writing, any unnecessary pain or scandal given to anyone,—and this also in specific instances that might occur to his memory. But he would, as decidedly, refuse any unlimited, absolute retraction, any unbounded submission; and would, sadly but firmly elect to die without the sacraments if such a solution were insisted on.[20]

On this understanding, Dessoulavy entered the room where Tyrrell was lying. The dying man was roused, recognized Dessoulavy, and greeted him gladly. Using Maude Petre as an interpreter because of his slurred speech, he commented: 'You surely won't let me die like a dog.' Dessoulavy reassured him that he would give him absolution, whereupon Tyrrell joked: 'He's as bad as I am.' Dessoulavy then responded, 'You are a real old Catholic at bottom', before he was left alone with the dying man. Tyrrell spoke for a long time making his confession, probably so indistinctly that Dessoulavy was unable to follow. Certainly Dessoulavy did not insist upon any 'recantation'. He later told von Hügel:

It is an unheard of thing to require recantation in a case where no definite heresy has been officially pointed out . . . Every priest in this country has written 'Faculties' to absolve from all cases 'even from those reserved to the pope in virtue of the Constitution Apostolicae Sedis', and neither the Faculties, nor the rules elsewhere laid down say a word of any recantation being required.[21]

Tyrrell, then, was under no pressure from Dessoulavy to retract what he had written; only to repent of his sins, a position he would have appreciated. Dessoulavy, unsure of what Tyrrell was saying but determined to respond to his need, gave him conditional absolution, but not Communion or extreme unction. Since he thought there was no immediate danger of death, and since Tyrrell was barely conscious, he thought these could wait until a lucid interval or a crisis. It is clear that Dessoulavy considered the condition of Tyrrell's absolution—his heartfelt penitence for sin—to have been in all likelihood fulfilled, and that he thought painful intellectual debates over *Lamentabili* and *Pascendi* to be beside the point. He intended to return to give Tyrrell Communion and, if necessary, extreme unction. When Dessoulavy left, Tyrrell said: 'He won't let me die without the sacraments.'

For two days Tyrrell was distinctly better, though he was still paralysed on his left side and troubled by pains in his head. He was able to recognize friends like Norah Shelley, who had now arrived. Then, on 12 July, he suddenly relapsed.

Thinking he might now be very near the end, and that Dessoulavy might not arrive in time, Maude Petre reluctantly sent for the Prior, calling him away from high mass. While she held Tyrrell's head, the Prior recited several acts of faith and exhorted him to submit himself totally to the teaching of the Church.[22] It is possible that Tyrrell could hear, but he did not respond. The Prior concluded by giving him extreme unction, but not Communion, as he probably could not swallow. After that he fell into a peaceful sleep.

The next morning Bremond arrived, just in time to be recognized. He put on a surplice and stole, and gave Tyrrell absolution. That evening also, at the bidding of the Bishop of Southwark, John Pollen came from Farm Street, since Thurston was away. He was allowed to see the unconscious man three times, to pray for him, and to give absolution. By 4.00 p.m. on 14 July he found him 'quite collapsed, motionless; only kept alive by skilful holding the head up and tongue on one side etc.'.[23] The next morning, a little after 9.00 a.m., Tyrrell died.

Shortly after his death Tyrrell was dressed in the borrowed apparel of a priest. Wilfrid Blunt described what he saw when he visited Mulberry House the next day:

There lay the dead heresiarch, as sad a little shard of humanity as ever my eyes saw. I could not have recognised it as the man I had known so brilliant in his talk, so full of combative life, or indeed, hardly as a man at all. The face was shrunk and the features seemed to have fallen in though he had been only thirty-six hours dead, for he died at nine yesterday morning, and the body with its poor small fingers was more like an accidental handful of shapeless clay than anything that had been alive. Pious hands had clothed him in surplice and stole, as befitted the priest he was, and there were two tapers lighted at his head. I knelt a minute or two beside him and recited a 'De Profundis' and kissed the hem of his garment, or rather the stole, and rose and went out, moved, as one could not help being moved, to tears of pity, it was so utter an ending.[24]

For Maude Petre, von Hügel, and Bremond, the immediate fear was that, since Tyrrell was known to have died 'fortified by the rites of the Church', it would be assumed, and trumpeted by Rome, that he had finally recanted. For this reason they sent a carefully worded letter to *The Times*, signed by Maude Petre, in which they explained how he had received absolution without recanting his views.[25] It was this letter that made a Catholic funeral impossible. On 16 July the Bishop wrote to Maude Petre informing her that such a funeral was out of the question unless Dessoulavy or Bremond could assure him in writing of a 'definite retraction' on Tyrrell's part.[26] As plans for the funeral advanced, no such statement could be made, and the Bishop's mind hardened. Despite aggression from Maude Petre, and diplomatic approaches from family and friends, it became clear that there would be no Catholic funeral. The best that could be done was to bury Tyrrell in the Anglican churchyard.

On 21 July a cortège headed by Bremond, von Hügel, and William Tyrrell assembled at Mulberry House. Bremond, who wore no vestments, asked that all remain silent throughout the burial and that there be no hint of protest or of unseemly behaviour. The sad little procession of forty or fifty mourners then proceeded down the lane to the Anglican churchyard. Bremond read the *Pater Noster, Kyrie Eleison, De Profundis*, and, on arrival at the grave, he blessed both the coffin and the earth in which it would lie. Then he delivered a remarkable funeral speech in which he reminded Tyrrell's friends how, all his life, 'the very word "Catholic" was music to *his* ears, and summoned before *his* eyes the outstretched, all-embracing arms of Him Who died for the *orbis terrarum*'.[27] The next day Bishop Amigo wired the Prior: 'Do not allow Bremond to say Mass.'[28]

In a sudden burst of creativity earlier that year, Tyrrell had translated a number of German and Italian poems, adding typical adaptations of his own.[29] One such ran:

> Two chambers hath the heart
> Wherein do dwell
> Sorrow and joy apart.

When in the one joy wakes
Then in the other
Sorrow her slumber takes.

Hush joy! oh hush! refrain
Laugh not too loud
Lest sorrow wake again.

To these three verses of Neumann's Tyrrell added a fourth, which might well serve as his epitaph:

Let sorrow when she weepeth
Weep low and know
Joy is not dead but sleepeth.[30]

Despite the pain, the depression, the fighting, the labour, the fatigue, and the emptiness, the hope of joy yet remained. 'I am glad', said Tyrrell in one of his last letters, 'God is to judge me and not any of his servants.'[31]

NOTES

1. J. Thorp, *Friends and Adventures* (London, 1931), p. 41.
2. Tyrrell to von Hügel, 7 Apr. 1909 (BL, Petre Papers).
3. W. Blunt, *My Diaries*, 2 vols. (London, 1919–20), ii, p. 245.
4. Tyrrell to Lilley, 26 Nov. 1908 (SAUL, Lilley Papers).
5. Tyrrell to G. E. Newsome, 17 July 1908 (*AL2*, p. 377).
6. A. Houtin, manuscript life of Tyrrell (BN, Fonds Houtin, n.a.f. 15743) p. 272.
7. Tyrrell to 'William Scott Palmer', 23 Aug. 1908 (*AL2*, p. 416).
8. Tyrrell to Boutwood, 13 Jan. 1909 (*GTL*, p. 119).
9. A. Boutwood (pseud. Hakluyt Egerton), *Father Tyrrell's Modernism* (London, 1909).
10. 'Revelation as Experience', ed. T. M. Loome, *Heythrop Journal*, 12 (1971), pp. 117–49 (MS in BL, Add. MS 52369).
11. Tyrrell to Loisy, 16 Mar. 1909 (BN, Fonds Loisy); see 'The Point at Issue', in 'Jesus or Christ', *Hibbert Journal Supplement* (1909), pp. 5–16.
12. 'Jesus or Christ', p. 15.
13. Tyrrell to von Hügel, 9 Apr. 1909.
14. *Christianity at the Cross-Roads* (London, 1909). Quotations are from pp. 10 ('Former heresies . . .'); 44 ('the hope of . . .'); 103 ('a frank admission . . .'); 104 ('Any construction . . .'); 273 ('Christianity has

but brought...'); 275 ('not merely a society...'); 281 ('the true Catholicism...').
15. Tyrrell to Houtin, 13 Dec. 1907.
16. *EFI*, pp. 245–77.
17. 'Revelation as Experience', introd., p. 122.
18. Tyrrell to Kitty Clutton, 18 May 1909 (CP).
19. Norah Shelley to Kitty Clutton, 4 Apr. 1911 (CP).
20. There are a number of accounts of Tyrrell's death which, despite the bitterness between Maude Petre and von Hügel on the one hand, and Kitty Clutton and Norah Shelley on the other, agree in major details. For the sake of the narrative I have conflated these accounts: Maude Petre, 'Journal of each Day' (BL, Add. MS 52368); diary (BL, Add. MS 52374); 'A Short Account of Father Tyrrell's Death' (copy in CP); *AL*2, pp. 422–33; letters of Maude Petre and von Hügel to *The Tablet*, 31 July 1909; von Hügel to Lilley, 13 July 1909 (SAUL, MS 30556); von Hügel to Osborne, 16 July 1909 (SAUL, MS 37018/2); Bremond (BN, Fonds Bremond); Norah Shelley to Osborne, 3 Sept. 1909 (SAUL, MS 37018/8); statement by Norah Shelley in CP; Pollen to Sykes, 14 July 1909 (ARSJ, ANGL. 1021, VII–IX); Kitty Clutton, 'The Death of George Tyrrell', the *Modern Churchman*, 22 (1932–3), pp. 678–86 (typescript in CP); M. Clifton, 'New Light on Tyrrell', *The Tablet*, 22 Jan. 1983, pp. 55–7.
21. Von Hügel to Lilley, 13 July 1909 (SAUL, Lilley Papers).
22. Dessoulavy to von Hügel, 30 July 1909 (SAUL, MS 2390).
23. De la Fourvière to Amigo, 13 July 1909 (SDA).
24. Pollen to Sykes, 14 July 1909 (ARSJ, ANGL. 1021, VII–IX).
25. Blunt, *My Diaries*, ii, p. 265.
26. *The Times*, 16 July 1909.
27. Amigo to Maude Petre, 16 July 1909 (SDA).
28. *AL*2, p. 444.
29. Amigo to de la Fourvière, 22 July 1909 (SDA).
30. *Versions and Perversions of Heine and Others* (London, 1909).
31. Blunt, *My Diaries*, ii, pp. 231–2.
32. Tyrrell to Kitty Clutton, 17 June 1909.

Select Bibliography

MAJOR UNPUBLISHED SOURCES

Archive of the Archdiocese of Westminster, London
Vaughan Papers, including letters of Tyrrell to Vaughan.

Archive of the Diocese of Southwark, London
File marked 'Tyrrell'.

Archive of the English Province of the Society of Jesus, London
Manuscript sermons by Tyrrell (CD/1).
Letters of Tyrrell to his superiors (CD/2).
Typescript of letters of Tyrrell to Mathew (CD/3).
Letters of Tyrrell to Thurston (CD/4).

Archive of the Society of Jesus, Rome
Volumen ANGL. 1021, 'Tyrrell'.
Registrum Epistolarum ad Provinciam Angliae, v (1897–1907).
Registrum Epistolarum ad Externos Prælatos et Ecclesiasticos, iv (1898–1908).

Bibliothèque Nationale, Paris
Fonds Bremond: Letters of Tyrrell to Bremond.
       Letters of von Hügel to Bremond.
Fonds Houtin (n.a.f. 15743): Letters of Tyrrell to Houtin.
Fonds Laberthonnière: Letters of Tyrrell to Laberthonnière.
Fonds Loisy (n.a.f. 15662): Letters of Tyrrell to Loisy.

Blackfriars, Oxford
Letters of Tyrrell to Raffalovich (7 letters from the correspondence are in the John Gray Papers, National Library of Scotland, Edinburgh).

Borthwick Institute, York
Halifax Papers: Letters of Tyrrell to Halifax.

British Library, British Museum, London
Petre Papers: Letters of Bremond to Maude Petre (Add. MS 52380).
 Letters of von Hügel to Maude Petre (Add. MSS 45361–2).
 Diaries of Maude Petre (Add. MSS 52372–9).
 'Journal of each Day', concerning Tyrrell's last illness (Add. MS 52368).
 Tyrrell–von Hügel correspondence (Add. MSS 44927–31).
 Letters of Tyrrell to Maude Petre (Add. MS 52367).
 Letters of Tyrrell to his superiors (Add. MS 52368).
 Manuscript of 'Beati Excommunicati' (Add. MS 52369).
Waller Papers: Letters of Tyrrell to Waller (Add. MSS 43680–1).

Cambridge University Library
Collection of press cuttings, deposited by Maude Petre.
Clutton Papers, Oxford (in the care of Dr A. W. Adams)
Letters of Tyrrell to Kitty Clutton.
St Andrews University Library
Von Hügel Papers: Diaries.
Lilley Papers: Letters of Tyrrell to Lilley.
MS 37018/9–18: Letters of Tyrrell to Osborne.
Wilfrid Ward Papers: Ward–von Hügel correspondence.

PUBLISHED SOURCES

Books by Tyrrell

Autobiography, vol. i of Maude Petre, *Autobiography and Life of George Tyrrell*, 2 vols. (London, 1912).
Another Handful of Myrrh: Devotional Conferences (London, 1905).
The Church and the Future (London, 1910), originally published under the name of 'Hilaire Bourdon'.
Christianity at the Cross-Roads (London, 1909).
The Civilizing of the Matafanus: An Essay in Religious Development (London, 1902), published under the name of A. R. Waller.
Essays on Faith and Immortality (London, 1914), arranged by Maude Petre.
External Religion: Its Use and Abuse (London, 1899).
George Tyrrell's Letters (London, 1920), selected and edited by Maude Petre.
The Faith of the Millions: A Selection of Past Essays, 2 vols. (London, 1901).
A Handful of Myrrh: Devotional Conferences (London, 1902), published anonymously.
Hard Sayings: A Selection of Meditations and Studies (London, 1898).
Lex Credendi: A Sequel to Lex Orandi (London, 1906).
Lex Orandi: Or Prayer and Creed (London, 1903).
Medievalism: A Reply to Cardinal Mercier (London, 1908).
A Much-Abused Letter (London, 1906).
Notes on the Catholic Doctrine of Purity (Roehampton, 1897).
Nova et Vetera: Informal Meditations for Times of Spiritual Dryness (London, 1897).
Oil and Wine (London, 1907).
Religion as a Factor of Life (Exeter, 1902), published under the name of 'Dr Ernest Engels'.
The Soul's Orbit: Or Man's Journey to God (London, 1904), published under the name of Maude Petre, compiler and part-author.

Through Scylla and Charybdis: Or the Old Theology and the New (London, 1907).
Versions and Perversions of Heine and Others (London, 1909).

Other Books

Abbott, C. C. (ed.), *The Correspondence of Gerard Manley Hopkins and Richard Watson Dixon* (London, 1935).
—— *The Letters of Gerard Manley Hopkins to Robert Bridges* (London, 1935).
—— *Further Letters of Gerard Manley Hopkins to Robert Bridges*, 2nd edn. (London, 1956).
Barmann, L. F., *Baron Friedrich von Hügel and the Modernist Crisis in England* (Cambridge, 1972).
Barry, W., *Memories and Opinions* (London, 1926).
Blanchet, A. (ed.), *Henri Bremond et Maurice Blondel: Correspondance*, 2 vols. (Paris, 1970–1).
—— *Henri Bremond 1865–1904* (Paris, 1975).
Blondel, M., *The Letter on Apologetics, and History and Dogma*, presented and translated by A. Dru and I. Trethowan (London, 1964).
Blunt, W., *My Diaries*, 2 vols. (London, 1919–20).
Boutwood, A. (pseud. Hakluyt Egerton), *Father Tyrrell's Modernism* (London, 1909).
Bremond, H., *The Mystery of Newman* (London, 1907).
—— (pseud. Sylvain Leblanc), *Un Clerc qui n'a pas trahi*, ed. E. Poulat (Rome, 1972).
Butterworth, R. (ed.), *A Jesuit Friendship: Letters of George Tyrrell to Herbert Thurston* (London, 1988).
Campbell, R. J., *The New Theology* (London, 1907).
Crehan, J., *Father Thurston* (London, 1952).
Crews, C. F., *English Catholic Modernism: Maude Petre's Way of Faith* (Tunbridge Wells, 1984).
Daly, G., *Transcendence and Immanence: A Study in Catholic Modernism and Integralism* (Oxford, 1980).
David, A. L.- (ed.), *Lettres de George Tyrrell à Henri Bremond* (Paris, 1971).
De la Bedoyère, M., *The Life of Baron von Hügel* (London, 1951).
Falconi, C., *The Popes in the Twentieth Century* (London, 1967).
Gout, R., *L'Affaire Tyrrell* (Paris, 1910).
Harnack, A., *What is Christianity?* (London, 1901).
Hogarth, H., *Henri Bremond: The Life and Work of a Devout Humanist* (London, 1950).
Hollis, C., *A History of the Jesuits* (London, 1968).
House, H., and Storey, G. (eds.), *The Journals and Papers of Gerard Manley Hopkins* (London, 1959).

Hügel, F. von, *Essays and Addresses on the Philosophy of Religion*, 1st Series (London, 1921).

—— *The Mystical Element of Religion as Studied in Saint Catherine of Genoa and her Friends*, 2nd edn., 2 vols. (London, 1923).

—— *Essays and Addresses on the Philosophy of Religion*, 2nd Series (London, 1926).

—— *Selected Letters (1896–1924)*, ed. B. Holland (London, 1928).

Ignatius of Loyola, *The Spiritual Exercises*, trans. T. Corbishley (Wheathampstead, 1973).

Kendall, K., *Father Steuart* (London, 1950).

Laubacher, J. A., *Dogma and the Development of Dogma in the Writings of George Tyrrell* (Louvain, 1939).

Leonard, E., *George Tyrrell and the Catholic Tradition* (London and New York, 1982).

Lilley, A. L., *What We Want* (London, 1907).

—— *Modernism: A Record and Review* (London, 1908).

—— (trans. attrib.; in fact by G. Tyrrell), *The Programme of Modernism* (London, 1908).

Loisy, A., *L'Évangile et l'Église* (Paris, 1902).

—— *Autour d'un petit livre* (Paris, 1903).

—— *My Duel with the Vatican* (New York, 1924).

—— *Mémoires pour servir à l'histoire religieuse de notre temps*, 3 vols. (Paris, 1930–1).

—— *George Tyrrell et Henri Bremond* (Paris, 1936).

Loome, T. M., *Liberal Catholicism, Reform Catholicism, Modernism, Tübinger Theologische Studien*, 14 (Mainz, 1979).

McCool, G. A., *Catholic Theology in the Nineteenth Century: The Quest for a Unitary Method* (New York, 1977).

Marlé, R. (ed.), *Au coeur de la crise moderniste* (Paris, 1960).

Mathew, A., '*An Episcopal Odyssey*' (Kingsdown, 1915).

Maxwell-Scott, Hon. Mrs, *Henry Schomberg Kerr* (London, 1901).

May, J. L., *Father Tyrrell and the Modernist Movement* (London, 1932).

Meadows, D., *Obedient Men* (London, 1955).

Nédoncelle, M., *Baron Friedrich von Hügel* (London, 1937).

Newman, J. H., *An Essay in Aid of a Grammar of Assent* (London, 1870).

—— *Essays Critical and Historical*, i (London, 1871).

—— *On Consulting the Faithful in Matters of Doctrine*, ed. J. Coulson (London, 1961).

—— *University Sermons (1826–43)*, with an introd. by D. M. MacKinnon and J. D. Holmes (London, 1970).

—— *An Essay on the Development of Christian Doctrine*, ed. J. M. Cameron (1845 text, republ. by Penguin Books, Harmondsworth, 1974).

Norman, E., *The English Catholic Church in The Nineteenth Century* (Oxford, 1984).

Osborne, C. E., *The Life of Father Dolling* (London, 1903).

Our Dead: Memoirs of the English Jesuits who Died between June 1939 and December 1945 (Manresa Press, 1947–8).

Papers Read before the Synthetic Society 1896–1908 (London, 1909).

Perrin, M.-T., *Laberthonnière et ses amis* (Paris, 1975).

Petre, M. D., *Modernism: Its Failure and Its Fruits* (London, 1918).

—— *My Way of Faith* (London, 1937).

—— *Von Hügel and Tyrrell* (London, 1937).

Pollen, J. H., *The Life and Letters of Father John Morris of the Society of Jesus* (London, 1896).

Poulat, É., *Histoire, dogme et critique dans la crise moderniste*, 2nd edn. (Paris, 1979).

Ratté, J., *Three Modernists: Alfred Loisy, George Tyrrell, William L. Sullivan* (London, 1968).

Reardon, B. M. G., *Roman Catholic Modernism* (London, 1970).

Rivière, J., *Le Modernisme dans l'Église* (Paris, 1929).

Sabatier, A., *Esquisse d'une philosophie de la religion d'après la psychologie et l'histoire* (Paris, 1897).

—— *The Vitality of Christian Dogmas and their Power of Evolution* (London, 1898).

—— *Les Religions d'autorité et la religion de l'ésprit* (Paris, 1904).

Sagovsky, N., *Between Two Worlds: George Tyrrell's Relationship to the Thought of Matthew Arnold* (Cambridge, 1983).

Schoenl, W. J., *The Intellectual Crisis in English Catholicism: Liberal Catholics, Modernists, and the Vatican in the Late Nineteenth and Early Twentieth Centuries* (New York and London, 1982).

Schultenover, D. G., *George Tyrrell: In Search of Catholicism* (Shepherdstown, 1981).

Schweitzer, A., *The Quest of the Historical Jesus* (London, 1954).

'T' (Thorp, J.), *Friends and Adventures* (London, 1931).

Thomas, A., *Hopkins the Jesuit* (London, 1969).

Vidler, A. R., *The Modernist Movement in the Roman Church* (Cambridge, 1934).

—— *A Variety of Catholic Modernists* (Cambridge, 1970).

Ward, M., *The Wilfrid Wards and the Transition*, i. *The Nineteenth Century* (London, 1934); ii. *Insurrection versus Resurrection* (London, 1937).

Ward, W., *W. G. Ward and the Oxford Movement* (London, 1889).

—— *Witnesses to the Unseen and other Essays* (London, 1893).

—— *Problems and Persons* (London, 1903).

Weaver, M. J. (ed.), *Letters from a 'Modernist'* (London, 1981).

Weiss, J., *Jesus' Proclamation of the Kingdom of God*, trans., ed., and with an introd. by R. H. Hiers and D. L. Holland, Lives of Jesus Series (Philadelphia, 1971).

White, A. D., *A History of the Warfare of Science with Theology in Christendom* (1 vol. repr., London, 1955).

Articles

A comprehensive list of Tyrrell's many articles can be found in T. M. Loome's bibliographies and in D. G. Schultenover's, *George Tyrrell: In Search of Catholicism.*

Archbishop and Bishops of the Province of Westminster, 'The Church and Liberal Catholicism', *The Tablet*, 5 Jan. 1901, pp. 8–12; 12 Jan. 1901, pp. 50–2.

Butterworth, R. (ed.), 'A Perverted Devotion (II)', *Heythrop Journal*, 24 (1983), pp. 379–90.

Chapman, R., 'The Thought of George Tyrrell', in *Essays and Poems Presented to Lord David Cecil*, ed. W. W. Robson (London, 1970), pp. 140–68.

Clarke, R. F., 'The Training of a Jesuit', the *Nineteenth Century*, 40 (1896), pp. 211–25.

Crehan, J., 'More Tyrrell Letters: 1', *The Month*, NS 40 (1968), pp. 178–85.
—— 'Tyrrell in his workshop', *The Month*, 2nd NS 3 (1971), pp. 111–15, 119.

Daly, G., 'Some Reflections on the Character of George Tyrrell', *Heythrop Journal*, 10 (1969), pp. 256–74.
—— 'Tyrrell's "Medievalism"', *The Month*, NS 42 (1969), pp. 15–22.

Duffy, E., 'George Tyrrell and Liberal Protestantism', *King's Theological Review*, 2 (1979), pp. 13–21.

Fawkes, A., 'Modernism: A Retrospect and Prospect', *Hibbert Journal*, 8 (1909–10), pp. 67–82.

Gardner, P., Review of TSC, *Hibbert Journal*, 6 (1908), pp. 923–6.

Hügel, F. von, 'Father Tyrrell: Some memorials of the Last Twelve Years of his Life', *Hibbert Journal*, 8 (1909–10), pp. 233–52.

Hurley, M., 'George Tyrrell: Some Post-Vatican II Impressions', *Heythrop Journal*, 10 (1969), pp. 243–55.
—— 'George Tyrrell: Some Post-ARCIC Impressions', *One in Christ*, 19 (1983), pp. 250–4.

Inge, W. R., Review of CCR, *Hibbert Journal*, 8 (1909–10), pp. 434–8.
—— 'The meaning of modernism', *Quarterly Review*, 210 (1909), pp. 571–603; repr. as 'Roman Catholic Modernism', in *Outspoken Essays*, 1st Series (London, 1919), pp. 137–71.

Lash, N. L. A., 'Modernism, Aggiornamento and the Night Battle', in A. Hastings (ed.), *Bishops and Writers* (Wheathampstead, 1977), pp. 51–79.

Loome, T., 'A Bibliography of the Published Writings of George Tyrrell (1861–1909)', *Heythrop Journal*, 10 (1969), pp. 280–314.
—— 'A Bibliography of the Printed Works of George Tyrrell: Supplement', *Heythrop Journal*, 11 (1970), pp. 161–9.

—— (ed.), ' "Revelation as Experience": An Unpublished Lecture of George Tyrrell', *Heythrop Journal*, 12 (1971), pp. 117–49.

Osborne, C. E., 'George Tyrrell: A Friend's Impressions', *Hibbert Journal*, 8 (1909–10), pp. 253–63.

Root, J. D., 'English Catholic Modernism and Science: The Case of George Tyrrell', *Heythrop Journal*, 18 (1977), pp. 271–88.

Weaver, M. J., 'George Tyrrell and the Joint Pastoral Letter', *Downside Review*, 99 (1981), pp. 18–39.

Index

Printed in the United Kingdom by
Lightning Source UK Ltd., Milton Keynes
137323UK00005B/7/A

9 780198 267287